The Lives of Colonial Objects

The Lives of Colonial Objects

EDITED BY

Annabel Cooper, Lachy Paterson
and Angela Wanhalla

OTAGO

Published by Otago University Press
Level 1, 398 Cumberland Street
Dunedin, New Zealand
university.press@otago.ac.nz
www.otago.ac.nz/press

First published 2015

ISBN 978-1-927322-02-4

A catalogue record for this book is available from the National Library of New Zealand.

Publisher: Rachel Scott
Editor: Anna Rogers
Design/layout: Fiona Moffat
Index: Diane Lowther

Front cover: The Haberfield family's kahu kiwi, showing the tāniko border and first rows of kiwi feathers (see p. 253).
Above: One of the 'Smiling Boys' (see p. 292). *Frontispiece*: Heel of tāniko slipper (see p. 224).
Contents pages: Detail of the Weller Brothers' Medicine Chest (see p. 52). *Opp. Glossary*: Interior, Toko Toru Tapu, 1889 (see p. 218).

Printed in China through Asia Pacific Offset Ltd

Contents

Acknowledgements

With this book's numerous and varied assemblage of authors it is not surprising that the editors have many people and institutions to acknowledge. The project came out of a conference held at Toitū Otago Settlers Museum, Dunedin, in 2013, so we would like to thank all who supported the event by presenting papers and attending. Special mention must be made of the financial support from the University of Otago's Centre for Research on Colonial Culture, Humanities Division staff for administrative support, and the student helpers Emma Gattey, Raechel Hunt, Hope Wilson, Kirsty Clarke and Caroline Leeming for making sure the conference ran so smoothly. The task of co-ordinating the images for 50 essays, and arranging the photography of a number of objects, was always going to be difficult and so we were fortunate to have the services of Katie Cooper to take on this burden. We thank the Humanities Research Committee at Otago for enabling us to employ her in this role. Katie's calm and supremely efficient assistance went well beyond her job description.

We consider ourselves very lucky too, to have the assistance of Michael Hall, who took a number of the beautiful photographs in this book, in Wellington, Christchurch and Dunedin. In Dunedin, for example, he photographed items in the University of Otago's Hocken and Special Collections and from the Otago Peninsula Museum, but also a number of privately held objects. We would like to acknowledge the help received from the Hocken staff, as well as that of Katie Cooper and Jane McCabe, in enabling Michael's work in Dunedin. Other photographers included Michele Pointon, Daniel List and Catherine Jehly. We would like to thank those contributors who provided photographs from their own or their families' private collections.

Most of the numerous existing photographs, however, came from a number of libraries, archives, museums and other institutions in both New Zealand and abroad. We would like to acknowledge the Alexander Turnbull Library; Auckland Art Gallery: Toi o Tāmaki; Auckland War Memorial Museum: Tāmaki Paenga Hira; Christ's College Archives, Christchurch; Corbis Images; Cornell University Library Digital Collections, Ithaca, New York; Experience Mid Canterbury; George Eastman House, International Museum of Photography and Film, New York; Sir George Grey Special Collections, Auckland Libraries; Hawke's Bay Museums Trust: Ruawharo Tā-ū-rangi; Robert Heenan and Family; Hocken Collections: Uare Taoka o Hākena; Hokonui Heritage Research Centre; Lloyd Homer, GNS Science; Katherine Mansfield Birthplace, Wellington; Manatū Taonga: Ministry for Culture and Heritage; Museum of Fine Arts, Boston; Museum of New Zealand Te Papa Tongarewa; National Library of New Zealand; National Trust of Australia (Victoria); NewsBank Inc; Nelson Provincial Museum; Richard Nunns; Peabody Essex Museum, Massachusetts; Puke Ariki; Rotorua Museum: Te Whare Taonga o Te Arawa; Smithsonian Institution: National Anthropological Archives; Special Collections, University of Otago; St John's in the City, Wellington; Solent Preservation Society, Auckland; State Library of New South Wales; Tairāwhiti Museum: Te Whare Taonga o Te Tairāwhiti; Te Aroha Museum; Te Rūnanga o Ngāti Awa, Whakatāne; Trustees of Toko

Toru Tapu; Toitū Otago Settlers Museum; Tokomairiro Historical Society; Wainuiomata Historical Museum Society; Whanganui Regional Museum.

This project would not have been completed without the on-going financial support from the Centre for Research on Colonial Culture. We would like to thank the director, Professor Tony Ballantyne, and Sue Lang, who provides administrative support. Similarly indispensible has been Otago University Press, whose publisher, Rachel Scott, has been enthusiastic from the start. In particular we would like to acknowledge OUP's designer, Fiona Moffat, for all her invaluable assistance and Anna Rogers and Imogen Coxhead for their careful editorial work. Last, but not at all least, this book would not have come to fruition without the fine scholarship and good humour of the contributors, who have given their time and energy so freely.

Glossary

`afa plaited coconut fibre, sennit (Samoan)
`ato baskets (Samoan)
ahikā ancestral fires, long-held right to land
aho string, cord, weft thread in weaving
Aonui pattern triangular-shaped tukutuku pattern
fale house (Samoan)
fautua adviser (Samoan)
hapū kin group, sub-tribe
harakeke New Zealand flax, *Phormium tenax*
Hauhau Pai Mārire followers
hei tiki foetus-shaped pendant
heru comb
hongi Māori greeting of pressing nose and forehead
hui meeting
huia extinct wattled bird, *Heteralocha acutirostris*, valued by Māori for its tail feathers
hura kohatu unveiling of gravestone, normally undertaken a year after the burial
iwi tribal grouping, composed of hapū
kahu huruhuru feather cloak
kahu kiwi kiwi feather cloak
kaitiaki guardian
kākahu cloak, clothing
karakia incantation, prayer
kaumātua elders
kaupapa topic, matter, main body of the cloak
kauri large forest tree, *Agathis australis*
kete huruhuru basket covered in kiwi feathers
kilikiti Samoan version of cricket (Samoan)
kīnaki relish
Kīngitanga Māori King Movement, pan-tribal movement seeking autonomy from mid-1850s, under an appointed king
kiwi flightless bird, *Apteryx* species
korowai cloak
Kotahitanga pan-tribal movement seeking autonomy that flourished in the 1890s
kōtare kingfisher, *Halcyon sancta*, coastal bird
kōwhaiwhai scroll-painted rafters inside a wharenui
mahara memories
mākutu sorcery
mana power and authority, control, influence
mana whenua authority over land
manaia a design from Māori art
marae complex comprising buildings including a wharenui, and marae ātea, an open space in front of the wharenui where whaikōrero takes place
matikara finger
Mau Samoan resistance movement seeking independence
mauri life force
mere pounamu greenstone hand club
moko tattoo
moko kauae chin tattoo, normally worn by women
mōrehu remnant, people remaining
mōteatea ancient classical chant
muka fibre from harakeke, *Phormium tenax*
pā fortified village
paepae bench at which orators sit
Paikea ancestor of Ngāi Tahu and Ngāti Porou
Pākehā European
Palagi European (Samoan)
papa kāinga original home
papahou treasure box
pare lintel
pātaka elevated food storage building

pate cricket bat (Samoan)
pātiti hatchet
pāua abalone, univalve shellfish, *Haliotis* species
pipi bivalve shellfish, *Paphies australis*
pītau perforated spiral carving
pōua grandfather
pounamu greenstone, nephrite jade
poutokomanawa central ridge pole in a wharenui
pūtōrino flute-like musical instrument
rangatira chief
raupō bulrush
remu bottom edge of a cloak
rewarewa New Zealand honeysuckle, *Knightia excelsa*
rimu red pine, *Dacrydium cupressinum*
rūnanga council
siva dances (Samoan)
siva afi fire dancing (Samoan)
takapū calf of the leg
tangata whenua hosts, Māori people
tangi funeral
tāniko patterned border of a cloak, embroidered patterns
taoka/taonga treasured item, object, item or thing (tangible or intangible) that has been passed through the generations and is recognised as being of ancestral importance
taonga pūoro musical instrument
tapu under spiritual restriction, sacred, set apart
tauā army, war party
tauihu prow of a canoe
te ao Māori the Māori world
te reo/te reo Māori the Māori language
Te Rūnanga o Ngāi Tahu Ngāi Tahu tribal council
tikanga procedure, custom, practice
tīpuna ancestors
toetoe tall native grass, *Cortaderia* species
Toko Toru Tapu Holy Trinity
tokotoko walking stick
tōtara tall forest tree, *Podocarpus* species
tūī parson bird, *Prosthemadera novaeseelandiae*
tuku ceremonial gifting
tukutuku ornamental lattice panels inside a wharenui
tūpāpaku corpse
upoko ariki paramount chief
urupā graveyards
wāhi tapu sacred or restricted place
waiata song
waka canoe
whaikōrero formal oratory
whakaaraara weaving technique
whakamīharo surprise, amazement
whakapapa genealogy
whānau family grouping
whanauka relative
whare house, building
whare rūnanga council house
whare whakairo decorated, carved meeting house
wharenui meeting house
whenu warp threads in woven fabric
whenua land
whenua tīpuna ancestral land
whenua ūkaipō original home
whio blue duck, *Hymenolaimus malacorhynchos*
whītau flax fibre

Introduction

A Scheme of Things

Annabel Cooper, Lachy Paterson and Angela Wanhalla

Things – beautiful or simply practical, expensive or everyday, fragile museum objects or robust items that have withstood years of use – things invite us into the past through their tangible, tactile and immediate presence. *The Lives of Colonial Objects* is a collection of short essays in which objects serve as pathways into New Zealand's colonial history. Inspired by Neil MacGregor's *A History of the World in 100 Objects* and the study of object histories it has initiated, we tell New Zealand history 'through things'.[1] We do so because attending to objects and their stories enriches our understanding of the material circumstances of colonial life, of how Māori, settlers and sojourners lived and related to each other and the natural environment, shedding light on beliefs and social structures, institutions and cultural practices.

In 2013 we convened a conference on 'Colonial Objects' at Toitū Otago Settlers Museum, Dunedin. We defined 'colonial' broadly, ending with New Zealand's involvement with World War II, and we invited contributors to 'think beyond the museum' if they wished, and to tell the stories of their objects from the perspective they felt suited them best. Offers poured in from academics in a variety of disciplines, archivists and librarians, professionals in the heritage sector, and independent scholars, ready to talk about everything from tents to tokotoko to flying boats. From the 70 papers given at the conference we had the difficult task of selecting contributions for this book, adding a small number of essays on objects that were not the subject of conference presentations, but helped to provide the balance we sought.

The diverse range of the authors' backgrounds and disciplines has meant that this volume contains not only a wide range of objects but of approaches to looking at them, from history, art history, social anthropology, visual culture, material culture and gender studies. We asked contributors to set aside overly theoretical or methodological approaches to their task. Rather, authors have focused on telling the stories of how people used or interacted with these items, and perhaps continue to do so.

Restricted to a single item, some authors have selected something precious or significant to them, things kept carefully in top drawers or on family mantelpieces, whose stories have been preserved in the memories of their owners or kaitiaki. A number of essays discuss objects gifted to museums, archives and art galleries, whether provincial or specialist museums, or national or international institutions. Others focus on mundane objects, such as a tin billy, or those that are part of the built environment, such as a road or a cottage. Given this collection's focus on colonial history, the inclusion of such practical objects draws attention to important aspects of colonial development. Roads, for instance, were essential to economic progress, as well as opening up Māori-held regions to colonial domination. Other objects draw attention to New Zealand's presence in the Pacific, or illuminate histories of migration and mobility, gender relations, and aspects of colonial childhoods and family life or working conditions, as well as race relations. They highlight histories of colonial taste, dress and consumption, collecting practices, patterns of leisure, the breadth of colonial visual and print cultures (portraiture, photographs, illuminated manuscripts, scrapbooks, albums, diaries, journals, registers and minute books) as well as the evolution of medical and scientific knowledge. As a collection, the objects illuminate the richness and variety of colonial society and culture – its opportunities – but also its limits and constraints.

The stories of many of our objects include the journeys they have made, in time and place, and the new meanings they acquired as they changed hands within families or across generations, or moved from one institutional setting to another, or, in some cases, disappeared without trace. How did some things become broken, mistreated, hidden away, lost or discarded as obsolete, while others were treasured and collected? Several essays discuss items that drew public attention in their own time, like the stereopticon, but have since disappeared. Tracing the ebb and flow of the function, use and value of an object reveals a great deal about evolutions in taste and patterns of consumption, as well as the development of new knowledge and the impact of technological change.

The colonial institutions that held some objects were fundamental to unravelling the relationship between the items and their life stories. Several objects in this book relate to the establishment of vitally important scientific institutions, notably museums, where the sharing of ideas and new knowledge took place. These institutions contributed to a colonial intellectual culture based on classification, collection and display. Some of the first objects to enter colonial museums were rocks, testifying to the importance of fostering knowledge about the natural world. Rocks had the advantage of being easy to collect and to display, which cannot be said for whale skeletons, sought after by museums around the world but not straightforward to obtain or exhibit.

Because a single object may tell many stories, object histories can usefully complicate interpretations of the major drivers of historical change, such as colonialism or migration. Generic, common and everyday objects, such as registers, minute books, diaries and scrapbooks, can contain histories quite distinct from their initial purpose, and come to life in new ways for later generations. Māori Land Court Minute Books, for instance, which from 1864 underpinned the court's work to break up communal ownership of Māori land, are records of colonialism in practice, providing important source material for historians. But they are also rich repositories of whakapapa and oral traditions, and they resonate with the voices of Māori, marking their contents and the books, their containers, as precious taonga. Looking at them as objects draws attention, too, to the mechanisms of colonialism, demonstrating that precise recordkeeping was a hallmark of colonial governance, but could also be turned to other purposes.

A single object may direct attention to historical processes, or well-known events, from the vantage point of ordinary people. Objects may 'speak' for people and families who may not have left an imprint on the written record, adding richness, diversity and complexity to New Zealand's colonial story. Through a church lectern we come to know of William Ah Gee, a Chinese furniture maker who lived in Blenheim;

Egerton Peters' polo trophy is a tangible trace of the networks between former British colonies, in this case between India and New Zealand.

and the affection between Percy Heenan and Martha Cranstoun is recalled through a gift of ostrich feathers. And, like the portrait of Mrs Humphrey Devereux and Marian Sargood's music album, the stories these objects tell also point to the connections of ordinary New Zealand people to the wider world, tracing the colonial networks that linked this country to China, South Africa, the United States and Australia.

As we made our selection and thought about the structure of the book, we contemplated various kinds of thematic ordering. We were keen, however, for the collection to 'tell colonial history', so we put the essays in chronological order according to the time period of each, and then rearranged them a little so that, as far as possible, they sat beside neighbours with which they had some thematic link. We liked this structure immediately, and have not made a single change since. Indeed, as we read through from beginning to end, we saw more and more connections, and we warmed to the sense of a history through 'glimpses', and the alternation of large political themes and smaller domestic realities, which the ordering revealed.

The objects in this book range from examples of familiar historical patterns to the much less known or typical. Some of our contributors approached the major narratives of New Zealand colonial history through important items that sat at the heart of such themes as literacy, economy, land and law, religion and high culture, while others traced the same ideas through less recognised objects. William Colenso's composing stick, used to set the type for the Treaty of Waitangi and the Māori New Testament, takes us into the history of the arrival of printing, while the *Pihoihoi* press chirping against the Kīngitanga in the 1860s reveals its ongoing political uses. A harpoon head reminds us of the early resource economies. The voluminous minute books of the Land Court refer us to the processes through which land sales were effected, but the *Te Wananga* ledger shows us one way in which they were resisted. Another official book, Bishop Harper's register, enables us to follow his travels as he disseminates Christianity in the south, while a Noah's Ark shows us how the word was spread through play in a domestic setting. A piano marks the cultural connections settlers cherished as they left the Old World for the New.

Some objects handed down through families continue to be used. Here the kahu kiwi passed down through generations of the Haberfield whānau frames Emma Wyeth's bouquet on the day of her marriage to Michael Stevens. *Private collection. Photograph by James Newman*

Other histories, such as warfare, intercolonial trade and exchange, migration and health, sometimes emerge through surprising items. The commitment of hearts and minds to imperial warfare is signalled by Florence Nightingale's memorial tree in Ashburton Domain, while Phillip Tapsell's cannon reminds us of wars at home. The ostrich feathers bring us World War I through soldiers shopping in South Africa, and a hand-carved dog is a memento of Japanese prisoners of war confined at Featherston during World War II. A portrait is commissioned from Boston to remind a son of his mother across the ocean, a polo trophy points to a family's dispersal across England, India and New Zealand, and a cricket bat links England, New Zealand and Sāmoa. Health was maintained with the aid of a whaler's medicine chest, improving education from travelling lecturers and 'taking the waters' in the eastern North Island, and unwittingly threatened by the more dubious effects of feeding bottles and radium activators.

Objects in the book originate from Māori and Pākehā worlds, and show the extraordinary diversity of the criss-crossing between cultures throughout the colonial period, in stories of both relations and ruptures. In Bluff and Dunedin, Kāi Tahu families hold onto their taoka – a kahu kiwi and a tokotoko – through changing times and uses and as the families themselves incorporate Pākehā members. A pūtōrino travels from New Zealand to Sydney and ends up in a museum in Salem, Massachusetts. In the messy aftermath of the Taranaki Wars (1860–69), Wiremu Kīngi's tauihu passes out of Māori hands and it, too, turns up in a museum; Kīngi himself may, or may not, have been the subject of a photographic portrait in a New Plymouth studio. Katherine Mansfield, in a half-conscious appropriation, gestures to her birthplace by wearing a hei tiki, and is photographed on a journey through Te Urewera. In Auckland, Māori viewers warmly appreciate Bohemian artist Gottfried Lindauer's rendering of Māori subjects in the unfamiliar medium of oil, and despite the separate visitors' books, Māori sign in the 'Pākehā' book, and vice versa. Te Keepa's tāniko slippers deploy the technical skills of both cultures to create a cross-cultural domestic artefact. A memorial to the chief, however, commissioned by Māori but rendered by a colonial sculptor, satisfies no one. In the Poverty Bay settlement of Manutuke, Toko Toru Tapu Church stands as vivid testimony to the creative energy released through cultural exchange.

Unravelling the stories attached to objects also gives precedence to dimensions of past lives not always made prominent in historical writing, such as the senses, for many objects discussed in *The Lives of Colonial Objects* were designed to be touched, worn, held, exchanged and gifted, or to be heard, played or read. Musical instruments and albums register the importance of paying attention to sound in history, helping to identify potential approaches to uncovering the aural experience of men and women in the colonial era. Objects could also excite emotions, telling stories of tragedy and grief, of joy and happiness, or in the hope of maintaining connections, as when photographs were sent to family far away. Many function as aids to private or family memory: scrapbooks, which were common objects in Victorian homes, allowed anyone to become a collector, with the

Tents were items of necessity for many settlers in the early colonial decades. For these young Christchurch men at the turn of the nineteenth century, however, they meant leisure – opening up the prospect of a summer at the beach and escape from urban workplaces.

Maclay, Adam Henry Pearson, 1873–1955: Negatives. Ref: 1/1-023660-G. Alexander Turnbull Library, Wellington, New Zealand

items made valuable through personal associations or memories of places visited.

As we move towards and into the twentieth century, some earlier themes continue but new ones emerge. In 1892 Herries Beattie's diary documents his young life in serious boyish handwriting, prefiguring a life of earnest scholarship; by 1912 Nola Pratt chooses wittily posed snaps as her autobiographic medium, signalling modernity in the rise of leisure; and in the intervening two decades, the pursuit of pleasure flowered in the summertime tent settlements of Sumner and New Brighton. As faster and easier travel and communication broke down the tyrannies of distance tourism promoted spas for recreational use, Evelyn Bond travelled abroad, her sense of the newness of the experience recorded in her travel diary, the whare whakairo Mataatua was exhibited around the world, the latest British photographic conventions appeared in Wellington exhibitions and flying boats connected colonies with a speed that anticipated the future.

Contributors to this collection have approached their object in a range of ways. Some chose to employ a material culture approach, stressing the physicality of the object, placing weight on its dimensions, size and composition to reveal aspects of its lived past. Looking closely at the materials and techniques used to create an object can tell particularly local stories about the crafting of everyday items, like the tāniko slippers owned by Te Keepa, and the kiwi feathers stitched into an embroidery depicting a Māori village on the Whanganui River in 1885. These things could have been created only in New Zealand. Modifications draw attention to changing function and use, enabling the survival of an object. Often survival happened by chance, or circumstance, or because an item possessed particular properties that made it collectible or gave it commercial value – or because, like Spinks Cottage, it lent itself to a variety of functions.

Where objects have disappeared, or are manufactured items, the context of their historical past is important, and traditional historical research methods have been employed. William Colenso's composing stick, brought to New Zealand from England, was hardly unique in its manufacture, but its owner and how he made use of it makes it special. Health stamps became ubiquitous, but their story, which can be identified from written records, is what makes them significant. For some objects, their aesthetics and decorative elements give them appeal, and make them collectable. Collectors themselves, such as Wellington's Walter Cook, fascinated by colonial taste, are also part of our story. Taonga Māori maintain connections to the past, but their meaning in the present ensures continued use. Several essays demonstrate that objects endure because they are energised by whakapapa, and animated by the mana of former owners, ensuring that the kahu kiwi will continue to be worn, and the *Te Wananga* register visited and cried over by descendants.

The fiftieth and final essay, a collaboration between two of the keynote speakers at the Colonial Objects conference, serves a particular purpose and has its own voice. When Jonathan Mané-Wheoki became too ill to write an essay for the volume, we resigned ourselves to the fact that the presentation which had entranced listeners could not be part of the book. But Conal McCarthy, meeting Jonathan by chance, suggested that he might incorporate the address within the reflective theoretical conclusion we had asked him to write, enabling it to be included in the collection. The final essay is the outcome of that meeting, which occurred only months before Jonathan's death in October 2014. Jonathan traces the life of the meeting house Mataatua, a taonga Māori with a quintessentially colonial history of appropriation, travel and loss of cultural meaning. In his richly nuanced treatment of the house as a taonga and ancestor, Jonathan offers a sensory and emotional insight into Mataatua's return home to Whakatāne, where it now looks forward to a long future. Conal then takes up the story of Mataatua, using it as a departure point for reflecting on how the essays in this volume contribute to a growing scholarship concerned with the history of objects and their stories, placing many of the preceding essays into a theoretical and historiographical context.

The taonga within *The Lives of Colonial Objects* initiate kōrero both small and large. Individually, many open a series of small windows into the material circumstances of colonial life and the everyday social aspects of the time: the clothes people wore, the work they did, the things that gave them pleasure and joy, the sounds they heard, the music they played, the houses they built and lived in, the words they wrote, the hardships they faced and the emotions they expressed. Many reflect the political forces at work in colonialism: the infrastructure that facilitated settler ideas of progress, Māori resistance and cultural exchange. Object stories bring attention to underexamined social and cultural practices, as well as a focus on the less familiar elements of emotion, feeling and experience in otherwise well-traversed dimensions of our history. While each object is the subject of a particular story, therefore, the objects in *The Lives of Colonial Objects*, taken as a collection, inform and enrich major themes in the colonial history of Aotearoa New Zealand.

1
Intimate Immensity
A Pūtōrino in the Peabody Essex Museum[1]
Lucy Mackintosh

The renowned Oceanic collection of the Peabody Essex Museum in Salem, Massachusetts, contains a number of early, unique and beautiful Māori objects collected by traders during voyages to China and the East Indies in the late eighteenth and nineteenth centuries. Captain William Richardson, who donated one of the earliest and largest groups of objects in 1807, was among the earliest Americans to enter Oceania and exchange goods, objects and ideas with Polynesians during commercial voyages of which little is known. His collection contains a number of impressive Māori objects, including a pare, a papahou and a shark-tooth knife. But it is a small pūtōrino in the collection that has caught, and held, my attention. The delicate instrument, carefully crafted for mouths, fingers and breath, draws me in to closely inspect its intricately carved surfaces and dark interior, and encourages an intimate and ephemeral connection with the past. This essay follows the pūtōrino as it weaves through space and time, tracing its logic of circulation, following the careful, tiny movements between musician and instrument and examining the object's potential to deliver glimpses of lived experience amid the archival silence surrounding these epic voyages and early encounters.

When Richardson sailed out of Salem harbour on the *Eliza* in May 1805, the town was in a period of enormous prosperity.[2] Salem traders had been among the first Americans to sail around Cape Horn and the Cape of Good Hope after the American Revolution (1775–83) and open up new trade routes with China and the East Indies. Vessels left Salem with rum, tobacco and clothing, and returned with sugar, coffee, pepper, porcelain, silks and other luxury goods. Following the scientific expeditions of Captain James Cook and others to Oceania in the late eighteenth century, some Salem traders began sailing via Oceania, picking up otter and seal skins, sandalwood and beche-de-mer (sea slugs) for trading in China.[3]

The incomplete logbook of the *Eliza*'s voyage records that Richardson travelled around the Cape of Good Hope and stopped in Mauritius, before following the new 'easternmost route' around the southern coast of Australia. He spent several months in Port Jackson (Sydney), then sailed to Canton via the Norfolk Islands and possibly Padang (Sumatra).[4] The *Eliza* left Canton on 25 December 1806 and returned to Salem by an unknown route in mid-1807.[5]

Pūtōrino (flute).

Cat. No. E5515, Peabody Essex Museum, Salem, Massachusetts

The vessel is not recorded as having visited New Zealand, so we do not know where Richardson obtained the New Zealand objects. Port Jackson is a strong possibility, since there was already a steady flow of trans-Tasman commercial traffic by 1805.[6] Richardson spent almost three months in Port Jackson, where he sold 27,275 litres of brandy and Jamaican rum and recruited ex-convicts as crewmen.[7] The artefacts may have been brought over from New Zealand by whalers, who regularly visited the Bay of Islands in the first few years of the nineteenth century, and often collected small, portable, carved objects.[8] Researchers believe the Māori objects originally came from Tai Tokerau (Northland), an area frequently visited by Europeans around 1800.[9]

The pūtōrino is a cylinder about 40 centimetres long, made from a single piece of kauri or tōtara split in two, hollowed out, then bound together again with rows of flax fibre. In the middle of the cylinder is a carved face with an opening in the shape of a mouth. To play the pūtōrino, a Māori musician placed his mouth over the end of the flute or over the carved face in the centre of the instrument, and adjusted his hand over one of the openings, producing a quiet, deep sound that trembled as the finger moved.[10] The instrument had a number of different voices, including a male and female voice and a third voice that produced unpredictable sounds, which was considered to be the sound of Raukatauri, the goddess of flutes, and her daughter, Wheke, who reside in the interior of the pūtōrino.[11] According to some traditional music experts, musicians may also have recited or sung words into the pūtōrino.[12]

A musician's performance on the flutes could break down spatial and temporal distance, connecting distant places, ancestors and gods with the present. A nineteenth-century Tai Tokerau song written for the pūtōrino describes a journey from New Zealand to Tonga, Tahiti and Hawaiiki, naming ancestors, events and places along the way.[13] The song was part of an oral tradition that transmitted information from generation to generation about past migrations across the Pacific, navigating techniques and genealogies.[14] It shows the Pacific as a place of connections and crossings between ancestral homes, the gods and the underworld, most unlike the nineteenth-century European notion of a vast unconquered territory on the 'edge' of the world, measured in lines and grids.[15]

The pūtōrino further encouraged the collapse of space and time by requiring an intimate engagement between player and instrument. Each flute was unique and carefully carved, its shape determined by its place in Māori cosmogony and its carvings materially incorporating the shapes of the sounds, ancestors and stories associated with the flutes.[16] Flutes were often carved with a face at the blown end, so that the nose of the instrument met the player's nose in a hongi. A face could also be carved at the end of the flute, where the breath exits, which was considered to be the face of the music.[17] These intimate, momentary interactions – the joining of a performer's lips and nose with those of the flute, the flow of breath in and out of the flute's interior and the mingling of saliva with wood – created a mutual involvement that challenged the separation, or boundaries, between person and thing, subject and object, and meaning and materiality.

China Goods.

FOR Sale at the House of
WILLIAM RICHARDSON,
Bridge Street,
25 chests of Hyson Tea,
25 chests Hysonskin do.
25 chests Padra Souchong,
100 Tea Setts of assorted China, handsome figures,
1 chest of 30 yard piece black Satin,
1 chest of black silk Handkerchiefs,
500 pieces blue Nankeens,
[illegible]00 pieces snow white do.
400 pieces short yellows, all of the first quality, and entitled to certificate and debenture.
The above articles will be sold cheap, and a liberal credit given. June 12.

Above: *Captain William Richardson, c. 1800.*

Cat. No. M2773, Gift of Miss M. Helen Tibbetts, 1923, Peabody Essex Museum, Salem, Massachusetts

Left: *Captain Richardson advertises trade goods from Canton for sale in the* Salem Gazette, *12 June 1807.*

Courtesy of NewsBank Inc.

Richard Nunns playing a pūtōrino.

Courtesy of Richard Nunns

When Europeans began visiting New Zealand regularly in the late eighteenth century, Māori already had a well-established trading system and showed interest in the new items on offer, particularly metal objects, which could be incorporated into their own systems. In exchange for these items, Māori sometimes offered taonga.[18] While Europeans viewed a transaction as the final stage in a relationship between two peoples, Māori viewed the gift of taonga, which instantiated ancestors and the power and prestige of a lineage, as the beginning of an ongoing relationship between the peoples and their lineages.[19] Even though the object had been removed physically, it continued to generate ties across territorial and cultural boundaries, stitching the two groups together, then and in the future.

For Richardson, the objects served a very different purpose. He was a founding member of the East India Marine Society, a unique and exclusive organisation established in 1799 for the few mariners who had made it around the Cape of Good Hope or Horn.[20] The society maintained 'a museum of natural and artificial curiosities', a practice that was closely linked with late eighteenth-century Enlightenment notions of collecting and categorising things in the name of science and reason.[21] But Salem was primarily a place of enterprise, and the members of the society were particularly interested in 'useful and entertaining' knowledge that might help them to understand and control foreign cultures and markets.[22] At the society's annual banquet in 1804, six months before Richardson embarked on his journey, a toast was proposed to 'A Cabinet: That every mariner may possess the history of the world'.[23] Richardson's collection declared him a man of the Enlightenment, of commerce and of independence, all virtues that helped Salem men move along their life course from mate to captain and, finally, to merchant.

Before the pūtōrino reached Salem, it paused for a year or more on board the *Eliza*, as the vessel crossed vast distances, weaving in and out of different worlds. Goods collected during the journey were stored in boxes, crates, barrels and chests in the cargo hold, a giant cavity at the bottom of the ship. Down there, things gathered together from a variety of distant places and cultures constantly moved and knocked against one other with the motion of the waves. Disconnected from their original context, they had not yet reached the European world of markets and scientific classifications. The *Eliza* was a borderland of sorts, a place where objects such as the pūtōrino, surrounded by commercial goods in the hold and beneath the feet of the crew on deck, were in the process of being assembled, quarantined and redefined under the banner of the expanding Salem empire. In June 1807 the *Eliza* docked at one of the dozens of wharves that lined Salem Harbour. Richardson died six months later, leaving his wife pregnant with their eleventh child.[24] Shortly before his death, he handed the Māori objects over to the East India Marine Society.

The pūtōrino was erroneously entered into the museum accession notebook as a musical instrument from New South Wales, Australia.[25] For much of the nineteenth century it was kept in one of the curiosity cabinets lining East India Hall, along with the society's other objects from China, the East Indies and Oceania.[26] Objects were arranged by type (and later function) rather than by geography, and served to entertain the huge number of visitors, who described the museum as 'whimsical', 'wonderful' and a 'fairy land'.[27]

Over 130 years later Ernest Dodge, a curator at the Peabody Museum (as the East India Marine Society was now known), and Edwin Brewster, a science teacher, picked up the pūtōrino. Their intention was to study its 'acoustics and operation', but playing the instrument was no easy task. By this time traditional Māori musical instruments were scarce and many of the playing techniques had been lost after missionaries and teachers in New Zealand had consistently discouraged Māori music throughout the nineteenth century.[28] Dodge and Brewster turned to New Zealand research: Pākehā and Māori ethnographers had recently consulted with Māori about traditional songs, instruments and games.[29] They also practised in front of a mirror as they attempted to re-enact the movements of Māori musicians.[30] Their efforts were rewarded when they managed to produce music, probably for the first time since the instruments had left New Zealand.

Over the last 30 years, New Zealand musicians and carvers have examined, played, recorded and composed with Māori traditional instruments from museums around the world, initially focusing on recording and preserving existing traditional songs, but more recently composing new songs based on the styles of the tradition.[31] According to Wonu Veys, these musicians and researchers have literally blown new life into traditional Māori instruments.[32] Performing with taonga pūoro (singing treasures) from museums can reanimate a kin group's ancestral landscape, encourage new creative encounters, initiate relationships between curators and members of the Māori community and activate imagined communities that experience the sound of the flutes as part of New Zealand's unique soundscape and collective identity.[33]

The pūtōrino, connected intimately with life, resists being represented as an inert, fixed object. The instrument reaches beyond its small frame, encouraging a close yet ephemeral entanglement between musician and flute, subject and object, idea and thing, and present and past.

A new generation of Ngāti Whakaue takes aim toward Te Tumu with the cannon named Te Haupapa. This is the last of 12 cannons once in Maketū. Originally owned by the Danish trader Te Tapihana (Captain Phillip Tapsell), Te Haupapa now rests on Whenua Akura, famed landing place of the Arawa waka. Photograph by the author

2
Te Haupapa
Pāora Tapsell

Takiri mai ko te ata e
i runga o Whakapou,
ko te hoa ia au e
tenei ka ora mai

Hoki mai e tai e
ki te au kaha ia Te Arawa e
maunga tu noa e
Kauae e uta ra

Ka riro ra ia e
nga totora whakahi o te wao
e ahu ki te muri e
nga rake pingao waho Te Tumu e

I roto i te paroa
kai tomo kourua
Te whare o Kiharoa
ka rau ta mitia e
ka toenga kaitia

E ahu ra waho e
te whare o Whakatiarere
ko Taharangi ko Hikareia e

Mau ana to patu ko Te Waharoa
ka nui te taonga e
ka hoki mai ki te iwi na e.[1]

This is the story of a very special taonga named Te Haupapa.[2] Before he was a cannon, Te Haupapa was born in human form around 1790 to a chiefly lineage of Ngāti Whakaue of the Te Arawa tribal grouping. Raised in the pā of Ōhinemutu (on the southern shores of Lake Rotorua) and Kaiweka (on Mokoia Island in the centre of the lake), he was initially named Te Kiore. On coming of age he became better known as Te Haupapa, a Ngāti Whakaue fighting leader to be both respected and feared. On learning that their neighbouring enemy, Ngāi te Rangi, had received a musket trader into their midst in 1829, he and a small group of Ngāti Whakaue warriors, including Tipitipi, Tohiteururangi and Pipipipi, risked death by going into the Tauranga district to meet the Danish-born trader, Te Tapihana or Hans Homan Jensen Falk, better known as Captain Phillip Tapsell,[3] daring to invite him to consider establishing his flax station at Maketū. Hongi Hika's devastating musket attacks were a recent reminder to all the Bay of Plenty tribes of the urgent need for firearms. After some tense negotiation Ngāi te Rangi accepted that the flax-abundant region of Maketū was ideal, but not before Te Haupapa agreed, with equal reluctance, that their leader Tūpaea had the mana to transfer the requisite Maketū land to Te Tapihana.[4] With Te Haupapa's assistance Te Tapihana built his homestead on the southwest corner of Maketū Pā at Pūtangaru. Below it was erected the Bay of Plenty's first trade station, complete with a jetty for loading dressed flax onto visiting cutters. Over the coming months trade of dressed flax for guns was fierce, as iwi competed to acquire Te Tapihana's firearms.[5] Within weeks of his arrival the population of Maketū had exploded. Ngāti Whakaue took up residence in the main pā alongside Te Tapihana. Aware of the continuing tensions, Ngāi te Rangi chose to live on the other side of the Kaituna at Te Tumu, strategically controlling access back to Tauranga. According to Te Tapihana, in those first months he could hear 'the sound of scraping pipi shell on flax night and day, for so anxious were these erstwhile enemies gathered about him to obtain guns and ammunition that rest was a minor consideration, until they thought they had acquired sufficient arms to make them secure against aggression'.[6]

George French Angas sketched this house, named Maketū, in 1844. Puatia initially built it at Ōtāwhao pā, Te Awamutu, to commemorate Waikato's success at the Battle of Maketū. The house also came to memorialise those whom Puatia fought alongside at Maketū, but who died at later battles. *Ref: PUBL-0014-25, G.F. Angas,* The New Zealanders Illustrated *(1847), Alexander Turnbull Library, Wellington, New Zealand*

With the backing of Te Haupapa on one hand and Tūpaea on the other, Te Tapihana ensured that all the Bay of Plenty tribes prospered equally from his musket trade.[7] By the end of 1830 he had established satellite trade stations along the coast at Tauranga, Matatā and Whakatāne and inland at Rotorua and Matamata. Although he succeeded in preventing any one iwi gaining an arms advantage, tensions still simmered, not least between Ngāti Whakaue and Ngāi te Rangi. Gunpowder and shot were in high demand and Maketū soon became the prize.

By 1831 tensions in the region had escalated. Wanting to protect his livelihood, Te Tapihana purchased a number of cannons, which likely arrived from Australia on the Sydney cutter, *Fairy*.[8] His most impressive cannon appears to have been an 1815 naval gun. Equally interesting were two small swivel cannons, later used in 1832 by Ngāti Whakaue while laying siege to Ngāi te Rangi's pā at Ōtūmoetai. These were innovatively mounted on the front end of war canoes in place of the carved prow or tauihu and fired upon the enemy from offshore. The majority of Te Tapihana's guns, however, were probably late-eighteenth-century Napoleonic carronades – short, large-calibre, 20-pounder muzzle-loaded ship's cannons. By his own account, Te Tapihana strategically positioned 12 of these along the harbour side of Maketū pā (above today's village store) from Pūtangaru to Maraekura (above Whenua Akura, where the Arawa monument is located) in an effort to deter potential attacks from the Tauranga direction.[9] From this point Te Tapihana was on high alert and his cannons at the ready. In early 1833 Te Haupapa cemented his friend's loyalty by presenting him with a

Artist H.G. Robley served with the 68th Regiment, which saw action at Pukehinahina (Gate Pā) in 1864. During this time he visited Maketū and sketched his famous image of a Te Arawa warrior in front of Te Kiore, an 1836 Maketū Pā gateway near Pūtangaru, one of seven gateways or kūwaha erected by Ngāti Pikiao after the Battle of Te Tumu.

Ref: B-139-016, H.G. Robley, Tattooed gate, Maketu, 1865, Alexander Turnbull Library, Wellington, New Zealand

TE ARAWA

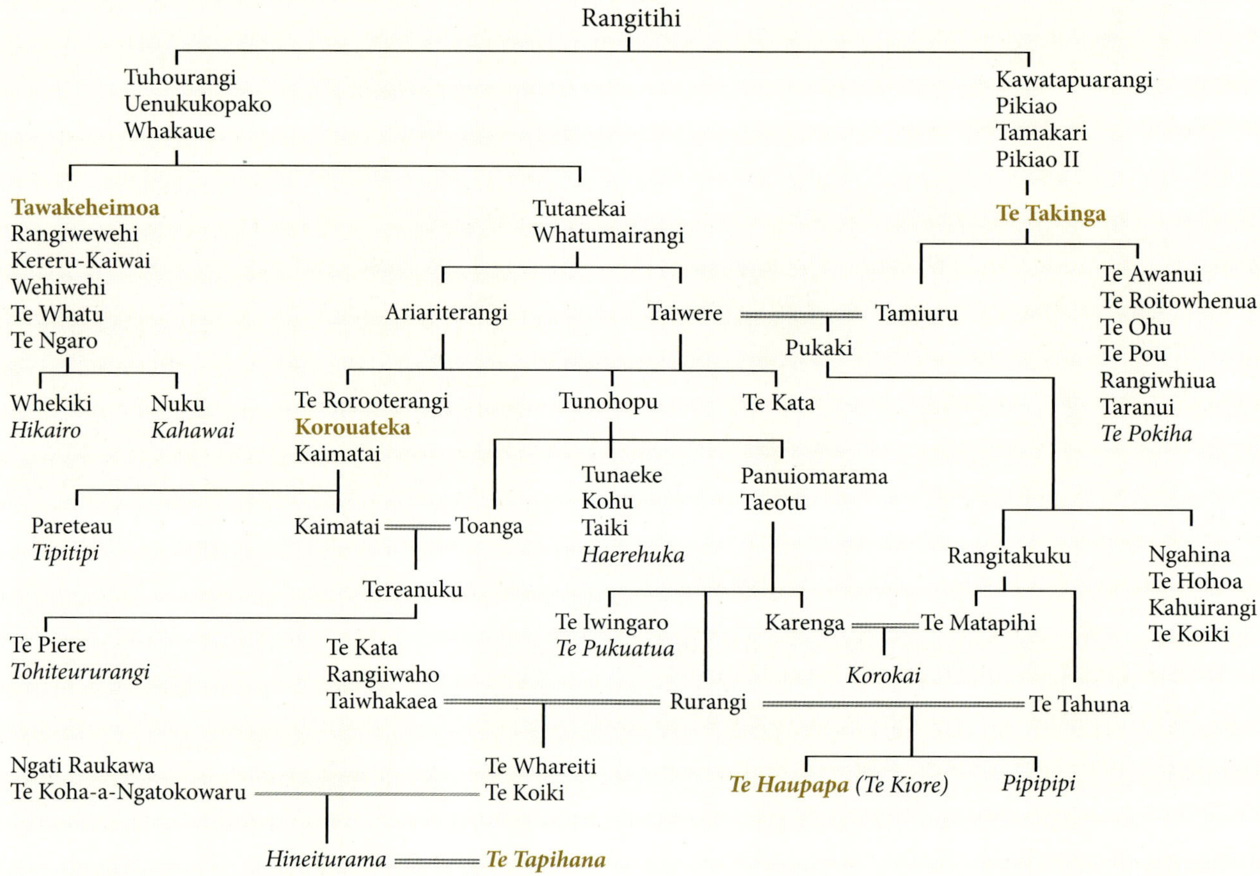

NGATI RAUKAWA

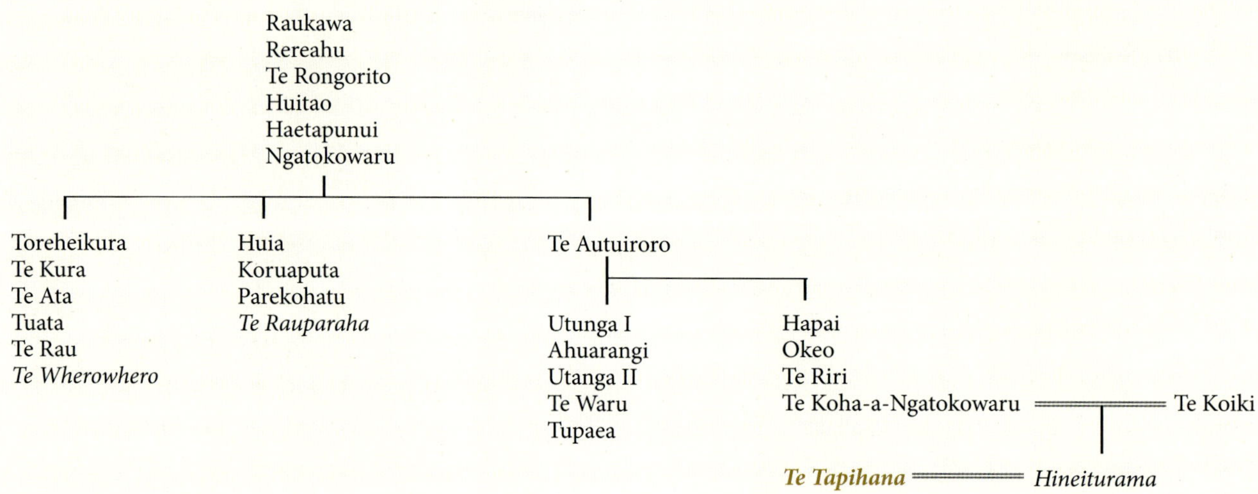

Whakapapa of the kin-context associated with the cannon Te Haupapa. These genealogies are neither complete nor do they necessarily account for seniority, spouses, full names or aliases. They may also differ from one kin group to others, and hence do not claim authority over and above any other versions that may exist. Italics denotes those ancestors mentioned in this essay; ***bold*** *indicates those after whom five of the cannons were named.*

new bride, Hineitūrama, after the loss of his previous wife, Karuhi. The latter, and her Ngāpuhi brother, Wharepoaka, were diplomats of the highest order and instrumental in bringing Te Tapihana to the Bay of Plenty.

Karuhi's death by illness was the beginning of Te Tapihana's turn in fortunes. After taking her body home to Rangihoua he returned to the escalating war between Ngāti Whakaue and Ngāi te Rangi. While Te Tapihana was away Tūpaea had prevented wider Ngāi te Rangi from destroying his stores. Fortuitously, Te Tapihana's new wife, Hineitūrama, was not only Te Haupapa's niece, but also Tūpaea's close relation, a connection that proved to be invaluable in the tumultuous years to come.

In late 1833 Ngāti Whakaue gave up their siege of Ōtūmoetai and, with assistance from wider Arawa tribes, conducted a surprise attack on Ngāi te Rangi, who were living in Te Tumu, as utu for an earlier skirmish. Tipitipi was killed. Tūpaea, his uncle Hikareia and a handful of survivors retreated to Tauranga, and Ngāti Whakaue took occupation of Te Tumu. Tensions were also heightening in Rotorua and Matamata as petty jealousies developed among lesser chiefs and new musket-armed leaders surfaced, challenging the rangatira of old by being able to deliver death from a distance. They were turning Māori warfare and custom upside down.

In 1835 a Ngāti Haua chief named Te Waharoa emerged from the Matamata–Waikato region to lead a formidable army, feared by all. Around the same time a bitter dispute erupted in Rotorua when a man named Haerehuka accused his Ngāti Whakaue relations of cheating him of his due share of Te Tapihana's muskets. Convinced he was the victim of treachery, Haerehuka took his revenge on Christmas Eve 1835 by killing Te Waharoa's nephew, Te Hunga, to bring war on his relations.[10] Ngāti Whakaue, furious, immediately stripped Haerehuka of all his earthly possessions: personal adornments, a pātaka, weapons and carvings. Thereafter Ngāti Whakaue congregated at Ōhinemutu, expecting Waharoa's assault at any moment from nearby Matamata. Ōhinemutu was refortified to repel muskets, including the carving of Te Haupapa's direct ancestors, Pānuiomarama and Pūkaki, as gateways that could be shut like doors.[11]

Te Waharoa, however, cunningly organised a surprise strike on the more distant target of now-undefended Maketū with the aim of ripping out the trade heart of Ngāti Whakaue. Three months after Te Hunga's murder, over 1000 of Te Waharoa's warriors marched across the Kaimai Range to Tauranga. This number swelled to over 1500 when Hikareira's 500 Ngāi te Rangi men joined in. Early on the morning of 29 March 1836 Te Waharoa's formidable army congregated at Te Tumu, ready to plunder Maketū.

Since 1831 Maketū's main line of defence had been Te Tapihana's cannons. As it was, Te Tapihana's guns did not frighten Te Waharoa. While he was intent on destroying Te Tapihana's trade and killing all those who got in the way, Te Tapihana was equally confident he could take out the majority of the assembled army and give the inhabitants a fighting chance of living another day. Before the attack Te Waharoa sent word that if Te Tapihana did not fire his cannons he and his family would be spared. By Te Tapihana's own account he waited for the opportune moment when the army was in range and lit his cannons. To his dismay, they did not fire. Overnight Ngāti Pūkenga, a Te Arawa grouping, had secretly emptied them of their powder and shot to use in their muskets. Needless to say, Te Tapihana rued the missed opportunity to call Te Waharoa's bluff. Without the cannons Maketū's depleted force was no match and those who did not flee were killed and eaten. Te Haupapa and his brother Pipipipi were not spared. The latter was beheaded on what is known today as Pipi's Rock; Te Haupapa was mortally wounded. In the morning, a Ngāti Haua leader, Murupara, discovered Te Haupapa's body in Te Tapihana's house. He immediately severed the head in front of the trader's family, claiming mana over Ngāti Whakaue's paramount fighting leader. This attracted much attention, resulting in a fight over the rest of Te Haupapa's mortal remains.[12]

Fortunately, Tūpaea prevented a similar fate befalling Te Tapihana and his family by successfully negotiating their safe passage out of Maketū. On arriving at Ōhinemutu a few days later, Ngāti Whakaue learned of Te Waharoa's unforeseen attack. Most alarming for all was the death of Te Haupapa. A grief-stricken Haerehuka, knowing his action had directly contributed to the loss of his fighting leader, composed his lament, urging Ngāti Whakaue to strike back.

Te Tapihana was also distraught. Te Waharoa had set fire to his station and buildings, and sacked all his trade items, including tonnes of scraped flax bales awaiting shipment to Sydney. Personal property, furniture, clothing and muskets had been fought over, claimed and carried away. Most important to the victors were the cannons, which were rolled down the pā and then ferried to Te Tumu. Te Waharoa disposed of his share of the guns in the Kaituna River. Ngāi te Rangi, however, inserted five of their claimed guns into the rebuilding of Te Tumu pā, readying themselves for the inevitable counter-attack by Ngāti Whakaue. A sixth cannon was carried back to Tauranga.

Three weeks later, on 20 April 1836, a massive war party of Ngāti Whakaue, supported by wider Te Arawa tribes, attacked Te Tumu. As was custom, everything in the captured pā became the possession of the victors, regardless of origin. The three principal Arawa tribes, led by Te Pukuatua, Tohiteururangi, Te Pokiha and Hikairo, among others, reclaimed the five cannons, giving three of them ancestral names in honour of the victory. Ngāti Whakaue named theirs Korouateka (eldest son of Te Rorooterangi); Ngāti Pikiao's was named Te Takinga (eldest son of Pikiao II); and Ngāti Kererū gave theirs the name Tawakeheimoa (revered grandfather of Kererū-kaiwai), honouring Kahawai, who fell while leading the initial engagement. The largest cannon, the naval gun, was set aside for Te Tapihana's return and the remaining cannonade was dedicated to Te Haupapa, in memory of his demise at the hands of Te Waharoa. This cannon was laid to rest in the vicinity of Te Tapihana's burnt-down home at Pūtangaru, where Te Haupapa's blood had soaked into the earth.[13]

On 4 August Te Waharoa eventually counter-attacked Ngāti Whakaue at their stronghold of Ōhinemutu. Although the Battle of Te Mataipuku resulted in deaths on both sides, Te Waharoa failed to breach the pā.[14] After a month of frustration he returned to Matamata, where he fell ill and eventually died in 1839. In 1842, after 10 years of fighting, Ngāi te Rangi and Ngāti Whakaue finally made peace, making Te Tapihana's cannons obsolete relics of a bygone war era.

In 1872 Te Tapihana requested Ngāti Whakaue/ Te Arawa to retrieve whatever cannons they could find and prepare to fire them at his tangihanga when he died. Te Haupapa was fetched from the pā and another was retrieved from the Kaituna River, where Te Waharoa had dumped his share of cannons in 1836. Both were mounted outside the homestead of Te Tapihana's son, Retireti – the site of Bay of Plenty's original trade station. They were fired immediately after the old man died, at 10 pm on 6 August 1873, and then many more times until he was buried two days later.

In 1928 the cannon recovered from the Kaituna for Tapsell's tangi was placed on the new Tapiti (Ngāti Whakaue) marae and remained there until it disappeared one night during a World War II scrap-metal drive. The cannon named Te Haupapa, however, was more fortunate. After the tangi he was returned to his resting place, hidden away under an old hedgerow at Pūtangaru. In 1965 Maketū elders Dick Wickliffe (a descendant of Tipitipi) and Wahawaha Tapsell (a descendant of Tohiteururangi) assisted Te Tapihana's great-grandson, Quentin Taiporutu, to mount Te Haupapa at Whenua Akura. Positioned beside the Arawa Memorial, Te Haupapa again stands guard at Maketū and is visited daily by his many descendants still living in and beyond the old pā. Young children play around and over him, and sit on him, imagining enemies now long past.

The dawn is breaking high
over Whakapoungakau[1]
and with it the weariness within me
comes back to life

(Te Haupapa) return upon the tide[2]
and strengthen Te Arawa over yonder[3]
as I stand like a mountain
trapped here at Kauae[4]

He (Te Haupapa) departed
like the most lofty totara of the forest
destined to join
the tufts of golden sand sedge[5]
found outside Te Tumu (Pā)

While within the long-stronghold
lurks a well of peril/treachery
represented by the house of Kiharoa
that seeks to capture, enslave
and consume you[6]

The threat of war blows forth
from the house of Whakatiarere,
Taharangi and Hikareia[7]

Take hold (of them) and strike a mortal blow
against Te Waharoa[8]
so our great taonga[9]
might return to the people.[10]

1 A mountain range on the eastern shores of Rotorua.
2 From his ancestral homeland of Tawhiti.
3 To the east, preparing to attack Te Tumu.
4 A mountain on the western shores of Rotorua.
5 i.e., past Arawa leaders killed on Te Oneonenui o Tama.
6 i.e., if Ngāti Whakaue's authority at Maketū is not restored.
7 Tauranga leaders.
8 Te Haupapa's killer.
9 Maketū.
10 Ngāti Whakaue/Te Arawa.

3

Voyaging Taonga

The Kīngi Tauihu

Kelvin Day

A magnificently carved tauihu held in Puke Ariki's heritage collection has journeyed not only through time but also between the Māori and Pākehā worlds. Its whakapapa points to a strong connection to Te Ātiawa rangatira Wiremu Kīngi Te Rangitaake and the pre-Treaty of Waitangi era of shifting iwi alignments. Its trajectory out of iwi hands and into a Pākehā museum collection mirrors the fate of many significant Māori taonga in Taranaki following colonisation – loss to their original owners and appropriation by Pākehā. This essay traces the narratives and different meanings that have been attached to this important taonga and how, in a post-treaty settlement environment, its story is being reclaimed by its community of origin.

The tauihu's origins lie in the 1820s and 1830s when a number of iwi relocated, driven by the changing cultural and political landscape. One iwi, Ngāti Toa, under increased pressure from other Waikato-based tribes, left their ancestral homeland of Kāwhia and travelled down the west coast of the North Island to settle at Kāpiti and along the Wellington coastline. Owing to whakapapa and strategic alliances several Taranaki tribes – Ngāti Tama, Ngāti Mutunga and Te Ātiawa – journeyed with them.

Tauihu.

Ref: A78.128, Collection of Puke Ariki, New Plymouth

A tauihu display at the New Zealand and South Seas Exhibition, Dunedin, 1889, with the Kīngi tauihu at the top.

Ref: P1910-008, Hocken Album No. 45, Hocken Collections, Uare Taoka o Hākena, University of Otago

These new locations were a staging point for trade, providing direct access to European traders who were a source of firearms and other goods. The alliance between Ngāti Toa and the iwi from Taranaki displaced local tangata whenua groups. There were several raids to settle old scores and push for new lands at the top of the South Island. Waka large enough to cross Cook Strait were needed, and though the alliance had several vessels, more were required. Some of the new waka were made of tōtara from the Waikanae area. Ngāti Toa called upon their Te Arawa (Rotorua) relations, principally Ngāti Tuara, who were known for their carving, to assist with the building. At least one of the waka that Ngāti Tuara carved apparently came later into the possession of Te Ātiawa living at Waikanae: the waka that carried what we now know as the Kīngi tauihu.

The whakapapa relationships between Te Ātiawa, Ngāti Toa and Te Arawa allowed the tauihu to be created for mutual benefit. The Kīngi tauihu bears the signs of its creation: its design expresses and celebrates iwi bonds. Te Ātiawa carving expert Hemi Sundgren describes 'its blend of carving styles, including elements of Te Ātiawa designs based on common tauihu conventions of the central and eastern North Island'. This suggests, he notes, 'that either Wiremu Kīngi Te Rangitaake or another Te Ātiawa craftsman had significant input into the design'.[1] There is no evidence to suggest that Kīngi was a carver, but given his whakapapa and tribal knowledge, it would not be inconceivable that he contributed to the form and design elements used. It is said that Te Rauparaha directed his nephew, Te Rangihaeata, to undertake the 'main carving of the canoes'.[2]

It is likely Te Ātiawa came into possession of either the entire waka or perhaps just its carvings through a practice of gift-giving. As Paul Tapsell notes, 'On one level, the more valuable the taonga given, the greater the mana bestowed on the receiver and on the occasion. By the same token, the mana of the gifting kin group is elevated in proportion to its generosity, obligating the recipients to reciprocate sometime in the future.'[3] In this instance, the gift of the tauihu was likely to be in recognition of kinship relationships and the role Te Ātiawa played in assisting Ngāti Toa in their South Island raids. If it was indeed Ngāti Toa who made the tuku, this would align with other recorded examples of Ngāti Toa gifts.[4]

The first recorded use of the tauihu, however, is associated with a later migration. In the early 1840s English settlers, recently arrived in New Plymouth, applied pressure to obtain Māori land in the Waitara area. In response, leading Te Ātiawa rangatira Wiremu Kīngi Te Rangitaake led a return migration to Taranaki from Waikanae in April 1848, aboard five boats and 44 canoes. The Kīngi tauihu is said to have come from the waka in which he travelled on this momentous journey. But there is a mystery here. The names of the vessels, principal chiefs, number aboard and hapū were recorded by two Pākehā observers, who counted 580 and 587 people respectively;[5] one named Kīngi's waka *Kapakanui,* and the other *Kaupahanui*.[6] Both sources agree that *Kaupahanui* carried three men, eight women and three children, indicating that this was a small vessel. On the basis of other ethnological evidence, we know that a waka with a large ornate tauihu would be substantial,

requiring a crew in the vicinity of 80. If Ngāti Toa gave Te Ātiawa a waka carrying this tauihu then it cannot have been *Kaupahanui*. Rather, the tauihu – with the associated mana that would have warranted its place on such a significant journey – appears to have been removed from its original waka and reused on *Kaupahanui*, a not unusual practice. We will probably never know to which waka this tauihu was originally attached.[7]

Through the late 1840s and 1850s Te Ātiawa thrived economically, selling agricultural produce to New Plymouth settlers, but the situation deteriorated in the late 1850s. Governor Thomas Gore Browne agreed to purchase a 243-hectare block of land on the banks of the Waitara River from a junior chief, Te Teira Manuka, against the wishes of Kīngi. The latter vehemently opposed the sale of Waitara lands and was forced to take up arms. Browne declared martial law in February 1860 and on 17 March the opening shots of the First Taranaki War were fired. This conflict lasted for nearly a year, until a peace deal was brokered. Kīngi then left Taranaki, staying with Rewi Maniapoto at Kihikihi in the Waikato. After returning to Taranaki some time later, he lived up the Waitara River until 1872, when he moved to Parihaka. In 1877 he shifted to the village of Kaingaru on the Waitara River, where he died in January 1882.

Local iwi were dispossessed not only of their land, but of their taonga. In April 1883 the *Taranaki Herald* listed items that had been gifted to the newly established New Plymouth High School Museum. Among them was 'William King's canoe head (in which he came from Waikanae, in the Wellington Province) … from Mr W. Lawrence, Waitara'.[8]

Collectors obtained taonga through a variety of means – purchasing, exchanging, gifting or fossicking.

The Kīngi tauihu depicted as a fine ethnological specimen for a 1970 calendar.

Ref: PHO2012-0180, Charters and Guthrie Associates Ltd Collection, Collection of Puke Ariki, New Plymouth

In 1880, when the Taranaki Education Board was establishing the museum at the high school, it sought 'Maori curiosities'.[9] Collector and later museum founder W.H. Skinner wrote to 'W. Lawrence asking if he had any old Maori curios for sale',[10] indicating that Lawrence was a known collector. William Lawrence was a foundation member of the Taranaki Volunteer and Militia Band in 1867, and of the Waitara Rifle Corps. From the mid-1870s until 1880 he kept a boot and shoe shop in Waitara.[11] How he obtained the Kīngi tauihu remains unclear. It is hard to imagine that such an important taonga, with its links to key events and people, would have been abandoned lightly. There are areas of decay and one of the pītau (central spirals) is damaged, suggesting that the tauihu had been exposed to the elements sometime before 1883.

The tauihu has been in the Pākehā museum world for 130 years and for most of that time has been categorised as a fine ethnological 'specimen'. It was selected for the 1889–90 New Zealand and South Seas Exhibition in Dunedin. A photograph titled 'Native carved canoe prows' shows one of the curio displays: a tiered, pyramid-like arrangement of five tauihu with the Kīngi prow at the apex, signifying its superiority in carving and form. The other four tauihu are of similar form, but none displays the fine carving style of the Kīngi prow. On its return to New Plymouth in 1890 it went back into the high school museum, where it remained until about 1901 when, along with other exhibits, it was transferred to the newly established Taranaki Museum in the New Plymouth Town Hall.

Admired as a 'fine example' of its type, the tauihu has been effectively severed from its surrounding Māori narrative, which was largely seen as irrelevant. Its connection to the Māori community yielded to 'the colonizing culture of Pakeha settlers'.[12] This disconnection of the tauihu from its Māori history is reflected in the museum's documentary record of the tauihu, which begins in the 1918 Taranaki Museum registration book. When it was accessioned in 1919, the accompanying short entry stated that it was from 'Taranaki', a 'Figurehead of canoe, finest old Maori carving known' and that it was presented by 'Wm Lawrence, Waitara'. In 1946 two new pieces of information were added to the record: an acquisition date (1880/90), and that the tauihu was associated

The Kīngi tauihu positioned next to the figurehead of HMS Eclipse at the entrance to the Te Ahi Kā Roa, Te Ahi Kātoro Taranaki War 1860–2010: Our legacy – our challenge *exhibition held at Puke Ariki in 2010.*

Collection of Puke Ariki, New Plymouth

with Wiremu Kīngi Te Rangitaake. The source of the additional information is unclear but was most likely Skinner.

The establishment of New Plymouth's Puke Ariki museum and library in 2003 provided the opportunity to rethink how the tauihu was understood and presented, and to link it back to its community of origin. The museum label, written by Māori researchers, now states the iwi origin of the carvers who commissioned the carving, and its subsequent relationship to Kīngi. This extended narrative was further developed in 2010 when the tauihu was displayed at the entrance to Puke Ariki's major exhibition marking the 150th anniversary of the beginning of the Taranaki Wars.[13]

Throughout this essay the tauihu has been referred to as the Kīngi tauihu. Naming greatly influences the interpretation of objects. This tauihu was carved by one group (Ngāti Tuara) for another (Ngāti Toa), and then passed on to an allied group (Te Ātiawa), who subsequently not only relocated to their ancestral lands but also incorporated the tauihu into another waka. After a few decades the tauihu was removed from one cultural setting to another, and a new set of values applied.

Created in the turmoil that accompanied European arrival, the tauihu's story has been repeatedly entangled with the colonisation process. For some 50 years it remained comfortably within the Māori world, one of a number of taonga that linked 'the myriad of interconnecting relationships within the genealogically patterned universe of Maori society'.[14] It is no coincidence that the tauihu left te ao Māori in the early 1880s. In November 1881 the village of Parihaka was invaded by the military, in the last act of the Taranaki Wars, and in 1882 Kīngi died. The wars resulted in the confiscation of Māori land, which in turn led to the loss of economic prosperity and of a whole generation of Taranaki Māori leaders. Also lost were many of the wāhi tapu and other taonga that were so important to the wellbeing of Māori. Given these circumstances, it should be no surprise that the tauihu was not only lost to another cultural setting, but that its original narrative was replaced with a Pākehā one. Viewed in this light, it is a powerful symbol of the path colonialism has taken in Taranaki.

4

William Colenso's Composing Stick

Sydney J. Shep

On 27 July 1920 Sophia Sarah Harding, née Blackmore, donated a printer's composing stick to the newly established Alexander Turnbull Library. 'Curios-008-007' had belonged to the so-called father of New Zealand printing, William Colenso, who had bequeathed it to her late husband, the printer, typographer and journalist, Robert Coupland Harding. Described in Colenso's will as 'my sole composing-stick, with which I did so much work both in England and New Zealand',[1] it was an unremarkable metal stick with a ferrous metal screw and copper nut to adjust line length. But it had marshalled the lead type used to typeset and print such defining icons of New Zealand's early print culture as the Māori New Testament and Te Tiriti o Waitangi.[2] It also had a pre-history in London, having travelled out with Colenso in 1834 and, after his death in 1899, it became an object synonymous with the memory of 'New Zealand's Caxton', exemplifying the power of the printed word.

Printers' composing sticks have fascinating past lives and were always objects of affection, memory and status. They started as the simplest frame cut out of a stick of wood, hence their name, and were later made of metal. The stick was an essential tool for the typesetter, originally known as the compositor. He picked out individual metal or wooden letters and spaces from the type case and lined them upside-down and backwards in the stick, which was adjusted to a fixed width. As he composed each line of text he added it to the stick until, after three to five lines of type, he transferred them out of the open end of the stick and onto a galley tray, ready for printing and proofing. With the gradual stratification of the trade through the late eighteenth and early nineteenth century into newspaper, book and jobbing printing, various styles of composing sticks followed suit. Fixed-width sticks for newspaper column setting were joined by adjustable sticks that accommodated variable widths using a screw and nut or clamp system. The double-knee stick, which could set main body text and marginal notes at the same time, was a boon to the frazzled compositor, while long wooden sticks facilitated the setting of multi-line wood types for posters and broadsheets.

Generally made, given or purchased on entry to an apprenticeship, a composing stick assumed the idiosyncrasies of its owner. Once a printer completed his training and became a journeyman, the composing stick might

KO TE

RONGO PAI KI TE RITENGA O RUKA.

UPOKO 1.

6 He hunga tika raua ki te aroaro
o te Atua, e wakarite ana raua i nga
ture katoa i nga tikanga o te Ariki,
kahore hoki i riria.
7 A kahore o raua tamariki, he pa-
koko hoki a Erihapeti, kua kaumatua-
tia hoki tokorua tokorua.
8 A i a ia e minita ana ki te aroaro
o te Atua, i te takanga o tona wiki,
9 Ki te ritenga o te mahi tohunga,
ka taka te rota mona kia tomo ki te
tino o te temepara o te Ariki ki te tahu
i te mea kakara.
10 Na, ko te nuinga katoa o te iwi

hine ma Erihapeti e wanau he tamaiti

tika; kia wakaritea mo te Ariki he
hunga ka oti te wakariterite.
18 ¶ A ka mea atu a Hakaraia ki
te anahera, Me pehea ka matau ai a
hau ki tenei *mea?* he koroheke hoki
a hau, ko t … hitia.
19 Ka ki … mea atu
ki a ia, Ko K … ana ki
te aroaro o te … ka tonoa mai ano
hoki a hau … a koe, ki
te wakapuaki i tenei rongo pai ki a koe.
20 Na, e turi koe a ekore e ahei
te korero, kia tae mai ra ano te ra
i enei *mea*, no te mea kahore koe i

William Colenso's composing stick, that deceptively simple device to marshal the 26 soldiers of lead for old-style typesetting.

Ref: Curios-008-007, Robert Coupland Harding: Printer's composing stick, c. 1832, Alexander Turnbull Library, Wellington, New Zealand

be replaced with a newer model perhaps, but was never discarded. The tools of the artisan were invested with an emotional attachment unexpected, to the outsider at least, for ostensibly inanimate objects. As Martin Speckter remarks in his *Disquisition on the Composing Stick*,

> the stick was emblem of a proud craft, and his stick signified his full membership in a brotherhood of the elite. He wore it with smug ostentation on his watch chain, or planted it on his lapel. You might say he also wore it on his sleeve – for he was not too self-conscious to write verse in praise of it and to articulate his fondness for it. Odes to the composing stick are commonplace among the numerous poems about printing.[3]

In October 1876 Thomas Bracken, who wrote the words to 'God Defend New Zealand', published his latest poem in the *New Zealand Press News and Typographical Circular*: 'The Printers' Stick: A typographical lyric'.[4] Like many such poems, it celebrates the power of the press in militaristic rhetoric and refers to the composing stick as the printer's rifle. Reprinted throughout the colonial newspaper press, anthologised in *Flowers of the Free Lands* (1877) and finally collected in his magnum opus, *Musings in Maoriland* (1890), the poem obviously resonated with the journalist politician and his public. Bracken's apostrophe to this most essential tool of the printing trade follows a tradition of paeans to the composing stick, including the 'Song of the Printer', by Thomas MacKellar of the MacKellar, Smiths and Jordan typefoundry of Philadelphia, and author of *The American Printer* (1860–67).[5] The *Scottish Typographical Circular* published 'The Adventures of My Composing-Stick. As Told By Itself. (From an Old Ballantonian's MS)', and 'The Song of the Setting Stick' appeared in the *Australasian Typographic Journal* in 1895.[6] By the time Colenso was apprenticed for a six-year term to master printer John Thomas of East Street, Penzance, Cornwall, on 5 September 1826, he may have been given one of the newer models available in the British market. Seven years later, however, it was obviously not enough for the newly minted journeyman printer and religious zealot. If we believe Colenso's story about his 'sole composing stick', purchased when he arrived in London in late 1833 to start work at Richard Watts & Son, Crown Court, Temple Bar, printers to the British and Foreign Bible Society, we can understand how acquiring a new stick epitomised the aspirations of the progressive printer.

Colenso's purchase of a new composing stick represented a substantial investment. As Bagnall and Petersen's biography notes, 'Out of a wage averaging with overtime less than £1 per week William contrived to satisfy his landlady, clothe himself, pay his church dues, repay at least part of his indebtedness to his friends in Cornwall, and make comparatively generous donations to charity.'[7] To obtain a sense of the contemporary value of such an item, we can trace the way sticks travel through the court records. The Old Bailey Online is full of stories of wayward apprentices, nimble-fingered thieves and charming textual highwaymen. From 1807 to 1891 the court heard a total of 15 cases, mostly theft, involving

William Colenso, the posed and pensive ex-printer, reinvents himself as a man of the world and politician.

John Crombie (photographer), Gifted by Mrs W.M. Simcox, Collection of Hawke's Bay Museums Trust, Ruawharo Tā-ū-rangi, m66/53

composing sticks, which ranged in value from 1 to 10 shillings; punishments ranged from several months' imprisonment to penal servitude or transportation. James Yates, for example, was confined for six months in 1866 for stealing 42 sticks from James Smith Cook, the celebrated brass-rule maker, and inventor and manufacturer of the Improved, Invariable Composing Stick, advertisements for which circulated in the New Zealand typographical press.[8] 'These,' Cook testified, 'are my property – they are worth from 4*s*. 6*d*. to 10*s*. a piece – I have lost forty that I know of, and chiefly within the last three months – two of them are German silver – the value of the whole is 14*l*. [pounds] or 15*l*. – they are used by compositors for setting the letterpress.'[9]

That Colenso purchased his own stick was certainly fortuitous. While in London, he met with Dandeson Coates, the secretary of the Church Missionary Society, and expressed a fervent interest in becoming a missionary. When the CMS advertised for a printer to New Zealand, Colenso volunteered. But after arriving in Paihia in 1834, charged with the task of printing the Māori Bible, he discovered several significant omissions in his print shop supplies: no type cases,

Gospel of St Luke from the 356-page Māori New Testament *completed by Colenso on 30 December 1837. His day book entry says it all: 'Finished printing the New Testament, 5,000 copies demy 8vo. Glory be to God alone!'*

Ref: 0042, Williams Collection, Hocken Collections, Uare Taoka o Hākena, University of Otago. Photograph by Michael Hall

no paper, no furniture, no imposing slab and no composing stick, 'save a private one of my own that I had bought two years before in London'.[10] Undaunted, Colenso proceeded to set, it is estimated, some 600,000 words in that same stick; by 1840 he had contributed over 74,000 books and pamphlets in both Māori and English to New Zealand's print culture.[11]

In 1900, a year after Colenso's death, Robert Coupland Harding wrote 'Relics of the first New Zealand press' for the journal of the Wellington Philosophical Society. In this article he indulged in some posthumous hero worship, elevating his great mentor and friend William Colenso to the role not only of the country's first printer but also to the status of the 'New Zealand Caxton', the father of antipodean printing. Harding based his hagiography on his assessment of Colenso's hitherto unrecognised role in bringing print, that agent of colonisation, to New Zealand. Although there had been earlier attempts at printing in New Zealand, Colenso's contribution was undeniable. The same stick that was used to compose the Bible, the Treaty of Waitangi and various secular and religious pamphlets and proclamations, also contributed to the dissemination of literacy and the spread of the Māori language in print. Given this legacy, it is no wonder that Harding comments eloquently on the ignoble fate of Colenso's stick: 'For a long time the composing-stick could not be found by the executors. It was at last discovered – alas! – partly embedded in the earthen floor of a damp shed, where it had lain neglected for probably thirty years, and was so corroded by rust as to be almost unrecognisable.'[12]

Colenso's stick not only entered the popular imagination through Harding's article, but has since been publicly exhibited. First loaned, in the 1960s, to the National Museum, where it appeared in the colonial history gallery and part of the print shop display, it was repatriated to the Alexander Turnbull Library in 1990, where it immediately went on display and bore witness to the sesquicentennial *Nga Kupu Korero/The People of the Treaty Speak* (1990–91). It then featured as one of the *Treasures in Trust* (1995), followed by *Posted Love: Love letters from the Turnbull Library and beyond* (1999), and finally *Books in Māori* in 2005. Today it resides in at least two places: in a digital image available online and in a twenty-first-century cabinet of curiosities along with Colenso's lead type, a reed book in Malayalam script, a set of quill pens, an ivory paper knife, a semi-precious partly cut gemstone, carved fruitstones in a miniature bamboo basket, a cut-glass stamp wetter and a paper knife from the Eastern Telegraph Company. Now too fragile to touch or hold, Colenso's 'sole composing stick' remains a potent witness to the power of print and its role as agent of colonisation and conversion, instrument of literacy and preserver of language.

KO TE

RONGO PAI KI TE RITENGA O RUKA.

UPOKO 1.

NO te mea he tokomaha te hunga
kua wakamatau i te korero i nga
mea ka tino rite nei i roto i a tatou,
2 Pera hoki me ta te kai titiro no
te timatanga, ko nga minita ia o te
kupu, i ho mai ai ki a tatou;
3 I pai hoki ki hau, noku i tino
rapu ki nga mea katoa no te tima-
tanga, kia tuhituhi marie atu ki a koe,
e Tiopira *te tangata* pai rawa,
4 Kia matau ai koe ki te tikanga o
nga korero i wakaakona ai koe.
5 ¶ I nga ra o Herora te kingi o
Huria, tera taua tohunga karakia ko
Hakaraia te ingoa, no te wiki o Apia:
ko tana wahine hoki no nga tamahine
o Aarona, ko tona ingoa ko Erihapeti.
6 He hunga tika raua ki te aroaro
o te Atua, e wakarite ana raua i nga
ture katoa i nga tikanga o te Ariki,
kahore hoki i riria.
7 A kahore o raua tamariki, he pa-
koko hoki a Erihapeti, kua kaumatua-
tia hoki tokorua tokorua.
8 A i a ia e minita ana ki te aroaro
o te Atua, i te takanga o tona wiki,
9 Ki te ritenga o te mahi tohunga,
ka taka te rota mona kia tomo ki te
tino o te temepara o te Ariki ki te tahu
i te mea kakara.
10 Na, ko te nuinga katoa o te iwi
i waho e inoi ana i te haora o te *tahu-
nga* mea kakara.
11 A ka kitea e ia te anahera o te
Ariki e tu ana ki matau o te ata o te
mea kakara.
12 A ka poheua a Hakaraia i tana
kitenga ai, ka tau te wehi ki a ia.
13 Ka mea atu te anahera ki a ia,
Kaua e mataku, e Hakaraia: kua ra-
ngona hoki tau inoinga; ma tou wa-
hine ma Erihapeti e wanau he tamaiti
mou, a me hua e koe tona ingoa ko
Hoani.
14 Ka hari ka koa ano hoki koe; ka
hari te tokomaha ki tona wanautanga.
15 E nui hoki ia ki te aroaro o te
Ariki, ekore ia e inu i te waina i te
mea wakahaurangi; e wakakiia ano
ia i te Wairua Tapu no te kopu mai
o tona matua.
16 A he tokomaha o nga tamariki
o Iharaira e wakatahuritia e ia ki te
Ariki to ratou Atua.
17 Na, e haere ia i tona aroaro me
te wairua me te kaha o Iraia, kia wa-
katahuritia nga ngakau o nga matua
ki nga tamariki, me te *hunga* ekore e
rongo ki te matauranga o te *hunga*
tika; kia wakaritea mo te Ariki he
hunga ka oti te wakariterite.
18 ¶ A ka mea atu a Hakaraia ki
te anahera, Me pehea ka matau ai a
hau ki tenei *mea?* he koroheke hoki
a hau, ko taku wahine kua ruruhitia.
19 Ka ki atu te anahera ka mea atu
ki a ia, Ko Kapariera a hau e tu ana ki
te aroaro o te Atua; ka tonoa mai ano
hoki a hau ki te korero atu ki a koe, ki
te wakapuaki i tenei rongo pai ki a koe.
20 Na, e turi koe a ekore e ahei
te korero, kia tae mai ra ano te ra
i enei *mea*, no te mea kahore koe i
wakapono ki aku kupu e wakaritea
nei ki to ratou taima.
21 Na, e tatari ana te iwi ki a Ha-
karaia, ka miharo ki a ia ka wakaroa
nei i te temepara.
22 Ano ka puta atu ia, kihai ia i
ahei te korero atu ki a ratou: a ka
mahara ratou he moe tana i kite ai i
te temepara: na, e tungou ana ia ki
a ratou, ka mau tonu tona turi.

23 A ka mea ano, ka rite nga ra o
tana minitatanga, ka hoki atu ia ki
tona ware.
24 ¶ A i muri iho i aua ra ka hapu
tana wahine a Erihapeti, ka wakangaro
ano i a ia i nga marama erima, ka mea,
25 Tenei ra te mahi a te Ariki ki
hau i nga ra i titiro mai ai ia, kia
tangohia te mea i wakakinoa ai a hau
e te tangata.
26 ¶ Na, i te ono o nga marama
ka tonoa te anahera a Kapariera e te
Atua ki tetahi pa o Kariri, ko Naha-
reta te ingoa,
27 Ki tetahi wahina i taumautia ki
tetahi tangata ko Hohepa te ingoa, no
te ware o Rawiri; ko te ingoa o te
wahina ko Meri.
28 A tomo atu ana te anahera ki a
ia, ka mea atu, Tena ko koe, *e te wa-
hine* e paingia ana, kei a koe te Ariki:
ko koe i roto i nga wahine te wakapai-
ngia ana.
29 Ano ka kite ia, ka raruraru ki
tana kupu, ka wakaaroaro ki te pehea-
tanga o tenei owatanga.
30 Ka mea atu te anahera ki a ia,
Kei mataku koe, e Meri: e paingia
ana hoki koe e te Atua.
31 Na, e hapu koe, e wanau koe he
tamaiti, a me hua tona ingoa ko IHU.
32 E nui ra hoki ia, e meinga ia
ko te Tamaiti o *te Atua* i runga rawa:
ka ho atu ki a ia e te Ariki te Atua te
torona o Rawiri tana matua:
33 Ko ia hei rangatira mo te ware
o Hakopa ake ake ake; a ekore e
mutu tona rangatiratanga.
34 Ka mea atu a Meri ki te ana-
hera, E peheatia tenei, kahore hoki
he hoa ki hau?
35 Ka ki atu te anahera ka mea atu
ki a ia, E tae mai te Wairua Tapu ki a
koe, e wakangaro i a koe te kaha ona i
runga rawa: ma konei hoki *tou* wanau
tapu te huaina ai ko te Tama o te Atua.
36 Na, ko Erihapeti tou teina, kua
hapu hoki ia he tamaiti i tona ruruhi-
tanga; a ko te ono tenei o nga ma-
rama ona i meinga he pakoko.
37 Kahore hoki he mea ekore e
taea e te Atua.
38 Ka mea atu a Meri, Na, ko te
pononga o te Ariki; kia pera ki hau
me tau i korero ai. A ka haere atu
te anahera i a ia.
39 ¶ Wakatika ana a Meri i aua
ra, haere porangi ana ki te wenua
pukepuke, ki tetahi pa o Hura:
40 Ka tomo atu ki te ware o Ha-
karaia, ka owa atu ki a Erihapeti.
41 A ka mea ano, i a Erihapeti e
rongo ana i te owatanga a Meri, ka
oho te tamaiti i tona kopu; a ka wa-
kakiia a Erihapeti ki te Wairua Tapu:
42 A ka karanga ki te reo nui, ka
mea, *E* wakapaingia *ana* koe i roto i
nga wahine, *e* wakapaingia *ana* hoki
te hua o tou kopu.
43 I nahea mai ano tenei ki hau,
kia haere mai te matua o taku Ariki
ki hau?
44 Na, i te panga mai hoki o te reo
o tou owatanga ki oku taringa, ka oho
te tamaiti i taku kopu i te hari.
45 A *e* hari *ana* a ia i wakapono:
e wakaritea hoki nga *mea* i korerotia
ki a ia no te Ariki.
46 ¶ Ka mea atu a Meri, E waka-
nui ana taku wairua i te Ariki,
47 E hari ana taku wairua ki te
Atua taku Kai wakaora.
48 Mo te mea hoki kua titiro ia ki
te nohinohinga o tana pononga: no
naianei ake hoki ka meinga ai a hau
e nga wakapaparanga katoa he *wa-
hine* hari.
49 Nana hoki e kaha nei i mea i
nga *mea* nui moku; *e* tapu *ana* ano
tona ingoa.
50 Ko tana mahi tohu kei te hunga
e wehi ana i a ia no tenei wakapapa-
ranga ki tera atu.
51 Kua wakaputaina he kaha na
tona ringaringa; ko te hunga waka-
kake i te wakaaro o o ratou ngakau
kua wakamararatia e ia.
52 Kua wakataka e ia te hunga
kaha i nga torona, kua meinga te hu-
nga nonohi ki runga.

5
The Harpoon's Head

David Haines

In January 2004 a harpoon's head with a section of its shaft intact was uncovered beneath the ruins of Oashore whaling station on Banks Peninsula. Encrusted with over 150 years of dirt, dust and rust, it is notable for being the most complete item of whaling equipment found to date in similar excavations across Australasia.[1] The arrow-like head of the whaler's harpoon is an instantly recognisable emblem of the global whale hunt, and of the broader struggle for human mastery over the natural world; works of art depicting its use date back to the fourteenth century. Yet in New Zealand, the harpoon is associated not only with global resource extraction, but also with the very beginnings of Pākehā life in these islands. Shore whaling in particular was intimately connected to colonialism, forming the context for interaction and settlement around much of our coastline. Taking the Oashore harpoon as its inspiration, and exploring the object's significance in a range of other settings, this essay makes an argument for the harpoon as colonial artefact.

The 'harpoon head with shaft', as it has since been labelled, was unearthed in front of a stone fireplace amid the foundations of one of three whalers' huts on the Oashore dig site. Measuring 28 by 12 centimetres and weighing just over 600 grams, the harpoon points provocatively back in time, its curved shaft bending like the tip of an unformed question mark, as if inviting us to speculate on its life story. Where in the world was this twisted rod of iron forged and shaped, and by whom? Which of the globe's great oceans did it then traverse, before coming to rest on the remote southern Banks Peninsula shoreline? In whose hands was it held and hurled? How many whales did it pierce, hook and tow before it snapped in two and was cast aside? Did it break off when lodged in its target? What happened to the whale? Did it swim off, or was it caught, killed and processed for oil and bone? Where was the oil and bone shipped to, for how much and to what end?

Sadly, little is known about this particular colonial object, and not a lot more about the shore whaling station from which it came. Shore whaling at Oashore Bay, a narrow inlet on the far west of Banks Peninsula, began in 1840 under the prominent Weller Brothers' firm, based in Sydney and Ōtākou. The initial crew of 24 included Weller employees Samuel Brown and Thomas Brown, and the short-tempered Irishman William 'Paddy' Woods. When

Harpoon head with shaft, excavated from site of Oashore whaling station, Banks Peninsula, 2004.

Courtesy of the Department of Anthropology and Archaeology, University of Otago. Photograph by Michael Hall

the Wellers went bankrupt soon afterwards, Woods took over the running of the station and developed a reputation for hard drinking and brutality towards his men, and towards neighbouring Kāi Tahu. Despite this ill repute, the Oashore station was profitable for close to a decade, with production peaking at 80,000 litres of oil and 4 tonnes of whalebone in 1844. By 1848 whales had become scarce and commercial whaling in the region ground to a rapid halt, though Kāi Tahu and local farmers continued small-scale operations until the mid-1870s.[2] One of the few things we can say with any certainty about the Oashore harpoon head is that, as a tool of the colonial whaling trade, this object and those like it were all too successful at skewering their quarry.

Oashore was just one of roughly 100 stations operating at various times on the New Zealand coastline from the late 1820s to the mid-1960s, to which must be added many hundred more whaling ship visits, both in bays and far out in the open ocean.[3] Any attempt to quantify the impact of this activity on whale populations must address a crucial problem: that its subjects live chiefly underwater. This makes them hard to count, and may be one reason why environmental history in New Zealand has tended to focus on the land, so that maritime and marine environments remain largely 'uncharted waters'.[4]

In the last 10 years scientists have begun to shed light on the legacy of marine extraction for our waters, as part of the global History of Marine Animal Populations (HMAP) project. Historians would do well to look closely at the results. In the case of inshore whaling, we now know that the southern right whale (*Eubalaena australis*) population fell from some 27,000 in 1825, before the advent of whaling, to approximately 1000 in 1997. At its nadir in the 1920s, the species came perilously close to extinction, reduced to as few as 60 breeding females in the entire Southern Ocean, from South Africa to South America.[5] That the vast majority of these removals occurred under sail, mostly from rowboats, with handheld harpoons, is testament indeed to human determination to extract profit from the oceans, often at great personal cost.

Whaling at Oashore was little different from that carried out elsewhere. It is often forgotten that whaling, though adventuresome, was also hard and dangerous work, made more perilous by the fact that most sailors of the time were unable to swim. Injuries and drownings were common and, as the workforce was for the most part unskilled, the industry relied on strict hierarchy and discipline, sometimes verging on brutality and economic enslavement, in the whaleboat and on ship and shore. Moreover, despite the whalers' overall efficiency in wiping out entire whale populations in a few decades, the success of the whale chase was by no means guaranteed. Even once a harpooner had struck fast, the whale had been lanced and the long haul back to shore had begun, it was common for a prize to be lost altogether, either by slipping loose or through the carcass sinking and being abandoned.[6]

The global whaling industry, expanding in the mid-nineteenth century from the American seaports of New Bedford and Nantucket, was increasingly polyglot, with ships and men of many nations and

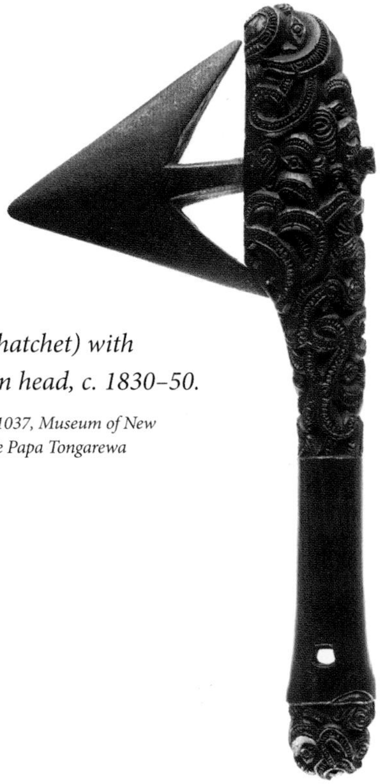

Pātiti (hatchet) with harpoon head, c. 1830–50.

Ref: OL001037, Museum of New Zealand Te Papa Tongarewa

cultures. This was also true of most whaling ships reaching New Zealand waters. Shore stations such as Oashore were similarly diverse, with numerous sailors from the multinational whaling fleet abandoning ship to join shore crews. These places did, however, have several distinctive features that set them apart from ship-based whaling. They were established almost without exception by merchants from the Australian colonies, backed by British capital, and their original crews were drawn primarily from the Sydney and Hobart docks. Shore whalers, too, had a far greater impact on coastal Māori populations and the future colony, because each station brought 30 foreigners, semi-permanently for eight months of the year, to areas of the country that had previously experienced little or no Euro-American contact. James Belich has described the social formation that resulted from these encounters as 'a Tasman World' and its wandering workers as 'Tasmen' – 'products of the space between the fragment and the frontier'.[7]

Not only were shore whalers a cosmopolitan group, but the commodities they produced were sent around the world. Thanks to searchable electronic newspaper databases and the digitisation of other source material, we now have a new level of access to innumerable lists of things that accompanied whaling to New Zealand – among them harpoons and whaling irons, such as the one under discussion, as well as exotic articles of clothing such as monkey jackets and duck frocks and, not least, strange medicines and ointments such as those discussed by Jonathan West in this volume. Often we can also see exactly what was shipped in return: oil and whalebone as well as a variety of other trade goods, including sealskins, timber, dressed flax and potatoes. Indeed it may be possible to further trace at least some of these items to their ultimate destinations, for example the processing of whale oil and bone into streetlamp fuel and candlewax, fine machinery lubricant, corsets, umbrellas, furniture and various other modern products in Europe and America.

We may assess, too, the significance of material objects introduced through the whaling industry to iwi and hapū of central and southern New Zealand. In considering material culture, we would do well to keep in mind what Nicholas Thomas calls the 'promiscuity of objects': 'Objects are not what they are made to be, but what they become.'[8] Nowhere is this better illustrated than in the 'pātiti (hatchet) with harpoon head', a weapon fashioned and spliced in wood and cast iron and likely employed in tribal warfare in the Cook Strait region sometime between 1830 and 1850, now held at the Museum of New Zealand Te Papa Tongarewa.

Māori made up a quarter or more of the workforce at many, if not most, shore stations in the 1830s, and several rose to the rank of harpooner or first mate aboard whaling vessels. Their reputation for strength and good seamanship was celebrated in the work of Herman Melville, whose novels *Omoo* (1847) and *Moby-Dick* (1851) both feature heroic Māori harpooners aboard American whaling voyages.[9] Māori at home also benefited from a close association with whaling. Until the early 1840s it was standard practice for indigenous leaders to form ongoing relationships with shore whaling proprietors; in exchange for protection and permission to use and occupy land, they received various objects from the stations' material networks, notably muskets, powder and ball and whaleboats. Thereafter, each station received a steady stream of Māori visitors, offering cargoes of whalebone, pigs, fish, potatoes and other produce, and the companionship of female relatives, in return for a range of everyday items, including tools, medicine, tea, sugar, tobacco and alcohol. In southern New Zealand these arrangements amounted to commercial partnerships, and there is evidence that Kāi Tahu ran their own whaling operations in Otago and Southland. Kāi Tahu were also active in shore whaling on Banks Peninsula, including at Oashore; there is every likelihood that the Oashore harpoon was at some stage held and thrown by Kāi Tahu hands.[10]

The world-famous Bettman photographic archive contains a striking 1936 portrait of an unidentified East Coast Māori man posing with a whaler's harpoon, subtitled 'a heroic (but vanishing) figure'. As the photograph suggests, shore whaling continued well into the twentieth century, concentrated in Northland, on the East Coast, in Marlborough and periodically in Canterbury and Otago. The last whale was taken by the Perano whalers off Kaikoura in 1964. The image also reflects a disproportionately high level of Māori participation in post-1840 whaling. This may be explained, in part, by their concentration in remote coastal communities, as well as a reluctance by Pākehā to carry on a seasonal and economically marginal activity that remained hard and dangerous work. It nevertheless also signifies a lasting cultural association with the whale hunt, and the passing down of family tradition, especially in those parts of New Zealand where extended contact with whalers resulted in intermarriage and enduring whakapapa ties.

The ongoing Māori connection with whaling can also be seen in the 1932 gifting of the whaleboat *Maori Girl* and a collection of harpoons and other whaling gear by a group of prominent Kāi Tahu whānui including the Ellison, Bradshaw and Parata families, to Dunedin's Otago Settlers Museum. In the 1860s and 1870s these items had been used for the short-lived revival of whaling at Waikouaiti and Ōtākou.[11]

The harpoon's legacy in New Zealand is, fundamentally, a colonial one. Shore whaling, especially, is best regarded as the extension of settler commerce from one developing sphere of British influence – the Australian penal colonies – to another, coastal New Zealand. Relationships of trade and co-existence between Māori and shore whalers emerged not in a vacuum, but within this colonial context. Further, to consider whalers and their methods as somehow separate from colonial settlement is to

Left: *Standing beside the* Maori Girl *whaleboat in 1933 are James 'Tiemi' Apes (right), an original Kāi Tahu crew member, and Kenneth Ross, who restored the vessel.* *Ref: F-609, Collection of Toitū Otago Settlers Museum*

Below: *Whaleboat showing position of crew, early nineteenth century.* *Ref: A-032-025, Alexander Turnbull Library, Wellington, New Zealand*

Bottom: *A Māori man aims a harpoon in 1936. The photograph was captioned: 'A heroic (but vanishing) figure. With their almost obsolete methods, the natives achieve excellent results.'* Courtesy of Corbis Images

ignore the significant history of whaling by Māori and non-Māori in the decades after 1840. Rather than thinking of those who wielded the harpoon as foreign, prior and 'other' to our settler past, we must come to terms with the fact that colonialism in this part of the world was founded on the exhaustive extraction, if not pillaging, of natural resources. We must also face the uncomfortable reality that the colonial urge to slaughter marine mammals endured long into the twentieth century, even after several whale species had become so rare as to be virtually extinct.

Archaeological excavations at Oashore and elsewhere, the prominence of the *Maori Girl* and Kāi Tahu harpoon collection at the entrance of the recently relaunched Toitū Otago Settlers Museum, and historical fiction such as Fiona Kidman's *The Captive Wife* are all evidence of a continuing fascination with the history of whaling.[12] An object-focused approach has the potential to move us past romantic portrayals, to consider instead a new history of harpoons: of artefacts embedded in colonial ground, of long-submerged marine environmental histories, of wandering workers in the Tasman world, of colonial commodity circuits, of the persistence of Māori whaling traditions and, ultimately, of overlapping and entangled categories of indigenous and colonial in nineteenth- and twentieth-century New Zealand.

The Weller Brothers' Medicine Chest.

Courtesy of the Otago Peninsula Museum. Photograph by Michael Hall

6

'Keep the head cool, the feet warm, and the bowels open'

Octavius Harwood and the Weller Brothers' Medicine Chest

Jonathan West

Octavius Harwood did not write in his usual diary on 25 October 1838. It was the first time, in six months as clerk at the Weller Brothers' Ōtākou whaling station, that he had not jotted just a few terse words on the wind, the whales or perhaps a ship's arrival. This might otherwise be unremarkable, but on this occasion Octavius had a rather more delicate task: to document his employer Edward Weller's brutal assault on one of the station's most valuable members, Dr Joseph Crocome. He took up a new notebook and penned the following account:

> October 25th, 1838 [Weller] took a bludgeon from under a jacket laying alongside of him … and deliberately made a blow at the Ds [Crocome's] head, which completely stunned him and cut his head severely, he then repeated the blow a second time and would have killed him when I interfered … The D. fell dead, and staggered down bleading profusely … He [Weller] then appeared to consider what he had done and enquired what was to be done … I recommended cold water … he [Weller] then said he had better bleed him, which he did. By that time Mr. P came in and assisted the bleading … he [Weller] then enquired of him [Crocome] what had better be done if he got any worse. The D. recommended cold applications to the wound, aperient [opening, or laxative] medicine and bathing feet in warm water. Mr P. and myself then washed his head and shaved the hair off round the wound … about 2 inches in length and right in to the bone … We then put sticking plaster to keep the wound together and put him on the sofa … very unwell, took no refreshment of any sort whole day except water. At 4 gave him Does [dose] of opening medicine …

Dr Joseph Crocome, of the Ōtākou and Waikouaiti whaling stations, perhaps the first doctor to live in Te Wai Pounamu (South Island).

Ref: S06-1891, Hocken Collections, Uare Taoka a Hākena, University of Otago

Harwood's testimony makes clear that young and hot-headed Edward Weller, suspecting Crocome of inciting doubt about his authority as manager of the whaling station, had made a premeditated but promptly regretted assault. It is rather wonderful that Weller then had to ask his victim how he should help him – but Crocome was then the only doctor in all of Te Wai Pounamu, or the South Island.

Even a little medical knowledge meant much in this distant edge of empire, despite, and even in some ways because of, the very patchy nature of that knowledge: when all doctors were more or less faith healers, who

Detail of the Weller Brothers' medicine chest, showing compartments holding equipment such as the truss, splints and probangs, alongside assorted medicine bottles.

Photograph by Michael Hall

could but believe in them? As Robert Fulton observes, 'Pathology could hardly be said to exist, the very meaning of disease and the explanation of its processes was a sealed book ... Can one picture what [Crocome's] difficulties were, and what his limitations?'[1] Oxford-educated Harwood had gained the rudiments of medical training as a novice first mate on his voyage out to Sydney the year before,[2] and now he followed Crocome's advice: the good doctor received regular doses of laxatives over the next few days. This, in fact, was long-standing best medical practice. As the apocryphal but powerful story goes, when the celebrated physician Hermann Boerhaeve died in 1738 a book in which he had reputedly set out all the secrets of medicine was opened; its pages were empty save for the very treatment Crocome self-prescribed: 'Keep the head cool, the feet warm, and the bowels open.'[3]

Crocome revived, left, understandably, and later returned to Otago to work for the Wellers' rival, Johnny Jones.[4] Harwood could call on Crocome for especially serious cases but he was now the makeshift physician to the whaling station, and to the Māori communities in which it was embedded.[5] Harwood relied, as Crocome had before him, on the contents of the Weller Brothers' medicine chest.

Today the chest sits propped against a wall of the Otago Peninsula Museum. A solid wooden box, about 50 by 30 centimetres, its heft is tolerable for one person, though much more comfortable for two. A sheet of cracked glass now covers the chest, under which its contents are arrayed in cork-stoppered glass bottles, each in a small compartment. These surround a larger space filled with a jumble of string-bound paper packages, and a belt-like leather object which, a typed list tacked to the lid describing the chest's 'original contents' suggests, must be a truss.

The chest embodies the state of European medical knowledge in the 1830s. Its central compartment holds basic paraphernalia such as splints and dressings for binding people back together after accident or surgery. The truss was used to treat hernia, caused perhaps by the terrible strains of towing a whale, sometimes for a considerable distance. Probangs (perhaps made of whalebone) and gum bougies were tubes to clear the throat or secure airways. Numerous glass bottles contain drugs and other medicines, their diversity highlighting the patchiness of medical knowledge. Several were effective painkillers: extract of belladonna (deadly nightshade), tincture of henbane and paregoric, or opium. Without anaesthetic these were indispensable. Other bottles contain all-purpose medicines such as hartshorn, peppermint and cinnamon; some have specific uses, such as smelling salts and quinine. There are emetics, expectorants and purgatives – emetic of tartar, ipecacuanha and rhubarb – reflecting the consensus that disease had to be evicted from the body. Māori and European shared this belief, differing only in how best to effect the ejection: Māori used karakia to try and drive illness out, whereas Europeans used purgatives alongside prayer. Balm of Gilead, meanwhile, was probably not the biblical herb but Dr Samuel Solomon's extraordinarily popular quackish miracle cure-all which, as one advertisement puffed, 'warms and enlivens the heart, raises the spirits

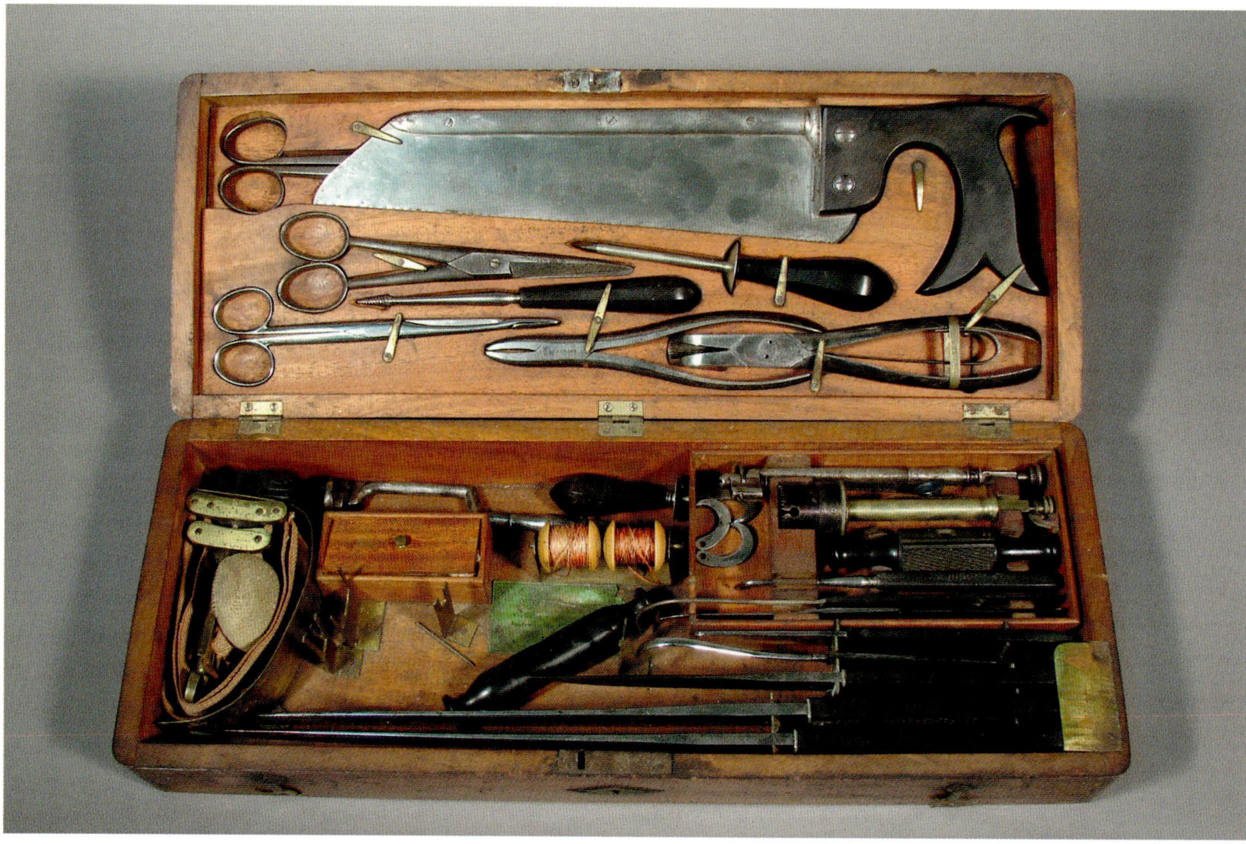

and provides digestion, eases or cures nervous, hypochondriac, consumptive and female complaints, and lifts lassitude, debility and weakness rising from juvenile imprudences'.[6]

Although Harwood at some point acquired a fine surgical kit, now in the Toitū Otago Settlers Museum, his journal never mentions its use.[7] His journal tells us how he used the medicine chest, and its role in the life of the whaling station. He regularly dispensed medicine to both Māori and Europeans, but there is never any suggestion of payment for his services.[8] His help was needed for the injured and the sick, and for mothers in childbirth. On Saturday 11 May 1839, Harwood recorded that 'Mr. Cureton came over from Tyarie [Taieri] bringing with him two men hurt by whales, one his leg broke, the other struck about the head and back. Had killed 7 whales up to this date. Reported Mr. Whylie to be very ill of fever.'[9] Illness recurrently debilitated Ōtākou, and Harwood 'gave physic' while the whaleboats stayed ashore.[10] Harwood named his European patients and over time came to name Māori too; Cowtier [Kautea] was one such. Still, Māori were more often sick, and in greater numbers, and so Harwood more typically records that he 'Gave physic to 6 natives' or to 'Price's Mowrays'.[11]

Four Kāi Tahu villages lay within a few hundred metres of the whaling station in the late 1830s, and Harwood had important roles in brokering relationships with these communities. He traded with Kāi Tahu leaders for goods, engineered their transport to the wider world and employed Kāi Tahu as whalers and as general labourers. His written archive is terse testament to such work, so it is telling that he recorded a detailed list of Māori words for parts of

Left: *Surgical instruments belonging to Octavius Harwood, and possibly given to him by Dr Crocome.*

Collection of Toitū Otago Settlers Museum

Right: *Octavius Harwood (1816–1900).*

Ref: S06-189m, Hocken Collections, Uare Taoka a Hākena, University of Otago

the body, many of which suggest the distinctive Kāi Tahu dialect: Harwood names finger as 'migarra', for example, which in modern Māori would be rendered as matikara, while 'calf of leg' is tarkaw rather than takapū.[12]

Octavius had to gain and maintain the trust of Māori while working in that most intimate of settings: as physician examining patient. Ōtākou Māori had great need of such care as waves of epidemic disease devastated their communities during the 1830s and 1840s.[13] This placed Harwood in a powerful yet precarious position, as is attested to in his brief mentions of his own wife, Tītapu. Her father was Kāi Tahu rangatira Pokene, displaced from Canterbury to Ōtākou by Te Rauparaha. Harwood and Tītapu had married according to Māori custom in about 1839, but in 1842 Tītapu sickened, perhaps with tuberculosis.[14] She was bled by a French whaling surgeon but tended by a 'very much troubled' Harwood,[15] and died on 14 June. Pokene had told Harwood two days before that 'he would be revenged' should this happen. There is no sign that he exacted this toll, but the threat suggests the risk undertaken in dispensing hope in the form of medicine.

The chest is an apt prop, too, for considering the wider fate of whaling in our colonial history. Whaling's disappearance, epitomised in the Weller empire's sudden disintegration, has obscured its significance. Although whales and Wellers vanished, their employees did not: many melded into colonial life. The chest stayed with Octavius Harwood at his farm on the Otago Peninsula until he died there in 1900. By then eight of his descendants also ran farms on the peninsula. Other whaling families such as the Clearwaters share a similar story.[16]

Harwood retained an interest in medicine. In 1857 his brother Thomas wrote from Sydney to reassure him that he had sent 'the books on Mineralogy and Medicology which you ordered'.[17] And perhaps Harwood still acted as physician to his own family in some small way. But the very fact that the chest's 'original contents' could later be listed, probably by Lucy Harwood (who cared for the chest after her grandfather's death), suggests just how quickly it became an antiquarian object: a thing retained unchanged to honour the memory of Octavius Harwood's role as makeshift physician, through which he both helped to keep old New Zealand alive, and played midwife to colonial Otago.

7
Colonising Through Play
The Crowthers' Noah's Ark

Lynette Townsend

Mary Crowther aged 12, c. 1881.

Photograph by W.H. Clarke, courtesy of Mrs Joy Johnson and the Wainuiomata Historical Museum Society

Opposite: *The Crowthers' Noah's Ark, made between 1840 and 1875.*

Ref: GH011702, Museum of New Zealand Te Papa Tongarewa

It is a very basic flat-bottomed type of Noah's Ark, plainly painted with stencilled features typical of cheaper mass-produced nineteenth-century arks and it is missing the dove that was sometimes painted on the roof. There is a set of 40 roughly carved and painted animals and figurines, although there may originally have been more. Once owned by the Crowther children, the ark, now in the Museum of New Zealand Te Papa Tongarewa, connects us to the experiences of colonial children and the hopes and dreams of parents for their families. While these toys represent one of the ways Christian values were transferred through play and storytelling, the tale of their production also draws attention to another, less idealised picture of childhood labour in the colonial era.

The Crowther family was among the first of the almost 10,000 settlers, including 3846 children under 13, who migrated to New Zealand under the auspices of the privately organised New Zealand Company scheme.[1] The family of Thomas and Judith Crowther and their children, John aged nine, Frederick aged eight, Emma aged seven and Anna aged four, arrived at Port Nicholson (now Wellington) in 1841 on board the *Slains Castle*. They lived first in the Hutt Valley, then later settled in Moores Valley near Wainuiomata.[2]

Thomas became an active and involved member of the settler community, operating a successful tailoring business in Lambton Quay and Willis Street between 1841 and the 1860s. When he died in 1872 at the age of 69, a notice in the *Wellington Independent* described him as 'An early settler and an excellent man, one who, at the commencement of the colony, had to "rough it", but who always bore the burden', while 'his uniform temper and cheerfulness endeared him to all who knew him'.[3]

Thomas Crowther's involvement as a committee member in the 1848 Evangelical Alliance, established to open a Bible depot, is recorded in Louis Ward's account of colonial life in Wellington.[4] It is evidence of the family's religious activities, and hints at their commitment to continuing the Christian values and beliefs they brought with them. Owning a Noah's Ark would certainly have been in keeping with the Crowthers' convictions.

For many of New Zealand's early settler families the continuation of the religious practices they had followed in their country of origin was an

important part of the 'better life' they hoped to have by emigrating. The desire to give children more opportunities and a quality education, seen as a tool in the reform of society, prevailed. This combination of enlightened and religious interests in education transferred easily to the colonies, which settlers believed offered land and opportunities not to be found in Britain.[5] Religious ideology also justified the settlers' presence in New Zealand. As Philippa Mein Smith writes, the 'pioneers tamed the land and, they believed, made it productive as God intended'.[6]

It is unclear whether the Crowthers brought their Noah's Ark with them to New Zealand or purchased it here. It is conceivable that they bought it in Wellington because by 1845 there were already many well-established shops in the growing city and a relatively large variety of goods available. Toys could also be acquired at local auctions. Wholesale catalogues for German-made arks show the availability of a variety of styles and sizes.

Noah's Arks, with their biblical theme, were considered the most suitable Sunday toy for Victorian Christian families. Restrictions on Sundays included no whistling, jumping or climbing trees, but quiet play was permitted between the morning church service and Sunday school in the afternoon,[7] and children were encouraged to use the Noah's Ark to recite and act out the biblical tale. Apart from the religious

Penny beasts or misery beasts? Carved animals from the Crowthers' Noah's Ark.

Ref: GH011702, Museum of New Zealand Te Papa Tongarewa

lessons, children learned classification by arranging the animals in pairs, and by identifying the species they broadened their knowledge of the animal world. The popularity and tremendous commercial success of arks can be attributed to the toy's ability to satisfy the demands of both adults and children.[8]

For inventive children, however, the story of Noah could be a springboard for other games and stories. Recalling her childhood in Victorian England, Eleanor Acland wrote that 'We began our play with the traditional "animals went in two by two", and then branched off into variations of Treasure Island or Swiss Family Robinson, or stories made up by ourselves, any of these being tolerably sabbatical so long as we remember to call the leading characters Mr and Mrs Noah, Shem, Ham and Japheth.'[9] Perhaps the Crowther children, too, acted out stories of their own experience of travel by ship or even played games that made a connection between the biblical story of Noah and their own situation as colonial settlers – both were settling new lands.

Thomas Crowther's religious convictions and connection to the Evangelical Alliance suggest that the Crowther children would have played with the Noah's Ark now held in Te Papa. Crowther's granddaughter Mary, who gave the ark to the museum, would certainly have played with it. Her parents were clearly eager for her to be well educated. As a young girl she had joined her cousins, the Woods, at Northbrook House in Wainuiomata to be taught by a governess until she went on to Miss Ellen Greenwood's School for Young Ladies on The Terrace in Wellington. Her diaries, which begin in 1885 when she was 16, provide insight into the family's daily activities and religious commitment. Every Wednesday she attended Bible class; and every Sunday she went to church services in the morning and evening, and Bible class after that.[10]

The Noah's Ark toy also fitted dominant theories about early childhood education, which perhaps added to its popularity with astute colonial settlers like the Crowther family. German educationalist Friedrich Froebel, for example, proposed the development of a system of education for the very young based on the concept of self-activity.[11] Play, the highest phase of child development, helped children to grow into 'well rounded individuals'. Froebel devised a series of educational tasks and games he named 'Gifts'. These activity-based playthings for self-directed free play encouraged both imaginative and scientific learning in much the same way as the Noah's Ark toy did.

The joy and luxury of play enjoyed by the Crowther children did not extend to the German children involved in making toy Noah's Arks. The story behind their production illustrates another side to nineteenth-century childhood where long hours of hard work ensured there was very little time for play.

By the 1840s the mass production of Noah's Arks was well under way and the villages of the Erzgebirge Mountains had become the worldwide centre for their production and distribution. Specialist machinery enabled 60 to 100 identical animals to be created at a time and the availability of cheap labour, which involved entire families working from home, kept costs low. Child labour was integral to the process. Each animal was cut, rounded by hand, sanded, painted and shellacked; children were assigned the task of

sanding and glueing on ears, horns and tails. The more competent were also allowed to do some carving and painting.[12] The production of the arks was the most prestigious work. An ark builder made the raw ark and then sold this to the master ark painter, who was assisted by a child who applied the undercoat. The master painter then stencilled the façade and painted the finishing details and a child assistant added the final layer of shellac.

The cheap and abundant supply of animals using the Erzgebirge method meant that wholesalers could assemble and export thousands of sets of Noah's Arks during the nineteenth and early twentieth centuries. The small animals, known as 'penny beasts' by the wholesalers, were less fondly nicknamed 'misery beasts' by the families who worked long hours for a pittance to create them.[13] A family making 6000 animals a week earned barely enough to keep them supplied with bread and potatoes. Malnutrition and disease were common.[14]

Many different styles of ark were made, each in several sizes, meaning that there could be hundreds of variations. The easiest arks to make, and the least expensive, were stained, stencilled and filled with the crudest turned animals. The well-loved dove with its olive branch is missing on many of these inexpensive arks,[15] like the Crowthers'. These cheaper models allowed wholesalers to broaden their market by providing a more affordable option for lower-income families. They were also a deliberate attempt to compete against other European toymakers and the developing toy industry in the United States and Britain.

World War I brought an end to the golden age of the Erzgebirge toy industry. As pioneers in the mass production of children's toys, the craftspeople of Erzgebirge played an integral part in the transformation of the international toy industry, which resulted in a move away from small-scale, expensive toys affordable only for wealthy families, to toys that were mass-produced and available to the majority of children, including young colonials like the Crowther children.

Now the arks are celebrated in museums and private collections all over the world. For some, they are reminiscent of a life fraught with poverty and child labour but for others they signify a childhood guided by Christian values and filled with imaginative play. Each ark has associated with it the lives of the children and families who owned and enjoyed it, and like the Crowther children, many were among New Zealand's early colonial settlers. For Mary, the last of the Crowther family to live on the family farm, Brookfield, this Noah's Ark had other, more personal associations. When she died in 1958 the ark was in her possession and had by then become much more than a toy; it was also a precious family heirloom.

8
The Bishop's Register
F. Jane Teal

The first Bishop's Register for the Anglican Diocese of Christchurch began its working life in 1856 with a copy of the letters patent granted to Henry John Chitty Harper, and concluded 407 pages and 33 years later with the resignation of a lay reader from Governors Bay.[1]

The register succinctly records those parts of a bishop's official daily life that are associated with buildings, people and parishes. It is a direct consequence of an episcopal consecration when the bishop is given liturgical tasks that only he or she has the authority to undertake, and must be recorded for posterity. For this reason it is still a primary reference document for the diocese.[2] In New Zealand these registers have been in existence since the appointment of George Augustus Selwyn as Bishop of New Zealand and Melanesia in 1841. As New Zealand was divided into dioceses, each bishop began to record their individual official acts. This register, covering Harper's episcopate, bridges the imperial and colonial worlds.

Harper was consecrated a bishop at Lambeth Palace on 10 August 1856 by John Bird Sumner, Archbishop of Canterbury,[3] following Selwyn's partial resignation of his see. On his arrival in New Zealand Harper was installed as Bishop of Christchurch in the pro-cathedral – the Church of St Michael and All Angels – on 25 December 1856.[4] It was not until 1871 that the Diocese of Dunedin was formed, so the register contains entries from the Otago–Southland region until that date.

The role of registers has changed over time. Heresies, contributions for the repair of roads and bridges and even wills are no longer recorded as they were in the medieval registers, but the registers still retain the long link with the past with their documentation of confirmations, licensing, appointments, ordinations, consecrations and deconsecrations. Financial matters, the calling of synods, letters of dismissal and recommendations to bishops in other New Zealand dioceses and overseas, commissions and inquiries, all of which are now recorded elsewhere, can be found in this early volume. Each subsequent register therefore has a relationship to its predecessors. For example, Harper's volume includes the consecration of the second church at Lyttelton, the Church of the Holy Trinity, on Easter Day, 10 April 1860; just over 150 years later its deconsecration on 11 October 2011, following damage in the earthquakes of

Henry John Chitty Harper, first Bishop of the Diocese of Christchurch (1856–90) and Primate of New Zealand (1869–90).

Dr A.C. Barker photograph, Christ's College Archives, Christchurch

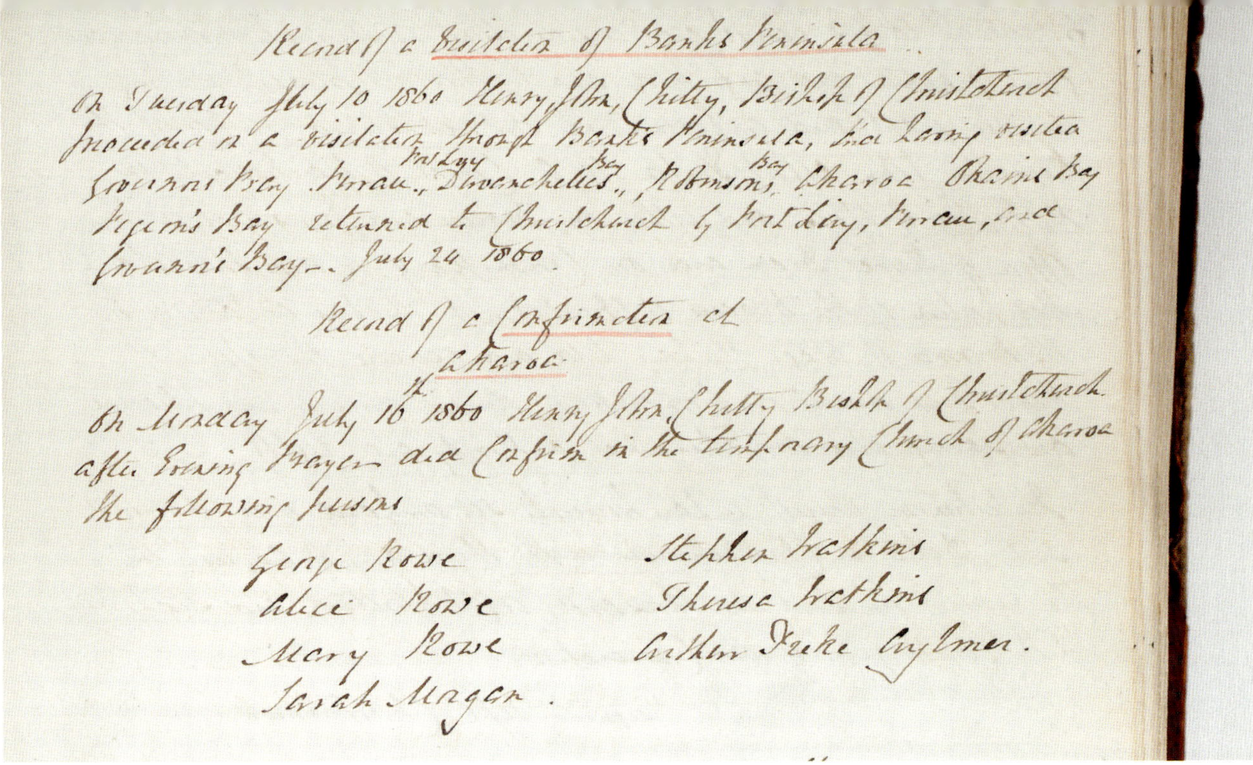

Record of a Visitation of Banks Peninsula

On Tuesday July 10 1860 Henry John, Chitty, Bishop of Christchurch proceeded on a visitation through Banks Peninsula, and having visited Governors Bay, Port Levy, Akaroa, Duvauchelles Bay, Robinsons Bay, Akaroa, Okains Bay, Pigeon's Bay returned to Christchurch by Port Levy, Akaroa, and Governor's Bay – July 24 1860.

Record of a Confirmation at Akaroa

On Monday July 16th 1860 Henry John, Chitty Bishop of Christchurch after Evening Prayer did Confirm in the temporary Church of Akaroa the following persons

George Rowe — Stephen Watkins
Alice Rowe — Theresa Watkins
Mary Rowe — Arthur Drake Aylmer.
Sarah Morgan.

2010 and 2011, can be found in the official acts of the eighth bishop, Victoria Matthews.[5]

The responsibility for keeping the register accurate and up to date initially lay with Harper. It then devolved to his clerical secretaries, Robert Simeon Jackson and then Francis Knowles, as the centre of diocesan administration moved first to Bishopscourt and then to the Diocesan Office and Synod Hall on the eastern edge of the Christ's College site in Rolleston Avenue.

The volume is far more than a collection of facts. It sits not only within the context of Anglican tradition and the New Zealand Anglican Church's Constitution and Canons but also in the world in which it was created. The register therefore provides a very accurate account of the changing role of the bishop. Much of Harper's time in the early years was spent as a parish priest to his whole diocese. So, as he made his way around his extensive see, he baptised, and officiated at marriages. At the end of July 1857, after initial visits to Little River, Avonside and Hororata, he set off on Dick, his strawberry roan, for the first of his southern visitations.[6] Accompanied by his son, Henry William, and with a telescope, pocket compass and a packhorse, it took him 18 days to get from Christchurch to Dunedin, visiting sheep and cattle stations on the way. Father and son then spent 10 days in and around the town, before heading south towards Jacobs River (Riverton). In the course of the visitation the pair almost drowned, were lost in a storm over Flagstaff and returned in mid-October just in time for the 5 pm service at St Michael and All Angels. Later Henry William wrote, 'Riding up to the gate that led into the church grounds, we found there one or two clergy, who at first could hardly recognize the Bishop in his travelled stained clothes; from head to foot he was mud-coloured, his gaiters bound together with flax, his Episcopal hat quite disreputable.'[7]

Harper's first visit to the West Coast was in late August and September 1865 in preparation for the appointment of Henry William Harper to an area that stretched from the Teramakau River to Ross. On horseback, and in the company of his son George and the many miners who were following the same route,

Harper's visitation of Banks Peninsula, 10–12 July 1860, included a confirmation in the temporary church in Akaroa.

Photograph by Michael Hall

they took a week to reach Hokitika.[8] The bishop made subsequent visits by coach, and although the register records his official business, unofficially his presence was a good reason for a concert and for gathering together people from scattered communities.

From the mid-1860s the register shows that more and more of Harper's visitations were organised around consecrations and confirmations. Although churches had been built before this time and people were worshipping in them, all debt had to be paid off before they could be formally consecrated for permanent ecclesiastical use. Many of the churchyards surrounding the buildings and portions of public cemeteries were consecrated at the same time.

Confirmation enabled individuals to take Holy Communion and this was seen, along with the words of commitment in the service, as a sign of adult involvement in a congregation. Local clergy increasingly prepared individuals, but it required the presence of the bishop and the laying on of hands to complete the process. The adoption of the seasonal rhythms of the southern hemisphere can be seen most clearly in the dates of these services. They gradually become more frequent in late spring and early summer, to fall away in January and then resume in the autumn months of March and April.

The greater number of consecrations and confirmations was also associated with the appointment of clergy to clearly defined parishes. Clergy were acquired by various means. When Harper arrived some of the chaplains from the Canterbury Association ships had been licensed by Selwyn for specific localities. Others took services as and when they were required, but had almost all turned to farming as a means of actually making a living. After Harper's arrival some clergy wrote directly to the bishop enquiring about positions, while others were vetted by his English commissaries. There were also a few who just turned up from all parts of the world and exhibited their letters of orders in the hope of acquiring a position. The bishop, however, wanted clergy who were locally trained and physically and spiritually fit for the diocese's conditions.[9] This led to the gradual development of the Upper Department of Christ's College as a place for theological education. The register records the increasing number of ordinations of these locally trained men in the pro-cathedral and from 1881, with the opening of ChristChurch Cathedral, these occasions took place almost exclusively in the mother church of the diocese.

Harper had responded realistically to the initial shortage of clergy by licensing lay readers. Selwyn had envisaged this as a possibility and the register shows Harper taking it up with enthusiasm from the 1860s. He not only placed potential ordination candidates in a range of localities as a means of testing their vocation and giving them pastoral skills, but also licensed men the local community recognised as appropriate for this task. This acknowledged the informal practice on many rural stations, where workers and family had regularly gathered together for morning and evening prayers. Although he could not converse in their language, Harper understood the need for Māori to be ministered to by Māori and appointed local lay readers.[10]

As well as having a responsibility towards people, a bishop is also responsible for authorising the temporal

This faculty, issued on 21 December 1879, sanctioned the placing of a brass cross and two candlesticks in the Church of St Augustine, Waimate.

Photograph by Michael Hall

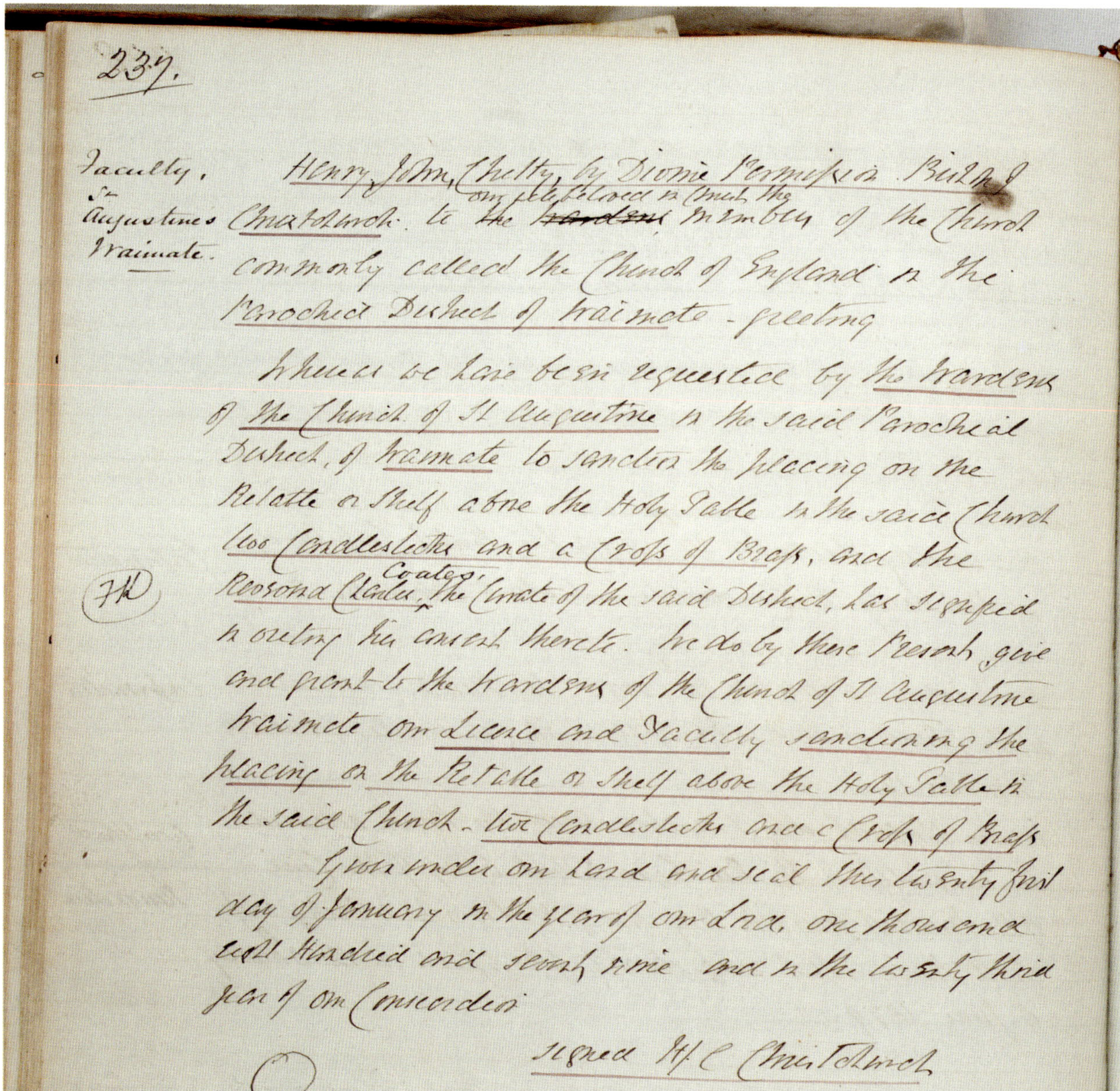

237.

Faculty. St Augustines Waimate.

Henry John Chitty, by Divine Permission Bishop of Christchurch: to ~~the Wardens~~ our well beloved in Christ the members of the Church commonly called the Church of England in the Parochial District of Waimate - greeting

Whereas we have been requested by the Wardens of the Church of St Augustine in the said Parochial District of Waimate to sanction the placing on the Retable or Shelf above the Holy Table in the said Church two Candlesticks and a Cross of Brass, and the Reverend Charles Coates, the Curate of the said District, has signified in writing his consent thereto. We do by these Presents give and grant to the Wardens of the Church of St Augustine Waimate our Licence and Faculty sanctioning the placing on the Retable or Shelf above the Holy Table in the said Church two Candlesticks and a Cross of Brass

Given under our hand and seal this twenty first day of January in the year of our Lord one thousand eight hundred and seventy nine and in the twenty third year of our Consecration

signed H J C Christchurch

possessions held and used on church property. The Diocesan Archives holds terriers that include details of an individual church and lists of artefacts from the early 1870s. It was not until 1879, however, that Harper actually began recording faculties for individual items held within a church. Once issued by faculty, an item cannot be removed from a church without another faculty; this guards against the whim of an incumbent or a congregation. The formalising of the process at this particular time was a carefully considered response following the objections of some Kaiapoi parishioners to the rites and ceremonies introduced by Hubert Carlyon, and what he taught. One parishioner went so far as to throw a cross into the River Cam.[11]

Harper was appointed primate by General Synod and his fellow bishops in 1869. Much of the increased workload that this new position entailed can be seen in the accounts of General Synod,[12] but he also had to formally record episcopal resignations, the arrangement of electoral synods and the consecration of their successors. His correspondence shows just how widespread his communication was with bishops of the whole Anglican Communion, and he also attended the first (1867) and second (1878) Lambeth Conferences in England.[13] These two extensive periods of time away from his diocese enabled him both to converse with fellow bishops and to be part of decision making at an international level. During his absence, the register records his appointment of commissaries to deal with urgent administrative matters, but consecrations, ordinations and confirmations necessarily had to wait until his return.

Clues about the bishop's extended family are few, but they are there to be found in the register. For example, a diversion to Holincote, the home of the Acland family at Mt Peel in Canterbury, was added to a southern visitation in November 1859 for the baptism of Charles Howard Tripp, the first of the many grandchildren of Harper and his wife Emily. Again in April and May 1864 he headed inland to baptise more grandchildren, Emily Dyke Acland and Percy Harper Cox. Five years later he baptised Lucy Alice Dyke Acland, Robert Ernest Irvine and Margaret McLeod – the latter two were children of Mt Peel shepherds.[14] There is only one entry in the official acts between 5 September and 3 October 1869, for during this time Herbert Harper, Henry and Emily's seventh son, died from consumption on 7 September, aged 22. There is also a notable gap between 10 and 27 June 1888. Emily Harper, whom Henry described in a letter to his brother Leopold as his constant 'companion and helper', died on 10 June.[15]

This first volume of the Official Acts of the Bishops of Christchurch records the formative years of the Anglican Diocese of Christchurch. Parallel and intertwined within the register is the life, work and vocation of one man, Henry John Chitty Harper. It was a diocese that initially owed much to its English heritage and ecclesiastical structures. It was during Harper's years as bishop and primate, however, that the Anglican Church developed its New Zealand identity and, more particularly, the Diocese of Christchurch established its ongoing Canterbury and West Coast distinctiveness.

9

The Face on the Wall

Mrs Humphrey Devereux as Object, as Art, as Family

Charlotte Macdonald

Mrs Humphrey Devereux is a long-lived and much-travelled object. Painted in Boston in 1770, the portrait now resides in the collection of the Museum of New Zealand Te Papa Tongarewa. The artist's signature was barely dry on the canvas when the work was shipped across the Atlantic to London in late January 1771. It went on public display in the same year, before taking a place on the wall of the sitter's son's London home. The portrait remained in private hands in England until 1842, when it was stowed among the boxes belonging to John and Sarah Greenwood, who were embarking on the *Phoebe* as New Zealand Company settlers to Nelson. For the next century it hung on walls in Greenwood family homes in Motueka and later in Eastbourne, Wellington, until being 'discovered' in 1952, when it was recognised as the work of the pre-eminent artist of colonial America, John Singleton Copley (1738–1815).[1] The portrait was extensively restored in New York before being generously gifted to the New Zealand national art collection by the Greenwood family in 1965. Since that time *Mrs Humphrey Devereux* has been exhibited to the New Zealand public as a rare eighteenth-century beauty, and within major Copley and Colonial America exhibitions in leading United States galleries.[2]

As a face on the family wall, a work of art and a valuable collection item, *Mrs Humphrey Devereux* has transcended the circumstances and purposes of its creation, and long outlived its subject, artist and patron. In crossing the oceans several times, the portrait has connected the worlds of eighteenth-century colonial America on the cusp of revolution, mid-nineteenth-century British settler colonialism, New Zealand national life in the later twentieth century and contemporary global art. In doing so it has linked Mrs Humphrey Devereux to her family and their successors across the separations of space and time created by colonial histories. At either end of its life, in 1771 and from 1965, the portrait has been an object of admiration as a transcendent work of art.

Mrs Humphrey Devereux began life in 1770 as a means of bridging the familial distance between colony and metropole. Now that he had settled permanently in London, American-born John Greenwood, Mary Devereux's son from her first marriage, knew that his recent marriage and flourishing business as an art entrepreneur made it unlikely he would ever return to America or see his mother again, so he commissioned a painting of her.[3] As

John Singleton Copley painted Mrs Humphrey Devereux (Mary Charnock) in the summer of 1770 as a commission from her London-based son John Greenwood. The painting was created in the year in which Mrs Devereux celebrated her sixtieth birthday.

John Singleton Copley, Mrs Humphrey Devereux*, 1771, oil on canvas, 1020 x 810 mm, Ref: 1965-0013-1, Museum of New Zealand Te Papa Tongarewa*

Details of John Singleton Copley, Mrs Humphrey Devereux, *1771.*

Greenwood explained to Copley, the portrait would be the next best thing: 'seeing the good Lady's Face as she now appears, with old age creeping upon her.'[4] Having her face on the wall was both an expression of his affection and a mark of his status as head of a reputable London household. The ageing mother's image bestowed a sense of both lineage and domestic virtue.[5]

For Copley the portrait bridged the cultural gap between Boston and London. The commission was a welcome opportunity to press his claims for recognition among the 'Elustrious Artists' at the 'summit' of the art world. London, and Europe generally, compared very favourably with 'this Country', which he considered 'destitute … of every affection' for the 'Arts'.[6] Even as he enjoyed the status and income of New England's premier artist, Copley's ambitions lay beyond the colonies and the lucrative but aesthetically lowly 'trade' of portraiture. With this commission he was particularly eager to show that he was a true artist and not simply an accomplished maker of 'likenesses'.[7] The two previous works Greenwood had exhibited for him in London had been admired, but also criticised for being 'too liney', wrongly coloured, overdetailed in their precision.[8] Copley's work impressed in its exactitude, but lacked feeling. Preoccupation with the material substance at the cost of the human presence of the subject exposed a lack of training and sophistication; commercial portraiture rather than the higher realm of Art. *Mrs Humphrey Devereux* was Copley's attempt to turn colonial specificity and materialism into universal metropolitan idea.

Painting the face of an older woman in informal pose served both Copley's and Greenwood's needs. Of the sitter's part in the portrait's creation we know least. Mary Devereux turned 60 in 1770.[9] We can only conclude that she agreed to her son's request and was sufficiently committed to make the 30-kilometre journey from Marblehead to Boston more than once to sit for the 32-year-old artist.

The half-length portrait with the subject sitting at a table, head resting on a hand under the chin, was a conventional late-eighteenth-century portrait pose, the same Copley had used in painting silversmith Paul Revere two years earlier.[10] Greater emphasis, and light, fell on the face, while the surroundings were sparser than in Copley's lavish full-length portraits of Boston's mercantile elite. The work's restraint is also evident in the darker and more limited palette. Yet the social status of Mrs Devereux and the skill of the artist are fully demonstrated here. The silk sheen of sleeve, the transparent shawl, the lightness and shade in the white frill on the resting and upraised arms, along with the reflections cast on the polished surface of the gateleg table, all testify both to the artist's capacity to produce an immediacy in his work and to the subject's comfortable financial circumstances. Copley combines his realist precision with a skilful rendering of skin, face and expression. Mrs Devereux's plain countenance contrasts with conventional depictions of female beauty, wealth and power, or the youthful attractions of his earlier London pieces, *Boy with a Squirrel (Henry Pelham)* (1765) and *Young Lady with a Bird and Dog* (1767). The averted gaze adds to the painting's pensive, contemplative aspect. Copley has

created a highly convincing image, presenting the viewer with a person whose existence – whose 'life' – can be believed. The subdued material styling of the portrait may also be placed in the context of 1770 Boston, where everyday things – fabrics, furniture, tea, plate – had become highly political. Refusal to consume imported items was part of the growing colonial resistance to the British imposition of taxes and tariffs.

On its arrival in London, John Greenwood placed the work in the spring 1771 exhibition of the Society of Artists under the title *A Lady*. It drew favourable comment from eminent painter Benjamin West, among others.[11] Joshua Reynolds was later reputed to have remarked that the portrait showed Copley's art at its height.[12] *Mrs Humphrey Devereux*'s success, in fact, was a factor in Copley's decision three years later to leave America permanently. In 1774 he followed *Mrs Humphrey Devereux* to London, taking his family, business and ambition with him, and there embarked on what would become the second and distinctive phase of his career as a painter of contemporary history.[13] Although Copley's 1768 portrait of Paul Revere has become a powerful symbol of revolutionary America, the artist himself turned his back on the colony on the eve of its independence.

Mrs Humphrey Devereux remained with John Greenwood until his death in 1792, thereafter passing to his second son, also John Greenwood, and in turn to *his* son, John Danforth Greenwood. In the early 1840s *Mrs Humphrey Devereux* embarked on its second sea journey among the possessions packed by the third John Greenwood and his wife Sarah, as colonists destined for Nelson.[14] In its original frame, measuring over a metre in height and just under a metre in width, it was one of a great array of objects that would form the material foundation for the family's new economic and cultural life. The Greenwoods were among the 'anxious classes' to whom Edward Gibbon Wakefield addressed his appeal of systematic colonisation, with its radical promise of an improved version of English society.[15] In Nelson, where the Greenwoods raised 13 children at their home, Woodlands, near Motueka, they were known for their educational, social and artistic sensibilities. *Mrs Humphrey Devereux* was an object of continuity in the family's history, something valued in its careful shipment across the world, a face on the wall known by name and to whom the connection was one of kinship. The portrait brought something old to a place that was new; *Mrs Humphrey Devereux* spoke of age – of a person and an era – in a place that to settler eyes was fresh and young.

Copley painted silversmith Paul Revere (1734–1818) in 1768 as Boston seethed with revolutionary fervour. Longfellow's 1861 poem, 'Paul Revere's Ride', elevated the historical person into legendary folk hero.

John Singleton Copley, Paul Revere, *1768, oil on canvas, 89.22 x 72.39 cm, Gift of Joseph W. Revere, William B. Revere and Edward H.R. Revere. Ref: 30.781, Museum of Fine Arts, Boston*

The long period of private ownership and domestic display came to an end in the 1950s. On a visit to New Zealand, the American portraitist Charles Hopkinson recognised the work hanging in a private home as a Copley. After authentication, *Mrs Humphrey Devereux* was sent to the United States for conservation and subsequent public exhibition. In 1965, after its return to New Zealand, the Greenwood family gifted the work to the National Art Gallery.[16] This act of generosity is remarkable; it underlines the continuing significance of private philanthropy even as the nation state expanded to become a major patron of arts and culture in the mid-twentieth century.[17] As a valued item in the public and scholarly domain, *Mrs Humphrey Devereux* has travelled extensively on loan in the international art world within the custody and practices of professional curatorship.

In this most recent phase of its life, the portrait became part of a national collection of art, rather than a historical collection of colonial artefacts, and one that had few contextual works within which to situate a portrait from late-eighteenth-century revolutionary America. The relatively small body of eighteenth-century art works existing in New Zealand collections tend to be of English or European origin, framed within categories of European versus 'colonial' or 'national' art. Mary Kisler's *Angels and Aristocrats: Early European art in New Zealand public collections* (2010) further proclaims the definition.[18] *Mrs Humphrey Devereux* is an American face in our midst. The acquisition history and conceptual frameworks for New Zealand collections tend to contrast an English or European 'there' with a colonial or New Zealand 'here', which allows little cognisance of an earlier era of colonial relations. If *Mrs Humphrey Devereux* is a colonial object, she is one that draws attention back to the first British Empire, and to the era on the other side of the defining rupture of 1776, which established America as an independent republic.

Since coming into the public domain, *Mrs Humphrey Devereux* has been viewed by strangers in the reverent space of prestigious art galleries, rather than by a family at home. Copley's portrait is encountered as 'art', an object of appreciation, and of intrigue. The dress, furniture, and composition speak of a time and style that are historic, standing at a distance in time from the present. Such objects fascinate for their capacity to show us what we are not. Perhaps the portrait suggests a time that can be imagined as one of greater leisure and formality, and of impressively ornate if encumbering dress. The object has a history that can be traced, yet at the same time it defies the temporal and spatial contexts of its production and subsequent existence. The image in the frame continues to command attention. In part that is testament to Copley's skill: the face on the wall might turn and speak. But even as she does not, her averted gaze is looking somewhere, at something. In this sense *Mrs Humphrey Devereux* presents the continuing puzzle of long-lasting objects: for all that their lives trace the circumstances of their creation, their subsequent ownership, use and transmission, they also transcend these. For portraits, this may be especially so. Copley's *Mrs Devereux* continues to convince us of the presence of a person. For all that this is 'only a picture', the face on the wall looks out, as much as we look in.

Spinks Cottage, part of the St John's in the City Church complex, is one of the oldest cottages of its type in Wellington. Its appeal lies in both its picturesque façade and historic aesthetic. The history of its inhabitants is less well known.

Photograph by Michael Hall

10

Spinks Cottage

Heritage, History and Use

Catherine Bishop

Wellington is justifiably proud of a historic landscape of picturesque timber cottages on its steep, surrounding hillsides, providing a colourful backdrop to the city. Within the city centre itself, only a few historic buildings remain. Their architectural pedigree is treasured and their general ambience provides a comforting sense of establishment and romantic nostalgia. Gavin Mclean noted in 2001 that 'Heritage is sexy' and it has certainly become so in the last three decades.[1] Historic buildings are now more likely to be saved, even if only as a façade, hiding a modern, practical tower block behind. But what of the inhabitants of these heritage buildings? This essay considers how one particular colonial building illustrates the intersection of heritage, history and present use.

Spinks Cottage is part of the St John's in the City Presbyterian Church complex on the corner of Willis and Dixon streets. One of the very few mid-nineteenth-century buildings remaining in Wellington, it was probably built in 1858 or early 1859, competing with the nearby Colonial Cottage Museum in Nairn Street (c. 1858–61) to be the oldest surviving cottage of its type in the city. In August 1859 Spinks Cottage was noted as a recent addition to the city: 'a very pretty specimen of a colonial residence …[with] a very elegant appearance from the water'.[2] Now painted in heritage colours and carefully matched with other buildings on the site, the two-storey cottage exudes an historic aesthetic. A sign on one wall identifies it as 'Spinks Cottage c. 1860'. There is also a somewhat obscured New Zealand Historic Places Trust plaque, labelling it as Historic Building 19. There are no other signs or historical information.

The smaller and more portable colonial objects featured in this volume have been carefully preserved in museum collections, hidden away, perhaps forgotten, in a drawer somewhere, or lovingly treasured and passed down through families: their value has depended on their remaining much as they always were. Spinks Cottage has survived for most of its life only because of its continued usefulness, its historical associations largely irrelevant and at times inconvenient for its owners.

St John's in the City purchased Spinks Cottage in 1884, in order to expand its property. The original owner, William Spinks, sold the cottage for £1500, though he continued to live in it until his death a few months later.[3] Under church ownership the cottage has had a variety of uses – as a caretaker's cottage for 80 years, as a student hostel for over a decade from 1967, as offices for church staff in the 1980s and, most recently, as meeting rooms for the church youth group. The cottage has also been more portable than one might imagine, having been moved twice, in the 1880s and then a century later, from its original position, set back from the road on the right of the church, to its current position next to Dixon Street, in order to make room for other buildings. Until the early 1980s church authorities planned for its eventual demolition once funds to replace it became available. But this became an untenable position in the face of growing public consciousness of the importance of historic buildings from the late 1970s and an increasing awareness of the scarcity of such buildings remaining in Wellington. From this time the New Zealand Historic Places Trust took an active interest in the future of Spinks Cottage.[4] After an unsuccessful attempt by St John's to sell the cottage to Wellington City Council for removal, the church bowed to the inevitable and decided to make a feature of what was rapidly becoming a white elephant. In 1983 a dedicated team of volunteers with a very limited budget restored the cottage as a picturesque but useful part of the church complex, with staff offices upstairs.[5] A church staff member told me proudly that the cottage was 'probably the only one of its type remaining that has been in continuous use since it was built'.[6]

The 'white elephant' sense remains, however. The church, driven by budget considerations, requires that the cottage be useful, regardless of its historical significance. In 2006 a much-publicised and controversial proposal to create a youth club underneath the cottage involved raising it to create a basement.[7] This was eventually rejected and space inside the cottage is now used as a meeting place. Offices upstairs remain, although at least one staff member was pleased to move out of the dark cottage into a purpose-built modern building.[8]

As a colonial object, Spinks Cottage is essentially a shell. Modernisation of the interior, leaving few original features, followed the cottage's heritage listing in 1986, when it was described by the Historic Places Trust as 'in remarkable original condition', though exactly what this meant is unclear.[9] As recently as 2012 the downstairs was renovated. It was freshly painted and carpeted; there is a modern kitchen; doors and walls have been moved. Some ceiling cornices have been preserved, as have the original doors, windows and (unused) fireplaces but, other than that, this is a neutral space. There is no sense of history. Upstairs the offices are functional and efficient.[10]

What does such an object therefore tell us about New Zealand's past? That the cottage has been repeatedly renovated internally and has also been moved from its original position perhaps limits its 'authenticity' and value as a colonial object. The layers of its subsequent history as a caretaker's home, student hostel, church offices and youth centre have overwritten traces of the original inhabitants. In spite of this, in 2010 the Historic Places Trust noted that 'In its own right the cottage is considered invaluable because it is the only house that provides the evidence

St John's Church with Spinks Cottage in the background. This picture is one of the few surviving images of the building in its original location. It was reproduced in Alison Dangerfield's booklet, Spinks Cottage, *published by the Historic Places Trust in 2010, having been found in a church pamphlet produced by St John's in the City.*

Courtesy of St John's in the City, Wellington

of how a significant group of people, in the middle classes, lived in this part of the centre of Wellington.'[11] The Trust emphasises the construction of the cottage – its place in architectural history – and the evidence it provides of the outward materiality of people's lives. But recently discovered documents reveal a richer life. An auction notice from 1885 shows that the 10-room cottage contained furniture and furnishings 'pertaining to a comfortable house', including a loo table, a sideboard, 'four-post bedsteads', feather beds and a glass bookcase, along with pictures and about 300 books.[12] In a nation that emphasises its rural pioneer history, this site offers the opportunity to describe the lives of urban dwellers, particularly women.

Spinks Cottage was originally the home of respectable, aspiring middle-class William and Mary Spinks and their two daughters, Florence and Sarah Ellen Jane (known as Jane), who arrived in Wellington in 1843. William Spinks kept a general store on the corner of Manners and Herbert streets for 20 years, initially in partnership with Robert Langdon. He purchased land in Willis Street in 1854 but did not build the cottage until at least 1858. It was very much a symbol of the family's success. By 1862 William Spinks was a member of the Legislative Council and served as the first Provincial Government wharfinger or manager for Queens Wharf after it was built in 1863. The Spinks family was prominent in the local church with the daughters active in the choir and Sunday school. When William died in December 1884 vessels in the harbour flew their flags at half-mast in respect.[13] His wife died a week later.

This was not only a home, however; it was also a place of business. While still in their teens, in 1849 the Spinks sisters started a school, which continued when they moved to Spinks Cottage. They taught in the large front room, with boarders accommodated upstairs. After Jane's marriage in 1862, Florence continued teaching until 1880. When her parents died Florence Spinks moved to Nelson to be near her married sister. When she died in 1905, her estate was worth over £4000.[14] The school was a Wellington institution for over 30 years, advertised in newspapers and mentioned in trade directories. A history of the capital's schools noted in 1900 that 'all old settlers remember well the popular school of the Misses Spinks … a large percentage of Te Aro girls and small boys received in it their early training'.[15]

Jane Spinks kept a diary, though it sheds little

useful light on the school. She seldom mentions teaching, apart from a few references to music pupils' absences, holidays and meetings with parents. Most daily entries revolve around the weather, church-going, music practice with church groups, bill paying, walking and various people's health. Jane Spinks tells us that she sewed, made jam and cleaned rooms. In their detailed everydayness, these diaries breathe life into Spinks Cottage, adding to its significance as a colonial object. It is not only one of the oldest buildings of its type, but a visible location in which to imagine the Spinks family's ordinary lives.

A Wellington City Council's Heritage Trail brochure, which describes the cottage as 'a family home' but also notes that the sisters ran a girls' school there, emphasises the age of the building, valuing it as 'one of the oldest … in Wellington',[16] rather than the domestic or business lives that were lived there. But Spinks Cottage also provides a history lesson, by challenging popular images of women's participation in the colonial economy. Heritage sites or historic buildings are frequently public or industrial buildings, which have not lent themselves to the inclusion of women. Others are homes, suited to telling a domestic story, so women tend to appear in heritage settings only in domestic roles. The Spinks sisters, however, were businesswomen, and they were not alone in Wellington. Jane Spinks describes paying Mrs and Miss Farmer for the mangling (i.e. doing the laundry) and buying haberdashery from Miss Willcox's store, and she writes of Miss Fletcher's rival school. Her pupils included shopkeeper Mary Taylor's niece.[17] In fact, there were many female-run small businesses populating the streets of Wellington, and other colonial cities, well before the late nineteenth century, though they have been somewhat lost in historical narratives. Histories of colonial women have acknowledged their employment as domestic servants and as hardworking wives contributing to the family income, but scholarly discussions of women running businesses are recent and rare.[18] Investigations of women as independent economic entities have tended to focus on the period after 1870, when sources are more readily available and when employment opportunities for women expanded.[19] Mary Taylor, famously a friend of Charlotte Brontë, is one of the few known businesswomen from the 1850s and 1860s and has been assumed to be 'a novelty' because she worked for a living.[20]

As a colonial object, then, Spinks Cottage is unusual in that it is a rare surviving visible place of female entrepreneurship in the mid-nineteenth century. In combination with Jane Spinks' diary, this building takes us beyond the aesthetic appeal and architectural history of built heritage. Spinks Cottage also tells us a story about the serendipity of survival: it lasted only because it could be made useful. Ironically, however, that very usefulness has obscured its colonial history, leaving a picturesque heritage shell. Perhaps it is time to breathe new life into this object, to give it a new usefulness as a connection to New Zealand's colonial past.

Spinks Cottage was moved twice, first in the 1880s and then in 1982, when it was shifted to its present location, next to Dixon Street. This mobility has ensured its survival and it is now an appealing part of the landscape.

Photographs from the collection of St John's in the City, Wellington

11
The Piano at The Elms
Kirstine Moffat

The Elms' drawing room, featuring Euphemia Maxwell's Broadwood grand piano. The portrait to the top left of the photograph is of Euphemia in later life.

Photograph by Michele Pointon, with kind permission of The Elms Foundation

Just before the bustle of the Tauranga business district begins, beyond a sprawling overpass junction, there is a tranquil haven of serenity enclosed by a white picket fence. I push open the gate and wander down a curving shell path which admits me to the faithfully preserved historical precinct that is The Elms. When I step into the parlour a shaft of morning sunlight illuminates the gleaming rosewood case of an 1855 grand piano. The wood is polished to a high gloss, the grain apparent beneath the veneer, golden tones alternating with rich brown. Two octagonal carvings decorate the side of the instrument, a pattern repeated on the scrolls framing the brass pedals. Three tapering, but sturdy, circular legs end in a simple castor, but begin with wing-like carvings that attach them to the sinuous curves of the body. To the twenty-first-century New Zealand eye the spiral at the centre of each 'wing' resembles a koru. The top of the piano is shut, the lid a repository for a display of ornaments and knick-knacks. A Chinese plate, the photograph of a woman in Victorian dress, a small leather card case and a lorgnette rest on a cream cloth painted with flowers, ferns and mushrooms. Such is the mirror-like lustre of the wood that the photograph is reflected in the piano's surface, as are the faces of the family portraits on the wall behind.

I lift the cover to reveal the keys beneath. The ivory of the white keys is faded and slightly yellowed in places, where the fingertips of generations of pianists have left their mark. An inset panel above middle C reveals the instrument's origins: 'Patent Repetition Grand Pianoforte, John Broadwood & Sons, London'. I sit down on the piano stool, its leather seat cracked in places but its shiny surface, like the wood of the instrument, testimony to loving and careful preservation. I raise the ornate music stand. My fingers depress the first, haunting notes of Beethoven's 'Moonlight Sonata'. The bass notes sound, rich and resonant. The treble joins in, clear and true. A couple of keys stick a little and the instrument is not completely in tune, but I am content. The music transports me back through time, connecting me to the lives and stories of those for whom the piano was a treasured object and a familiar friend.

The first performer to sit at this keyboard was Euphemia Maxwell and the story of her relationship with the instrument is one of romance, tragedy and resilience. In the late 1840s Andrew Maxwell, a young Scottish divinity

LEFT *The rosewood lid of the piano is polished to a mirror-like gloss.*

Photograph by Michele Pointon, with kind permission of The Elms Foundation

RIGHT *Piano keyboard with the manufacturer's name-board declaring that the Patent Repetition Grand Pianoforte was crafted by John Broadwood & Sons of London 'Manufacturers to Her Majesty and the Royal Family'.*

Photograph by Michele Pointon, with kind permission of The Elms Foundation

FAR RIGHT, TOP *Euphemia Maxwell and her husband, Reverend Andrew Maxwell.*

The Elms Collection, Tauranga, reproduced with kind permission of The Elms Foundation

RIGHT *The harp-shaped pedals are decorated with octagonal carvings, a pattern that is repeated on the sides of the instrument.*

Photograph by Michele Pointon, with kind permission of The Elms Foundation

student, visited the home of an affluent Aberdeen banker, James Johnson. Invited into the drawing room, Andrew fell instantly in love with Johnson's youngest daughter, Euphemia, who was playing the piano. According to family legend, his wooing consisted not only of declarations of love but also of vows to buy 'his Angel' her own instrument should she consent to be his wife.[1] This consent was eventually granted and the couple married and emigrated to Australia in 1853. Nine years later Andrew honoured his promise, ordering a Broadwood grand to be sent to Melbourne from London.

When Andrew died in 1865 Euphemia was left with four children and little money. She travelled to New Zealand to stay with her brother, Alexander Johnson, a Supreme Court judge. In spite of her straitened circumstances her piano accompanied her. A year later, assisted by her brother, Euphemia bought a house in the Wellington hill suburb of Wadestown. The only access to the area was a bridle track following the Kaiwharawhara Stream, along which the carriers refused to transport the piano. Undeterred, Euphemia hired two bushmen to cut a new track. Her great-nephew writes that 'using quite good judgment she

ABOVE *The revolving leather piano stool bears the honourable marks of generations of pianists.*

Photograph by Michele Pointon, with kind permission of The Elms Foundation

picked out reasonable grades, avoiding big trees and had smaller ones felled'.[2] She then hired a bullock team and sledge and, as her daughter Alice recalled, 'with the true pioneer spirit of refusal to be daunted by difficulties ... loading upon it the piano and her other furniture, proceeded herself to pilot the team up the steep and rugged hillside'.[3]

Once the Wadestown house was safely reached, it was discovered that the piano was too big to fit in the rooms, but Euphemia remained undefeated and built an additional room to house the piano, complete with its own fireplace to keep the instrument warm, dry and in tune. When, in 1887, Euphemia inherited The Elms in Tauranga from her sister, Christina Brown, she reluctantly uprooted herself yet again. On this occasion more affluent circumstances ensured that both Euphemia and her piano could travel in style to their final resting place in a specially chartered boat.[4]

Euphemia's Wadestown and Tauranga parlours were focal points for the social life of their respective local communities. Alice Maxwell remembered that the first religious services in Wadestown were 'held in my mother's drawing room and the first Sunday school was organised by my sister Edith, the hymns being accompanied on the piano'.[5] Friends and visitors also gathered for musical entertainments and dinner parties. Much of Euphemia's collection of sheet music remains intact at The Elms and is indicative of the type of music she performed at the piano. The collection includes Franz Schubert's sonatas and Johannes Brahms' waltzes, but mostly consists of piano and vocal duets. The latter range from Mrs Felicia Hemans' moralistic 'The Landing of the Pilgrim Fathers', to the operatic duet 'Là ci darem la mano' from Mozart's *Don Giovanni*, to the Scottish ballad, 'My Love She's But a Lassie Yet'.[6]

Colonial music-making could be both improving and fun. The hymn-singing and Sunday school services in Euphemia's parlour reflect a commitment to bolstering and spreading what Lady Martin, wife of New Zealand's first chief justice, termed the 'divine work' of 'civilisation'.[7] Yet, for the Maxwells, the piano was also a central form of entertainment. Impeccably dressed, Euphemia hosted soirées and musical afternoons, her guests, including Sir George Grey, undeterred by the steep climb to her home. The music played by this 'unusually fine pianist' was a decided attraction and possession of a piano ensured that the Maxwells enjoyed a stimulating social life.[8] The words and phrases chosen to describe piano playing in colonial diaries, letters and reminiscences reinforce this association between the instrument and fun: 'treat', 'fabulous', 'en-chanted', 'great time', 'pure joyousness and good humour'.[9]

Euphemia's Broadwood grand is also the embodiment of the meticulous craftsmanship and technical innovations so fundamental to the piano's early history. Craftsmen and manufacturers were determined to make their instruments look, as well as sound, beautiful. The piano is the perfect object to showcase both the natural splendour of the chosen wood and the possibilities for carving, marquetry and embossing. Euphemia's grand is a simple statement about the majesty of wood.

Broadwood pianos were among the most sought after in the nineteenth century because of the manufacturer's technical innovations to improve sound quality, such as introducing a divided bridge to assist the bass tone and increasing the keyboard range to seven and a half octaves.[10] For settlers such as Euphemia the patented Broadwood bolted iron frame was particularly significant as it ensured the piano stayed more easily in tune, vital for instruments making jostling journeys through temperature extremes to find a home in a young colony where piano tuners were scarce. Euphemia's advanced and expensive instrument avoided the worst of the tuning problems that plagued instruments such as Sarah Selwyn's square piano, which reached its Waimate destination in 1842 with its keys 'much loosened' and the treble 'in a bad state'.[11]

The continuing story of The Elms piano is one of preservation, as the instrument receives regular tunings and repair. This reflects the way in which Euphemia's daughter Alice and great-nephew Duff saw themselves as caretakers of a past stretching back to the 1830s: Duff wrote of his 'duty' to 'preserve' The Elms 'as a whole'.[12] Euphemia's piano nestles in a setting where it seems naturally to belong. Alfred Nesbit Brown and his first wife Charlotte, who arrived in Tauranga in 1838 to establish a Church Mission Society mission, built The Elms. Passed on to the Maxwell family by Brown's second wife Christina, Euphemia's sister, The Elms is a relative rarity in New Zealand, a heritage site that was a beloved family home from 1847 to 1992 before becoming a museum.[13] Not only the structure but also the furnishings remain intact.

This was, and is, a home filled with music. Before Euphemia's arrival the 1835 William Allen square piano in the dining room entertained the family and helped the Browns in their mission. Brown's daughter Celia 'played very nicely' and used her skill to teach the Māori children in her father's mission to sing hymns.[14] This piano is also associated with a poignant occasion on 28 April 1864. Several military officers from the 43rd Regiment, including Lieutenant Charles Hill of HMS *Curacoa* and Captain John Hamilton of HMS *Esk*, were invited to dine at The Elms on the evening before the Battle of Gate Pā. After dinner and prayers, Christina Brown sat at the piano to play, everyone joining in to sing 'Abide With Me'.[15] By the next evening all the officers were dead; only the surgeon, Dr W.G.W. Manley, survived.[16]

These stories of heartbreak, courage and romance haunt me as I sit at the keyboard of the Broadwood grand. I am no longer the onlooker, the researcher, but part of an enduring tradition. I play Beethoven, Brahms and Schubert from Euphemia's dark-green piano books, embossed with the gold letters 'Music'. My fingers caress the keys of a 158-year-old instrument that has survived sea crossings, bush journeys, the deaths of three owners, the ravages of time. Above all, the music itself forms a continuum between then and now, a union of performers and music lovers. The emotive, intense music of the Romantics seems most truly in keeping with the imposing physical presence and dynamic range of a grand piano. As the C# minor bass octaves and treble triplets of the opening adagio sostenuto to the 'Moonlight Sonata' quietly fill the air I am transported.

6
Più animato.
Ped.
5821
THE
KANGAROO HUNT
POLKA
Composed by
C. M. WEINRITTER
MELBOURNE
Published for the Author by
JOSEPH WILKIE, 15, COLLINS ST

12

From 'Home Sweet Home' to the 'Kangaroo Hunt Polka'

The Colonial Voyages of Marian Sargood's Music Album

Kate Stevens

On 1 June 1914 the Wanaka home of Sir Percy Sargood was burnt to the ground.[1] Family anecdote recounts that the only item saved from the devastating flames was the piano, which also happened to be the only thing that was insured.[2] Although the piano is not the subject of this essay, this story illustrates the value and importance that the Sargood family placed on music. My subject is a music album owned by Percy's mother, Marian Australia Sargood (née Rolfe), wife of prominent businessman and politician, Sir Frederick Thomas Sargood of Rippon Lea, Melbourne.[3] Hardbound in black and brown, and comprising a compilation of sheet music for the piano, the album was inherited by Marian's eldest daughter Clara Wordsworth Webster (née Sargood) on her mother's death in 1879, and travelled to Canterbury with her when she married Henry Webster in 1889. The now-worn volume remains in the hands of descendants in New Zealand.[4] My mother currently keeps the album, and on occasions, it continues to be used.

While Marian Sargood's music album travelled from London to colonial Australia, she added to its contents before having it bound in Melbourne. As a collection of individual sheet music, the volume warrants attention because its creation highlights processes of cultural transition for the mid-nineteenth elite in the antipodean colonies, when ties to England remained strong but new cultural identities were simultaneously forming. Its use offers an insight into the importance of music, musical education and music performance for the Sargood family and others like them.

The album was not purchased ready-made, but collected and collated by Marian Sargood in the 1850s when she was in her early twenties and before her marriage – it was a personal 'Victorian playlist' of sorts. We know this because Marian's name is handwritten on the cover of many of the different pieces of music. The volume itself was bound in Melbourne, as were many books of the period, given the high costs associated with shipping and binding abroad. The spine of the album is adorned with the title 'MUSIC', followed by four harps in vertical succession. Inside the cover is the sticker of the bookbinder, William Detmold, who had come to Australia by way of Hanover, Germany and New York, and established his business in the colony in 1854. A craftsman of some renown, Detmold catered to notable individuals and important

OPPOSITE *Marian Sargood's music album showing the cover of Weinritter's 1857 composition, 'The Kangaroo Hunt Polka'.*

Private Collection. Photograph by Michael Hall

cultural institutions, including the Melbourne Public Library and the University of Melbourne.[5] Based on the time of Detmold's arrival in Melbourne, and Marian's handwritten inscriptions on some covers and the initial publication dates of songs included in the album, we can date the binding to the late 1850s or early 1860s, probably after her marriage in 1858.

The contents of the album reflect Marian's own musical tastes and interests, but also the broader cultural milieu in which she lived. All are compositions or arrangements for the pianoforte, and the majority are either dances or arrangements from operas. Three pieces were published in Melbourne, the rest in London. The majority reflect the musical culture that immigrants and settlers brought with them to Australia and New Zealand from England and continental Europe. To give an indication of the range, there are excerpts from Mozart's *Don Giovanni*, a series of 'household melodies' arranged by J.M. Gibson, including 'Home Sweet Home', and the 'Varsoviana Nationale' composed by Alphonse Leduc.[6] Perhaps the most famous of the compositions included in the album is Mendelssohn's 'Wedding March', which was played on the ballroom organ on the occasion of the marriage of Marian's daughter Clara Sargood to Henry Webster on 29 November 1889 at Rippon Lea.[7]

In contrast to the European sheet music, the three Australian-published works included in the album hint at the emergence of a new tradition, of new composers who drew influence from local politics, culture and the natural environment of the colony of Victoria. Despite the local points of reference, the style of these compositions is very much in the classical European tradition and shows little or no influence deriving from indigenous Aboriginal music. Two of the pieces are written by George Mitchell Weinritter, a Polish-born composer and music master who arrived in Melbourne in 1856, and published by Joseph Wilkie.[8] The first, amusingly titled 'The Kangaroo Hunt Polka', was issued in February 1857 and quickly commended as having 'already become deservedly popular. It is a spirited composition, well marked as to time, and by no means difficult, all points which are, of course, much in its favour.'[9] The second Weinritter piece was 'The Melbourne Varsovienne', probably produced around 1857 or 1858.[10] The third Australian composition, 'The Victorian Waltz', was by a Mrs Charles Terry and published in Melbourne by Cyrus Mason, the artist who provided the cover illustration for Weinritter's 'Melbourne Varsovienne'.[11]

The specifically Melbourne or Victorian flavour of these latter two pieces highlights the development of local music quite separate from that emerging in contemporary Sydney.[12] The 1850s saw a burgeoning of the music and theatre scene in Melbourne, associated with both the political independence of the colony from New South Wales and the gold-rush period, which brought a rise in disposable income. There was also the arrival of Joseph Wilkie's musical instrument warehouse, which sold sheet music of the kind that Marian purchased, and numerous other patriotic musical compositions and publications such as Wilkie's own 'The Separation Polka' and Charles Thatcher's 'The Victoria Songster'.[13] Added to this was the growing popularity of opera in Melbourne from

Exterior view of Marian Sargood's music album. Photograph by Michael Hall

the 1860s following the establishment of William S. Lyster's opera company in 1861.[14]

Music was a central part of the social life and education of the Sargood family. Frederick Sargood arrived in Melbourne with his family in 1850 and in the following decade rose through the ranks of his father's wholesale clothing and drapery firm, Sargood, King & Co. In 1858 he married Marian Australia Rolfe and over 21 years, until her death in childbirth, they had nine surviving children.[15] Both the couple's fathers were involved in early colonial politics, and Frederick Sargood followed in their footsteps. He first entered the Victoria Legislative Council in 1874 and went on to serve as Victoria's first Minister of Defence from 1883 – he was knighted in 1890 – while continuing to expand his business interests.[16] His early commercial success provided the Sargoods with the wealth to build, in 1868, a grand house on Melbourne's outskirts modelled on a stately English manor.[17] Rippon Lea served as a generous family home for the children's upbringing and education and the venue for social gatherings befitting the Sargoods' status and role as part of Victoria's commercial and political elite.

The memoirs of the eldest daughter, Clara, born in 1864, are peppered with references to music that demonstrate the many functions it had within this

Marian's album was handed down through the generations. Her eldest daughter Clara and her descendants: Henry Norman Webster, Clara Wordsworth Webster (née Sargood), Joan Elizabeth Wylde (née Webster) and Beverley Dawn Wylde (later Stevens) photographed in late 1953. *Private collection*

prominent colonial family: as part of education, religion and social life, and as a simple diversion. The Sargood children were largely taught at home by their mother, stepmother and an Irish governess, Mrs Ferguson, and musical training was a key part of their learning, as it was for many well-to-do families of the era. Clara's usual piano classes continued when the family lived in England between 1880 and 1882,[18] and there was even a piano at their seaside holiday home of Ellerslie, 'so our music was not neglected'.[19] Music was also a memorable aspect of religious education and practice: the family regularly gathered around the piano for hymn singing on Sundays.[20] As she got older, Clara's training in piano enabled her to contribute to the hosting of her father's guests at Rippon Lea. After the Sargoods returned to Melbourne in 1882 Clara had new responsibilities:

> I was no longer a schoolgirl but had to take my place as the eldest daughter and help Mother. I took lessons in music, drawing and French. Father's public position meant there was a good deal of entertaining in the home – still we were not allowed to run wild in our amusements. We had tennis parties once a fortnight, on a Saturday, the players remaining for tea, after which other friends came for a friendly dance. The music being provided by different families present, and very happy gatherings they were …[21]

The music album includes basic instructions for the steps to certain dances such as the 'Varsoviana' and the 'Polka Mazurka'. There were also occasional opera performances in the gardens, and on winter Saturday evenings the family hosted a glee club, for which Clara played the piano.[22]

Music was more than just cultural capital for Clara Sargood; it was a source of pleasure and entertainment from an early age. The excitement of attending concerts and operas stands out vividly among her recollections of youth. She particularly admired and was inspired by the professional pianists she heard during early visits to Dunedin, London and Paris.[23] Soon after the family's arrival at their new London

Marian with her husband Frederick Sargood, photographed around the time of their wedding in 1858.

Courtesy of Rippon Lea Estate, National Trust of Australia (Victoria). Photograph courtesy of Nicholas Vardaxis

Album detail showing Marian Sargood's signature and Joseph Wilkie's imprint.

Photograph by Michael Hall

residence, Aston House, beside the Crystal Palace, a bout of chicken pox almost thwarted one memorable occasion:

> I can remember how anxious I was to get better, for father had bought me a ticket to go with him to the great Handel Festival, held every three years at the Crystal Palace – and unless all the spots had gone, I must remain at home. What excitement, when the morning came, and I was told I could go. The thrill when in our seats, and the choir members entered they seemed to be a great white block with the black background – in front of the large organ – such a sight, as I had never seen – The volume of sound!![24]

Describing a trip to see the opera *Lohengrin* in Paris, she wrote, 'Father said afterwards, he got almost as much pleasure watching my face, as from the opera.'[25] Clara surely continued to play the piano after her marriage and subsequent move to Geraldine, Canterbury, and passed her mother's valued music album down to her own children.

While growing up, I was vaguely aware that Marian Sargood's album was one of my mother's most precious possessions, a tangible connection to our family's continued interest in music, which goes back at least four generations. Just like the family, the music album and its contents voyaged from London to Melbourne and then eventually to New Zealand. The Sargoods maintained ties to England, by adhering to English cultural norms such as musical taste and through continued travel between London, Australia and New Zealand. However, the range of music collected – from 'Home Sweet Home' to the 'Kangaroo Hunt Polka' – shows that the Sargoods retained their imperial British identity while beginning to refashion it into a more distinctly colonial one. Yet for Marian and Clara Sargood, music was simply a part of everyday life. They drew pleasure from learning and playing, from family and friends gathering around the piano, and from the magic of attending professional performances. The album continues to be treasured and used, a testament to the cultural and social significance of music.

Photograph of Richard and Augusta Webb, Waipori, early 1870s.

Ref: 1938/62/1, Collection of Toitū Otago Settlers Museum

13

Portrait of a Material Life

The Photograph of Richard and Augusta Webb

Jill Haley

A man has just returned home from a morning spent working his gold claim. He stops to contemplate the person standing in front of his house with a camera. His wife, hearing voices, sets aside her baking and steps outside to see who is there. In her haste, she has not bothered to take off her apron. Even the cat's attention is caught by the presence of the interloper.

To our twenty-first-century eyes, accustomed to the candid nature of photography brought about by amateur snapshots, digital images and the intrusive paparazzi, this is a plausible interpretation of the creation of the photograph of Richard and Augusta Webb at Waipori, in Otago, in the early 1870s. Colonial viewers, however, would have had a very different interpretation of the image. Understanding the constraints involved in nineteenth-century photography, they would not have seen this as a spontaneous moment caught by a passing photographer, but recognised it as a portrait taken by a professional and as structured and formally organised as a studio photograph. They would have seen a couple posed in front of their comfortable cottage and understood the respectability and prosperity communicated by the objects included in the image. And the Webbs would have intended this photograph to be a visual record of their commitment to Victorian values and achievements in the new colony.

Richard Webb's background was typical of many Cornish immigrants to New Zealand in the nineteenth century. In 1851 his father Thomas was a copper miner, as were 16-year-old Richard and his two younger brothers, Thomas, aged 15, and Henry, aged 14.[1] Living conditions for most Cornish mining families in this period were harsh, marked by poor sanitation, ill health and famine.[2] Overcrowded terraced houses rapidly replaced the cottages and smallholdings enjoyed by miners earlier in the century.[3] Constant mine closures forced families to be mobile and adaptable, moving around Cornwall or overseas in search of opportunities. In 1854, when Richard was 20, he, like thousands of miners, left Cornwall. He headed for Australia and mined in New South Wales and Victoria, then in 1863 moved on to Otago.

Augusta Buckthought enjoyed a very different background from Richard. She was born in 1850 in Liskeard, Cornwall, where her father, a millwright, employed three men.[4] Her grandfather and uncle were innkeepers with

Photograph of unidentified house, Edward Teague, late 1870s.

Ref: Box 25, No. 24, Collection of Toitū Otago Settlers Museum

household servants. Augusta appears to have had a somewhat genteel upbringing: her granddaughter Margaret recalled that she was a good musician and needlewoman.[5] In 1869, at the age of 19, Augusta immigrated to New Zealand to join her sister, Elizabeth Hancock, who had moved to the colony with her husband William in 1866. In December 1869, six months after arriving, Augusta married Richard, who was her brother-in-law's partner in a series of mining claims.

The Webbs settled at Waipori, where, in 1871, Richard became the manager of the Otago Pioneer Quartz mine and held a number of sluicing claims. He owned crushing batteries and was a member of the Waipori Miners' Association. The couple took part in community life. Richard became a member of the Odd Fellows Lodge and sat on local school committees, Augusta was involved in the Anglican Church, and both participated in school, library and hospital fundraising.[6]

Anne Webb, Richard and Augusta's eldest daughter, donated the photograph of her parents to the Otago Early Settlers Association in 1938. It measures 23 by 34 centimetres, but there is evidence that the association trimmed it down, presumably for display.[7] Discolouration around the edges indicates that it was once matted and framed. The fact that a daughter donated the image to the museum suggests that Richard and Augusta had this photograph taken for themselves, and that it was kept within the family. This is the earliest known photograph of the couple, probably taken between their marriage in late December 1869 and the birth of their first child in January 1873.[8] Taking it would have been a cumbersome and complicated affair. It would have been produced using a collodion wet plate, which would have required transporting a large camera to the site, along with a heavy tripod and fragile glass plates, chemicals for preparing the plate and a field darkroom for processing the negative immediately after the image was taken. The Webbs would have had to hold their pose for several seconds to prevent blurring during the plate's exposure time.[9]

No photographer's mark or other identifying information appears on the image. In the early 1870s at least seven photographers advertised in the *Tuapeka Times*, the newspaper published in Lawrence, a large township close to Waipori. Although the Burton Brothers operated in the region in the 1870s, and had the equipment and expertise for this type of outdoor photography, the fact that they ensured their products carried the studio's name rules them out.[10] A more likely candidate is Edward Teague, a Cornish immigrant who went to Australia and then later to Otago to chase gold. In the 1860s he was Richard Webb's partner in the Long Gully water races, but by the early 1870s he had given up mining for photography.[11] Two Teague photographs held in Toitū Otago Settlers Museum's collection are similar to the Webb image in that they feature houses set in the landscape. Given the personal association between Teague and the Webbs, and the fact that he was the only photographer known to be working in Waipori, it is reasonable to assume that he was responsible for this image.[12]

Depicted within the Webb photograph are highly symbolic objects that highlight the importance and power of the material world. The house stands centre stage, dominating everything else, including the Webbs. It demands the viewer's attention and suggests that this is as much a portrait of a home as of the people living in it. It was a house to be proud of, probably one of the first at Waipori.[13] Its construction – of cob (layers of clay mixed with straw or grass) with a stone foundation – was customary in Cornwall and would have been familiar to the Webbs, but it was also common throughout Central Otago owing to the availability of suitable building materials.[14] With its hipped roof, central front door, windows on either side of the door and end-wall chimney, it represents a local adaptation of a house type found in England and New Zealand in both rural and urban contexts. For Richard, a house like this might have symbolised a return to the smallholding past rapidly disappearing in Cornwall. For Augusta it might have been a step towards fulfilling her expectation of a New Zealand version of the life she had left behind.

Featuring an exceptionally ordered and uncluttered composition, the Webb photograph focuses the viewer's eye on the objects displayed. Household yards during the nineteenth century were extensions of the house and served as storage areas for tools, work areas for cooking and washing and general living areas. Here, however, there is a surprising lack of household items littering the yard, suggesting that the objects shown are carefully selected props, placed visibly but unobtrusively to communicate information about the couple. Tucked around the side of the house on the left is what could be a sharpening stone. Nineteenth-century miners used a variety of tools, many of which needed to be sharpened, and the presence of the stone could be intended to point to Richard's success as a miner. On the ground to the left of Augusta is a metal bucket, a symbol of her domestic role and place within the household. Women and buckets are not an unusual combination in such settings, appearing in other colonial photographs. Augusta's apron reinforces her role. Although this is a domestic setting, her hair and clothing are more formal, suggestive of best dress worn for a studio portrait.[15] Six-pane windows with glass, mounted into what are probably imported frames, speak of their middling comfort. Curtains offer an added touch of Victorian gentility.

One of the most curious and endearing 'props' in the photograph is the cat, whose engaging stare draws the viewer in. Domestic animals 'featured incidentally in photographs of houses', so the presence of this cat invites speculation.[16] On the Central Otago goldfields in the 1860s, where settlements were overrun with rats and mice, these working pets were in demand and worth between £1 and £5 each.[17] The Webbs' cat may have been an investment that other miners could not afford and included in the photograph as a display of their wealth. During the nineteenth century, Victorians transformed the cat from working animal to sentimental pet.[18] In addition to being a household help, the Webb cat could have been a valued member of the family to be included in a portrait.

The placement of the couple within the composition expresses the ideology of separate spheres for men and women prevalent in middle-class Victorian culture. Augusta and her domestic props are firmly centred on house and home while Richard is separated from her and slightly distant, suggesting his link with the outside world. He stands there casually, suggesting a man at rest and successful enough to afford moments of leisure.

In New Zealand Richard and Augusta Webb made for themselves a respectable Victorian life. The carefully structured, professionally taken portrait of the couple in front of their Waipori home is a visual record of the life they aspired to and achieved in the new colony. For thousands of immigrants, the possibility of this form of modest prosperity, with property ownership and the opportunity for social mobility, led the drive to leave their home country. The Webb photograph embodies a sentiment expressed by another immigrant a generation earlier: 'I have a house and garden of my own, and I never intend to be an English slave more.'[19]

Unidentified house, Otago, featuring a variety of household implements, tools and general 'clutter' in the yard.

Ref: Box 79, No. 212, Collection of Toitū Otago Settlers Museum

14

A Photograph, a Feeding Bottle and the Tragedies of Colonial Family Life

Alison Clarke

Rachel and Westwood Stewart, carte-de-visite by J. McGregor & Co., Dunedin, c. 1869.

Ref: S13-546b, William Downie Stewart Papers, Hocken Collections, Uare Taoka o Hākena, University of Otago

One day in the summer of 1869–70 Rachel Stewart, 24 years old, donned one of her best outfits, carefully arranged her hair and visited John McGregor's 'Portrait Rooms' in Stuart Street, Dunedin. This was not Rachel's first visit to a photographer's studio and nor was it her last. There are 10 studio portraits of her – some alone, some with other family members – dating from the 1860s and 1870s in her son's papers, which are held at the Hocken Collections.[1] All these portraits are cartes-de-visite, a relatively cheap format to produce. Another Dunedin photography firm, Clifford & Clifton, advertised their cartes-de-visite around this time as 'portraits for the million'; they would take photographs 'in first-class style' for 8 shillings per half-dozen, and could supply extra copies or celebrity cards for a shilling each.[2] This was not as prohibitively expensive as earlier forms of photograph, but 8 shillings would have been a sizeable sum to many people, corresponding to just over $100 in 2014 values.

The significant number of portraits of Rachel Stewart demonstrates her position as a woman in comfortable circumstances and a member of a prominent Otago 'early settler' family. Aged five, she had arrived in Dunedin from Scotland in 1850 with her parents, George and Rachel Hepburn, and seven siblings. George was a successful merchant in Scotland and then in Dunedin; in Otago he served in politics at both provincial and national level. In 1868 Rachel Hepburn married up-and-coming young lawyer William Downie Stewart, another Scottish migrant. Her elaborate and fashionable wedding gown is in the collection of Toitū Otago Settlers Museum and featured in their popular 2008 exhibition of 'fabulous frocks'.[3]

John McGregor had photographed Rachel previously and perhaps it was that attractive portrait that prompted her to select him from the half-dozen or so photographic studios in Dunedin for another sitting. This was to be a very different portrait, though, because she had brought along her firstborn child, Alexander Westwood Stewart (known as Westwood), born 28 August 1869. Obtaining a good portrait of a wriggly infant was no easy matter when a long exposure was required, but McGregor managed to capture a focused image of the young mother and baby.

I first encountered this photograph in a quintessentially mid-Victorian source, a beautifully elaborate carte-de-visite album in the Toitū archives. The album had come into the collection long ago from the Eunson estate, but was otherwise unidentified.[4] When the photograph was published in my book on the history of childbirth in nineteenth-century New Zealand, a descendant recognised it as a portrait of her great-grandmother, Rachel Stewart. This led me to another copy of the same carte-de-visite, this time identified, in the Hocken Collections; descendants also hold a copy. The former Toitū archivist, Jill Haley, identified many of the photographs in their album as belonging to members of the well-photographed extended Hepburn family; the Eunsons were descendants of Rachel's sister, Sarah Barr (née Hepburn).

The photograph McGregor took of Rachel and Westwood is striking and unusual, not because of the people in it, but because of an incidental feature: the baby feeding bottle, complete with milk, on the table next to them. We can only speculate about why it appears in this portrait. Had Rachel fed her baby to settle him, and the photographer simply forgot to remove the bottle from view? Or was it deliberately placed in the photograph to demonstrate that Westwood was being brought up on the bottle? One clue to Rachel's feelings about this photograph can be found in the several photographs taken later of her with her four younger children: instead of McGregor, she turned to some of his business competitors, the London Portrait Rooms and Clifford & Morris, for future portraits.

The message that breastfeeding is best for babies is one heard often in our own era. Most Victorian babies were breastfed. Those at either extreme of the class spectrum were more likely than others to be handfed, as it was then commonly called. Some elite women did not breastfeed their babies, believing this rather 'animalistic' activity was below them, or simply inconvenient; the poorest women often had to place their children in care while they worked and hence could not breastfeed them. Some mothers were physically unable to feed their babies, while of course babies whose mothers had died had to depend on either handfeeding or wet nursing by other women.[5]

For Victorian babies, the absence of breastfeeding was positively dangerous. Understanding of nutrition was not sophisticated and many of the substitutes fed to babies were nutritionally inadequate, making infants vulnerable to illness and, in some cases, even to starvation. Bottles like the one in this photograph added to the problem in an era when understanding of microbiology was primitive. This was the most popular sort of baby bottle in Victorian times, available in a range of styles and materials, as the trade advertisement shows. The design allowed the bottle to be placed upright beside a baby, who could then feed him or herself by sucking up through the tubing. But these bottles had a serious flaw: bacteria could build up in the long tubing unless it was very thoroughly cleaned, so babies faced a high risk of gastroenteritis. Malnutrition and gastrointestinal infection killed many Victorian babies. The 'banana' bottle dating from the late nineteenth century, with teat attached directly to the bottle, was a life-saving design improvement.[6] The photograph of Rachel and

S. MAW, SON & THOMPSON'S

FEEDING BOTTLES.

Patented in England, December 4, 1879;
Patented in the United States, April 27, 1880.

THE ALEXANDRA. (Earthenware Cap.) THE EXPORT. (Glass Screw Stopper.)

	White Fittings			Black Fittings		
Alexandra, Wood Top Corks ....per doz.	3/-	3/8	—	3/3	4/3	—
Alexandra, Glass Screw Stoppers .... ,,	—	4/-	—	3/9	4/6	—
Export, Wood Top Corks........ ,,	2/9	3/6	—	3/3	4/-	—
Export, Glass Screw Stoppers .... ,,	—	4/-	—	3/9	4/6	—

The following are sent out with Black Fittings unless ordered to the contrary.

	With Ordinary Fittings			With Valve and Patent Fittings		
Alexandra, Earthenware Caps ....per doz.	—	7/6	11/-	—	8/6	12/-
Alexandra, Glass Screw Stoppers .... ,,	—	7/6	11/-	—	8/6	12/-
Export, Earthenware Caps........ ,,	—	7/-	—	—	8/-	—
Export, Glass Screw Stoppers .... ,,	—	7/-	—	—	8/-	—

SPECIAL DISCOUNT FOR QUANTITIES.

Not less than £5 worth each or assorted... ... ... 15 per cent. off Invoice and 5 per cent. Cash.
Not less than £10 worth each or assorted... ... ... 20 per cent. off Invoice and 5 per cent. Cash.

Carriage paid to any part of the United Kingdom, Isle of Man, and Channel Islands, at the following discounts:—

Not less than 1 gross each or assorted ... ... 5 per cent. off Invoice and 5 per cent. Cash.
Not less than £5 worth each or assorted... ... ... 10 per cent. off Invoice and 5 per cent. Cash.
Not less than £10 worth each or assorted... ... ... 15 per cent. off Invoice and 5 per cent. Cash.

S. MAW, SON & THOMPSON, 7 to 12 ALDERSGATE STREET, LONDON, E.C.

63

Details of popular feeding bottles from the trade journal Chemist and Druggist, *2 November 1889.*

W.A. Baylis the Chemist records, 84-126, Hocken Collections, Uare Taoka o Hākena, University of Otago

Rachel and William Downie Stewart with William Downie Stewart junior, carte-de-visite by Clifford & Morris, Dunedin, 1878.

Ref: S13-546c, William Downie Stewart Papers, Hocken Collections, Uare Taoka o Hākena, University of Otago

The safer 'banana' bottle, developed in the late nineteenth century.

Courtesy of the Tokomairiro Historical Society

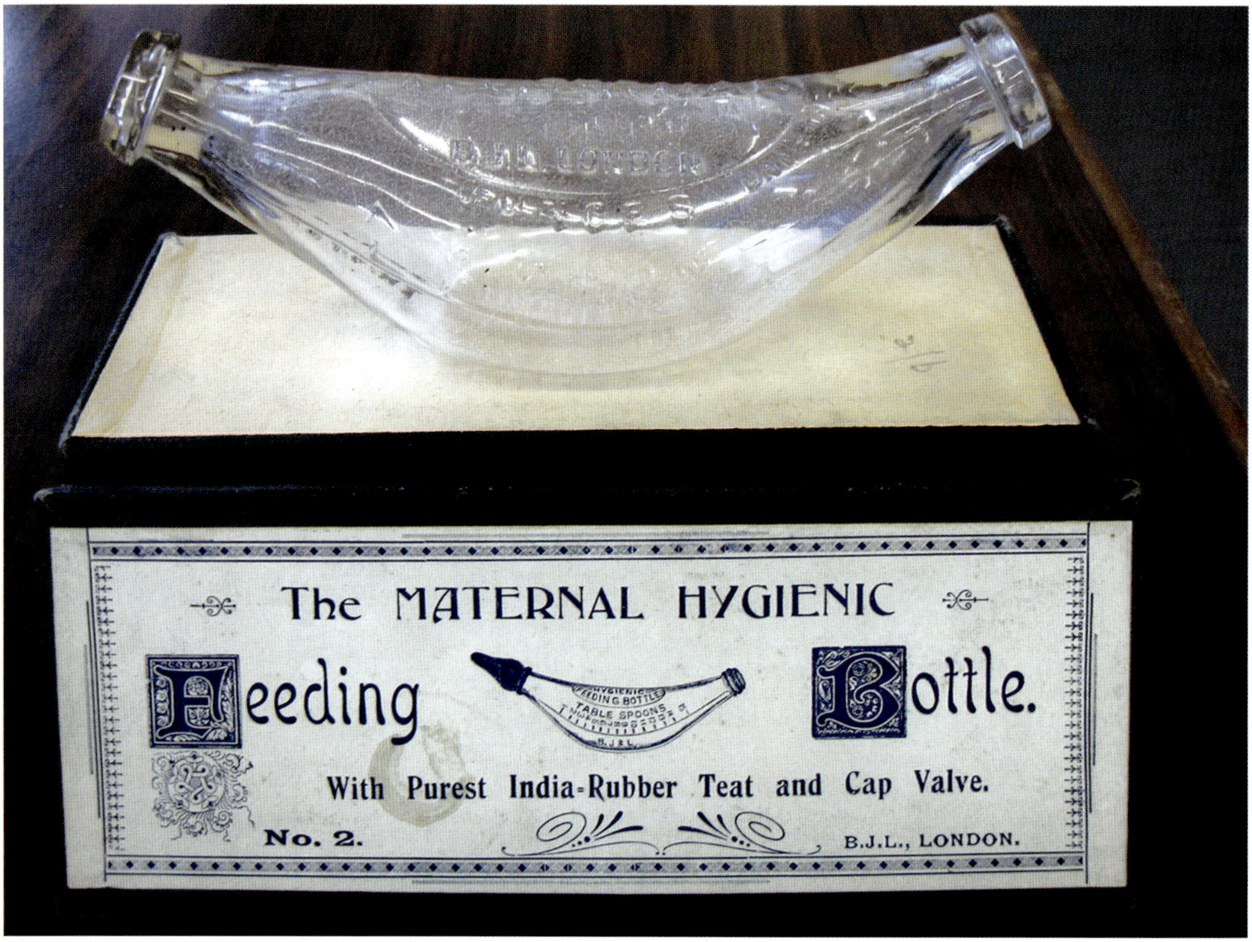

her son would prove to be an important keepsake for the Stewart family, as Westwood died when he was just five months old. His death certificate reveals the cause of his death as dysentery, giving added poignancy to the photograph: it is very likely that this feeding bottle contributed to his death, though his family may not have realised it.[7] Eight years later Rachel joined her son in the family grave at Dunedin's Southern Cemetery. Her youngest child, William Downie Stewart junior, was three months old when she died; she must have taken ill not long after the photograph of William and his parents was taken.

Rachel's death was not related to childbirth, but to erysipelas, a common form of cellulitis that could progress to potentially fatal septicaemia, untreatable in those pre-antibiotic days. Rachel's father George Hepburn wrote to his sister in Scotland that she had died 'of erysipelas in the face after only 10 days illness leaving 4 dear children … Rachel was also in good health about 2 weeks before only not very strong thro nursing.' She was treated by two doctors and attended by a nurse and her sister, but all the money and care in the world could not save her. George Hepburn's comment that she was nursing, or breastfeeding, baby William is interesting, and only adds to the intrigue about why the bottle appears in the photograph of Rachel with baby Westwood.[8]

Five years later George Hepburn again wrote to Scotland to report the death of a young mother. His daughter-in-law Janet, married to Andrew Hepburn, Rachel's brother, died in 1883, just two days after giving birth to her sixth child. This had a devastating impact on her husband, who had been struggling to get by on their farm near Tapanui, where the rabbits were eating all the crops. He abandoned the farm and went to live with his father in Dunedin, together with his oldest son. The other five children were divided among other family members. Three went to live with their father's sisters, while the other two children, including the new baby, were taken in by their maternal grandmother. George Hepburn also wrote of the fate of that new baby in a letter to Scotland: 'Mrs Healey [Janet's mother], took baby and nursed it up on the bottle. It got a little cold and it died in a few weeks after. Andrew very much cut up.'[9] The death certificate records that four-month-old Hector died of pertussis, or whooping cough, and pneumonia.[10]

The sad stories of Rachel Stewart and Janet Hepburn and their children lend a human face to the rather stark statistics of maternal and infant mortality in nineteenth-century New Zealand. They also remind us that prosperity and the best of contemporary healthcare did not invariably provide protection from illness. In the last four decades of the century, around one in 11 non-Māori babies died before reaching their first birthday, while one mother died as a direct result of childbirth for every 200 or so births (around 50 times the current maternal mortality rate for New Zealand).[11] No statistics are available for Māori infant and maternal mortality in the Victorian period. We do, of course, need to remember the overall context of mortality in this period. Rachel Stewart's death from an infection that would now be easily treated was not out of the ordinary, and the biggest single killer of women of childbearing age was not childbirth, but tuberculosis (three of Rachel's five brothers died of this disease).[12]

Various objects might hold the power of life and death, but there can be few as poignant as the Victorian feeding bottle. It was a common household item with a benign purpose: to nourish a baby. Yet, with the wisdom of hindsight and a greater knowledge of nutrition and microbiology, we now understand that such bottles and their contents could be fatal to the lives they were intended to nurture. When John McGregor included, perhaps through carelessness, a feeding bottle in his portrait of Westwood Stewart and his mother, he did not know that he was photographing an object that might end the baby's life.

15

William Speer's Album

A Scrapbook of Colonial Travel

Angela Wanhalla

With its leather binding and gold tooling, William Speer's album suggests a luxury object, but by the 1860s albums were easily integrated into the Victorian home, largely because of their affordability.

Ref: E-395, Alexander Turnbull Library, Wellington, New Zealand

It is not known precisely under what circumstances Speer obtained this lock of hair belonging to Ellen Kihau.

Ref: E-95-016, Alexander Turnbull Library, Wellington, New Zealand

William Speer's album appears to be a curiosity.[1] Its 40 coloured and gold-edged pages, bound in a blue leather cover, include photographs, several pencil and ink sketches, and watercolours, some created by Speer. Engravings, lithographs, newspaper clippings, writing specimens, fabric, several locks of hair and a pressed flower also appear. Sold commercially as an album, it originally consisted of blank pages without mounts or slots for photographs. Speer gathered the objects with little regard for chronology, producing something more reminiscent of a personal scrapbook than a carefully organised Victorian photograph album.[2] This is not a unique object. Because of their affordability scrapbooks and albums were common in Victorian households, and though at first glance the range of media gathered by Speer seems curious, when placed in the context of the practice of scrapbooking, this album sits squarely within popular nineteenth-century collecting traditions.[3]

Victorians created scrapbooks for a variety of purposes, ranging from the personal, such as collecting memorabilia or newspaper clippings, to the professional: they were widely used by organisations to archive their activities. Scrapbooks and albums also functioned as aids to memory.[4] Like other scrapbooks from the same era, Speer's album serves multiple functions: it draws on the commonplace book in which young men were encouraged to gather together inspiring words for self-improvement but also as a demonstration of their learning. Humorous references to university dons, including a nine-verse poem, suggest a person familiar with university life.[5] His collection of sketches and watercolours evokes the tradition of the portfolio, designed for display as a showcase of one's artistic skill.

Speer's album is also a travel journal detailing the adventures of a middle-class Victorian, the son of a minister, who journeyed to New Zealand in the 1860s. Speer travelled to a colony in the midst of a gold fever, arriving at Port Chalmers, Dunedin, on board the *Bombay*, a Shaw, Savill & Co. clipper, in September 1862.[6] He commemorated this event by making a sketch of the ship, which he then pasted into his album, inscribing his departure and arrival dates underneath. Images of ships appear regularly in Victorian albums, to remember and 'evoke a life of adventure and travel' during an age of increasing migration and mobility.[7] We do not know if Speer came to New Zealand to join the gold

Part of the winding sheet of a Malay, three years under-

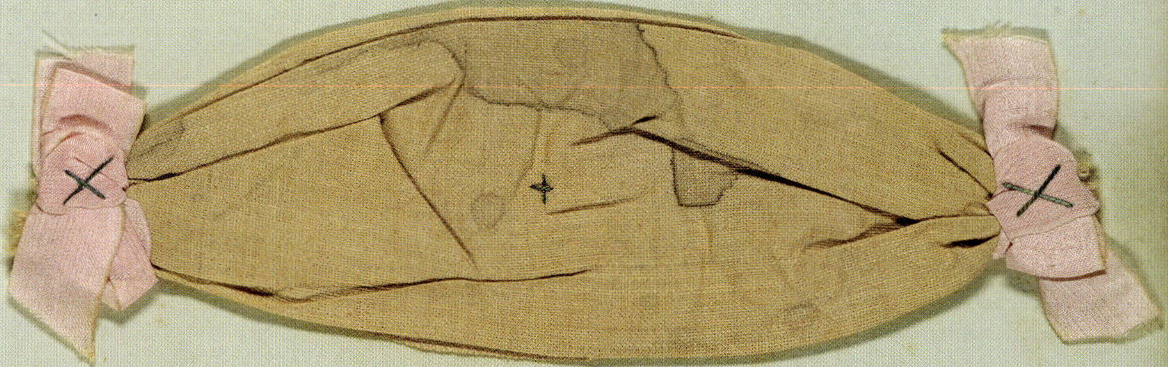

-ground, taken from the "Crommat" burial ground,
about 100 miles North of Cape town, Cape of Good Hope,
From - A. A. C. Octr 1864. -

Left: *This piece of linen, given to William Speer by 'A.A.C.' in 1864, was stolen from a Muslim burial ground in South Africa. Speer has sewn it onto a page of the album.*

Speer Album, Ref: E-95-028, Alexander Turnbull Library, Wellington, New Zealand

A small pencil sketch of a Māori woman, named as 'Gootie', sits at the centre of this page from Speer's album. At the top of the page is a folded sheet of paper containing a lock of hair belonging to 'H.R.H. Ellen Kihou Patuki Pihou'. Speer neither described the contents of the second piece of folded paper, which contains a piece of silk ribbon, nor offered any explanation of its provenance.

Ref: E-95-016, Alexander Turnbull Library, Wellington, New Zealand

rush, but he certainly took the opportunity to observe the gold towns of Central Otago, making sketches and watercolours of the Wakatipu region and its characters.

What we know for certain is that Speer hailed from the town of Thames Ditton, Surrey, where his father had been the vicar at St Nicholas' Anglican Church.[8] We also know where he travelled, for the photographs, clippings, sketches, engravings and watercolours of people and places record his movements through the ports, small towns, rural hinterlands and cities of the British colonial world. After disembarking at Port Chalmers, Speer spent time in Dunedin, travelled inland to take in the gold towns of Central Otago, then visited southern New Zealand, where he spent some time with the Māori community resident at windswept Ruapuke Island, a place few Pākehā visited. In 1864 he travelled across the Tasman to Sydney, before returning to England via Ceylon (Sri Lanka) in March 1865 on the Peninsular and Oriental steamer *Northam* which, like the *Bombay*, is commemorated visually and annotated with Speer's date of departure. Speer died in April 1868, only a few years after returning from his travels to the most distant parts of Britain's empire.[9]

Where Speer has taken the time to paste items onto the pages of the album, he has carefully annotated them, describing their provenance and dating their acquisition, as for any museum object. A number of items are loose, folded between pages, suggesting they were either added later by someone else after Speer's death, or that the album's creator never got the chance to fix them into place. This mixture of mounted and loose material is not unusual in scrapbooks and albums. The most common items in Speer's album are photographs. From the 1860s photographic and printing technologies enabled the mass production of photographic portraits in the form of cartes-de-visite, cabinet cards and albumen prints. These were of a size convenient for mailing to friends and family, and easily reproduced in large numbers for the purposes of collecting. As a result, portrait images dominated scrapbooks, which by the late nineteenth century offered greater freedom of arrangement than the formal photograph album.[10]

The first item in the album, a signature annotated 'The autograph of King Topie, Patuki Pihoa, his European name being John Topi.[11] Port Adventure, [Stewart Island], South Island, May 5th 1863', evokes the friendship album, popular in the nineteenth century and designed for collecting autographs, poetry, prose and letters or cards from friends. Short love letters, a Christmas card from a female friend in Sydney, the signature of Charles M. Cole who, according to Speer's annotation, acted as a second in a duel in Dunedin in October 1863 to Captain Crawford of the 40th Regiment, a 10-verse song written and gifted by a Mr Small, as well as a letter requesting the loan of a revolver, given to Speer by John Clerke on 18 June 1863, together testify to the album's function as a record of Speer's social network and associations.[12]

Speer also collected examples of Māori writing, beginning with Topi Patuki's autograph, two waiata from Ruapuke transcribed into te reo by Here Wete (Henry West) and letters to the album's compiler from several Māori women. While visiting Ruapuke, Speer also collected, or was given, a lock of hair from Ellen Kihau. It is one of three hair samples, all from women, in the album. How do we interpret these? Are they trophies? Or are they curios? Are they tokens of love? Each lock of hair is folded into thick paper, annotated and situated near an image of the woman who gave it, or, perhaps, from whom it was taken: two are sketches; the other a circular photograph that looks as if it may have once been housed in a locket. Is the hair a further aid to 'the memorial power of the image'? Victorian albums and scrapbooks commonly included tactile objects like hair, as 'a convenient and pliable stand-in for the body of the missing, memoralized subject'. While often associated with mourning, locks of hair could also be a 'metaphor for friendship and love or a discreet act of courtship', which may account for their presence in Speer's album.[13]

Speer collected items that would give his audience a taste of his travels and the people he encountered, ranging from the mundane, such as a laundry list, to items that appealed to his sense of humour, such as the clipping from the *Sydney Morning Herald* about the mayor of Sydney who shared his name. Invitations to balls and theatre tickets point to patterns of social life in the colonies, while letters and cards offer a glimpse into his networks in New Zealand and Australia. By the mid-nineteenth century, 'the word "album" referred to any blank book in which friends left a "memorial" to one another' and these personal messages were often set beside pressed flowers and locks of hair, also symbolic of social bonds and personal connections.[14] Like many Victorians, Speer dwelt on love, sentiment and memory, and his album reflects this.

The locks of hair, though, suggest a darker side to the album. Some of its content also demonstrates an interest in Victorian racial science, evoking a tradition of ethnographic collecting. Speer was in his late twenties when the locks of hair were collected, so they could certainly be mementoes of friendship or love, but they might also easily function as curios of colonial life, evidenced by his descriptions of the women as colonial 'types' – 'celestial Polly' and the 'convict bride', for instance – while a photograph of a Chinese woman is entitled 'Shanghai Mary', and the drawings of Fijian and Tongan women are rendered as ethnographic caricatures of sexualised 'savages' or 'cannibals'.

Speer's interest in ethnography is evinced by one of the most unusual items in the album: a piece of linen, given to him by A.A.C. in October 1864 and described as being from the 'winding sheet of a Malay, three years underground, taken from a Crommut burial ground, about 100 miles north of Capetown, Cape of Good Hope'. Each end is folded and tied with pink ribbon and the linen sewn onto the centre of an album page. Crommut is in fact *keramat*, a Malay word for a burial site and popular place of prayer for individuals who had gained standing and respect because of their learning and piety, which are found wherever Muslims migrated.[15] Colonists, scientists, ethnographers and travellers did not always treat sacred non-European sites with reverence, often plundering graves for treasures, bones or cloth. Speer's 'winding sheet' testifies to the practice of grave robbing, possibly in the hope of personal gain, or for 'curios' to add to a collection.

Although highly personal, Victorian scrapbooks and albums were also presentational objects, designed to be shown to an audience, or to be regularly opened, lingered over, discussed and debated. The inclusion of hair and fabric offered the added sensation of touch, for both the compiler and the audience. One can imagine Speer showing his album to family and associates in England, thrilling and titillating them with stories of exotic colonial peoples and their strange practices and customs.

I started this essay by describing Speer's album as an apparent curiosity, since at first glance his collection seems idiosyncratic and eclectic, but in many ways the varied contents of the album and their arrangement reflect a broader Victorian interest in science, race, imperial endeavour and colonial development as well as fantasies about indigenous peoples of the South Pacific. By focusing solely on the 'curios' in the album, though, we silence the multiple functions of the object. It was also a travel journal, commemorating his adventures in the colonies, and a friendship book providing evidence of his social connections and associations.

The histories of scrapbooks and albums are yet to be told in New Zealand, yet such items are common in our archival collections, suggesting that album making and scrapbooking were popular pastimes. For those interested in the study of the social and cultural practices of everyday life in the colonial past, scrapbooks and albums help us to understand what individuals valued and why. Writing of nineteenth-century American scrapbooks, Ellen Gruber Garvey characterises them as a portable embodiment of aspirations, but with the 'prestige of a bound book'.[16] She heralds them as portals into the social and cultural lives of people who 'did not respond to the world with their own writing' but who used scrapbooks to express their thoughts, ideas and their identity through the collection and containment of the things they valued.[17] Studied as a genre, placed in the context of their creation and read alongside the histories of their compilers, scrapbooks and albums are, as Juliana M. Kuipers suggests, a 'valuable container of cultural information' about the circulation of knowledge, patterns of consumption and an evolving visual culture, while also illuminating practices of collecting, archiving, memorialising and the fashioning of identities.[18]

16

Retrieved from Oblivion?

Wiremu Kīngi Te Rangitaake and the Photographic Object

Ruth Harvey

An unsmiling face with moko. A striking pale suit. An arm resting on a table decorated with distinctive tassels and a vase of flowers. A photograph, since disappeared, bearing the inscription 'William King'. From the time of its discovery in 1932, this vanished photograph – and its remaining copy – has been widely accepted as the only confirmed photographic portrait of Te Ātiawa chief Wiremu Kīngi Te Rangitaake. It has been reproduced extensively in publications, exhibitions and on websites, bearing his name without question. But is this photograph really of Wiremu Kīngi? Do the accounts of its making and discovery have merit? And why has the photographic object itself never been interrogated for what it can uncover about its subject? The image's story reminds us that photographs, just like other forms of historical evidence, require rigorous cross-examination.[1]

Despite his pivotal role in the beginning of the First Taranaki War (17 March 1860–18 March 1861), no photograph was known to exist of Te Ātiawa paramount chief Wiremu Kīngi Te Rangitaake. On 31 March 1932, however, Wellington's *Evening Post* declared that Wiremu Kīngi's face had been retrieved 'from oblivion'. A Mr E.C. Jones, searching for photographs of Waitara for an exhibition, had unearthed an album belonging to Lieutenant William Johnson of the Taranaki Mounted Volunteers, and his 'interest quickened when he saw on the back of [a] yellow portrait the simple words "William King"'. The portrait was shown to Kahu, a Te Ātiawa chief living at Manukorihi pā – Kīngi's birthplace – and Matewai Taituha, a descendant of Wiremu Kīngi's mother. Both had known Kīngi and both confirmed the identification. The article adds, 'Another and older Maori of Waitara, Totara, has confirmed that Wiremu Kingi was wearing a European suit of white cloth when he was photographed at Wellington.' The *Evening Post* had more. Kīngi was in Wellington and Waitara during 1846–47; Kahu thought that Kīngi's visit to Governor Grey before the Te Ātiawa migration in 1849 had been the occasion for the portrait. Grey himself was said to have arranged the sitting, which explained why Johnson, the governor's former attendant, had the portrait in his possession.[2]

The original 'yellow portrait' discovered by Jones has since disappeared. Puke Ariki in New Plymouth holds a silver gelatin bromide copy photograph

Unknown photographer, [possibly] Wiremu Kīngi Te Rangitaake (c. 1932), silver gelatin bromide developing-out paper print (copy photograph) from unknown original.

Ref: PHO2002-442, Collection of Puke Ariki, New Plymouth

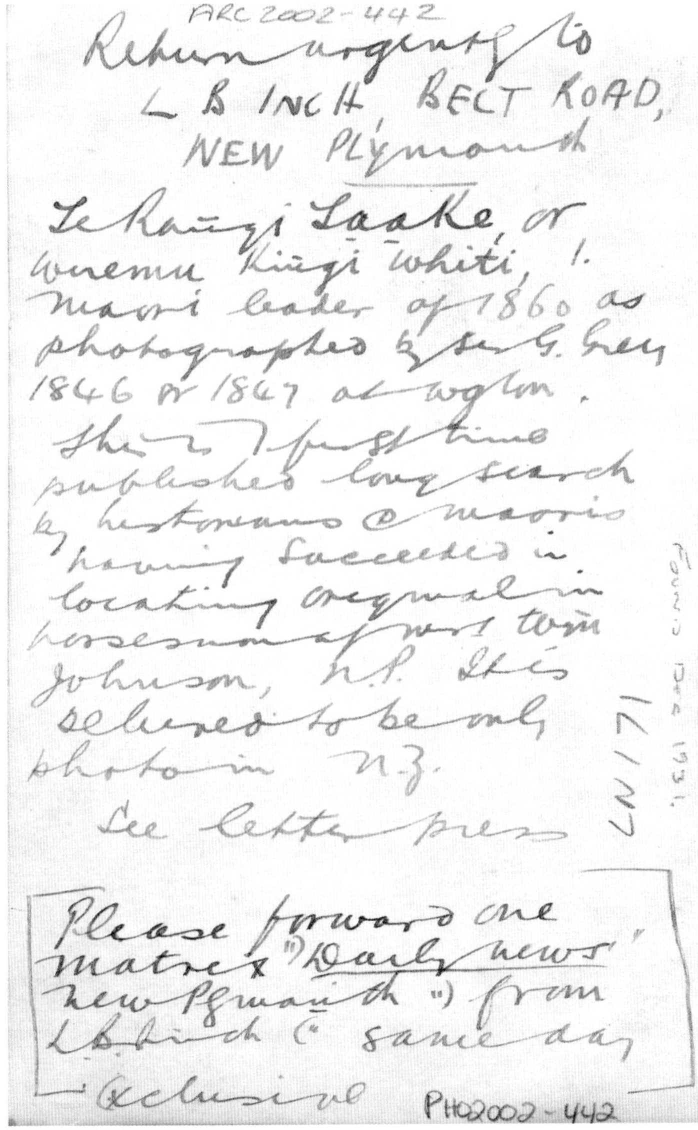

ARC2002-442

Return urgently to
L B INCH, BELT ROAD,
NEW PLYMOUTH

Te Rangi Taake, or
Wiremu Kingi Whiti, 1.
Maori leader of 1860 as
photographed by Sir G. Grey
1846 or 1847 at Wgton.
This is the first time
published long search
by historians & maoris
having succeeded in
locating original in
possession of Mrs Tom
Johnson, N.P. It is
believed to be only
photo in N.Z.
See letter press

LN/71

Please forward one
matrix "Daily News"
New Plymouth ") from
L.B. Inch (same day
Exclusive

PH02002-442

of the original, annotated extensively on the rear. Part of the inscription reads, 'Te Rangi Taake, or Wiremu Kingi Whiti, Maori leader of 1860 as photographed by Sir G. Grey 1846 or 1847 at Wgton.' Like the *Evening Post* article, further annotations suggest that it is the only photograph of Wiremu Kīngi and refer to a 'same day exclusive' forthcoming in the *Taranaki Daily News*. The inscription also reads 'Return urgently to LB INCH'. Inch was an Auckland-based lawyer known to deal in Taranaki Māori artefacts, but his involvement here is obscure.[3] Another copy of the photograph, featuring hand-drawn elements and likely copied and altered from Puke Ariki's version, exists in the Alexander Turnbull Library. Identified as 'possibly' Wiremu Kīngi, the photograph is dated c. 1847 and attributed to Sir George Grey.[4]

Wiremu Kīngi Te Rangitaake's central role in a contentious part of New Zealand's colonial history ensures a continuing desire to reproduce his likeness. Kīngi's steadfast refusal to sell Te Ātiawa lands, and his vehement rejection of the Pekapeka Block sale to the government, ultimately led to the First Taranaki War. He was a warrior, a man of principle, a diplomat and later a recluse. Owing to his great mana, a copy of this photograph hangs at the front of Ōwae marae's meeting house in Waitara, and many authors, curators and researchers have reproduced it without questioning its provenance.[5]

Perhaps blinded by the desire to know Wiremu Kīngi's appearance, we have taken this photograph – and the account of its finding – literally at face value. Yet the photograph itself throws the account of its creation into doubt. Any photograph taken before 1849 had to be a daguerreotype image.[6] Although there were daguerreotypists operating in New Zealand by 1848, the earliest extant New Zealand-made daguerreotypes date to the early 1850s.[7] This makes any date in the late 1840s, as suggested by the annotation on the back of Puke Ariki's copy photograph, improbable.

Nor does the photograph look like a daguerreotype. It looks like a carte-de-visite, a format not invented until 1854.[8] A carte-de-visite is a photographic print, usually an albumen print from a glass collodion negative, mounted on a card about the size of today's business card. The format became immensely popular in the 1860s and helped photography to proliferate throughout the world. Its small size was perfect for portraiture and cartes-de-visite adhered to a strict visual language that borrowed from portrait painting conventions. Typically, they presented a single person, often showing their full body, and used props such as tables, pedestals, chairs, curtains or painted backdrops. Daguerreotype portraits, by contrast, tended to frame the subject from the waist up and had a plain background with fewer props. The person being photographed was the primary subject; props were an unnecessary distraction. Wiremu Kīngi's portrait shows too much of his body to be typical of this format. His pose is casual, with one hand tucked into his pocket – not a common pose in daguerreotypes. The portrait also incorporates typical carte-de-visite props: a draped curtain, a chair, a table, a vase of flowers. The photographer has framed the view widely enough to show the patterned carpet.

Beyond what is depicted in the Wiremu Kīngi photograph, its physical appearance also gives clues to the process used to make the original image. Photographs copied from daguerreotypes 'look pretty distinctive' because of their highly reflective surface, but this trait is not evident in the Wiremu Kīngi image.[9] Further, Puke Ariki's copy photograph clearly shows a large crease or tear running from the top of the image, across Wiremu Kīngi's shoulder and down to his chest. At the very least this suggests that the original in Johnson's album was a paper-based photograph, confirmed by the *Evening Post*'s use of the words 'yellow portrait'. Most albumen prints yellow as they age. Further, a letter from Inch to the then Taranaki Museum director refers to 'the "cabinet" photographic print of Wiremu Kingi', implying that the lost original was a paper-based print.[10] Finally, the fact that it was found in an album suggests Johnson's photograph was more likely to be a carte-de-visite, which were commonly stored in albums, rather than a cased daguerreotype portrait.

Further clarification of the photograph's date is also possible through the discovery of six cartes-de-visite in Puke Ariki's Pictorial Collection that share the same props as those in the Wiremu Kīngi photograph, providing vital clues to the wider context of the image. All feature the same distinctive table with tassels seen in the Wiremu Kīngi photograph and the same patterned carpet. Where visible, the chair also seems to be the same. None of the cartes-de-visite bear studio information, but they were very probably photographed in a New Plymouth, or perhaps Whanganui, studio as the only clear commonality among them was the subjects' place of residence. All six subjects emigrated to New Plymouth between 1841 and 1854. All but two lived in Taranaki for the rest of their lives. The first to die was Mrs Elizabeth Faull in 1874.[11] Since the carte-de-visite format arrived in New Zealand in the very early 1860s, we can assume these photographs were made between then and about the mid-1870s.[12]

The visual evidence, in sum, suggests that the Māori man pictured in Puke Ariki's photograph, currently identified as Wiremu Kīngi Te Rangitaake, had his likeness taken in the same studio as six New Plymouth residents. But would Wiremu Kīngi have entered New Plymouth on the eve of the First Taranaki War and had his photograph taken? Or after the war began? It seems unlikely. After the war ended in March 1861, Wiremu Kīngi withdrew inland, becoming a virtual recluse. A lengthy account in the *Taranaki Herald* of his sole visit to New Plymouth after that date makes no mention of him being photographed while in the town.[13] Further, if Sir George Grey commissioned the photograph, as the story goes, there is no evidence Wiremu Kīngi Te Rangitaake met the governor after the 1840s – too early for a carte-de-visite portrait to have been taken. There is a definite possibility that this portrait is of a different 'William King'.[14]

An annotation on yet another photograph provides a further clue. On the rear of a different Alexander Turnbull Library photograph of a Māori man identified as 'Possibly Wiremu Kingi Te Rangitaake', a note written by ethnologist Stephenson Percy Smith says, 'Mr Gordon agrees with me, this is not a likeness of W Kingi Te Rangitake. He says that no likeness was ever taken of him, he always refused to be taken, which seems to me to be true, as it agrees with his character.'[15] The annotation was dated 18 February 1904. Yet at least three Māori who knew Wiremu Kīngi identified him as the subject of the portrait, though many years after his death.

On the evidence available, it is highly unlikely that the Māori man pictured in the striking pale suit is Wiremu Kīngi Te Rangitaake. One thing Puke Ariki's photograph does prove is our desire to believe a story for our own purposes. We have claimed to know Wiremu Kīngi Te Rangitaake's face by overlooking the flaws in the tale surrounding the photograph's discovery. Similar cases of dubious pictorial identification exist about other prominent Māori leaders, including Te Kooti and Tītokowaru, as they do for many historical figures worldwide. My hope is that the stern face staring out of the photograph will now remind us that 'To encounter the image *in* history … we must enquire about the circumstances of its making.'[16]

CLOCKWISE FROM TOP LEFT:

Unknown photographer, Mrs Ann Grylls (c. 1860s–1870s), carte-de-visite with albumen print.

Ref: PHO2008-1652, Collection of Puke Ariki, New Plymouth

Unknown photographer, Mrs Faull (c. 1860s–1870s), carte-de-visite with albumen print.

Ref: PHO2012-0502, Collection of Puke Ariki, New Plymouth

Unknown photographer, Mrs Samuel Curtis (c. 1860s–1870s), carte-de-visite with albumen print.

Ref: PHO2005-015, Collection of Puke Ariki, New Plymouth

Unknown photographer, James Thomas Davis (c. 1860s–1870s), carte-de-visite with albumen print.

Ref: PHO2012-0503, Collection of Puke Ariki, New Plymouth

Unknown photographer, Jim Johnson (c. 1860s–1870s), carte-de visite with albumen print.

Ref: PHO2012-0496, Collection of Puke Ariki, New Plymouth

Unknown photographer, Mrs Jane Harvey (née Rundle) (c. 1860s–1870s), carte-de-visite with albumen print.

Ref: PHO2012-0501, Collection of Puke Ariki, New Plymouth

HOPKINSON & COPE
FINSBURY
LONDON

17

'A Sparrow Alone Upon the House Top'

The Te Pihoihoi *Press*

Lachy Paterson

Until recently, two printing presses sat next to each other near the entranceway to Te Awamutu Museum. Much has been written about the larger press, now just a bare frame. This essay focuses on the smaller one, which was complete with all its working parts. Both are Albion presses, the nineteenth-century workhorse of pre-steam and pre-electric British and colonial printing establishments. Both bear the Hopkinson & Cope impress, which dates them from 1847 or later.[1] These machines were truly hand operated, requiring manual inking, placing the paper into a frame then upon the inked type, winding it into the press, pulling a lever to create the impression and extracting the paper from the machine. Although the presses were capable of excellent quality, they were relatively slow, limited to about 250 impressions per hour at best.[2] Notwithstanding this limitation, both machines were used in 1863 to print propaganda in two opposing Māori-language newspapers.

In early 1863 New Zealand was in the grip of an internal 'cold war'. Five years earlier, in 1858, central North Island iwi, through the drive and determination of Ngāti Haua chief Wiremu Tamihana, had come together to create the Kīngitanga, a loose coalition to stem the sales of Māori land to the Crown and to elect a Māori king. This land loss not only threatened Māori independence, but also generated significant internal conflict, often bloodshed, among the Māori owners, to which the government generally turned a blind eye. When the governor attempted to enforce a disputed sale of Te Ātiawa land in 1860, war ensued between Māori and the Crown, escalating as Kīngitanga warriors travelled south to assist the Māori cause. A year's fighting ended in an uneasy truce, with both Māori and Pākehā holding land that the other side believed was theirs.

Sir George Grey, recalled to the governorship, was not prepared to tolerate Māori forming an independent state across the centre of the North Island. The Kīngitanga waited defiantly as Grey manoeuvred politically to increase his influence over Māori, while also preparing militarily for the likely struggle to come. One of Grey's stratagems to undermine the Kīngitanga was to send John Gorst in 1862 to Te Awamutu, deep within the boundaries of the Māori kingdom. Gorst was primarily a magistrate, but his roles included

The Albion style of press, such as this Hopkinson & Cope model used to print Te Pihoihoi Mokemoke, *was ideal for colonial conditions. It was manually operated, with no need for steam or electricity.*
OPPOSITE: *A detail of the frame head.*

Courtesy of Te Awamutu Museum. Photograph by Catherine Jehly

This photograph was taken in 1958 when the press was donated to the Turnbull Library. It was loaned to Te Awamutu Museum until 2014, when it was returned to Wellington.

Ref: EP/1958/2210-F, Alexander Turnbull Library, Wellington, New Zealand

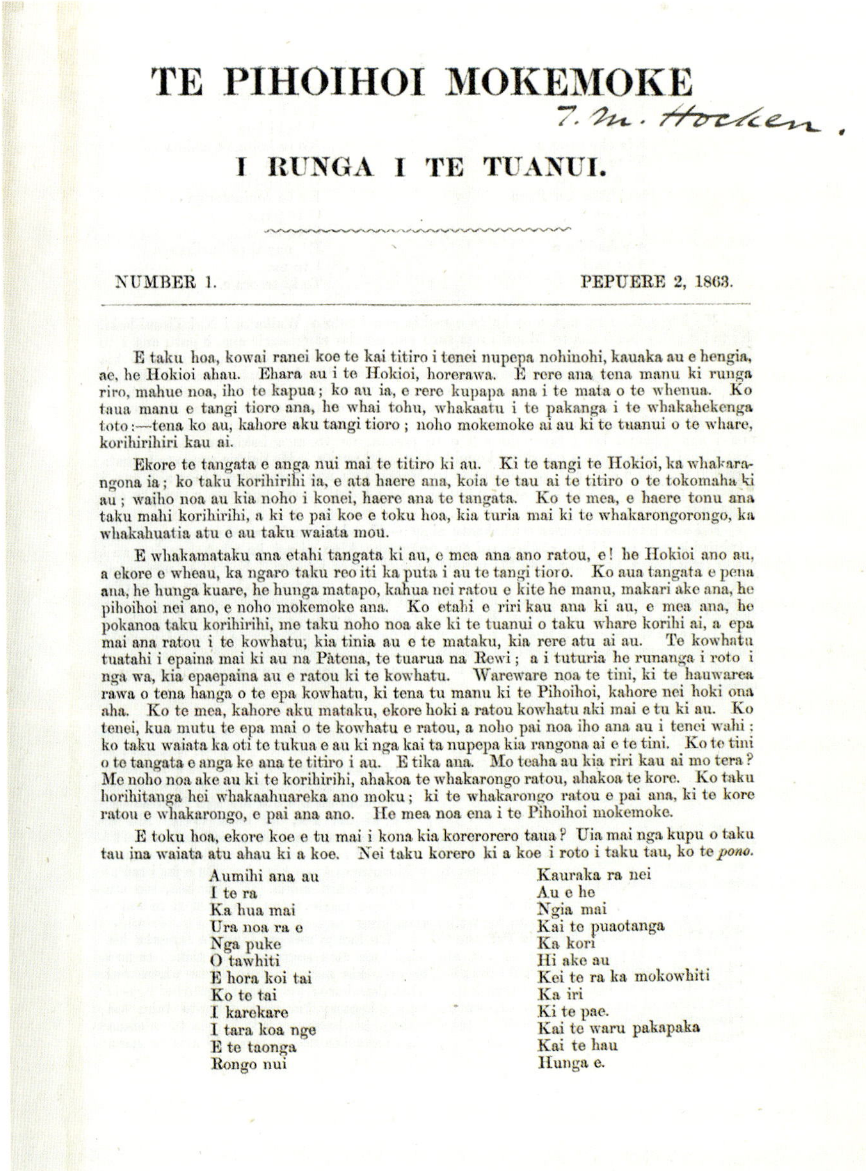

TE PIHOIHOI MOKEMOKE

T. M. Hocken.

I RUNGA I TE TUANUI.

NUMBER 1. PEPUERE 2, 1863.

E taku hoa, kowai ranei koe te kai titiro i tenei nupepa nohinohi, kauaka au e hengia, ae, he Hokioi ahau. Ehara au i te Hokioi, horerawa. E rere ana tena manu ki runga riro, mahue noa, iho te kapua; ko au ia, e rere kupapa ana i te mata o te whenua. Ko taua manu e tangi tioro ana, he whai tohu, whakaatu i te pakanga i te whakahekenga toto:—tena ko au, kahore aku tangi tioro; noho mokemoke ai au ki te tuanui o te whare, korihirihiri kau ai.

Ekore te tangata e anga nui mai te titiro ki au. Ki te tangi te Hokioi, ka whakarangona ia; ko taku korihirihi ia, e ata haere ana, koia te tau ai te titiro o te tokomaha ki au; waiho noa au kia noho i konei, haere ana te tangata. Ko te mea, e haere tonu ana taku mahi korihirihi, a ki te pai koe e toku hoa, kia turia mai ki te whakarongorongo, ka whakahuatia atu e au taku waiata mou.

E whakamataku ana etahi tangata ki au, e mea ana ano ratou, e! he Hokioi ano au, a ekore e wheau, ka ngaro taku reo iti ka puta i au te tangi tioro. Ko aua tangata e pena ana, he hunga kuare, he hunga matapo, kahua nei ratou e kite he manu, makari ake ana, he pihoihoi nei ano, e noho mokemoke ana. Ko etahi e riri kau ana ki au, e mea ana, he pokanoa taku korihirihi, me taku noho noa ake ki te tuanui o taku whare korihi ai, a epa mai ana ratou i te kowhatu; kia tinia au e te mataku, kia rere atu ai au. Te kowhatu tuatahi i epaina mai ki au na Pàtena, te tuarua na Rewi; a i tuturia he runanga i roto i nga wa, kia epaepaina au e ratou ki te kowhatu. Wareware noa te tini, ki te hauwarea rawa o tena hanga o te epa kowhatu, ki tena tu manu ki te Pihoihoi, kahore nei hoki ona aha. Ko te mea, kahore aku mataku, ekore hoki a ratou kowhatu aki mai e tu ki au. Ko tenei, kua mutu te epa mai o te kowhatu e ratou, a noho pai noa iho ana au i tenei wahi; ko taku waiata ka oti te tukua e au ki nga kai ta nupepa kia rangona ai e te tini. Ko te tini o te tangata e anga ke ana te titiro i au. E tika ana. Mo teaha au kia riri kau ai mo tera? Me noho noa ake au ki te korihirihi, ahakoa te whakarongo ratou, ahakoa te kore. Ko taku horihitanga hei whakaahuareka ano moku; ki te whakarongo ratou e pai ana, ki te kore ratou e whakarongo, e pai ana ano. He mea noa ena i te Pihoihoi mokemoke.

E toku hoa, ekore koe e tu mai i kona kia korerorero taua? Uia mai nga kupu o taku tau ina waiata atu ahau ki a koe. Nei taku korero ki a koe i roto i taku tau, ko te *pono*.

Aumihi ana au
I te ra
Ka hua mai
Ura noa ra e
Nga puke
O tawhiti
E hora koi tai
Ko te tai
I karekare
I tara koa nge
E te taonga
Rongo nui

Kauraka ra nei
Au e he
Ngia mai
Kai te puaotanga
Ka kori
Hi ake au
Kei te ra ka mokowhiti
Ka iri
Ki te pae.
Kai te waru pakapaka
Kai te hau
Hunga e.

that of overseeing the government's industrial school, formerly the Anglican mission station, at Te Awamutu.

The government had attempted to sway Māori opinion through print from its earliest days: the printing press was seen as a force for progress and civilisation. Its first Māori-language newspaper, *Te Karere o Nui Tireni*, appeared in 1842, just two years after formal colonial administration. In 1863 it was circulating its journal, *Te Karere Maori*, to Māori chiefs around the country, proffering an assorted mix of general news, moral and improving advice, and propaganda designed to engender Māori acquiescence to colonialism and Crown governance. In 1862 the Kīngitanga acquired its own press, now in Te

LEFT: *The first issue of* Te Pihoihoi Mokemoke *criticised and lampooned King Tāwhiao, arousing the ire of Māori who supported the Kīngitanga.*

Te Pihoihoi Mokemoke i Runga i te Tuanui, *No. 1, Pepuere 2, 1863, p. 1. Ref: S14-559a, Hocken Collections, Uare Taoka o Hākena, University of Otago*

Awamutu's museum, gifted to two Māori travellers to Austria.[3] It began to generate its own propaganda at Ngāruawāhia through its newspaper, *Te Hokioi e Rere atu na*, under the editorship of Ngāruawāhia chief Pātara Te Tuhi. This publication asserted the mana of the Kīngitanga, while disputing the government's claim to authority over all Māori. The Kīngitanga received few copies of *Te Karere Maori*, and tended to regard its content with disdain. In response to *Te Hokioi*, Gorst was instructed to publish his own newspaper, printed on the school's press – the smaller of the two presses – with the express aim of countering the Kīngitanga's rhetoric and belittling the movement.

Gorst's title for the new paper, *Te Pihoihoi Mokemoke i Runga i te Tuanui* ('a sparrow alone upon the house top'), derives from Psalm 102:7, a metaphor for one beset by enemies, its name contrasting with the Kīngitanga's 'Hōkioi', a large mythical bird of war. The biblical reference reflected Gorst's position: the Te Awamutu Māori were staunch Kīngitanga supporters, and the most militant of their leaders, Rewi Maniapoto of Ngāti Maniapoto, lived nearby. The press's first issue, overseen by Grey, 'was scattered broadcast over the whole of Waikato',[4] and asserted that, despite the throwing of stones by Rewi and others, the bird would continue to sing. 'If the call of the Hōkioi is false, this small thing, the Pīhoihoi, can beat it when its own chirping is true.'[5] The issue then proceeded with a deliberately provocative article, 'Te Kino o te Mahi Kingi' ('The Evil of King Activity'), which condemned Tāwhiao, the Māori king, for failing to suppress lawlessness within the lands under his mana.[6] According to Gorst, 'this article', its Māori polished by a daughter of missionary Benjamin Ashwell, 'produced an enormous and unlooked-for sensation. It was read in every Runanga house in Waikato, and was the subject of painful discussion at the King's Council at Ngaruawahia.'[7] The second issue comprised a single conversation between Grey and Wiremu Tamihana, from minutes taken by a Native Office official, designed to make the governor sound fair and reasonable and the kingmaker intransigent.[8] Each issue comprised but four small pages, and between 2 February and 9 March 1863 Gorst's printer, John von Dadelzen – not quite 18 years old – had managed to put out four issues, with most of the content designed to undermine the Kīngitanga.

Gorst's operation of the press for propaganda purposes was occurring at the same time as the Kīngitanga's relationship with the governor continued to deteriorate over larger concerns. Matters in Taranaki were still unresolved, and Māori also knew that Grey, while espousing peace, was constructing a military road and obtaining gunboats with which to attack the Waikato. As *Te Pihoihoi* disingenuously argued, the gunboat was armoured only lest Māori take potshots at it with their own guns.[9] Gorst further alienated Māori when he attempted to stop a Kīngitanga group removing from their territory sawn timber with which Grey was planning to construct a fortified barracks. More moderate factions were wary of any precipitous action against Gorst that might provoke a worse reaction from the governor, and *Te Hokioi*, published only once a month, publicly eschewed a 'newspaper war', despite its rival's provocations.[10] But the Kīngitanga's supporters were

TOP LEFT: *John Gorst, civil commissioner and magistrate at Te Awamutu in 1863, also edited the Māori-language newspaper,* Te Pihoihoi Mokemoke, *to counter the Kīngitanga's* Te Hokioi.

Ref: 1/2-038163-F, Alexander Turnbull Library, Wellington, New Zealand

ABOVE: *During his second governorship Sir George Grey was faced with rising Māori nationalism in the form of the Kīngitanga.*

Ref: PA2-1182, Alexander Turnbull Library, Wellington, New Zealand

LEFT: *Rewi Maniapoto led the militant wing of the Kīngitanga, and ordered the seizure of the* Te Pihoihoi Mokemoke *press on 24 March 1863.*

Ref: PA2-1359, Alexander Turnbull Library, Wellington, New Zealand

angry at the insults. Ngāti Maniapoto had already attempted to expel Gorst soon after his arrival in early 1862, when the chief Pātene Poutama and 30 warriors had descended on Gorst's establishment. Pātene accused Gorst and his staff of being 'worms, baits that Sir George Grey was fishing with'.[11] Gorst managed to argue his way out of eviction then, but a year later was not so lucky. Rewi Maniapoto had had enough of Gorst and his press, and decided to act.

On the afternoon of 24 March 1863, as Rewi watched at a distance, a Ngāti Maniapoto tauā broke into the printing room at the Te Awamutu industrial school, and overpowered Pineaha Te Mura, one of the employees at the complex. This time Pātene came in and physically tried to stop the tauā, but could not prevent them taking the printing press, the type and the fifth and final issue of *Te Pihoihoi Mokemoke*. Von Dadelzen was unharmed, but concerned that 'from the manner in which the press etc was handled it is exceeding likely, almost certain, that it is broken'.[12] Gorst, who had been out of town, found his press in the hands of Ngāti Maniapoto.

The moderate Kīngitanga leaders, including Wiremu Tamihana, were alarmed at this development. Although they had no desire for a magistrate in their territory, they did not want their relationship with the government to deteriorate any futher. They travelled to Te Awamutu to discuss with Rewi the ramifications of what he had done. Gorst refused to leave the town and contributed to the ensuing public debates. Rewi, unrepentant, wrote to the governor that Gorst had three weeks to depart on pain of death, giving the beleagured magistrate plenty of time to leave. Soon after Rewi also passed the mana over the press to Wiremu Tamihana. Despite this, and the government allowing Gorst the decision on when he might leave, he initially refused to accept the press back. His intention was to blacken the deeds of the Ngāti Maniapoto tauā, and to sow discord between them and the moderate Waikato leaders.[13] Three weeks after Rewi's ultimatum, however, and in response to the exhortations of Pātara Te Tuhi, the editor of *Te Hokioi*, Gorst returned to Auckland with the largely undamaged printing press.[14]

The settler press deemed the seizure of Gorst's printing press an 'outrage'. Tensions continued to increase, and several months later British troops crossed the Mangatāwhiri Stream into the Waikato in order to crush the Kīngitanga. Rewi Maniapoto led the Ngāti Maniapoto forces against the invaders. Gorst returned to England and wrote *The Maori King*, a book quite sympathetic to his former foes. The *Hokioi* press, evacuated from Ngāruawāhia as the troops advanced, was lost for many years.[15] The press on which *Te Pihoihoi Mokemoke* was produced returned to less exciting work for the New Zealand government, before finding a temporary new home in the Alexander Turnbull Library.[16] In 1984 the library transferred the press to the Te Awamutu Museum on loan, where until 2014 it resided alongside its ancient enemy.[17]

18

He Rau Mahara

The Te Wananga *Ledger*

Migoto Eria

A plain hard-bound office ledger purchased from Dinwiddie, Morrison & Co. Stationers in Napier some time in the 1870s contains a list of subscribers to a newspaper. '*Te Wananga* 1878' reads the handwritten label on its spine. Within this non-Māori object, set out in the lines and columns designed for the organisation of European commerce, are 771 Māori names. A mailing list of prominent Māori and their places of residence in 1878, the ledger documents their desire to be informed about Māori land issues. The *Te Wananga* ledger was created for a practical purpose, but it signalled the connection of many people to a cause. It is now a taonga valued as a record of tīpuna who were deeply involved in the most important issue confronting Māori at the time, and as a record of how crucial information about European law and commerce was circulated among Māori.[1]

Te Wananga was published by Hēnare Tomoana and printed by Hēnare Hira (Henry Hill), first at Pakowhai on 5 August 1874, and then re-established at Napier from 1874 to 1878. The first few editions were in Māori and included Tomoana's account of the paper's purpose;[2] later editions were published in both Māori and English. *Te Wananga* also aimed to unite iwi over land matters, discussing selling and leasing, mortgages, reserves and Crown grants. As the mouthpiece of the Repudiation Movement which, in the 1870s, sought to overturn fraudulent sales of Ngāti Kahungunu lands, it also reported on controversial land cases.

Te Wananga kept its readers informed on these pressing subjects in an attempt to foster unity. Although it was Ngāti Kahungunu-based, its discussion of Kahungunu land issues provided examples of what was happening throughout the country, and it sought to reach a wider audience. As it announced in its first issue, 'He Perehi tenei mo te Motu katoa, mo nga tangata Maori, kua huaina tona ingoa ko te Wananga o nga iwi katoa inaianei, hei ritenga ia mo te Perehi e huihui i a tatou ki te whakaaro kotahi, koia i huaina ai ki a Te Wananga, no te mea, mo tatou katoa tenei taonga.'[3] (This is a Press for the whole Island, for Māori people, it has been entitled *Te Wananga* for all the present day tribes, in the manner of the Press it will bring us to a consensus of opinion, hence the title *Te Wananga*, because it is an asset for us all.)

Te Wananga therefore invited information from all iwi, and all areas where

OPPOSITE *Close-up of H-page,* Te Wananga *ledger.*

Ref: 32460, Gifted by Mrs Gaisford, Collection of Hawke's Bay Museums Trust, Ruawharo Tā-ū-rangi. Photograph by Richard Brimer

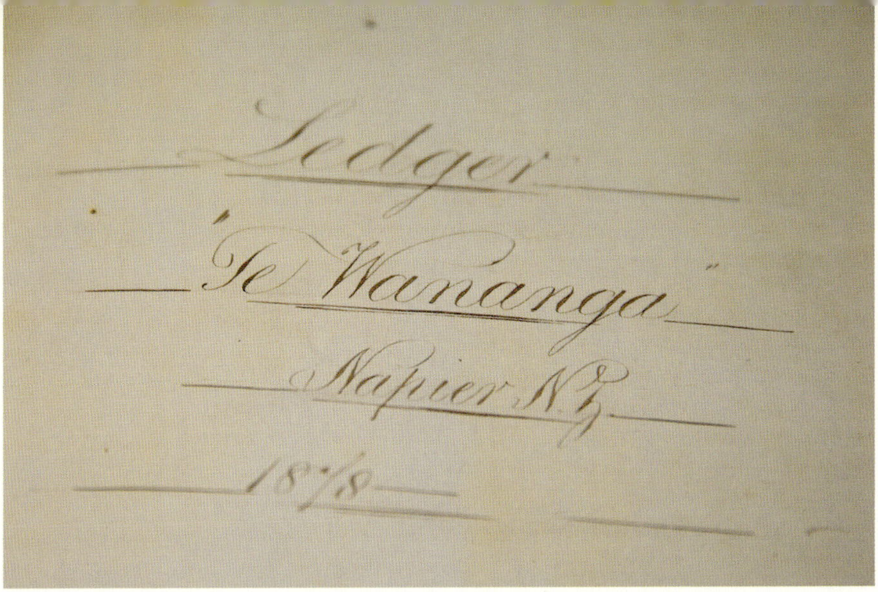

LEFT *Opening page of the* Te Wananga *ledger, established in 1874, and closed in 1878.*

Photograph by Richard Brimer

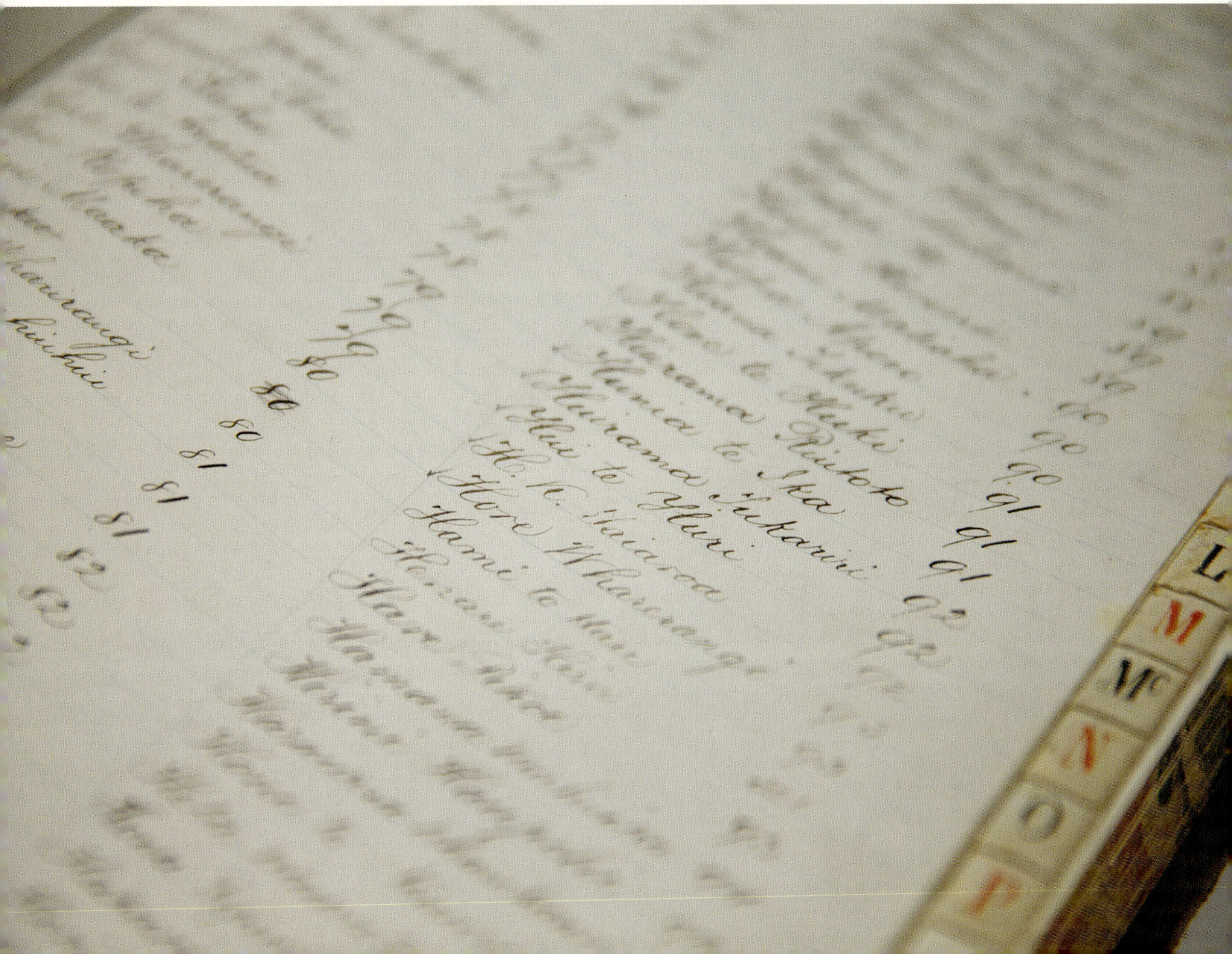

the government or private individuals were purchasing or leasing land. To assist people seeking redress, the newspaper allowed grievances to be aired publicly. Māori landholders could also advertise their land leases through *Te Wananga* so that Europeans could identify land available for lease and how to contact Māori owners. In one issue, *Te Wananga* stated that it aimed to settle antagonisms and promote goodwill between Māori and European: 'ko ta matou hiahia kia puta te pai ki nga iwi katoa o enei whenua, ahakoa Maori, ahakoa Pakeha a kia kore ai he amuamu a aua tangata ki a ratou.'[4] (We are anxious to do justice to both races; allay any irritation that may arise; and engender mutual feelings of forbearance and goodwill.)

Traditionally, the recollection and reciting of names and whakapapa were held within the mōteatea and mahara of our tīpuna (ancestors). Although missionaries documented some Māori births and deaths within church records, these were not generally recorded in the official register until 1913. The *Te Wananga* ledger created a record for a different kind of purpose, and many of the subscribers were prominent representatives of iwi and hapū authorities. Among the names are well-known individuals, such as Kāi Tahu leader Horomona Pōhio, but also many other Māori names with more local resonance, as well as a few Pākehā, including William Colenso and Sir George Grey. These tīpuna names included those involved in the Repudiation Movement, as well as others affected by land sales, those with an interest in Māori land sales, local government officials, lawyers and politicians. Their names were collated and their place of residence recorded in the back of the ledger for 1878, the same year *Te Wananga* ceased publication.

The transfer of Māori land to non-Māori was a threat to Māori landowners, as this meant that the mauri of the land was lost, and the ahikā could grow cold. Ahikā is defined as the mana whenua of a family, of a hapū, of an iwi, mana that has accumulated through residing on whenua for generations, and from the descendants continuing to return. The repercussions for the mana of the people through land loss were alarming: rangatira were no longer rangatira, and descendants could no longer interact with their whenua tīpuna, their whenua ūkaipō. The Repudiation Movement and *Te Wananga* were a line of defence. The ledger provides the identity of individuals related to this kaupapa. By their presence within this taonga, we know that our tīpuna struggled to maintain our mana whenua.

> Me kōmau te ahi kia pōnguru tonu ai.
> *Cover the fire so the embers continue to glow.*

The ledger's initial purpose was to employ a European business practice to distribute the newspaper to subscribers, and provide them with information about other such practices: it mediated between Māori and Pākehā worlds and interests. The ledger's journey is unrecorded after 1878, but it was gifted to the Hawke's Bay Museum in 1960 by Mrs Gaisford. Its significance has altered in the last 135 years. It is now a thing of intrinsic value to present generations, a window into the lives of our tīpuna and a source of empowerment and identity. This ledger

Ngāti Kahungunu chiefs ran the Te Wananga *newspaper (1874–78) to highlight dodgy land deals, and to advance Māori political interests.*

Collection of Hawke's Bay Museums Trust, Ruawharo Tā-ū-rangi. Photograph by Richard Brimer

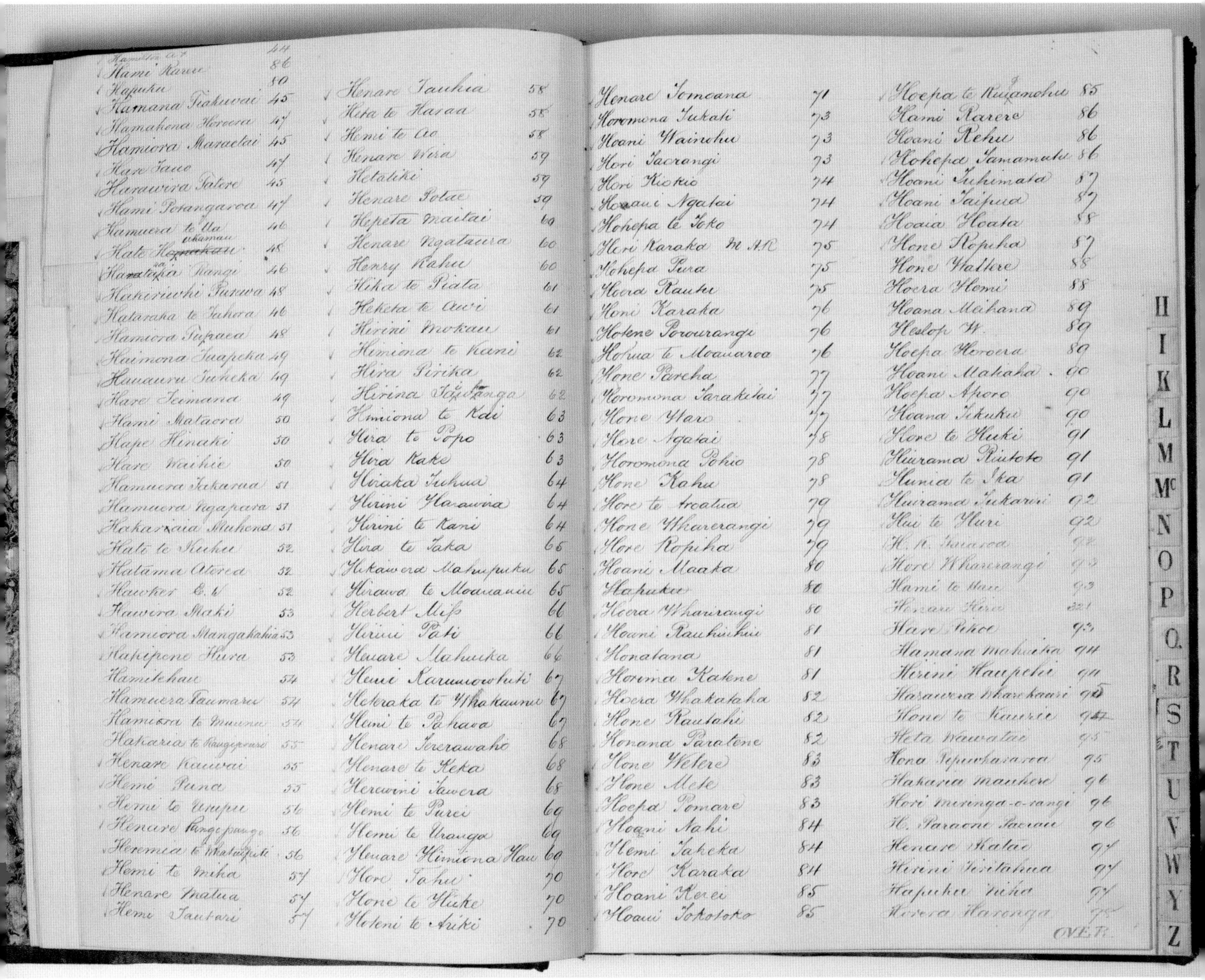
Hami Rawe 86
Hapuku 80
Hamana Tiakiwai 45
Hamahona Hereora 47
Hamiora Maraetai 45
Hare Tauo 47
Harawira Tatere 45
Hami Potangaroa 47
Hamuera te Uaa 46
Hati Hapukau 48
Hanatipa Rangi 46
Hakiriwhi Purewa 48
Hataraka te Tuhera 46
Hamiora Tupaea 48
Haimona Tuapeka 49
Hawaura Tuheka 49
Hare Teimana 49
Hami Mataora 50
Hape Hinaki 50
Hare Waihie 50
Hamuera Takarua 51
Hamuera Ngapara 51
Hakaraia Muhono 51
Hati te Kuhu 52
Hatama Atorea 52
Hawker E. W. 52
Hawira Maki 53
Hamiora Mangakahia 53
Hakipene Hura 53
Hamitehau 54
Hamuera Taumaru 54
Hamiora te Muunu 54
Hakaria te Rangipouri 55
Henare Kauwai 55
Hemi Puna 55
Hemi te Urupu 56
Henare Rangipungu 56
Heremia te Whatupite 56
Hemi te Miha 57
Henare Matua 57
Hemi Tautari 57
Henare Tauhia 58
Heta te Harao 58
Hemi te Ao 58
Henare Wera 59
Hetaliki 59
Henare Potae 59
Hepeta Maitai 60
Henare Ngataura 60
Henry Kahu 60
Hika te Piata 61
Heketa te Awe 61
Hirini Mokau 61
Himiona te Kani 62
Hira Pirika 62
Hirina Taitanga 62
Himiona te Kai 63
Hira te Popo 63
Hira Kake 63
Hiraka Tuhua 64
Hirini Harawira 64
Hirini te Kani 64
Hira te Taka 65
Hikawera Mahupuku 65
Hirawa te Moananui 65
Herbert Miss 66
Hirini Pati 66
Henare Mahuika 66
Hemi Karamaorahiki 67
Hetaraka te Whakaunu 67
Hemi te Pahara 67
Henare Tererawaho 68
Henare te Keka 68
Herewini Tawera 68
Hemi te Purei 69
Hemi te Uranga 69
Henare Himiona Hau 69
Hori Tahu 70
Hone te Huke 70
Hoteni te Aiki 70
Henare Tomoana 71
Horomona Tukahi 73
Hoani Wainohu 73
Hori Taerangi 73
Hori Kiokio 74
Hoani Ngatai 74
Hohepa te Toko 74
Hori Karaka M.H.R. 75
Hohepa Pura 75
Hoera Rautu 75
Hori Karaka 76
Hotene Porourangi 76
Hohua te Moanaroa 76
Hone Pareha 77
Horomona Tarakitai 77
Hone Waro 77
Hore Ngatai 78
Horomona Pohio 78
Hone Kahu 78
Hore te Araatua 79
Hone Wharerangi 79
Hore Ropiha 79
Hoani Maaka 80
Hapuku 80
Hoera Wharerangi 80
Hoani Rauhihi 81
Honatana 81
Horima Katene 81
Hoera Whakataha 82
Hone Rautahi 82
Honana Paratene 82
Hone Wetere 83
Hone Mete 83
Hoepa Pomare 83
Hoani Nahi 84
Hemi Takeka 84
Hore Karaka 84
Hoani Kerei 85
Hoani Tokotoko 85
Hoepa te Kuranohu 85
Hami Rarere 86
Hoani Rehu 86
Hohepa Tamamutu 86
Hoani Tuhimata 87
Hoani Taipua 87
Hoaia Hoata 88
Hone Ropiha 87
Hone Walters 88
Hoera Hemi 88
Hoana Mahana 89
Heslop W. 89
Hoepa Heroera 89
Hoani Mahaka 90
Hoepa Aporo 90
Hoana Tekuku 90
Hore te Huki 91
Huirama Riutoto 91
Hunia te Ika 91
Huirama Tukaru 92
Hai te Huri 92
H. K. Taiaroa 92
Hore Wharerangi 93
Hami te Hau 93
Hare Pihoe 93
Hamana Mahuika 94
Hirini Haupehi 94
Harawira Wharekauri 95
Hone te Kauru 95
Heta Wawatai 95
Hona Tepuwharaua 95
Hakaria Mauhere 96
Hori Meringa-o-rangi 96
H. Paraone Taurau 96
Henare Hatai 97
Hirini Teritahua 97
Hapuku Niha 97
Herera Haronga
OVER.
H I K L M Mc N O P Q R S T U V W Y Z

TE WANANGA.

HE PANUITANGA TENA KIA KITE KOUTOU.

"TIHE MAURI-ORA."

NAMA 14. NEPIA, HATAREI, 7 AKUHATA, 1875. PUKAPUKA 2.

Left: *Te Wananga* for 7 August 1875.

Collection of Hawke's Bay Museums Trust, Ruawharo Tā-ū-rangi. Photograph by Richard Brimer

Right: *Hēnare Tomoana (Ngāti Kahungunu), proprietor of* Te Wananga.

Ref: 1/4-022168-G, Samuel Carnell: Maori portrait negatives, Alexander Turnbull Library, Wellington, New Zealand

invites us to look for our tīpuna's names, and to feel represented within the discussion of mana whenua. It is physical proof of our tīpuna's interest in the subject of land. Its preservation shows that those who handled and cared for the ledger recognised its significance. Its physical form may have been its first survival advantage: it is large, well bound and of considerable weight. The records it contains reach across the generations to become a resource for whānau history and whakapapa research.

We have the opportunity to extend its story, to shed some light on its history and bring it to the attention of its descendants for the first time.

Ko te taonga he mea kei te tangata e mau ana, nāna ake, nōna ake rānei. He mea e kaingākautia ana, he nui rānei te utu, kāore rānei e tino kitea. *A taonga is something possessed by a person or belongs to them. It is something of importance, of financial value, or is rarely seen.*

This ledger may not possess typical taonga characteristics, as does a traditional mere pounamu or a korowai, but its empowering effect is just as significant. When descendants encounter this taonga, there is a sense of reassurance and pride, for they are represented through the names of their tīpuna, and this experience will continue for future generations.

South Island Minute Book 5, *which contains the proceedings of the Native Land Court in Bluff and Waikouaiti of February and March 1887.*

Photograph by Michael Hall

19

Minute Books

An Integral Part of the Māori Land Court

Paerau Warbrick

The history of the Māori Land Court is tied up with the colonial character of New Zealand in the nineteenth century, and from its genesis in 1862, it has recorded much of its proceedings in large sets of minute books. To this day cases regarding ownership or management, officially known as applications, are recorded in these books, which now total over 3000 and provide a wealth of information pertaining to Māori land titles and kin group relationships attached to the land. The Native Land Court, as it was originally called,[1] was created by the New Zealand parliament, partly as a result of an ever-increasing reluctance by Māori to sell any more tracts of land,[2] but also to avoid costly wars over the title to Māori land, as had happened at Waitara near New Plymouth in the late 1850s and early 1860s.[3] In order for a colonial system to operate, a well-oiled bureaucratic machine was needed and these minute books were part of that. From a sociological point of view, they played a crucial role in the Māori experience of colonisation in New Zealand by facilitating the transferral of land from Māori to Pākehā.

Generally, the minute books were hard-bound volumes around 20 centimetres long and 30 centimetres wide. They consisted of approximately 200 blank pages, or folios, on which handwritten notes were made of the evidence heard in court. In any given court hearing two minute books could be in use, one by a judge and one by a clerk of the court.[4] The latter tended to become the predominant minute book used by the court, though judges would sometimes also write up minutes.[5] If two sets of minutes existed for the court sitting, it did not matter from an administrative point of view, as the court determined any conflicts between minutes according to reliability and accuracy. Minute books were also sometimes kept by assessors, who were often Māori chiefs and were used as additional specialised clerks for complicated cases.[6] Informal court officials, who happened to record some of the proceedings, could also generate minute books. An example is that kept by South Island missionary, writer and Māori sympathiser Reverend James Stack.

The minute books recorded a range of cases involving claims to large blocks of land, subdivisions of land blocks and inheritance cases. A typical entry first set down such particulars as the date, time and place of the court sitting, and the officers of the court in attendance, such as the judge, an interpreter, a clerk

Owners of Block A, Taieri Native Reserve, Otago, listed in South Island Minute Book 5.

Photograph by Michael Hall

or an assessor.[7] The minute taker also wrote down the type of the case, and the various claimants and witnesses giving testimony and being cross-examined.

The particulars in the minute books could be quite detailed. As in the case involving the inheritance of land owned by Arapata Kooti at Kaiapoi in 1885,[8] Māori often made an exposition of their rights through historical narratives, genealogies and relationships between certain ancestors and various kin groups. Of course the recording of information was prone to inaccuracy, owing to the frailties of the human condition such as concentration span and accuracy of hearing, as well as the depth of understanding of the discussion in the court. Most of the testimony given by Māori in the court in the nineteenth century was spoken in te reo. Therefore the recorder had to rely on either their own proficiency in the Māori language or an interpreter. In the case of Judge Alexander Mackay, who was almost fluent in te reo Māori, *South Island Minute Book 2* contains his own handwritten interpretation of evidence spoken in the court. Despite the amount of evidence given in Māori, and the fluency of some judges, almost all the minute books are written in English. Fewer than 50 of the 3000, mostly belonging to assessors, are written wholly or partly in te reo Māori.[9]

The first court sittings were held in Northland and Rotorua in 1865. The first South Island sittings took place in Christchurch and Dunedin three years later.[10] By the end of the nineteenth century, the court had adopted the custom of sitting in towns and areas close to Māori communities. As the number of court hearings increased, it became necessary to give the minute books reference names, generally linked to the various places or geographical areas where the sittings were held. Eventually, the minute books were also assigned volume names. As time went on, many books, used constantly by court personnel to cross-reference land titles, heirs and other prior evidence given in the court over many years, became fairly well worn. In 1931, for instance, the Auckland firm of Collins Brothers & Company rebound 72 minute books at the cost of £15.[11]

Taken by themselves, the minute books look quite innocuous, but they possess other qualities. Some, for example, contain elegant handwriting, such as that found in the first 68 pages of *Nelson Minute Book 1*.[12] Aesthetics, though, cannot hide the fact that the minute books are an instrument of state control over Māori land. The recording of the title to land, however elegant the handwriting, creates a permanent record of knowledge that helps to define the extent and limits of power and control that a central authority can exercise over the land and its people. Because the court was an arm of this state control, Māori had to grapple with its substantive and procedural rules. Legal concepts based on traditional Māori values and principles quickly gave way to a hybrid set of rules and principles that straddled Māori law and British law defined by the state.[13]

More often than not, the court processes created conflict between Māori groups and individuals in a winner-take-all contest. Land rights were no longer negotiated flexibly as social circumstances changed. Rather, a third party, the state, wanted rigid British legal rules attached to the land and administered through the court.[14] Because the information in minute books

1/3/87 141A

10/3 O. L. — Taiari Blk. A. —

[Up]on inquiry made into the nature of the title to the [af]oresaid land and into the existence of any trust [aff]ecting the same the Court ordered that the under[m]entioned persons are the persons beneficially entitled [to] the said land and that a sufficient instrument [of] title be issued in their favor or of their representatives

1. Rawiri te Urawa
2. Werita Tuarea
3. Matene Karako
4. Tiaki Kona
5. Hapa te Kikitu
6. Wi Naihira
7. Hoani Hape
8. Papi Paraone
9. Tiaki te Karihi
10. Hamuera te Makahi
11. Tira
12. Natanahira Waruwarutu
13. Pita te Hori
14. Tiaki Parete
15. Tohitu
16. Tuineka Matene
17. Tare Matene
18. Makati
19. Pape Hapata
20. Makarita te Kako
21. Mere Hinehou
22. Rane
23. Hene Wharetia
24. Mate Whitio
25. Peti Parata
26. Tera Hapa
27. Sally Palmer
28. Peti Koe
29. Mere Kui
30. Hana Haukawe
31. Heni Parera
32. Eliza Brown
33. Harriet Palmer

[F]or Successors to deceased see Folio 315/16 Vol. 6

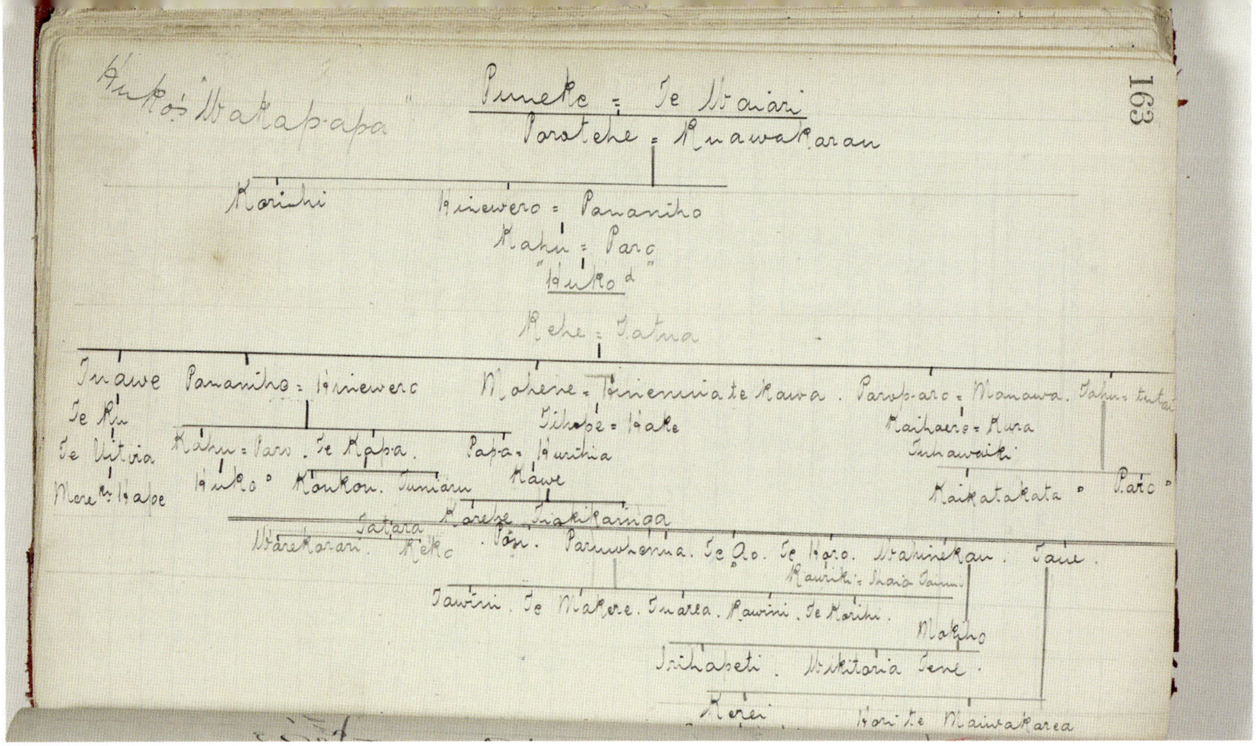

The minute book not only contains itemised land blocks and the names of the various landowners but also details intricate family genealogies. Photograph by Michael Hall

has always been a powerful tool for the assertion of land rights for Māori groups and individuals, conflicts and strained relationships have often arisen.[15] The inheritance case of Arapata Kooti mentioned earlier is just one of a multitude where the court became a medium for kinship conflict. It is no wonder that minute books were stolen from the court and at least one is known to have been destroyed to inhibit rival claimants to land.[16] Once cases were settled, however, the state or third parties could acquire such land titles from Māori in the confidence that they had the court's backing.

Over the years these minute books have been used by historians, social scientists and a number of Māori to research family and tribal histories.[17] They are rich repositories of oral histories and genealogies that would otherwise have been lost. For instance, Te Rūnanga o Ngāi Tahu has used the genealogies contained within *South Island Minute Book 2*, along with all other local minute book information, to construct a genealogical tribal database. The Waitangi Tribunal has also made extensive use of the minute book oral histories and genealogies to provide important historical information about Māori kin groups and their interaction with the Crown.[18]

For Māori, though, there is another dimension to the minute books, a particular allure, that arises from seeing what appears to be the direct oral testimony of their long-dead kin. This can have an intoxicating and spiritual effect: it is as if the dead are speaking directly to the reader.[19] Although the minute books of the court are a rich source of information, they were not created for historians or social commentators. What they recorded controlled and defined Māori relationships with their land, making it easier for the state or third parties to deprive them of it. The minute books are part and parcel of the bureaucratic machinery of settler colonialism. They belong to the genre of written material used for power and control by the state over the colonised – in this case, Māori and their lands.

Alexander Mackay (1833–1909), the main judge in Native Land Court hearings held in the South Island from 1886 to 1901.

Ref: PAColl-8550-29, Alexander Turnbull Library, Wellington, New Zealand

Below: *Detail of* South Island Minute Book 5. *Photograph by Michael Hall*

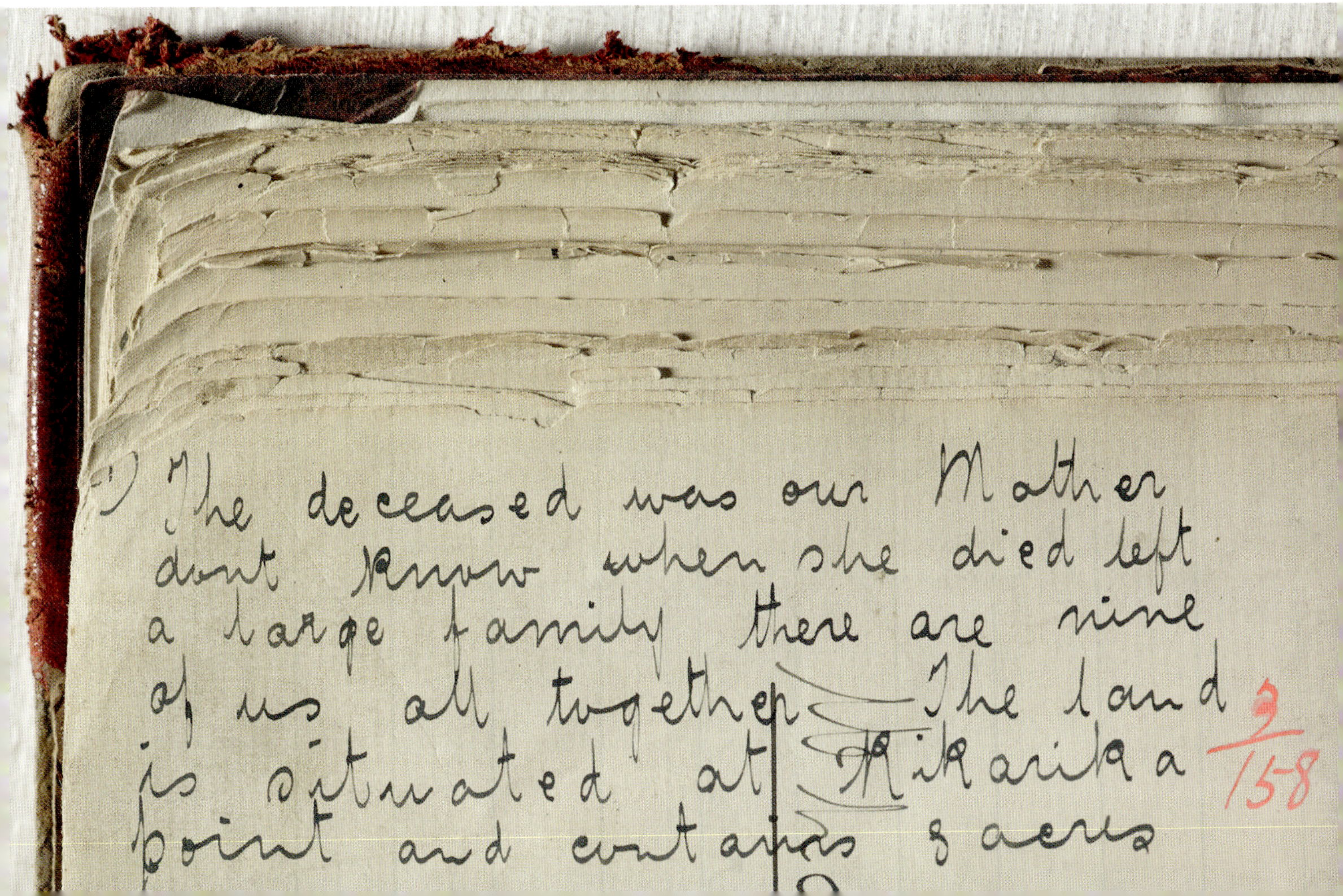

The deceased was our Mother
dont know when she died left
a large family there are nine
of us all together — The land
is situated at Mikarika a 2/158
point and contains 8 acres

20

A Road into Te Urewera

Annabel Cooper

In March 1904 Lord Ranfurly was the first governor to undertake a diplomatic journey through Te Urewera. As his party travels between Ruatāhuna and Te Whāiti, Native Minister James Carroll leads; George Preece's old comrade-in-arms Gilbert Mair also accompanied them. This section of road looks newly formed, with bare soil above and below the track. Although redevelopment after 1895 was designed for wheeled traffic, this path seems still suited only to horses.

Ref: PA1-q-634-23, Ranfurly family photographs, Alexander Turnbull Library, Wellington, New Zealand

Roads have long transported colonisation, and brought peoples into new, not always welcome, relationships. The first road into Te Urewera was one such avenue of change.[1] James Cowan's story 'Preece's Road' describes how the Tūhoe chief Paerau Te Rangikaitupuake confronted Lieutenant George Preece and halted this road in 1871.[2] This essay assesses the evidence for that encounter, which was not exactly the meeting Cowan imagined. It also considers the implications of this road for government and tangata whenua, and the ambivalence surrounding roads as both technologies and symbols of colonisation, enduring in Te Urewera to the present.

In the later part of the campaign against Te Kooti Arikirangi, George Preece commanded the No. 2 Arawa Constabulary, a unit of Crown-allied Māori from Te Arawa and several other Bay of Plenty iwi. Frustrated by over two years of chasing through Te Urewera, where both terrain and tangata whenua alike offered Te Kooti concealment and a base from which to raid, Preece wrote to Native Affairs and Defence Minister Donald McLean. He proposed a packhorse route, the first road into the region, right through the mountains, across Ngāti Whare lands including Ahikererū and Te Whāiti in the west, the Tūhoe territory of Maungapōhatu, Ruatāhuna and Waikaremoana, and over to Frasertown in Poverty Bay – over 200 kilometres in today's terms. Following existing Māori paths, the road would allow rapid movement from government forts into the enemy's territory. McLean responded readily. Roads already criss-crossed the North Island. General Duncan Cameron's Great South Road had 'kicked open the door to the Waikato' in 1863–64. A Scot, McLean knew only too well how effectively roads had subdued the Highlands.[3]

On 7 November 1871 Preece, aged just 25, noted in his diary receiving approval for the road.[4] Within a week work began from Fort Galatea, laying out willow and manuka fascines (bundles) through the coastal swamps.[5] Preece co-ordinated surveyors, road-building and bridge-building parties; ordered clothing and boots, timber, equipment and ammunition; paid the troops; and argued for his Māori troops to be paid extra for the arduous work as the Pākehā Armed Constabulary were. He waged war on drink and looked out for hot springs to cure his sore leg.[6] 'Old Tukehu' approached him to say that Preece 'should not go on with the Galatea road, that they the native owners of

George Augustus Preece in later years. He wears a constabulary uniform and the New Zealand Cross he won at the siege of Ngātapa during the Te Kooti campaign. No image of Paerau Te Rangikaitupuake was available for reproduction.

Ref: 1/2-049310-F, Alexander Turnbull Library, Wellington, New Zealand

the land wished to be employed on it'. Preece wrote to his superiors in support of this request.[7]

Once the road moved out of the swamps the work was vertical: the troops slashed through mountain forest, winding up and down precipitous slopes towards Ahikererū, pushing into lands that had been contested among iwi and hapū – Ngāi Tūhoe, Ngāti Manawa, Ngāti Whare and Ngāti Awa – for generations.[8] Ostensibly built for the pursuit of Te Kooti, the road's longer-term purpose had as much to do with increasing control of these Te Urewera iwi, 'the last stronghold of tribal hostility in the country', in Cowan's words. Te Urewera leaders understood this perfectly: 'they saw in it the breaking-up of the roadless isolation that had been their best defence.'[9]

By late 1871 Ngāi Tūhoe's experience of colonial encounter had been devastating. In the aftermath of the East Coast War, an unjust confiscation robbed them of their coastal strip, their most productive land, eroding their livelihood and sovereignty and fostering Tūhoe's subsequent support of Te Kooti.[10] From 1869 government troops pursued Te Kooti through Te Urewera itself, destroying settlements and crops in punishment for tangata whenua protection of the resistance leader. Confronted with starvation and disease, Ngāi Tūhoe and other Te Urewera iwi were pressed to cease support for Te Kooti; many 'came in', or surrendered, and were held on the coast in what were effectively prison camps.[11] Tūhoe chiefs Paerau Te Rangikaitupuake and Te Whenuanui 'came in' but in April 1871 were permitted to return to Ruatāhuna, on condition, as Judith Binney explains, that they 'forge co-operation among their own people with the government, against an enemy with whom they sympathised'.[12] Between the rock of starvation and the hard place of negotiation with a government whose actions had been so unjust, some Te Urewera chiefs supported cautious contact in the hope of peace and relief from deprivation; others argued for continued protective isolation. Roads, the pathways of colonisation with all its threats and opportunities, sat at the heart of the problem.[13]

Tūhoe and Ngāti Whare leadership debated roads during the early 1870s and again in the 1890s. The threats – faster military movement, transport of heavier firepower and troops' capacity to stay for extended periods; the loss of culture, language and chiefly authority; and perhaps Pākehā settlement and disease – were weighed against the potential benefits of greater production, trade, travel and knowledge. If roads *were* to be built, some argued, tangata whenua should embrace the inevitable and benefit from employment in this work.[14] But centuries-long protection by the steep forested terrain was at stake. The word 'fastness' occurs repeatedly in colonial reference to Te Urewera, conjuring the notion of a vast fortress. Isolation had created a distinctive culture which Pākehā and Māori outsiders alike saw as uniting place and people, popularly envisaged as 'wild'.[15]

Unusually for a European, George Preece traversed familiar ground on Urewera trails. His father, James Preece, had been the first missionary in Te Urewera, and George had lived at the Ahikererū mission between 1848 and 1853, one of very few Pākehā there.[16] In his diary of the Te Kooti campaign Preece records meeting his father's converts again and noting their care of the mission house. Some remembered him. After Colonel George Whitmore captured Te Harema pā at Te Whāiti in 1869, a woman whose husband had just been killed by soldiers recognised Preece as a child she had nursed. She 'rushed up … and threw herself at his feet, embracing his legs and crying'.[17] Such familiarity made him a particularly useful intermediary, and 'Pirīhi', like his colleague Gilbert Mair, often interceded with Urewera leaders, using his fluent Māori in negotiations, or in letters to persuade resistant tangata whenua to 'come in'.[18] This was the context for 'Preece's Road', published in the first of James Cowan's widely read collections of non-fiction stories, *Tales of the Maori Bush* (1934). The story tells how Paerau Te Rangikaitupuake came to stop the new track at Ahikererū. Using the journalistic language of his time, Cowan describes Preece going alone, ahead of his men, to meet Paerau and his 'twenty Urewera men, savage fellows with wild fuzzed-out hair'. 'War-dances' and fiery speeches against the road-making confront Preece, who in turn responds to Paerau as a 'knowing Pākehā'. He makes an elaborate speech, concluding that he will certainly not make a road, because – as he sees his men emerge from the distant bush – 'The road is already made! Look!' According to Cowan, Paerau 'raged and fumed', but before long they laugh together at the trickery, Paerau's people begin to use the road and Preece settles for stopping at Ahikererū.[19]

Cowan's narrative turns on a sleight-of-hand performed within cultural protocols, and on how anger and then laughter lead to compromise. The story reflects the young Preece's reputation as a skilled cultural go-between, but it tells us little about the elder Paerau's standing as a strategist against government incursion.

Cowan's story, however, appears to be something of a mixture of related events. Preece's diary actually records that, as the track neared Ahikererū, he arrived on 4 December 1871 to find 'Sergt. Hall and party at the old house, Paerau and party had stopped the road two days before'. He wrote to Paerau on the 11th and on 19 December met him at Whakatāne: 'Saw old Paerau, he seems all right about the road, he is quite agreeable to it.' Preece and Paerau did not, therefore, meet at Ahikererū. Cowan was probably drawing on other entries in Preece's diary alluding to meetings with 'war dances'.[20]

In Cowan's story, Paerau successfully halts the road. Preece notes, however, that road-making resumed within days. Paerau's objections were overridden – if he claimed sovereignty, in short, he could not enforce it. Nor was Paerau entirely 'agreeable', in Preece's words, about the road even to Ahikererū. Nine months later, in October 1872, Paerau's views were clear when he and Te Whenuanui wrote advising Captain Charles Ferris 'to make roads in your own territory … leave Waikaremoana to us, as well as all our territory, Te

Whaiti, Ruatoki, Waimana, and Ruatahuna, we are not agreeable for the road to enter these places'.[21]

Cowan's story centres on two key elements, neither of them present in Preece's record. First, there is a personal meeting between two emblematic figures, one a 'wild' and proud Tūhoe rangatira, the other a culturally literate Pākehā. Second, there is the outcome: not defeat, but compromise on *both* sides. In these respects, the story is a characteristic type of colonial narrative, recounting a passage through conflict to mutual understanding and respect between high-ranking Māori and 'insider' Pākehā. Cowan placed deep faith in such encounters, but in this case he had to stretch the evidence to create one.[22] Moreover, Preece's diary points not to mutual compromise and resolution, but to resistance reluctantly withdrawn, in recognition of impossible odds. Neither Preece nor Cowan conveys the depth of the threats confronting Te Urewera iwi, or the dilemmas posed by the paths of invasion.

Work began again in 1895, to improve the surface for wheeled traffic through to Waikaremoana. Judith Binney argues that the forcing through of this part of the road, together with the triangulation of Te Urewera, was 'a deliberate act of conquest', precipitating the 'small war', as Āpirana Ngata called it, of 1895.[23] The road was still strategic – government anxieties about Te Urewera endured – but by now it was economic too. Hopes, later dashed, of mineral wealth beneath the mountains circulated. As leisure travel developed, Waikaremoana was picked as a prime destination. Tūhoe and Ngāti Whare again vehemently resisted work on the road. Several times in 1895 they stopped surveyors and labourers, the latter unemployed men on relief work who lived in camps along the route as they widened and gravelled the road, blasting the hillsides to create sufficient passage. Tangata whenua expressed concern about higher taxes if the road went through, and objected to the route, which would have destroyed many miro trees; the enduring concern, however, was sovereignty.[24] Reluctant agreement was reached in the lead-up to the Urewera District Native Reserve Act (1896), and sections of roadmaking and maintenance were allocated to local people as a source of employment. By 1899, when Cowan rode through and wrote a travel feature for the *Auckland Star*, you could take wheeled transport 53 kilometres beyond Galatea, passing through Te Whāiti and on beyond the Tarapounamu Saddle. By then it had cost £30,000. Eighty kilometres and 30 years later it had reached the shore of Waikaremoana. In that time the region had been 'opened up' to the adventure tourists of the early twentieth century.[25]

Roads, however, had a limited impact on Te Urewera's isolation, for better and for worse. In 1894 Premier Richard Seddon had described Te Urewera as 'the most broken part of the country he had visited'.[26] In the early twentieth century Ngāi Tūhoe asked for roads, giving more than 16,000 hectares for roads to help develop farming and logging, but most never eventuated.[27] In 1928 Te Whenuanui III wrote to Ngata seeking to establish a butter factory at Te Whāiti to help develop dairying, but could not make headway.[28] Roads brought some opportunities as forestry and farming expanded, and bus and mail routes facilitated travel and communication. But these industries proved fickle sources of support. In

The roads opened up Te Urewera for tourism from the end of the nineteenth century. In 1907 these Pākehā travellers, including Katherine Mansfield (standing, left), posed for photographs to record their encounters with Te Urewera people.

Ref: 1/2-002584-F, Alexander Turnbull Library, Wellington, New Zealand

By the 1930s the road, now widened to take motor vehicles, enabled a regular mail service, which could also provide employment for locals such as this driver. Lee's Royal Mail served Rotorua, Murupara, Te Whāiti and Ruatāhuna.

Ref: APG-1672-1/2-F, Albert Percy Godber Collection, Alexander Turnbull Library, Wellington, New Zealand

2013, when National government ministers Chris Finlayson and Paula Bennett visited Minginui, once a forest company 'model village', they echoed Seddon's judgement on the area's poverty.[29] Roads remain potent symbols of sovereignty in the region: between 2006 and 2013, road blocks were set up in protest against forestry companies and contentious Treaty of Waitangi negotiations.[30] Government anxiety about Te Urewera 'wildness', and response by armed incursion, has also recurred. The invasions of 1869–72 were echoed in raids by police on Rua Kēnana's community at Maungapōhatu in 1916, and in October 2007, when the Armed Offenders Squad drove into Ruātoki and Taneatua.[31]

Hidden in this unremarkable sample of dunite from the Nelson Provincial Museum collections is a story that touches on the emergence of Nelson as a city in the colonial era. Ref: G.12.78-1, Nelson Provincial Museum Collection

21
Dunite
The Adventures of a Rock in Colonial New Zealand
Megan Wells

Dunite is a type of rock, at first glance perhaps not much to look at. It appears rough edged and feels like a solid weight but my white gloves denote its significance as a museum object and set it apart from any other rock picked up on the slopes of Dun Mountain, near Nelson.

Dun Mountain is named for its arid greenish-brown tops, a colour that comes from the dunite lying there, its oxidised surface a mottled brown and dull green. Yet closer inspection of this rock reveals detail and complexity. Freshly cut dunite is a brighter green although the air, in time, returns it to the same shade of dun. But this is not the only layer of brightness. A sliver of dunite with polarised light shone through it reveals a rainbow spectrum of colours edged in black.

There are no records of who found this sample of dunite, where exactly they discovered it or why they collected it and deposited it in the Nelson Provincial Museum. But after it was added to the museum's collection it was chosen as part of an educational set designed to be taken to schools during the 1990s to demonstrate the geographical make-up of the Nelson–Tasman region. After the school programme changed, the dunite sample, still clearly numbered to its position on the map showing its original location on Dun Mountain, was returned to its shelf in the dark of the storeroom. Brought back into the light, it sets us off on an adventure revealing dunite's importance to colonial science, its role in the economic development of colonial Nelson and its significance in the establishment of the Nelson Provincial Museum.

Microscopic image showing the bright colours that can be seen when polarised light is shone through a thin slice of dunite. The colours are from olivine, a mineral in dunite.

Catalogue No: P05728_dunite_XPL_5mm, Courtesy of Lloyd Homer, GNS Science

'I have called it dunite,' wrote Austrian geologist Ferdinand Hochstetter, prosaically recording his discovery of the new type of rock he had found on the slopes of Dun Mountain in 1859. Hochstetter visited New Zealand as part of the Austrian government-funded *Novara* expedition and, although based for most of his time in the Auckland province, he could not resist a chance to explore Nelson, 'the garden of New Zealand'.[1]

The discovery, naming and adding to western taxonomies seems to be an obvious starting point for dunite's story but, as a geological sample, the object is much older. Dunite is a kind of ultramafic basement rock called peridotite. Basement rocks normally form and remain in the Earth's crust but peridotite is an exception. It is formed in the Earth's mantle but can become a linear, snake-like line that stretches across the surface of the Earth. Called an

Ferdinand von Hochstetter has been styled the father of New Zealand geology for his work in the Auckland and Nelson provinces.

Ref: C849, Nelson Provincial Museum Collection

Opposite: *Ferdinand von Hochstetter's map, drawn after his visit to New Zealand, shows the geological foundations of the Nelson region.*

NZ Map 5694e. Sir George Grey Special Collections, Auckland Libraries

The new Nelson Institute and Museum lasted until 1906 when it was gutted by fire. It was replaced in 1911 by a larger brick building.

Ref: C821, Nelson Provincial Museum Collection

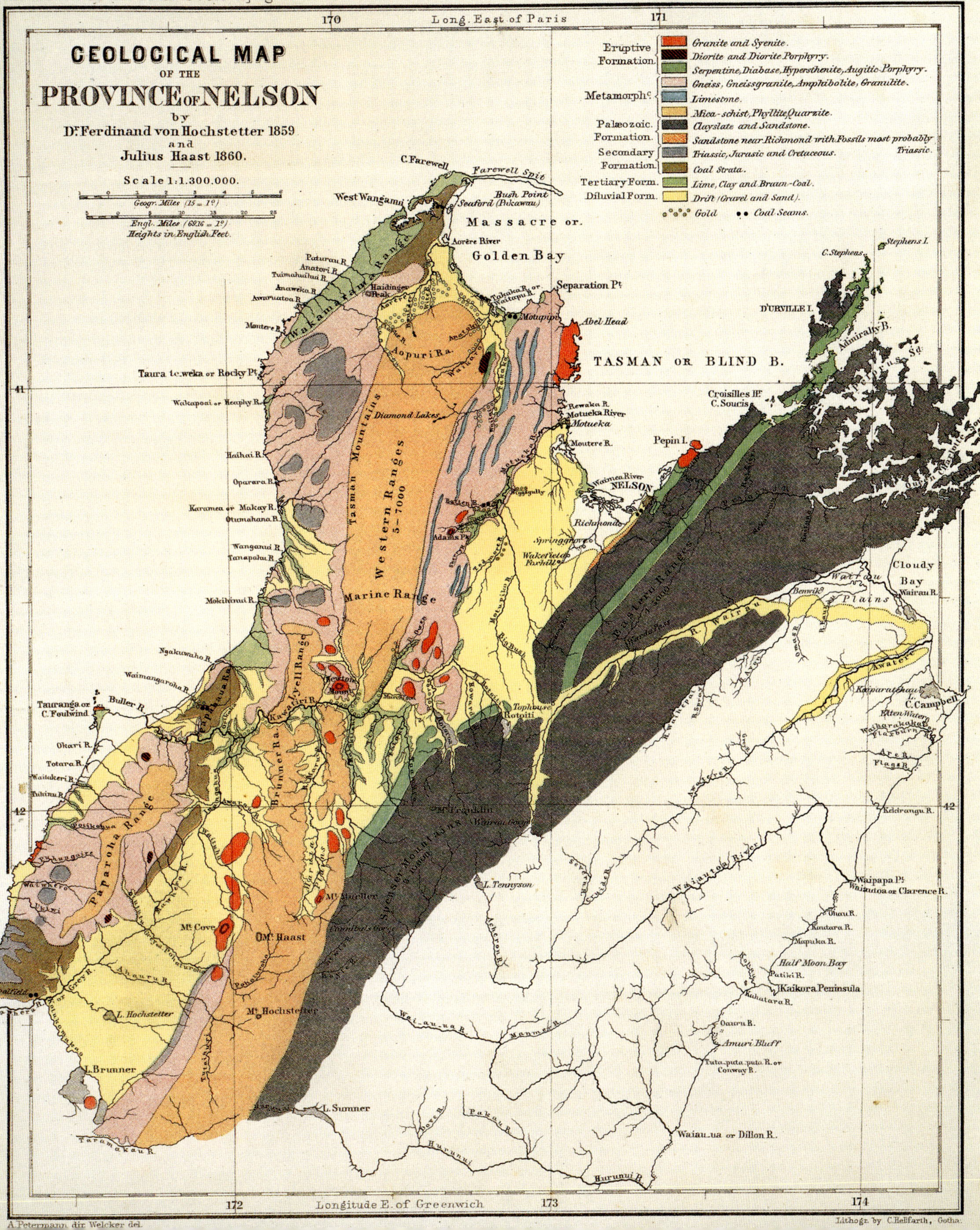
GEOLOGICAL MAP
OF THE
PROVINCE OF NELSON
by
Dr. Ferdinand von Hochstetter 1859
and
Julius Haast 1860.
Scale 1:1.300.000.
Geogr. Miles (15 = 1°)
Engl. Miles (69.16 = 1°)
Heights in English Feet.
Long. East of Paris
Longitude E. of Greenwich
Eruptive Formation.
Granite and Syenite.
Diorite and Diorite Porphyry.
Serpentine, Diabase, Hypersthenite, Augitic Porphyry.
Metamorphic.
Gneiss, Gneissgranite, Amphibolite, Granulite.
Limestone.
Mica-schist, Phyllite, Quarzite.
Palæozoic Formation.
Claystate and Sandstone.
Sandstone near Richmond with Fossils most probably Triassic.
Secondary Formation.
Triassic, Jurasic and Cretaceous.
Coal Strata.
Tertiary Form.
Lime, Clay and Braun-Coal.
Diluvial Form.
Drift (Gravel and Sand).
Gold
Coal Seams.
Massacre or Golden Bay
TASMAN OR BLIND B.
NELSON
Western Ranges 5–7000
Tasman Mountains
Marine Range
Spenser Mountains
Paparoha Range
Cloudy Bay
Kaikora Peninsula
A. Petermann dir. Welcker del.
Lithogr. by C. Hellfarth, Gotha.

ophiolite, it is created when two tectonic plates push against one another. A piece becomes detached from the subducting plate, the slab going downwards, and becomes part of the distorted continental crust. This process, which lifts the mantle rocks to the Earth's surface, is very rare.[2] The Dun Mountain Ophiolite Belt surfaces at Dun Mountain in Nelson, Red Mountain in Southland and Piopio in the King Country. Red Mountain and Dun Mountain were once joined before being forced apart by the Alpine Fault, and are now 460 kilometres distant from each other.[3]

We can situate Hochstetter's discovery of dunite within the larger nineteenth-century development of geology. He belonged to a tradition of natural historians attempting to rationalise the world. The Enlightenment saw an enormous boost in scientific activity, with particular emphasis on what can be observed. Later the research of men such as Charles Darwin, alongside Carl Linnaeus' system of taxonomy, set in motion a nineteenth-century hunger to collect, categorise and understand the world. Moreover, as historians of natural history have argued, the scientific ordering of the natural environment of colonies played a part in the taming and control exercised by expanding European empires.[4]

Rocks and minerals, among the most informative and simplest objects to collect and display, played a significant part in this process and formed the foundation collections of New Zealand's colonial museums. The Otago Museum began its collections with a geological display and when James Hector moved to Wellington in 1865 to become the first director of the Colonial Museum (now the Museum of New Zealand Te Papa Tongarewa) he brought with him the collection of rocks he made while he was the Otago provincial government geologist in Dunedin. At the time the removal of this collection of over 500 specimens caused an outcry and was considered a great loss to the southern museum. The Nelson Institute also had a substantial early geological collection, part of which was donated by Hochstetter after his visit to the region.

Institutions for the education and improvement of the mind were established quickly in early Nelson. The Literary and Scientific Institution was founded in May 1841 before the first settlers even set foot ashore in New Zealand. Officers of the Preliminary Expedition of the Second Colony formed an establishing committee on board the New Zealand Company ships *Whitby* and *Will-Watch* as they sailed through the Bay of Biscay. On arrival they set up shop in a small building in Trafalgar Street. By the time of Hochstetter's visit 18 years later funds had been raised for a new, substantially larger building in Hardy Street. Although still made of wood, it had two storeys and a more impressive façade.

The connections between the world of science and the aspirations of a thriving local economy are embodied in Hochstetter's laying of the foundation stone for the institute's new home. As part of the ceremony Hochstetter placed beneath the building a time capsule that included samples of the celebrated mineral wealth of the province – gold, Dun Mountain chromite, Pakawau coal and Current Basin copper – as well as coins, newspapers and a *Nelson Directory* for the year 1859.[5] Hochstetter had not yet discovered dunite; if he had, perhaps he would have included a sample along with the other minerals.

Hochstetter had been invited to visit Nelson partly to give his professional opinion about the economic viability of the Dun Mountain copper mines, then being developed. He quietly foreshadowed the company's ultimate failure, but while researching the copper resource, discovered dunite. The Dun Mountain mineral belt continued to foster economic speculation.

Although dunite continued to be mined commercially in other areas, notably the Green Hills in Southland, mining petered out in the Nelson area as the colonial period drew to a close.[6] It was not until the interwar period that its economic uses were explored. In the late 1930s it was found that powdered dunite, mixed with chromite and magnesium, could be made into corrosion-resistant bricks that could substantially extend the life of steel furnaces. Broken Hill Proprietary Company (BHP) of Australia began laboratory testing and Dun Mountain was chosen as a suitable source. It was proposed that the site could provide 12,000 tonnes of dunite annually, but this large-scale production never took flight. BHP mistakenly believed that Dun Mountain was in a mining district. There was confusion over who held the mining rights to the area and negotiations took place with the wrong parties; the Mines Department in Wellington was not even informed. This problem was finally resolved and work began in October 1939, with BHP quarrying enough dunite to complete their laboratory testing. At this point the Mines Department agreed to grant a mining licence, subject to a land survey. Although BHP supplied funding for the survey, it did not wish it to take place unless the licence was guaranteed – which created a convenient stalemate. BHP's testing was incomplete and World War II was causing shortages in labour and transport. The contract was allowed to lapse.[7]

During this same period dunite began to be used to make reverted superphosphate, a fertiliser designed to supply phosphorus to the soil and encourage plant growth, which continues to be centrally important to New Zealand farming. Although chemically dunite has similar effects to the more common lime superphosphate, the presence of magnesium means that it does not easily cake, an advantage during spreading, especially if the fertiliser has been stored for some time. However, reverted superphosphate made from serpentine, which has many of the same benefits, is more economical to produce. Specific to New Zealand, it was increasingly produced throughout the war, when it became more difficult to ship superphosphates from Europe. Although Dun Mountain has large deposits of serpentine, other, more economic quarries were preferred.[8] Since 1945 the Dun Mountain area has been less and less a focus for mining enterprises. Still under the control of the local council, it is instead used much more for recreation, especially mountain biking and walking.

During the colonial period dunite's story highlights the intersections between local economic development and wider international advancements in natural history. These two subjects tie the object back to the early Nelson Institute, forerunner to the Nelson Provincial Museum, which would undoubtedly have had a sample of dunite in its collection. And our sample of dunite? It has returned to the dark of the storeroom where, with the patience of a rock, it will wait until its next adventure.

22
Whale Tales
Rosi Crane

A skeleton of a fin whale has been hanging from specially designed and built iron girders in the Otago Museum since 1883. It has not moved from its original position – all dusting, cleaning and other maintenance has been carried out in situ – while other zoological specimens have moved between displays to laboratories and storage rooms. During a major refurbishment in 1973 the original three floors of the museum were floorboarded in and the whale became the centrepiece of a permanent maritime-themed gallery. The implied connections between the whale, and whaling, and the 50 model ships, flags and ship's bells that now surround it are left to the visitor to interpret. Contextual meanings of the skeleton may have changed since its installation but the bones themselves have remained static. This symbol of colonial interest in the natural world helps us to understand the importance of science carried out for its own sake, compared with earlier commercial exploitation of whales.

Fin whale suspended from specially modified railway girders, their weight supported by columns on the upper gallery. Note the ironwork and struts supporting the bones.

Ref: 1/1-025834-G, Otago Museum Interior, photograph by William Williams (1859–1948), Alexander Turnbull Library, Wellington, New Zealand

When zoology was the dominant science in the late nineteenth century each museum wanted its own drawcard. Large specimens fitted the bill and in New Zealand whales were an obvious choice. Complete skeletons were relatively rare; skulls, teeth and bones were more commonly preserved. By 1883 Otago, Wellington and Canterbury museums had skeletons but none matched the huge 27-metre skeleton of a black right whale which, because of its size, was mounted outside the National Museum at the University of Melbourne from 1867. In 1877 the Otago Museum opened in a newly built neo-classical building and the first sight that greeted visitors was a 'skeleton of a huge whale, and in close proximity the skeletons of moas and other large struthious [ostrich-like] birds, and the skeleton of a giraffe'.[1] Five years later, in 1882, the Dunedin correspondent for the *Tuapeka Times* noted that there had been many improvements but that the curator, Professor T. Jeffery Parker, had a 'mania for skeletons … [and] has procured some splendid and interesting specimens of birds and fish'.[2] It was a natural instinct for Parker, a renowned zoologist, to indulge his obsession so when the opportunity arose to acquire a second whale in 1883 he did not hesitate – it was the ultimate icon of civic pride and science.

Parker acquired his fin whale from Captain William Jackson Barry, a noted 'colonial character' who brought the whale skeleton to Dunedin on

GREAT BLUE SHARK
OTAGO HARBOUR

a cart in 1883. Barry had lived an adventurous life, which he outlined in great detail in a 200-page autobiography. Having arrived in Sydney as a 10-year-old child convict about 1829, Barry was later bailed up by Australian bushrangers, speared by Malays, attacked by cholera in Calcutta and afterwards by delirium tremens, and was, on average, shipwrecked about twice a year.[3] He took up work in the whaling industry but the tales continued, with more embellishment in each telling. On one occasion he was sent heavenward by a blow from the tail of a whale and on another was taken underwater after becoming entangled with a harpoon rope.[4] He supposedly rode on the back of a whale for several hours, or days, and/or around the whole of New Zealand. By the early 1880s he had established himself as a travelling lecturer touring throughout the country.[5] His lectures were highly entertaining and people flocked to hear his Munchausen tales. Barry's exaggerations were matched by newspaper reports, like those from Oamaru and Timaru, which detailed the numbers of eggs thrown, where they landed on the speaker and how long the mess took to reach the floor with a satisfying splat.[6]

While in Nelson Barry bought the remains of a whale that had beached itself in the area in May 1883. After having it defleshed and the bones cleaned, he exhibited the skeleton at a store in Nelson before carting it off, on show, to various towns, ending up in Dunedin. By June 1883 he had set up the whale at a warehouse in St Andrew Street, where he set to work joining its bones together before opening it up to public inspection, including hosting a dinner party for 'a number of ladies and gentlemen … in the jaws of the monster whale'.[7] It remained on display during June and July, attracting 'a considerable number of people, who all expressed astonishment at the dimensions'.[8] But by the middle of August a one-sentence newspaper report recorded that 'Captain Barry has disposed of his whale skeleton to the Otago Museum.'[9] And so Captain Barry's whale became Professor Parker's whale.

When Parker read a paper to the Otago Institute in October 1883 on the skeleton of a whale then being mounted in the museum, he gave the creature a new life by turning it into a sober means of edification rather than a prop valued for its entertainment appeal alone. The man who endowed the whale with such gravitas was Thomas Jeffery Parker (1850–1897), the first professor of biology at the University of Otago, a position he held concurrently with that of curator of the Otago University Museum. He arrived in Dunedin in 1880 from London where he had spent eight years teaching in the biological laboratory of Thomas Henry Huxley (1825–1895). Best known as 'Darwin's Bulldog', Huxley was a scientific educator and canvasser for a growing corps of younger men, like Parker, who made their living from scientific work.

Parker was clearly impressed with his new acquisition. He told his Christchurch-based friend and counterpart, Julius von Haast (1822–1887), that it was in 'very good condition except that a portion of caudal vertebrae were thrown away with the flukes and many of the phalanges are lost … The baleen is in beautiful condition, & the skeleton altogether will be a very fine one. It is to be slung from iron girders supported by

ABOVE: *Parker found his evolutionary ideas difficult to display. Fragile jars of invertebrates were arranged out of the reach of visitors.*

Ref: C.011759, Otago Museum Interior, Burton Brothers Photography Studio, unknown photographer, Museum of New Zealand Te Papa Tongarewa

TOP RIGHT: *Thomas Jeffery Parker (1850–97) was appointed curator of the museum and professor of biology at the University of Otago in 1880. He bought the whale to enhance the teaching capacity of the museum and to attract visitors.*

Ref: P1/1296, Photograph by David Alexander de Maus (1847–1925), State Library of New South Wales

RIGHT: *Captain William Jackson Barry (1819–1907) carted the fin whale on a lecture tour through the South Island, ending in Dunedin in 1883. It was the ultimate stage prop.*

Ref: 1/2-052803-F, Alexander Turnbull Library, Wellington, New Zealand

the columns. What size is your specimen? Mine is 54 ft 6 ins.'[10]

Measurement was an important observational and empirical methodology in Victorian zoology. As historian Lorraine Daston has explained, it was part of the collective nature of scientific endeavour.[11] Like other scientific workers, Parker established a persona of disinterested objective observer with the paper he wrote for the *Transactions and Proceedings of the New Zealand Institute*, recording that the bones were only 'roughly set up':

> Captain Barry … unfortunately was not sufficiently aware of the value of a complete whale's skeleton to give the proper amount of care to the smaller bones. The eight posterior caudal vertebrae were thrown away with the 'flukes'; the anterior epiphysis of the fifth cervical vertebra is missing; many of the phalanges and some of the carpals are lost and no trace of either pelvic bone reached Dunedin.[12]

The paper is full of close and careful observations written in what H.G. Wells, one of Huxley's biology students, called the 'dialect of science'.[13] By this means the hanging whale in the museum became a purveyor of knowledge, which was a world away from hosting a dinner party in its jaws. And yet Parker's published account hides his anxieties and angst. In a letter to William Henry Flower (1831–1899), the director of the Natural History Museum in London, he wrote: 'I send with this a photograph of the Museum showing a skeleton of Balaenoptera I had put up some time ago. I feel a little uncomfortable about the (artificial) pelvic bones, which are modelled from a figure of Haast's. Ought they to be reversed!'[14] Flower had a specialist interest in cetaceans and about a quarter of his published work was on the group. Parker compared his whale carefully with Flower's accounts and despite differences in the sternum, which Parker thought could be due to individual variation, came to the conclusion that it was a young specimen of a blue whale. But he agreed with Flower that more research on whales, particularly living ones, was needed to establish the links between northern and southern hemisphere species.

The members of the public who came to see Professor Parker's whale almost certainly included some of those who had gone to see Captain Barry's. But Parker's main target was his students, both those studying zoology and those doing medicine, for whom a course in comparative animal anatomy was compulsory: access to the bones served the purpose better than stuffed specimens. Even if the whole whale carcass had been available to make a taxidermic specimen, it would have proved particularly difficult. Whale skin could not be preserved like other mammalian skins. As Parker phrased it, 'the blubber passed insensibly into the cuticle', which made it 'so delicate as to be torn with the slightest traction', and in the words of one American taxidermist, the 'remarkably thin and fragile' skin tended 'to discolour and decay quickly upon its owner's death'.[15]

During the 1870s and 1880s there was much debate about the purpose of museums. Huxley suggested the primary objective was 'the public exhibition of a collection of specimens large enough to illustrate all the most important truths of natural history' and that only the serious student should have access to separate study collections.[16] In his ideal museum, curators and students could move about behind the public displays, sharing space with drawers and cabinets full of specimens, separated from visitors. The secondary benefits of such arrangements included conservation, the exclusion of dust and dirt and the provision of workrooms. This, historian Samuel Alberti points out, was part of Huxley's desire to construct a 'privileged space for the expert'.[17]

Part of the museum discussion concerned the maintenance of order, presenting items properly so they would not degenerate into a higgledy-piggledy jumble of curios. In the presidential address to the Newcastle meeting of the British Association for the Advancement of Science in 1889, Flower issued some instructions on how best to display specimens. Importantly, 'every specimen must be good of its kind … none must be placed too high or too low for ready examination. There must be no crowding of specimens one behind the other, every one being perfectly and distinctly seen, with a clear space around it.'[18] Parker had limited ability to separate study collections from those on display, and little physical room to follow Flower's advice on overcrowding. This explains why his whale could only be hung from the girders, since the floor space was still taken up with the original whale, moa and giraffe skeletons.

Parker's avowed evolutionary principles guided his work. Evolution dictated which specimens he should acquire and how he should display the collections. After all, 'organizing and displaying is a way of visualizing the invisible, of making ideas palpable'.[19] Surprisingly Darwin's *On the Origin of Species*, published in 1859, took several decades to permeate and affect the display ethos of museums.[20] Parker's scheme was, by his own admission, tentative. There was no fixed methodology by which to group specimens, or the order that they should fit. The audience relied on supporting textual information to make sense of the displays. Parker had to battle against both an inconveniently arranged building and a lack of space. 'It is practically impossible,' he wrote, 'to arrange the doors, passages, galleries, etc., [so] that the visitor is obliged to traverse them in a certain direction, and so to have forced upon him the natural sequence.' By this Parker meant a narrative of evolutionary progression through the animal kingdom. He did the best he could, but bemoaned the fact that the birds had to be accommodated in wall-cases on the upper gallery, mammals in the lower gallery, with smaller invertebrates 'exhibited in flat cases or desks, which could only be conveniently placed round two galleries and between the windows in the lower gallery, in places where wall-cases were inadmissible'.[21] This, he claimed, made the natural sequence unclear to an ordinary observer.

In its life-after-death the whale proved by turns a source of entertainment, edification and education. The unchanging exhibition of one skeleton has emphasised the changing shifts in focus and fashion, although its current location among ships and maritime artefacts is rather different from that intended by Parker, the evolutionist.

23

The Travelling Stereopticon

Barbara Brookes

We have no image of Frank Stanert, but we can imagine he was a consummate young showman like the man on the cover of this second edition of Roger Child Bayley's Modern Magic Lanterns: A guide to the management of the optical lantern, *published in 1900. Stanert turned 21 during the tour of New Zealand. In London in 1894 he formed his own travelling company of 'American comedy and musical entertainers' aptly named 'The Wanderers'.*

Courtesy of Cornell University Library Digital Collections, Ithaca, New York

Frank Stanert packed up his stereopticon, its attendant glass slides, gas cylinders and additional equipment, at the end of April 1892 and left Philadelphia for a summer camp in Minnesota. An 'experienced stereoptician', Stanert had learnt his trade in the city at the heart of the magic lantern business. William and Frederick Langenheim pioneered commercial photography in Philadelphia in the 1850s, and L.J. Marcy produced oil and gas 'sciopticons' in the 1880s.[1] The stereopticon, so named in the 1860s, was a form of magic lantern usually with a double lens that allowed images to dissolve, creating the illusion of movement.

The stereopticon was a sensation. The *Dayton Daily Empire* recorded the impact of its 'almost miraculous illusions and beauties' on crowds in Ohio in August 1864:

> Those who have not seen it cannot conceive how perfectly and satisfactorily it opens to view the scenes and objects upon which it is brought to bear. It adds to the beauty of the Photographic process, not simply expansion; but it has the wonderful power of lifting the shadow from the canvas or screen, and imparting to it the absolute intangible attributes of the *real object* … the stereopticon is one of the most interesting of modern discoveries, presenting the beholder, not with a mere *picture* but with absolute *counterparts* of the objects represented … The wire bridge over the Niagara river, the Niagara Falls, the Great Eastern, views in Paris, Rome, and throughout Europe, together with masterpieces of eminent sculptors, will be conjured into shadowy existence, and presented to the eye in such a manner as to impart in a large measure, the pleasure which would be enjoyed by beholding the real objects.[2]

In Stanert's hands the stereopticon continued this tradition of making visible the scenic sights of the world, while adding a new dimension to popular instruction. The magic lantern screen's handpainted slides had been associated with 'mystery and magic'. When the stereopticon came into use, photography largely supplanted painted slides and 'enhanced the lifelike quality of the screen image'. Photographic slides offered 'a much more accurate record of reality', which 'overwhelmed' audiences. In short, these new magic lanterns moved beyond magic to be seen as 'scientific'.[3]

We do not know the exact type of magic lantern that Frank Stanert operated but it may have been like this one made at 48 Waterloo Road, London, by Walter Tyler. It is a polished mahogany vertical biunnial dissolving lantern that has a metal chimney, four light viewing windows, and polished brass lenses with rack and pinion focus. It stands 61.3 centimetres high.

Ref: W231.00001, George Eastman House, International Museum of Photography and Film, Rochester, New York

This demure photograph of Mrs Anna Longshore Potts MD graced the frontispiece of the twelfth edition of her self-published book, Discourses to Women on Medical Subjects *(1897). Behind the image of the kindly aged woman lay a pioneer woman medical graduate, a shrewd businesswoman, a divorced mother, and an entrancing public speaker.*

Stereopticons soon made their way to colonial New Zealand: an Oamaru watchmaker advertised them as early as November 1868.[4] The stereopticon promised nineteenth-century New Zealanders virtual travel to places they might have left behind, such as Edinburgh and London, or an introduction to places they might never visit, such as India, Japan or the Rocky Mountains. These sights and scenes, as Elizabeth Hartrick has argued, helped to 'annihilate the challenges of time and space' that colonists 'routinely faced'.[5] What is more, this travel required no arduous and lonely sea voyage, but was undertaken in the comfort of a theatre and the company of others. Together viewers might appreciate great works of art unavailable in the colony, learn of advances in microscopy or geology or merely be entertained by comic scenes. They might also, however, be transported inwards to the hitherto unseen, and acquire anatomical knowledge that was usually the preserve of medical men. Education and amusement alike arrived on a grand scale through the stereopticon's illuminations. In addition, this 'modern discovery' provided a new means of livelihood for those in the theatre business. An instruction manual indicates how the stereopticon might be used:

> Suppose, for example, Saint Peter's, at Rome, is thrown upon the screen from [one lens] and a night view of the same is placed in [another]; then as the dissolver is changed, Saint Peter's with its surroundings continues on the screen, but an appearance of night comes over it; the windows glitter with a thousand lights, and the moon makes its appearance in the heavens. Now, suppose a chromatrope, suited to the purpose, is [used], then as the change proceeds fire-works will rise from the darkness, and illumine the sky.[6]

When all was in good working order, the stereopticon produced 'crisp, clear images of astonishing scale'. Most such lanterns were 'designed with transportation in mind', with 'collapsible screens and padded slide boxes'.[7]

Operating the stereopticon required expertise to set up the slides and ensure the relatively large machine worked properly. Lime made incandescent by a jet of oxygen through an alcohol flame provided the illumination for the lantern, and meant the risk of fire and explosions. Gas cylinders were an essential component to create a show. Stanert could not travel lightly and he needed to ensure that his equipment was packed properly. He and his stereopticon had a long way to go.

Stanert's travelling companion on the train from Philadelphia was Dr Anna Longshore Potts, an itinerant lecturer on health for whom he was the stereoptician and stage manager. One of the first medical graduates from Pennsylvania's Female Medical College in 1851, Longshore Potts had found her true vocation in lecturing. Having perhaps exhausted the lecture circuits in the United States, she had set her sights on an Australasian tour.

The doctor and Stanert met up with the rest of their party in Chicago: J. Charles Harrison MD, who gave lectures on men's health, his mother and his

These advertisements, which appeared in the West Coast Times *of 18 April 1893, typified the way the business manager generated interest for the Longshore Potts and Harrison lectures. The advertisement highlighted their qualifications, stressed the amusing and instructive content, and highlighted the spectacular size and colour of the 'limelight views'.* Courtesy of the National Library of New Zealand

brother George, who was the business manager, and George's wife. They set up camp in the Minnesota woods and rehearsed their show, Stanert screening the stereopticon slides, and the doctors practising their timing carefully so that the smooth integration of voice and image allowed audiences to be transported into new visual worlds.

At the end of the summer it was time to pack up the stereopticon again for the train trip to San Francisco. There the stereoptician and his equipment boarded the SS *Alameda* for Honolulu as the advance party for Drs Harrison and Potts. Soon the stereopticon was unpacked for lectures to women and men at the Royal Hawaiian Opera House. George Harrison made sure the lectures were well advertised, and the press notice reveals that the dual nature of the programme, providing entertainment as well as education, scenic and artistic wonders as well as instruction on the human body, was established from the beginning of the tour. The lectures would 'be magnificently illustrated with stereopticon views not only of the subjects discussed, but also of art and travel. They were especially prepared for these lectures, and most of them are in colors. There will be many views of scenery in Uncle Sam's domains, and among the finest are some of the famous Yellowstone Park.'[8] Dr Charles Harrison's lecture to 'old men, young men, and men of all sorts and condition of life' was 'made up of common sense, bright bits of humor, vivid dissolving views and a great mass of information'. Attendees had to be over 16 and a police officer manned the door to ensure that was the case.[9] 'Many

Notices:

PRINCESS THEATRE.

J. Chas. Harrison, M.D.

The Famous Traveller and Specialist.

Graduate of two leading Universities of the United States.

Will LECTURE to MEN ONLY as follows :—

THURSDAY NIGHT, April 20, at 8 o'clock. Admission Free.

FRIDAY NIGHT, April 21, at 8 o'clock. Admission 1s.

"Discarding too technical terms, he talked plainly and without offence . . . . The lecture was delivered fluently, clearly, and pleasantly, and interspersed with illustrative anecdotes, many of which caused much laughter, while there was frequent applause. There was also a succession of magnificent views, objects of art, splendid examples of the world's be t scenery, and mechanical views of marked excellence."—Evening Post, Wellington, February 14, 1893.

Both lectures illustrated with magnificent stereoptican views in colors, covering 600 square feet of canvas, 200 views at each lecture. Positively the most beautiful views in the world.

PRINCESS THEATRE.

Mrs. Longshore Potts, M.D.,

America's most famous woman physician, Graduate of the Woman's Medical College, Philadelphia,

WILL LECTURE ON

HEALTH AND DISEASE,

To women, only as follows :—

FRIDAY, APRIL 21 and 22, 24 and 25, at 3 p.m.

FIRST LECTURE FREE,

Illustrated with colored limelight views, including many of art and travel, 200 views each lecture.

MONDAY NIGHT, April 24 at Eight o'clock.

The famous leacture

ON

HEARTS AND HOMES

OR

IS MARRIAGE A FAILURE?

To both Sexes.

"Moral, instructive, and very amusing."
—London Truth.

PRICES—1s and 2s.

of the views,' the report continued, 'were very fine, and those of a medical character usefully illustrative, but not sensational.'[10]

Not everyone agreed. Soon a warrant was issued by the *Liberal* newspaper, perhaps in the interest of generating sales, for the arrest of Harrison 'for exhibiting foul illustrations'. According to the *Liberal*, 'The whole tone of the lecture and the pictures shown tended towards vileness.'[11] Harrison was tried on the charge of being a common nuisance for the public exhibition of 'certain obscene pictures, being a public outrage against common decency and good morals'. The stereopticon slides now became exhibits in the courtroom. A Dr Wood was sworn in and gave evidence:

> I ... saw pictures exhibited of males' and female private parts; they were stereopticon slides thrown on a screen; male organs were shown first, then sectional view of female parts; I thought they were objectionable before a promiscuous audience; thought such pictures of the opposite sex should not be shown before an audience that was not composed of medical or scientific people; thought it was out of place ... I have seen the same pictures used in lectures to medical students, shown in just the same way.

Although the stereopticon offered an unparalleled opportunity to educate the public on all aspects of science, some sights, according to Dr Wood, should be restricted to the male medical profession. In contrast, a number of other witnesses testified that there was nothing indecent or likely 'to create lustful thoughts in the minds of lads' in the lecture and the charge against Harrison was dismissed.[12]

Once again the stereopticon and its related equipment were packed up, this time for the voyage of the SS *Mariposa* to Auckland, where a seven-month tour of New Zealand began through the main centres and minor towns, enchanting audiences with the stereopticon views and expanding the public's knowledge about matters of health. Both doctors provided consultations as an adjunct to their lectures. The *Ashburton Guardian* reported on the first of Harrison's two lectures to men:

> A powerful stereopticon was mounted in position at the back of the hall, and there was a large white canvas sheet covering nearly the full expanse of the stage within the proscenium ... [as Harrison] diverged from more general remarks into more specific treatment of his subject, the lights were lowered and a succession of beautiful pictures began to appear upon the screen at his back, some of them views of notable places, or of choice statuary or paintings, and others being enlargements of anatomical charts illustrative of the lecture itself ... the exhibition of pictures, which are the best of the kind that have ever been seen in Ashburton, formed a capital entertainment of itself.[13]

Audiences were entranced by images shown on 55 square metres of canvas of 'Paris by day and illuminated at night', 'a thunderstorm in the Rockies with realistic effects' and 'Vesuvius in eruption'.[14] The last, 'immensely popular' as a subject for 'the dissolving view technique', had been in the lantern slide repertoire since the 1850s. Paired and matched slides were used to illustrate the 'Bay of Naples, smiling in the serenity of sunshine, with Vesuvius at rest lowering grandly in the distance ... Clouds

T.H. McAllister was a manufacturing optician based in Nassau Street, New York, who in 1887 issued a free Catalogue of Stereopticons, Dissolving-View Apparatus and Magic Lanterns with lists of several thousand ARTISTICALLY FINISHED VIEWS for the illustration of all subjects of popular interest. *Customers could order equipment and slides from the catalogue. This illustration from the frontispiece enables us to see how the stereopticon entranced audiences when the images accompanied a lecture.*

and thick darkness [then came] over the scene, and the volcano belche[d] forth its red fires and gloomy vapours.'[15] Spectators sitting safely in their local theatre or community hall were transfixed by the power of nature and the horror of the unexpected.

Crowds came to Anna Longshore Potts's lectures partly because of the novelty of a woman doctor. Dressed in 'charming gowns' and carrying a long rod that gave her 'the appearance of a Sybil gone fly-fishing', she pointed out 'the ulcers on the drunkard's throat, a picture we took great interest in, and other delicate pictures, together with some beautiful ones of art and travel which are projected by a handsome and powerful stereopticon'.[16] Without the projection of the physiological drawings, a Blenheim reporter claimed, 'the lectures would not be complete'.[17] Whereas past itinerant health lecturers had used papier-mâché or wax models to demonstrate anatomy and physiology, requiring an intimate venue, the stereopticon could illuminate the finer points of anatomy spectacularly on a large screen in vast theatres and opera houses. Both Potts and Harrison used the stereopticon to democratise their medical learning, attract audiences and line their pocket books.

The travelling stereopticon created a new kind of theatrical experience in which a lecture was enhanced by spectacular visual display. Perhaps in a unique combination, Stanert's slides threw light on both scenic splendours and bodily parts in order to enlighten and entertain. The stereopticon's illusions served to expand the mental landscapes of colonists' worlds in expansive and unexpectedly intimate ways.

The Lord's Prayer in Maori with literal English translation with illuminated = border &c. representing ancient Maori carvings, by W. Gordon Whanganui N.Z. 6/6/79.

24

Unanswered Prayers

The Failure of W.F. Gordon's Self-Promotion

Rebecca Rice

In July 1879 it was widely reported that a 'curiosity' was on display in a shop window in Whanganui.[1] The object was an illuminated manuscript by William Francis Gordon titled *The Lord's Prayer in Maori* or *Te Inoi a te Ariki*, destined for the 1879–80 Sydney International Exhibition. It was described as the 'first picture of its kind ever attempted' and reporters also noted that Gordon intended to have the picture copyrighted and photographed.[2] Forty-four years later Gordon presented a photographic copy of *Te Inoi a te Ariki* to the Smithsonian Institution in Washington.

OPPOSITE: *William Francis Robert Gordon (1846–1936), Te Inoi a te Ariki (The Lord's Prayer in Māori).*

Ref: MSO-Papers-4853, Alexander Turnbull Library, Wellington, New Zealand

The original work and its reproduction are as much 'curiosities' for contemporary art historians as they were for those who first encountered them, for three reasons. First, the original art work manifests a complex incorporation of Māori text and imagery into a European art form. Second, Gordon's desire to secure copyright for and to reproduce the manuscript was unusual in colonial New Zealand. Third, considered together, the original work and its copies provide an opportunity to consider Gordon's ambitions in the colonial world.

The execution of *Te Inoi a te Ariki*, as is typical of an illuminated manuscript, is painstakingly attentive to detail. First letters of words are picked out, enlarged and embellished with colour, ranging from vermilion to green, mauve and gold. The prayer is surrounded by a decorative border, interpreted by former soldier and fluent te reo speaker Gilbert Mair in an accompanying text. According to him, the decorative scheme is derived from the full range of Māori arts: greenstone mere and tiki, ancient Māori carving/whakairo, tattooing or tā moko, kōwhaiwhai rafter patterns, tukutuku panels and representations of male and female heads with tā moko and huia feathers in their hair. Mair also writes that the 'tracer under the words "Prayer of the Lord" is suggestive of rays of glory'.

Portrait of William F. Gordon, 1888.

Ref. 1935.59.3, Whanganui Regional Museum Collection

Te Inoi a te Ariki, then, has an ambitious decorative scheme that incorporates Māori design and text into an art form with a distinguished pedigree in western culture – the illuminated manuscript. It is a highly unusual product for an artist working in 1870s colonial New Zealand. A survey of holdings of the major colonial libraries and galleries shows that illuminated manuscripts produced in the colonies largely took the form of the illustrated address, commemorating the service of a notable individual who was on the point of retirement or departure.[3] There is little evidence of any other attempt to integrate the colonial and the indigenous, to produce a thoroughly hybrid work within the genre of the illuminated manuscript.

What adds further to the curiosity of this work is that Gordon places the Māori version of the Lord's Prayer above a *literal* English translation. This arguably serves those Pākehā who wish to read the Māori as it is written. In this respect Gordon seems to be attempting something more than the superficial borrowing of Māori design and culture that dominated nineteenth-century European art and craft. As Nicholas Thomas has stated, such indigenous references often proclaim the 'native' status of the new settler 'in a fashion that perforce draws attention to real natives who are excluded'.[4] But the literal English translation here suggests that Gordon conceived of an audience that included members of both races with an interest in Māori language and culture.[5] It is arguably a genuinely bicultural product, equally accessible to Pākehā and Māori. It also highlights the ambiguous meaning of terms whose misinterpretation would later generate conflict: rangatiratanga, for example, is translated as both 'kingdom' and 'chieftainship'.

The original work both is and is not the focus of this essay. The photographic reproduction of the art work, currently held by the National Anthropological Archive of the Smithsonian Institution in Chicago, is equally interesting. What intrigues me most about Gordon's work is that, as was widely reported at its time of production, *Te Inoi a te Ariki* was copyrighted and photographed.[6] While the original work of art was on the display circuit, shown at international exhibitions in Sydney, Melbourne and Dunedin, photographic reproductions could be viewed in New Zealand. In September 1879 there was a reproduction in the window of E.H. Haslett's Music and Stationery Warehouse in Shortland Street, Auckland, where copies could also be purchased. It was recommended that 'lovers of the beautiful and the curious should not fail to procure a copy',[7] and that 'a more unique or characteristic memorial of Maoridom could not be offered to English friends'.[8]

By copyrighting and photographing his art work, Gordon reveals his understanding of the nineteenth-century art world, in which artists were more likely to reap financial reward for reproductions, or for the sale of copyright to dealers, than they were through the sale of works alone.[9] Although he did not make money through the sale of copyright, he obviously anticipated that *Te Inoi a te Ariki* would have public appeal, so protected himself in advance of any illegitimate copies being made.

Gordon, who had worked as a wood engraver at the Colonial (later Dominion) Museum not long after his arrival in New Zealand in 1867 and also produced cartoons for the *Sydney Punch*, understood the intricacies of the reproductive world. His manipulation of such systems was also made clear during his protracted negotiations with the Dominion Museum over his 'splendid collection of photographs of officers and men who served in the New Zealand Wars'.[10] After purchasing the set, the museum subsequently heard a 'rumour' that Gordon was offering to sell copies of

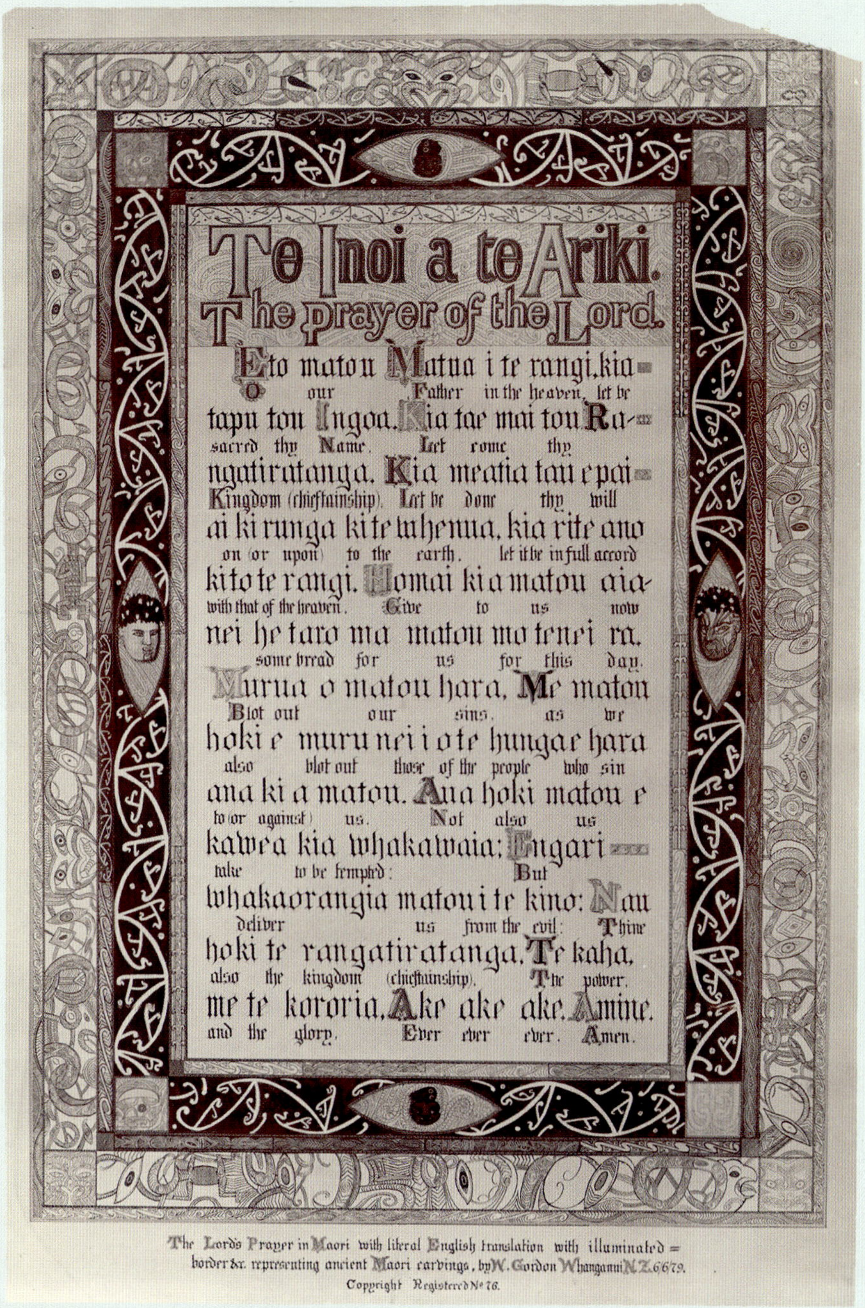

Te Inoi a te Ariki.
The prayer of the Lord.

E to matou Matua i te rangi, kia
O our Father in the heaven, let be
tapu tou Ingoa. Kia tae mai tou Ra-
sacred thy Name. Let come thy
ngatiratanga. Kia meatia tou e pai-
Kingdom (chieftainship). Let be done thy will
ai ki runga ki te whenua, kia rite ano
on (or upon) to the earth. let it be in full accord
ki to te rangi. Homai ki a matou aia-
with that of the heaven. Give to us now
nei he taro ma matou mo tenei ra.
some bread for us for this day.
Murua o matou hara, Me matou
Blot out our sins. as we
hoki e muru nei i o te hunga e hara
also blot out those of the people who sin
ana ki a matou. Aua hoki matou e
to (or against) us. Not also us
kawea kia whakawaia: Engari
take to be tempted: But
whakaorangia matou i te kino: Nau
deliver us from the evil: Thine
hoki te rangatiratanga, Te kaha,
also the kingdom (chieftainship). The power,
me te kororia, Ake ake ake. Amine.
and the glory. Ever ever ever. Amen.

The Lord's Prayer in Maori with literal English translation with illuminated = border &c. representing ancient Maori carvings, by W. Gordon Whanganui N.Z. 6/6/79.

Presented by W. F. Gordon
New Plymouth
New Zealand
June 18th 1923

W.F. Gordon, The Lord's Prayer in Maori with literal English translation with illuminated border representing ancient Maori carvings, photograph, 1879.

Ref: NAA INV 05092501, Smithsonian Institution: National Anthropological Archives

photographs to other individuals and institutions.[11] The museum eventually purchased the negatives for £5, but not before Gordon had also furnished the New Plymouth museum, now Puke Ariki, with an extensive collection.

It is perhaps curious that Gordon chose to photograph *Te Inoi a te Ariki*, rather than reproduce it by some other means, such as chromolithography, which might have allowed the colour to be replicated. But photographic rather than engraved reproductions of works of art, which became increasingly available to the Victorian public from the 1860s, were cheaper and quicker to produce and eliminated the artistic intervention of an intermediary. A number of New Zealand shops imported photographic reproductions of works of art in the 1860s.

In this respect, it is significant that Gordon felt *Te Inoi a te Ariki* was most worthy of such treatment. He had had success with an earlier painting, *Stray Leaves*, but it was not reproduced and made available on the market in the same manner. I suggest that Gordon was aware of both the uniqueness of the Māori content and the potential power of the religious content, of *Te Inoi a te Ariki*. It was reproduced both as a 15- by 20-centimetre photograph, and in cabinet card size.[12] This smaller version could function more as a portable religious talisman, or something that might be readily incorporated into a collection of such cards depicting notable personalities, or, as was common, something that might be regarded as 'curious' – Māori, of course, were a key subject for such collections. It is also worth noting that the description by Mair, widely accepted as a Māori 'expert', nearly always accompanied reproductions of the illuminated manuscript, suggesting that Gordon wanted to keep the informative, and perhaps authenticating, aspect of his work to the fore.

This brings us to the final point for consideration: Gordon's ambitions in the colonial world. The *Grove Dictionary of Art* suggests that 'since the middle of the sixteenth century it has only been in isolated and eccentric cases that the hand-produced illustration of texts has been a focus of artistic attention'.[13] Gordon's writings and oeuvre definitely speak of an eccentric at work. He produced few large-scale art works, all of which tended to be obsessive in nature, as is the case with *Stray Leaves* (1878), a trompe l'oeil study of colonial ephemera.

He was, however, obviously proud of this work. As well as being copyrighted and photographed, it was widely exhibited and generally well received. At Sydney in 1879 it was catalogued under 'Engravings, Lithography and Photography' and given an honourable mention. In Melbourne in 1880 it was prominently placed in the New Zealand Court, and though catalogued under 'Printing and Books' was awarded a prize under 'Fine Arts'. In 1881 *Te Inoi a te Ariki* was exhibited in the Fine Arts Gallery at the Dunedin Industrial Exhibition, and finally, also in that city, at the New Zealand and South Seas Exhibition of 1889–90, in the Early History, Maori and South Seas Court. Clearly, this work challenged those attempting to classify and order culture and nature. The same, it seems, is true of Gordon.

As is evident in his many and varied enterprises, he was a tireless self-promoter. As well as producing works of art, Gordon wrote biographies of the recipients of

Opposite: *This detail of Gordon's work demonstrates clearly the very literal translation he employed in the illuminated manuscript – 'Te Inoi a te Ariki' is translated word for word as 'The Prayer of the Lord'. The delicate patterning derived from Māori designs and described by Mair as being 'suggestive of rays of glory' is evident in the background.*

Ref: MSO-Papers-4853, Alexander Turnbull Library, Wellington, New Zealand

Left: *The New Zealand Court, Melbourne Exhibition 1880, albumen print.*

Photographer unknown, Ref: O.009429, Museum of New Zealand Te Papa Tongarewa

the Victoria Cross, photographed officers and men who had served in the New Zealand Wars and visited and drew many of the battlefields. He also collected depictions of the Māori flags associated with the wars and wrote a history of the Pai Mārire religion. By night, he was a musician and public caricaturist, by day he worked at the Telegraph Department in Whanganui, before settling in New Plymouth where he was employed as a draughtsman for the Lands and Survey Department. Gordon is one of those figures who surfaces on multiple fronts in the museological world, partly because he placed his work in institutions in Australasia and beyond, and partly as a result of his ready co-option of the press to aid his self-advertisement.

On the mount of the photographic reproduction in the Smithsonian is an inscription reading 'Presented by W.F. Gordon, New Plymouth, New Zealand, June 18 1923'. A copy for sale through Webb's auction house in 2010 had an inscription 'with W F Gordon's compts Oct 31 1923'. Nineteen twenty-three was clearly a year for action on this front. Copies of *Te Inoi a te Ariki* have been identified not only in the Smithsonian and the Alexander Turnbull Library (along with the original), but also in Te Papa, the Mitchell Library in Sydney and several other institutions. In spite of this, Gordon himself has, until recently, been a largely unknown figure, absent from histories of the time. Nonetheless, through considering his eclectic and varied work we can begin to understand how partial and limited the standard histories of colonial art in New Zealand have been to date. But we can also start to recognise that the colonial art world was a more complex place than acknowledged and that artists such as Gordon were canny, even if ultimately unsuccessful, operators in that system.

25
Embroidering the Whanganui
Claire Regnault

Detail of the Whanganui River embroidered by Maud Brown in 1891 and framed in rewarewa. Feathers, silk thread, glass beads and water colour on silk, 620 x 410 millimetres (including frame).

Ref: PC000832, bequest of Mrs Wickenden, 1963, Museum of New Zealand Te Papa Tongarewa

In 1963 the Dominion Museum, now the Museum of New Zealand Te Papa Tongarewa, received a bequest of an embroidered picture stitched by Maud Stuart, née Brown. Framed in rewarewa, and rendered in thread, chenille, glass beads, feathers and watercolour on silk, it depicts a New Zealand river scene featuring a group of Māori. The only information provided by the solicitors was that the picture was worked when Maud 'was a young girl in 1891'.[1] A resident of Wellington's Te Aro area, she would have been 18, more a young woman than a girl.[2] Although the picture was faded from decades of exposure to light, the museum's curator, Dr Terence Barrow, declared it a 'valuable addition' to the collection.[3]

Barrow never elaborated on his rationale, but it may have been because the picture, though unusual, was not unique. Just over a decade earlier, an almost identical picture had been gifted to the museum. Its original object tag records it as a scene of the Whanganui River worked by Alice Clapham[4] at 'Mrs Murray's School in Lower Molesworth Street', Wellington, in 1880. Alice, whose parents ran the hotel in Ngāūranga, would have been just 14.[5] These remarkable embroideries document two young women's engagement with indigenous culture at an important transitional moment in the history of the Whanganui River.

Needlework both plain and fancy formed an integral part of a girl's education in colonial New Zealand. In 1881 the Board of Education declared that all school committees be 'recommended to cause needlework to be taught in their schools'.[6] Needlework was viewed not just as a feminine accomplishment, but also a practical skill. 'Pretty shows' of needlework frequently accompanied school prize-givings throughout the country,[7] and were reviewed in the December papers yearly. Describing such a display in 1893, 'Elsie' of Otago's *Bruce Herald* observed that 'A point in the education of a girl that is of vital importance in making her an efficient self-reliant woman, is the training of eye and hand as well as of memory. In every case the hand should be as carefully trained as the brain … The State by insisting on needlework being taught in schools is doing its share in making girls notable …'[8]

Embroidered pictures such as Maud and Alice's are rarely listed among the types of 'pretty shows' displayed. This is not surprising, as stylistically they are akin to the needlework paintings of the 1830s, which often featured romantic, allegorical or pastoral scenes. By the late nineteenth century, this pictorial style was no longer fashionable. Berlin work, more ornamental embroidery executed from paper patterns, had become the most popular form of illustrative needlework, and the technique was not without its critics. One lady columnist blamed it for stopping 'the execution of any needlework requiring the intervention of the brain' and cultivating 'nothing beyond mechanical accuracy'.[9]

Although the draughtsmanship of the Whanganui River is rudimentary, suggesting it was drawn by an amateur rather than a professional, in stitching terms, it is more complex than a Berlin pattern. Commercially, embroidery patterns featuring Māori did not become available, or fashionable, until the first half of the twentieth century. The unusual pattern could have been drafted by Mrs Murray, a teacher about whom nothing is known. Thorndon boasted a range of private schools for girls, including the well-known Mrs Swainson's,[10] but Wise's directories, electoral rolls, educational histories, rates books and even *Papers Past* have all failed to provide even a hint of Mrs Murray or her school. Alternatively, the

According to the donors, Alice Clapham stitched this embroidery of the Whanganui River in 1880. It is worked in feathers and silk thread on silk. The frame is kauri with a bird's eye maple veneer and velvet surround. 730 x 610 millimetres (including frame).

Ref: PC000798, Gift of the Clapham Family, 1951, Museum of New Zealand Te Papa Tongarewa

pattern could have been drawn by one of her students, perhaps even Alice Clapham.

A comparison of Maud and Alice's embroidery pattern reveals prescribed lessons in chenille and feather work, beading, stitches and knots. But what else did the teacher seek to cultivate in her pupils, beyond technical skill, through her choice of pattern? Within a girl's education, needlework had a range of pedagogical ends. Samplers were not only about learning and recording types of stitches, but often reflected lessons in scripture, literacy and numeracy. White on white work emphasised the importance of cleanliness. In 1884 a teacher at Auckland's Girls' High School required students to come up with suitable mottoes to stitch onto clothes destined for children less fortunate than themselves: 'Wisdom is better than rubies', 'Use before beauty', 'With economy few need to be poor'.[11]

The Whanganui River scene presented opportunities for lessons in native flora and fauna. Both embroideries feature recognisable plants, such as cabbage trees, tree ferns and toetoe, and birds, including kiwi and whio, the little blue duck that inhabited the river's upper catchments. Alice's also features a parson bird, Maud's a kingfisher – although perhaps they called them by their Māori names, tūī and kōtare. Mrs Murray may have been following the Arts and Crafts philosophy – if not style – of using native flora and fauna to cultivate a sense of 'New Zealandness' in her pupils.[12] Unlike a straightforward botanical study, however, a whole scene lends itself to storytelling, and narratives of geography, native life and even race relations. One wonders if Mrs Murray's schoolroom was silent with concentration as knots were carefully looped around needles, or if it was peppered with conversation inspired by the picture that was taking shape in front of them, from the textile skills of Māori women to talk of events on the Whanganui.

Alice was certainly aware that she was stitching the Whanganui River and not a generic river scene. There is even an eel weir, a common sight on the eel-filled

Mary Tyer, Alice Clapham's younger cousin, stitched this Berlin work rug around 1885. Wool on linen, 1530 x 630 millimetres. *Ref: PC000250/1, Bequest of Mrs Mary H. Quin, 1956, Museum of New Zealand Te Papa Tongarewa*

river. However, when Alice Clapham is said to have worked her picture in 1880, the Whanganui River was not a comfortable subject for Pākehā, who knew neither the river nor its inhabitants well. The area had experienced Hauhau disruptions in the 1860s, and its situation on the edge of the King Country meant that the government's authority was still weak.[13] Pākehā who entered the uncharted upper reaches of the river without permission faced the risk of imprisonment or death.[14] Few images of the region existed in the public sphere. Symbolically and practically, the Whanganui River in 1880 seems an improbable subject for a 14-year-old schoolgirl.

When Maud Brown reputedly stitched her version, in 1891, it was a different story. Ten years earlier, King Tāwhiao had declared that 'this is the end of warfare in this land'.[15] He emerged from exile and, dressed in his 'habitual tweed',[16] became a recognisable identity among Thorndon residents. Schoolgirls soon learned to distinguish the king from the other Māori chiefs arriving at parliament to discuss the restoration of their land.[17] By 1885 Pākehā had been given access to the King Country and work had begun on the main trunk railway line.[18] By 1891 eel weirs were becoming a thing of the past, as the government removed them to make way for paddle boats. In the decade between Alice's and Maud's embroideries the Whanganui River underwent significant physical as well as political change, as it was progressively transformed into the picturesque 'Rhine of the Maoriland'.[19]

In 1885, in particular, the Whanganui was prominent in the public imagination, especially in the capital. From May to June 1885 photographer Alfred Burton travelled through the region with railway engineer John Rochfort, seeking to reveal 'the scenery' and 'native life' of this 'terra incognita' to the wider public and photograph Māori 'at home'.[20] Burton published a syndicated diary of his trip, 'Through the King Country with the Camera', and in August displayed a selection of photographs at the New Zealand Industrial Exhibition in Wellington.[21] The Claphams would certainly have visited the

The Whanganui River pattern features a range of Māori cloaks, which enabled the girls to show off both their feather work and their stitching skills. Maud Brown used albino kiwi feathers for this impressive chief's cloak, whereas Alice Clapham opted for a multifeather approach, including kākāpō feathers.

OPPOSITE: *The Whanganui River pattern includes popular 'types', including the Māori mother and child, alongside more surprising objects such as this naively rendered eel weir.*

exhibition, for Alice's uncle was an exhibitor,[22] as was a younger cousin, 15-year-old Mary Tyer, who swept the prize pool in the Juveniles Home Industry section with her skilful needle and leatherwork; the jurors declared her the 'very personification of "home industry"'.[23] Compositionally the Whanganui River pattern shares similarities with Burton's photographs, including the horizontal arrangement of figures and a lack of standard scenic framing devices.

A secondary influence on the pattern maker may have been Gottfried Lindauer's portraits of King Tāwhiao and other Māori, which also featured in the exhibition. The Whanganui River scene, like Lindauer's paintings, is peopled with Māori 'types', depicted in 'characteristic costume': the statuesque chief holding a taonga, a crouched figure and classic Māori mother and child.[24] Burton's Māori subjects, by contrast, wear European dress.

As art historian Rozsika Parker has observed, embroidery is all too often treated in terms of technical developments, rather than in terms of iconography, which sits in a social and historical context.[25] Placing the Whanganui River embroideries in a wider historical context not only throws received 'facts', such as dates, into question, but also sheds light on possible intent. When mapped against events of the day, a date between 1885 and 1891 seems more probable for Alice Clapham's embroidery for a number of reasons: the source material existed, public interest was high and there was a colonial sense of triumph over a region considered the 'final frontier', which was visualised in widely distributed photographs and paintings. Colonial Treasurer Sir Julius Vogel confidently expressed this sense of progress in his speech at the opening of the Industrial Exhibition in 1885, when he asserted that 'now all the Native difficulties had been surmounted', Māori could be safely viewed as 'a people who promised to assist with the reputation of the colony'.[26]

Within the context of the second half of the 1880s and the early 1890s, Mrs Murray could, through her choice of pattern, be seen, like Burton, to be instructing her pupils in 'the great and substantial progress made towards the pacification of the country'.[27] Armed with needle and thread, Alice and Maud were domesticating the Whanganui. As they stitched, they transformed the once unknown territory into a garden-like environment. Whanganui Māori were no longer subjects of fear, but subjects tamed – framed in native timber of kauri with a bird's-eye maple veneer and rewarewa, to be hung in the drawing room. When Maud placed a white feather in the hair of one of her chiefs, she may well have been aware that it was a symbol of peace. Knowingly or not, both girls were contributing to an emerging body of imagery intent on memorialising what was popularly believed to be a 'dying race', while at the same time celebrating the march of colonial progress.[28]

26
Te Tokotoko
Megan Pōtiki

Paikea figure on the tokotoko handle.

Photograph by Megan Pōtiki

An old tokotoko has long sat in the hallway in our family homestead at Ōtākou. To my knowledge, for the last three generations it has not been used in the manner for which it was originally created. This essay addresses, first, the tokotoko's past use as a kīnaki to whaikōrero and, second, my family's acquisition of the tokotoko which, according to our whānau, was gifted to my great-great-grandfather Rāniera Ellison (Erihana) through our tribal ties with Tainui and Te Ātiawa. Finally the essay discusses the tokotoko's recent history – for the past 20 years it has sat in our home, treated with trepidation as our family's knowledge of tikanga and te reo Māori dissipated.

The tokotoko is beautifully carved. It has a well-nourished, naked Paikea-type male figure lying flat, with his legs in the air to form a handle. The stick has two distinctive female faces further down, one with a moko on the lips and the other with a moko kauae. Next to them is a male figure with a full facial moko. All three faces have pāua-shell eyes. The body of the tokotoko is intricately carved with a three-dimensional curved shape. It is less than a metre in length, pointing to its use as a 'talking stick' rather than an aid to walking.

Poia Rewi observes that the tokotoko, although sometimes referred to as the common walking stick, is the most common hand-held prop during whaikōrero, or formal Māori oratory.[1] Tokotoko, though, were sometimes used as walking sticks to help physically support kaumātua. I recall my grandfather sitting on the paepae and leaning on the tokotoko for support. Judging from the size of many tokotoko, however, including ours, we should give greater emphasis to the other function Rewi identifies: 'symbolic, in that it is employed primarily for use during whaikōrero'.[2] At Ōtākou marae and the larger Kāi Tahu tribal area, though, it was not common, in recent history, to see the tokotoko used with whaikōrero. The only time I ever saw a tokotoko used on my marae was by my grandfather. After his death in 1993 my family totally abandoned the use of this tokotoko in Māori speechmaking and other oral traditions.

My grandfather's generation was the first not to speak te reo Māori and as a result knowledge of whaikōrero and the employment of objects like tokotoko was lost. Our tokotoko became a relic of the past, not to be meddled with because its role was no longer understood.

Rangi Ellison with the tokotoko at Ōtākou.

Author's Collection

LEFT: *The carved central detail of the tokotoko.*

Photograph by Megan Pōtiki

Tokotoko in whaikōrero had a variety of purposes: to act as a prop for a dramatic performance, to repel mākutu or black magic, to punctuate the speaker's remarks, to help him to stand, to imbue the orator with thoughts and ideas and spiritual support of his forebears, to signify rank and, as a weapon, to protect the speaker.[3] The function of a tokotoko undoubtedly varied across all tribal groups but on all occasions it was used to embellish the art of oratory.

Our tokotoko was acquired by my great-great-grandfather, Rāniera Ellison, the pioneering patriarch of the Ellison family of Ōtākou. Rāniera was born on 15 November 1839 at Korohiwa in Porirua, Wellington. His father was an English whaler named Tom Ellison and his Māori mother, Te Ikarāua, was of Taranaki lineage. Rāniera, the youngest of three children, was raised by his mother's people in the greater Wellington area after his father drowned in Tītahi Bay in 1840.

In 1861 Rāniera came south to Otago to search for gold. His initial efforts in Waitāhuna were unsuccessful, so he returned to Dunedin and sought work on the pilot boat operating at Taiaroa Heads. According to family accounts he was a powerful man: on one occasion he became a local hero when he saved eight crew members after the pilot boat capsized. In 1862 Rāniera and his dog returned to the goldfields at the Shotover River near Queenstown. Early one morning as Rāniera and his friend Hakaria swam across the swift river to the other side, his dog was swept downstream. Rāniera went to rescue the dog and as he pulled him out of the river found gold nuggets in the crevices in the rocks. By the end of that day he had gathered 300 ounces of gold, significant wealth that allowed Rāniera and his descendants considerable freedom to enjoy good education, housing and careers, as well as clout in politics, both Māori and Pākehā. Rāniera was later able to financially assist the rebuilding of Parihaka, one of his papa kāinga in Taranaki.

After his windfall, Rāniera returned to Ōtākou on the Otago Peninsula and entered into a strategically important marriage to Nāni Weller, the grandchild of Chief Te Matenga Taiaroa and of Hinewhareua, the sister of Chief Karetai. Rāniera and Nāni had 12 children, many of whom achieved highly in sport, professional careers and politics. The couple built a large homestead at Ōtākou and farmed land there and at Waikouaiti, as well as at Waikanae in the North Island. Rāniera, raised with a deep awareness of Māori issues, was profoundly committed to the social and political changes facing his people and was active in supporting both Kāi Tahu and Taranaki iwi in their confrontations with the Crown. Rāniera's activism is evident in his prolific writings, including many of the journals, mainly in Māori, that our family hold. These journals include detailed accounts of his conversations with the Parihaka prophets, Te Whiti and Tohu Kākahi, which, according to senior members of my family, most likely occurred during Rāniera's journeys back to the North Island.

Rāniera was a serious traveller, making trips to all parts of the North Island in support of the Parihaka kaupapa and also the pan-tribal Te Kotahitanga movement. Although Rāniera wrote about many of his political journeys in his diaries he did not reveal how

Far left: *Portrait of Rāniera Ellison (Erihana), the author's great-great-grandfather, who was gifted the tokotoko.*

Author's Collection. Photograph by Michael Hall

Left: *Portrait of Nāni Ellison (née Weller), wife of Rāniera.*

Author's Collection. Photograph by Michael Hall

he came to possess the tokotoko. It is clear, however, from the intricate carvings, that this tokotoko is of North Island origin. As noted earlier, the two female faces carved into the tokotoko have moko kauae, and there is no tradition of Kāi Tahu women with moko kauae, although historical accounts tell of women with full half-face moko.[4] The moko kauae represented on the tokotoko illustrate tā moko techniques consistent with those of the North Island.

Family tradition maintains that this tokotoko was given to my great-great-grandfather by King Tāwhiao. Along with other leaders from the South Island, Rāniera Erihana attended various Te Kotahitanga meetings,[5] so the acquisition may be related to his involvement in the Te Kotahitanga movement. Kāi Tahu, represented by political leaders such as Hōri Kerei Taiaroa and Pita Te Hōri, was also particularly involved in discussions with Tāwhiao leading up to the Kīngitanga making peace with the government in 1881. Importantly, Rāniera's wife Nāni was politically significant, not only directly through being related to the Kāi Tahu political leaders of the time, but through her own involvement in fighting for the Kāi Tahu claim, the 150-year legacy left to her generation and those who followed.

Kāi Tahu also had other noteworthy interactions with the Kīngitanga and the Tainui tribe. For example, Pita Te Hōri, a Kāi Tahu leader from Kaiapoi,[6] had lived in the Waikato for a time during the 1830s, and in 1871 again made his way north to Waikato with other Kāi Tahu to meet with King Tāwhaio. While there, the group discussed the various political peace movements, and it is highly likely that Rāniera, who had a close political relationship with these Kāi Tahu men, was part of these coversations.[7] Rāniera's connection with Tāwhiao is further cemented through his whakapapa connections to Kāwhia and Tainui, laid out in his journals.

Rāniera's relationship with Kīng Tāwhiao also flows out of his close association with Parihaka leaders Tohu Kākahi and Te Whiti whom, according to his many diary accounts, he met regularly throughout their time of imprisonment. He subsequently gave a great deal of support to the Taranaki prisoners in Dunedin.

It is through these various relationships that Rāniera made a connection with King Tāwhiao, and although our whānau cannot be sure of the details of the actual acquisition, the tokotoko remains as an embodiment of Rāniera's passionate political involvement with Taranaki, Kāi Tahu and Waikato. Furthermore the tokotoko is a symbol of the political and genealogical alliances Rāniera made and which continue to this day.

When Rāniera died the tokotoko was passed on to Rāniera's son, Te Iwi Herehere Erihana, also known as Davy Ellison. He lived in the Ellison family homestead with his wife Ōriwia Karetai and their six children. As a fluent native speaker and noted orator, Davy used this tokotoko in his speeches. It was then passed on to his son, my grandfather, George Grey Tūkitaharangi Weller Ellison, who used it when sitting at the paepae and in his speeches. When George returned from serving in the Māori Battalion during World War II he reluctantly took on a leadership position within the tribe. His misgivings were the result of his not speaking Māori: nevertheless he used the tokotoko as a prop to stress words and meaning in his speeches. Undoubtedly his memory of his forebears informed his attempts to imitate their use of tokotoko and oratory. I grew up on the family farm and had a close relationship with my grandfather. He was a very guarded man, and in his final years I frustrated him by insisting on asking far too many questions. He ultimately responded as if I would never understand his world, te ao kōhatu, the world past.

The recent story of this tokotoko is quite dark. George decided, when I was quite young, to deposit it in the Otago Museum for safekeeping. One night he had a dream about his own head being severed and woke in quite a distressed state. He went in to the museum, demanding to see the tokotoko, and was taken to a back room where it was discovered that a number of boxes had been laid on top of it and the head of the tokotoko had been broken. He took it home, repaired it and told the family that it should never leave the house. When he died a few years later, Rangi, George's younger brother, arrived from Auckland and after the tangihanga asked to have the tokotoko. As he was now the tuakana, the eldest son, it was difficult to refuse him and he took it away to Auckland. A year later we learned that Rangi had died of a heart attack. My father flew to Auckland to his tangihanga and arrived at the family home to a cold reception. His aunt thrust the tokotoko on him, stating that she never wanted to see it again.

The tokotoko now remains in the family homestead in the place it occupied when I was young. I believe it needs a new lease of life and should be used in tandem with the words, idiom and metaphor it understands and moves to. The few proficient speakers we have in our whānau, including my father, are ultimately responsible for reinvigorating a treasure like this beautiful tokotoko, allowing it to serve the purpose that it was given when its maker painstakingly carved each genealogical line and story into it.

Carved details of the tokotoko.

Photographs by Megan Pōtiki

27

A Church Lectern Made by a Celestial of Industry and Ingenuity

Steve Austin

The eagle lectern in position for the reading, with Bible and ribbons.

Courtesy of St Luke's Church, Spring Creek. Photograph by Daniel List

Sometimes a humble context can harbour an object of great interest. The rural church at St Luke's, at Spring Creek on the outskirts of Blenheim in Marlborough, contains a carved wooden eagle lectern with a unique and fascinating story. Created by the Chinese carver William Ah Gee in 1890, for the Church of the Nativity in central Blenheim, the lectern was moved out to the smaller St Luke's around 1906, when an impressive new bronze eagle lectern was given to the Church of the Nativity.

Ah Gee's lectern is modest in scale. The tips of the eagle's outstretched wings are just 47 centimetres from each other. From the edge of the beak to the end of the exquisitely carved tail feathers is a distance of only 56 centimetres. The base of the lectern at is 61 centimetres square. We do not have to look long at this eagle, however, to realise that the carving is of an extraordinary standard.

Eagle lecterns, common in Anglican churches, date from the time of the earliest Christian monasteries, when the first large scrolls and heavy books needed to be supported while open. One of the most notable early eagle lecterns, where the Bible would rest on outstretched wings, was commissioned in the mid-twelfth century by Abbot Suger of St-Denis, near Paris. His example was made of bronze, and inlaid with ivory. Eagle lecterns in Britain are recorded from the thirteenth and fourteenth centuries, and these inspired the typical Gothic Revival examples of the late nineteenth century: Ah Gee's lectern follows this style. Then, as now, the lectern was placed to one side of the chancel between the priest or the lay reader and the rest of the congregation.

A rich symbolism is attached to the eagle. Long regarded as the supreme ruler of the air and the messenger of deities, it was associated with Zeus, Jupiter and Odin. The ancient Jewish symbolism of the golden eagle (*Aquila chrysaetos homeyeri*) associated it with the power of God and his shelter of the Jews in exile, and this significance predominates in the Old Testament: 'You have seen what I did to the Egyptians, and how I bore you on eagle's wings, and brought you unto myself' (Exodus 19:4) and 'But they that wait upon the Lord shall renew their strength; they shall mount up with wings as eagles; they shall run, and not be weary; and they shall walk, and not faint' (Isaiah 40:31).

In New Testament iconography the eagle connotes a variety of ideas but is specifically linked to St John the Evangelist. The bird was, and indeed still is, understood by Anglicans as the bearer of tidings, representing the spread of the Christian gospels around the globe.[1] Such associations may well have resonated for parishioners in colonial Blenheim at the turn of the nineteenth century.

Ah Gee was an accomplished craftsman with a well-established local reputation; the eagle lectern in St Luke's is just one example of his varied output. He worked in a number of styles, across many forms, and in stone, plaster and wood. The pulpit, sanctuary chair and kneeling stool at St Mary's Catholic Church in Blenheim were made of tōtara and elaborately decorated by Ah Gee.[2] For St Mary's he also designed and made an Oamaru stone font in 1880, and he created similar fonts for the Anglican churches of Blenheim (Church of the Nativity) and Picton, commissioned by the head of the local police, Inspector Smith.

Ah Gee was famous for his church furniture, but also for household furniture, fire surrounds, gravestones, picture frames and low relief scenes, such as that of Mt Taranaki, c. 1905, in the collection of the Museum of New Zealand Te Papa Tongarewa. He also made figures for the façade of the Government Buildings in Blenheim, a fragment of which is in the collection of Marlborough Museum. None of Ah Gee's works are signed, so it is very likely an acknowledgement of the high regard for his work that the items now known to have been made by him have had their provenance recorded and remembered.

Three-quarter view of the eagle.

Courtesy of St Luke's Church, Spring Creek. Photograph by Daniel List

His reputation for delivering exactly what was ordered was undoubtedly enhanced by the kind of report that heralded the completion of our lectern. The *Church Messenger* reported:

> Some of Mr Grace's friends in England sent contributions, which have found expression in a carved wood eagle lectern, carved by a Chinaman of Blenheim. It is a bold bird, its anatomy is decidedly heraldic, and it is the second of its kind by the same cunning hand. If any other church requires an eagle, the Bishop will be ready to send to the sculptor a good pattern, for the Chinaman is an accurate follower of his model, as all the subjects of the 'Celestial Empire' are![3]

The report reveals something of the circumstances, and reception, of the lectern itself, but also how the Chinese were viewed by British setters at this time.

William Ah Gee, like the vast majority of Chinese who came to New Zealand in the nineteenth century, was originally from Guanggong, China. He was one of the first six or so Chinese people to have settled in New Zealand, bought property, married a British woman and had children. After arriving in Wellington in 1868, he applied for, and received, naturalisation in 1870. He married Jane Melbourne the following year.[4] A 1910 *Evening Post* article about Haining Street in Wellington recalled Ah Gee as a notable individual:

> At the time when Europeans began to live in Haining-street there were only about two Chinese in Wellington. They had their abode in Manners-street … and earned their rice at cabinet making. One of them, known as Ha Gee, was a clever carver, and his skilful hands made him widely known in the settlement. In the course of time Ha Gee went to the Hutt, and lived in a little house just over the river. His devotion to art spurred him to ornament the walls with carvings in Chinese designs, and these memorials of his residence are still visible … Many years ago his picturesque life nearly came to an abrupt close. Another Chinese quarrelled with him, and stabbed him deeply just above the heart, but Ha Gee, as time proved, made a good recovery.[5]

Sometime in the 1870s Ah Gee moved to Blenheim, where he started advertising for work in 1877 as an ornamental carver and cabinet maker, located at the premises of Mr E. Bythell, Builder &c., near Maxwell Bridge.[6] The supplier of the wood for the eagle lectern was almost certainly Elijah Bythell himself. Mayor of Blenheim in 1892–93, Bythell was a successful builder and wood merchant, and accounts of his business show that Ah Gee was one of his clients. Bythell and Ah Gee were old acquaintances, having first met on the goldfields of Ballarat, in Victoria, Australia, where Ah Gee had made furniture for joss houses (or miu – places for making offerings to ancestors) in the community of Chinese men. Elijah Bythell and Ah Gee formed a family connection when Bythell married Jane Gee's sister Jessie in 1877; subsequently they had a close family and business relationship.

This cross-cultural family connection was a happy one, but wider public attitudes were not so tolerant by the end of the nineteenth century. The end of slavery meant the increasing global export of labour from

China to the rest of the world. Immigration policies were the tool to control desirable population growth. Although the 1871 Select Committee on Chinese Immigration, which Ah Gee had attended, had concluded that there was no reason to exclude or tax the Chinese, and that they were industrious, frugal and orderly,[7] the political development of institutionalised racism promoted by Seddon meant that the position of Chinese changed seriously for the worse by the 1880s, and deteriorated further by the early 1900s.[8] A poll tax for Chinese was introduced with the Chinese Immigrants Act of 1881. Initially set at £10 per head, by 1896 the poll tax had risen to £100. Although Chinese paid their taxes, they were not always eligible for the pension. Old age for early Chinese settlers was extremely difficult even with considerable extended family support.

From the very outset Ah Gee was respected and publicly praised for the quality of his work, but with growing concern over the numbers of Chinese coming to New Zealand, he was not immune from extreme racist action. In 1888 an arson attack on his Blenheim workshop destroyed the work he was doing at the time and all his tools, but he continued operating from his home. Members of the community, including 'Messrs. Fowler, Howard, Bythell, and Sowman', gave him tools.[9] He almost certainly used these donated tools, still in the possession of his descendants, to make the lectern.

Ah Gee returned to work in Wellington some time in the mid-1890s. A 1906 newspaper story situates him in the context of public hostility towards Chinese immigration, and particularly local fears that work would be 'lost' to the new arrivals:

> The other day a story went round that John Chinaman had cut into the furniture trade in Wellington, and would monopolise it and turn it as yellow as the furniture trade in Sydney, or the fruit trade in our own city … But so far as can be discovered, the only approach to a Chinese furniture-maker in this city is one ancient Celestial who does carving, and who is a specialist, and who cannot be said to interfere to any profound extent with the established trade of white workers.[10]

The 1910 *Evening Post* story referred to earlier, however, casts him in a no doubt more acceptable light, characterising him as 'the patriarch of the Chinese clan, a wizard of ninety'.[11] William Ah Gee's carved lectern signals the optimism and the challenges of colonial enterprise. The labour and skills embodied by the carving demonstrate the diversity of connections – between the southeast coast of China, the Australian goldfields and New Zealand towns, and between Chinese and European settler communities – woven into the larger network of British colonialism.

Tools used by Ah Gee. These are now in the collection of his grandson, Max Gee.

Photograph by the author

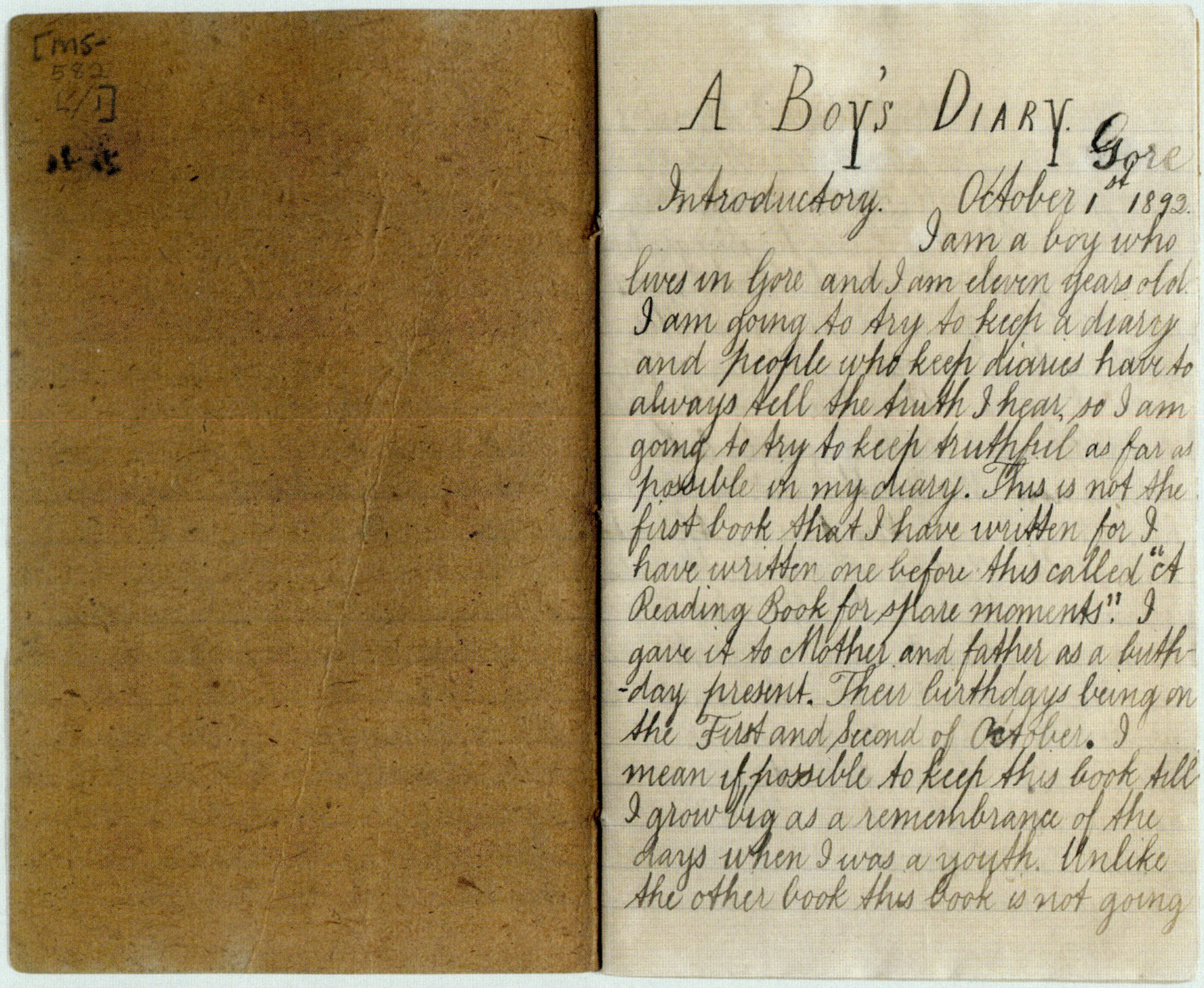

A Boy's Diary. Gore

Introductory. October 1st 1892.

I am a boy who lives in Gore and I am eleven years old. I am going to try to keep a diary and people who keep diaries have to always tell the truth I hear, so I am going to try to keep truthful as far as possible in my diary. This is not the first book that I have written for I have written one before this called "A Reading Book for spare moments". I gave it to Mother and father as a birth-day present. Their birthdays being on the First and Second of October. I mean if possible to keep this book till I grow big as a remembrance of the days when I was a youth. Unlike the other book this book is not going

The opening page of Beattie's first boyhood diary.

James Herries Beattie Papers, MS-582/L/1, Hocken Collections, Uare Taoka o Hākena, University of Otago. Photograph by Michael Hall

28
The Boyhood Diary of Herries Beattie
Tony Ballantyne

James Herries Beattie (1881–1972) was an indefatigable collector of material relating to the natural and human history of southern New Zealand. Raised in Gore, Beattie led a life framed by books: he worked as a clerk, reporter, librarian and bookseller, and was a voracious reader and writer. He produced over 50 books and pamphlets on the 'pioneer' colonists of the south, its Māori history, place names and flora and fauna – topics he wrote about extensively in local newspapers. He was also an enthusiastic collector of natural history specimens, particularly relating to birds and shellfish.

Within the large Beattie archive in the Hocken Collections is an object that illuminates his emergence as a collector and the family values that influenced his collecting practice and his intellectual sensibility. The earliest extant piece of Beattie's writing, it is the first of four childhood diaries that he kept intermittently until 1895. Beginning on 1 October 1892, it opens:

> I am a boy who lives in Gore and I am eleven years old. I am going to try to keep a diary and people who keep diaries have to always tell the truth I hear, so I am going to try to keep truthful as far as possible in my diary. This is not the first book that I have written for I have written one before this called 'A Reading Book for spare moments'. I gave it to Mother and Father as a birthday present. Their birthdays being on the First and Second of October. I mean if possible to keep this book till I grow big as a remembrance of the days when I was a youth. Unlike the other book this book is not going to contain poetry. Now I think I will tell you about the History of the family ...[1]

The grave of four of Herries Beattie's older siblings, three of whom who died within a month of each other in 1882, in the West Taieri Cemetery, Outram. Beattie's maternal uncle farmed at Maungatua and the Beattie family maintained strong ties to these Taieri kin.

Photograph by the author

This paragraph immediately establishes several concerns that run through Beattie's voluminous writings: family, the value of reading and writing and a deep investment in history. Later in life Beattie suggested that J.A. Forbes, printer, stationer, and president of the Gore Young Men's Temperance Mutual Improvement Society, prompted his interest in history and collecting. The diary, however, suggests that Beattie's interest in history was well established at the age of 11. This first entry records the outlines of both his father's and mother's history: their origins in Scotland, migration to Otago, work (in his father's case), their marriage, early family life in Invercargill and move to Gore.

It ends by describing Herries' four siblings, noting that four other children had died. These deaths – three of which occurred in the space of three weeks

Postcard showing a view of the Hokonui Hills from the Gore Cemetery, c. 1890s. This cemetery was established in 1878 in Crewe Street, close to the Beattie family home.

Courtesy of the Hokonui Heritage Research Centre and Neil Sleeman

in 1882 when Herries was 10 months old – had a traumatic effect on the family. In their shadow, Herries' boyhood writings express deep anxiety about illness, especially during the 1893 measles epidemic, and worry about his own strength and masculinity. They intermittently exhibit a preoccupation with death.

That is clear in his first diary. The entry for 8 October notes that he wandered into the Gore cemetery on the way to his cousin's house: 'I went in to the cemetery and had a look at the tombs. There were some very pretty ones. I noticed that the grave-yard was fast filling up with tombs.' In a way this observation blends Beattie's concern with death with the civic pride he took in Gore: a rapidly filling cemetery also surely signalled the growth of the town known by some at least as the 'Chicago of the South'.[2]

The diaries have a kind of inwardness entirely unlike anything in his adult writing. From the 1940s on Beattie produced some summative pieces reflecting on his life, but these dwell on the development of Gore and key public events; his own interior emotional terrain is seldom laid bare. Much of his published writing was necessarily about the negation of his authority – he was the 'Collector' – the authority of his work rested on the 'authority' of his informants. This, I think, helps to explain another distinctive feature of the diary: it is an unusually clean text for Beattie, with no annotations, explanatory notes, corrections or amendments. The older Beattie glossed much of his earlier work, but these diaries remained untouched.

Herries' boyhood journals show that reading and writing were important vehicles for building family bonds, a thread that runs through the entire collection of his papers. Together with fruit like pineapples and dates, books were the typical family gift at Christmas and birthdays. They not only tied siblings and parents and children together, but were also a palpable connection to family origins. A treasured collection of the books of Beattie's mother, Mary Roden Thomson, was kept in the family home. Many were prizes she had received before migrating to Otago from Kirkpatrick Durham, in Galloway and Dumfriess, in 1862. But others were gifts, mostly improving religious books from female friends as well as the sentimental *The Wide, Wide World* (1860) by Elizabeth Wetherall (pen name of the popular American evangelical novelist Susan Warner). The inscription in this volume, 'To Mary Thomson from her devoted admirer Neil McFiee', suggests that books could carry significant emotional freight across time and space. This small collection also points to the family's self-conscious investment in a Scottish heritage, including a collection of the poems of 'Ossian' and Henry White's much-reprinted *History of Scotland* (1857).

More broadly, the diary gives a very strong sense of Herries' broad range of boyhood pursuits in Gore: his immersion in the Congregationalist Church and the essentially Presbyterian culture of his family, bird-nesting (really the genesis of his object collecting), skating, playing rugby, cricket, gathering berries, rabbiting, fishing, floundering, schoolyard marbles games and a love of reading, especially the local newspapers and the works of James Fenimore Cooper. Although Beattie's taste for adventure stories suggests a liking for frontier life and 'native culture', his newspaper reading reveals a deep interest in both

local and international events. This involvement in the world through reading is explained in the second volume of the diary, where Herries writes that he likes newspapers because they tell him what 'what is going on in public'; and in the third volume he adds that after reading the papers boys 'come to school & tell the news to their mates'. These discussions informed a robust civic culture: debating clubs, mutual improvement societies, Sunday school, sermons, church meetings, public lectures, magic lantern shows, Caledonian sports, A & P shows, circuses, sports matches and visits to the athenaeum (including to a display of objects and 'curiosities' from Fiji and the 'South Sea Islands').

Although this diary is extraordinary in that we have very few extended pieces of such writing by children from nineteenth-century New Zealand, as an object it is not at all unusual, representing the kind of mundane stationery central to everyday colonial life. Of standard size, 16.5 by 10 centimetres – in bibliographic terms, octodecimo – it has a heavy brown cardboard cover with glossy burgundy coating and pages of slightly coarse ruled newsprint. Beattie made his entries in black ink with a pen, with the exception of the third diary, where all the dates are in a vivid red.

The book has 28 leaves, but may originally have been a larger volume of perhaps 36. This suggests the repurposing of a partly used notebook, with some pages removed. This is a common feature of all four volumes of the journals. The second volume, a purple memo book with 15 leaves, exhibits clear evidence of pages being torn out. Although the cover suggests this second volume was a more specialised and expensive piece of stationery, it, too, was in fact cheap – the vertical pink lines inside are misprinted and blurred. The third volume, again of coarse paper with light grey card covers wrapped in light purple fabric, has clearly had pages removed. It is a larger volume of 44 leaves but the final five are taken up with business notes, specifically an inventory of spices and baking ingredients – presumably from Thomson & Beattie Ltd, the drapers and general merchants run by Herries' father.

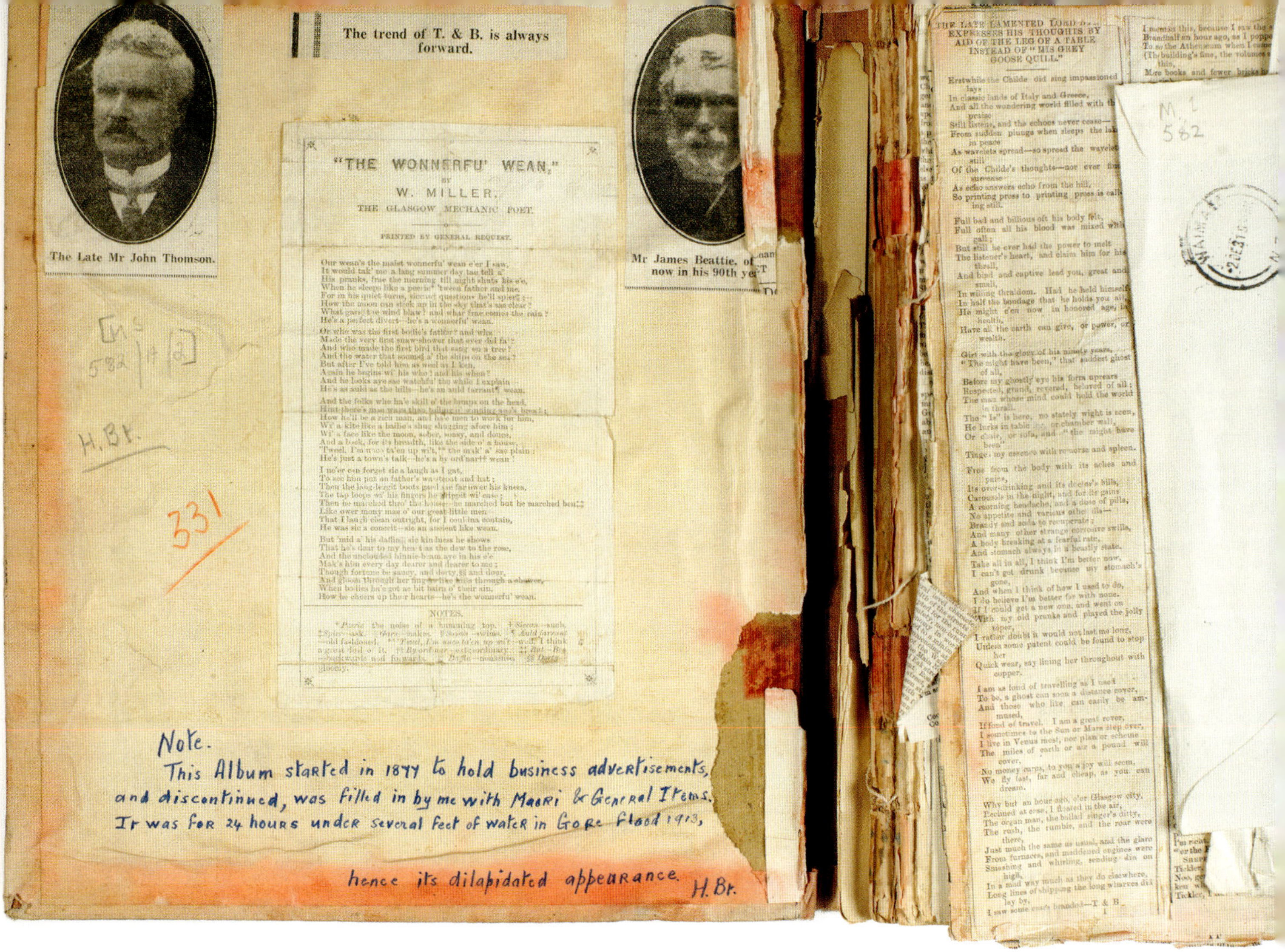

This book of newspaper clippings initially began life as a volume in which Herries' father, James Beattie, used to keep commercial advertisements for his successful drapery business. As with many volumes in the Beattie collection, Herries repurposed it, in this case as a volume of newspaper clippings which he particularly used for his writings on Māori history. *James Herries Beattie Papers, MS-582/A/2, Hocken Collections, Uare Taoka o Hākena, University of Otago. Photograph by Michael Hall*

These diaries suggest that thrift was important to the Beattie family, and remind us that paper and stationery remained comparatively expensive in the colony: from newspapers to ledger books, paper was frequently repurposed, recycled and reused.[3] Even in the 1890s most colonial writing paper was imported. Although Gore was close to the Mataura paper mill, that operation mainly produced rough brown paper and wrapping paper.

Thus the notebooks themselves are anonymous objects – even the memo book lacks any clear indication of where it was produced. In all cases, the paper is machine-made newsprint lacking any watermarks, and belongs to the broad family of cheap industrially produced paper imported into New Zealand for everyday use. In the Beattie collection some exercise books bear the imprint of the local stationer, J.D. Forbes, but again these seem to be imported notebooks with a locally printed cover affixed. This paper and these notebooks sit solidly in the middle range of what was circulating within the colony: they were not fine writing paper but nor were they the torn notepaper or even butter paper, which the itinerant labourer James Cox used to keep his diary.[4]

The repurposing suggests something significant about colonial intellectual history and cultural production more generally: the need to 'make do', which was found even in colonial families such as the Beatties of Gore, who liked to demonstrate their wealth and status through nice things, including their library. In many aspects of their lives they repurposed, reused, recycled, upcycled and downcycled.[5] Several leading scholars of colonial Africa, including Isabel Hofmeyr, have suggested that colonial intellectual activity often had an improvised, homespun quality,[6] which in part reflected the material constraints and cultural contradictions of the period. I think this is a productive line of thought worth exploring in New Zealand. It certainly fits well with Beattie's boyhood journals, and illuminates his collecting and writing as an adult. He was no great theorist but he had deep knowledge of the multiple narratives that recorded the history of the south and its peoples; this knowledge was produced by conversations in numerous locations, the exchange of letters with many correspondents and a voluminous collection of clippings books. His writing was largely skilful collation and juxtaposition: he was a cutter and paster of the highest order. If we wish to understand the birth of one of the richest collections of colonial objects found in these islands, this diary is a key place to start.

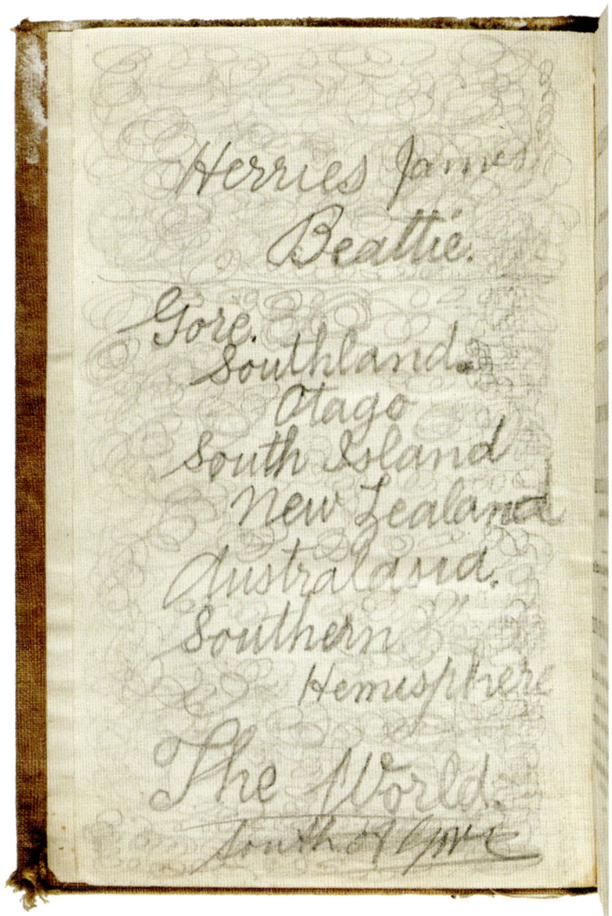

Herries Beattie's spelling textbook. As a mature collector and writer Beattie was an enthusiastic and careful annotator of newspaper articles, his clipping volumes and his own manuscripts. Here as a youth we see him, like many subsequent schoolchildren, reciting a sequence of increasingly broad spatial locations to locate himself geographically and culturally, a list which he finally subverts by ending his list with a return to 'south of Gore'.

Special Collections, University of Otago. Photograph by Michael Hall

29
Billies in Colonial Australia and New Zealand
Helen Leach

It was the tenth second-hand shop in Dunedin where, in 2012, I had enquired, 'Do you have any old billies?', and the first where I was successful. Although old billies proved scarce, the shopkeepers knew exactly what I was seeking. In Australia a similar enquiry would produce a similar outcome, but not in Britain. The *Oxford English Dictionary* lists several glosses for 'billy' – fellow or mate in Scottish and northern dialects in the eighteenth and early nineteenth centuries, club or truncheon, male goat, a slubbing machine (for creating unevenness in yarn) and, under the unequivocal heading '*Austral.* and *N.Z.*', 'A cylindrical container, usu. of tin or enamel ware, with a close-fitting lid and a wire handle, used for making tea and for cooking over fires in the open, and for carrying food or liquid.'[1] The accompanying quotations include both Australian and New Zealand sources from the nineteenth and twentieth centuries. Can there be any doubt, then, that the billy is a colonial object?

Only the widespread application of the name to this particular type of artefact is colonial, not the artefact class (a tin pot) and not the name (applied to a pot). The name itself could be derived from the word 'billy-pot' recorded in the ballad 'Willie Doo' in northern Scots dialect in 1828.[2] Alternatively it could be derived from an originally French term bouilli, meaning boiled, applied to canned boiled beef and soup throughout the nineteenth century. As for the cylindrical pot that colonials called a billy, it had a long prior existence as a tin pot.

Stamped into the lid handle of my tin billy is the numeral one. For over a century, billies have been sold in a range of sizes according to their volume. This is a one-quart billy, the smallest in most ranges.[3] There is no obvious manufacturer's stamp, but a previous owner has scratched his or her name on both lid and side. I suspect this billy was bought to take on a school camp. As yet I have no clues as to its age – it may even be post-colonial! It looks older than my aluminium billy, which dates from the 1950s,[4] but that may be because it is made from prefabricated tin plate with soldered seams, and such tinware has a longer history of use than aluminium ware. Most kitchen items that are made of aluminium and plastic in the twentieth and twenty-first centuries were made of tinware in the preceding two centuries.[5]

My No. 1 billy is basically a tin pot with a swinging wire handle that fits it for use suspended from a hook over a fire. A swinging handle is a disadvantage for

One-quart capacity tin billy purchased second hand in Dunedin, 2012.

Author's Collection. Photograph by Michael Hall

a pot that sits on a hot plate: the handle lies too close to the heat source and the side of the pot. But this type of handle is an advantage when there is no available stove, and also when the pot has to be hung from a pack, or carried over rough ground, or by a child. A billy is both a portable cooking pot and a container for liquids. You could, of course, make a portable pot from cast or wrought iron, or from copper, but tin pots weigh less than iron pots and are much cheaper than copper. Although cheapness and lightness in a pot were important considerations for a swagman, shepherd or prospector, in towns in the late eighteenth century the need to substitute a tin pot for a silver tea-kettle meant a drastic fall in social standing.[6]

Under the name tin pot, these kitchen objects have a long history in Europe. Tinware goes back to medieval Bohemia and subsequently Germany in the seventeenth century. Britain began tin plate manufacturing on a commercial scale in 1728. Kettles and pots were stamped out of the tinned sheets, along with many other types of tinware. Tin plate was non-toxic and resistant to corrosion so it became a useful material from which to make storage containers for food, and eventually the foundation of the food canning industry. We know that tin cooking pots accompanied late-eighteenth-century visitors to New South Wales, for one of them, Watkin Tench, described how, in the winter of 1791, drops of water froze on a tin pot beside the camp fire.[7] Australian newspapers carried advertisements for tinware from the early nineteenth century. Teapots made from heavy-grade double block-tin were the subject of advertisements in 1826,[8] but many merchants simply stated that they had too much tinware to itemise. For the first half of the nineteenth century, tinware was imported to Australia from Britain. Then in 1847 Sizar Elliott began to can surplus meat in Sydney, using tin plate to make the cans, and the following year his products crossed the Tasman to Wellington.[9] This documentation of meat canning in Australia is important evidence for local manufacture of tinware containers and the potential for the production of large quantities of tin pots when the Australian gold rushes began in 1851.

As a possible source of the name billy to describe the tin pots, canned boiled meat known as bouilli had a long history on both sides of the Tasman. Sydney residents would have been familiar with advertisements for canned 'Soup and Bouilli' from 1833, if not earlier. In New Zealand, a ship's cargo put up for auction in 1841 included '90 cans soup and bouilli'.[10]

The first Australian mention of a tin pot called a billy is recorded from 1849. In *The Australian National Dictionary*, W.S. Ransom quotes a passage from George Blakiston Wilkinson's *The Working Man's Handbook to South Australia*: 'Singing, near the wooden fire, is what is called the billy, or tea kettle.'[11] This entry suggests the source of the name was South Australia, just before the gold rushes of 1851. On checking the full text, I found that this billy heated water inside huts used by shepherds and hutkeepers in the course of their evening meal.[12] The fireplace where Wilkinson saw the billy in use may have been in the outback but it was not outside.

London-born John Rochfort, who would later become a well-known surveyor in New Zealand,

In the early twentieth century billies remained in use in back country settings, such as in this Department of Lands and Survey camp, photographed by Hubert Girdlestone between 1907 and 1909.

Ref: PA1-q-915-10-1, Alexander Turnbull Library, Wellington, New Zealand

visited the Victorian goldfields in 1852 as a 20-year-old. In his *Adventures of a Surveyor in New Zealand and the Australian Gold Diggings* (1853), he described how he and his mates found enough gold at Ballarat to buy some necessary equipment. This included a billy to 'make our tea in'. In parentheses he explained that this was 'a tin pot for boiling tea, coffee, meat, or anything you may have luck to get'.[13] Clearly Rochfort had not encountered this name for a tin pot before his visit to Ballarat, and had not heard it in New Zealand. Wilkinson was also unfamiliar with the name when he recorded it, and his book was published before the beginning of the gold rush, which would create a large market for tin billies. We cannot, however, attribute the initial naming to prospectors or miners, be they of Scottish origin or users of canned bouilli. Tin pots were well suited to the prospectors' living conditions and mobility, so it is not surprising that advertisements began to include them with prospectors' equipment.[14] By 1855 Melbourne merchant H. Leon had adopted the name 'Tin billys' for his tin pots and this practice soon spread.[15]

The first appearance of the name billy in New Zealand is dated to 1858, when surveyor John Turnbull Thomson published an account of his reconnaissance surveys south of Dunedin in February 1857. 'As we have gradually lost plates, knives, and forks,' he wrote, 'we are now existing in the manner of savages, boiling our flesh or fowl in our tea-can (called a *billy*), kneading our dough in waterproof cloaks, and baking our bread in the embers of our camp-fire.'[16] It is clear that the word billy was in use both in Australia and New Zealand before their respective gold rushes began in 1851 and 1861, but the influx of Australian miners to New Zealand's goldfields in the 1860s undoubtedly aided its spread. The *Otago Daily Times* carried three advertisements in December 1861 that listed 'Billeys' or 'Billies' together with pannikins and shovels.[17] References to tin billies, boiling the billy and drinking billy tea are numerous in Australia from the late 1850s, and in New Zealand from the 1860s. In Banjo Paterson's 1895 ballad 'Waltzing Matilda', the jolly swagger waited till his billy boiled, and this unofficial anthem made the billy an icon of

RECIPE NAME	KEY INGREDIENTS	1ST KNOWN NZ RECIPE	1ST KNOWN AUS RECIPE
Billy Cake [1]	1c butter, 2c sugar, 3c flour, 4 eggs, cream of tartar, baking soda,1c milk [1, 2, 3, 4 Cake]	1891	1913
Billy Bread	wheatmeal + white flour, golden syrup or treacle, baking powder, milk, small amount of fat	August 1916	November 1916
Billy Loaf	similar to Billy Bread	1920	[1924]
Billy Sponge or Billy Cake [2]	4 eggs, ½ lb sugar, ¼ lb flour [a true sponge]	November 1915	1930

Australians' love of the outdoors that persists into the twenty-first century. The billy stands for freedom, adventure and exploration. New Zealand's adoption of the term appears to be confirmed now that an 1839 New Zealand quotation from whaler James Heberley has been redated to 1878.[18]

By the start of the twentieth century, billies were serving new roles in cities and towns. Until milk was pasteurised and sold in bottles, lidded billies kept it covered in transit from the dairy, on doorsteps wherever home deliveries occurred and in safes or larders. In 1897 residents of Perth could buy 'Tea or Milk Billies' in sizes from one pint to 1½ gallons.[19] Milk billies were still in use in Australia in the 1950s. In New Zealand in 1913 a Christchurch firm advertised a 'new hygienic milk billy' that 'strains the milk, keeps out the dust, and yet admits fresh air'.[20] Although milk bottles began to replace billies in our main cities from the early 1920s,[21] billies remained in use in country towns until the 1950s.

Although the naming of the billy had occurred in Australia by 1849, New Zealand led rather than followed in one other aspect of the tin billy's colonial history – the practice of baking loaves and cakes in a billy with the lid on. From the late nineteenth century this use amounted to a domestication of the outdoor billy because the baking took place in the kitchen range. There are three different types of recipe and four different recipe names (see table).

Whoever first thought up the idea of using a billy as a cake baking tin did not have to develop a new recipe. The first recipe, for a billy cake, published in 1891,[22] was a classic American plain cake, sometimes referred to as a cup cake because it used cup measures. During the later nineteenth century cooks came to value light sponge cakes ahead of heavier plain cakes. In late 1915 a billy sponge cake recipe was published that required 20 minutes' vigorous beating of eggs and sugar, then the folding in of a small quantity of flour.[23] No additional raising agent was required. This recipe was reprinted in New Zealand cookbooks into the second half of the twentieth century, but is less common in Australia.

Within a year of the billy sponge's appearance, a healthy and more economical billy bread recipe was in circulation, also referred to as a billy loaf. Commonly without eggs and containing only a small portion of fat (butter, dripping or cream), it was sweetened with golden syrup or treacle and moistened with milk. Australians made this same billy bread in the same year and it would be foolish to speculate on its country of origin.

Throughout World War I a common destination for billy cakes, sponges and loaves was the fundraising cart or table run by local Red Cross women's committees.[24] After the war, A & P and winter shows included billy-baked items in their competition schedules well into the 1930s.[25]Although the jolly swagman would have appreciated any of these billy loaves or cakes, it would not have been possible for him to bake them in his billy over an open fire: a heavy camp oven might be more suitable. And the maker of a light billy sponge

Left: *Aluminium 'Hard Wear' billy, made in New Zealand c. 1950s.*

Author's Collection. Photograph by Michael Hall

Below: *A boy scout boiling his billy featured on this 1953 New Zealand health stamp (kindly provided by Terence Dennis).*

Photograph by the author

would not have been keen to cook it in the blackened, tea-stained billy used by a swagman. It could be argued that at the end of the nineteenth century the colonial billy of outback and bush evolved a feminine offshoot first through its use as a container for milk, and then as a cake tin for a sponge or loaf. Trampers and backcountry workers preserved the billy's outdoor associations in the twentieth century.

Scouts and Girl Guides helped the billy to become internationally recognised. Scouting books confirm that it was adopted for camp cookery from the movement's beginnings, and not just in Australia and New Zealand. Scouting founder Robert Baden-Powell wrote in his 1908 manual, 'For boiling water a scout would usually have his tin "billy", and in that he can boil vegetables or stew his meat.'[26] This material confirms that the world beyond Australia and New Zealand perceived the billy as a colonial object. Philip Carrington, a Scoutmaster in New Zealand before his departure for Britain in 1914, wrote a manual entitled *The Boy Scouts' Camp Book*, in which he said, 'If you find any difficulty in getting the round colonial "billy" of tin, an effective substitute in the larger size is an oval "fish kettle".'[27] For Scouts and Guides, the billy was transformed from a colonial object into an international aid to self-sufficiency and preparedness outdoors.[28]

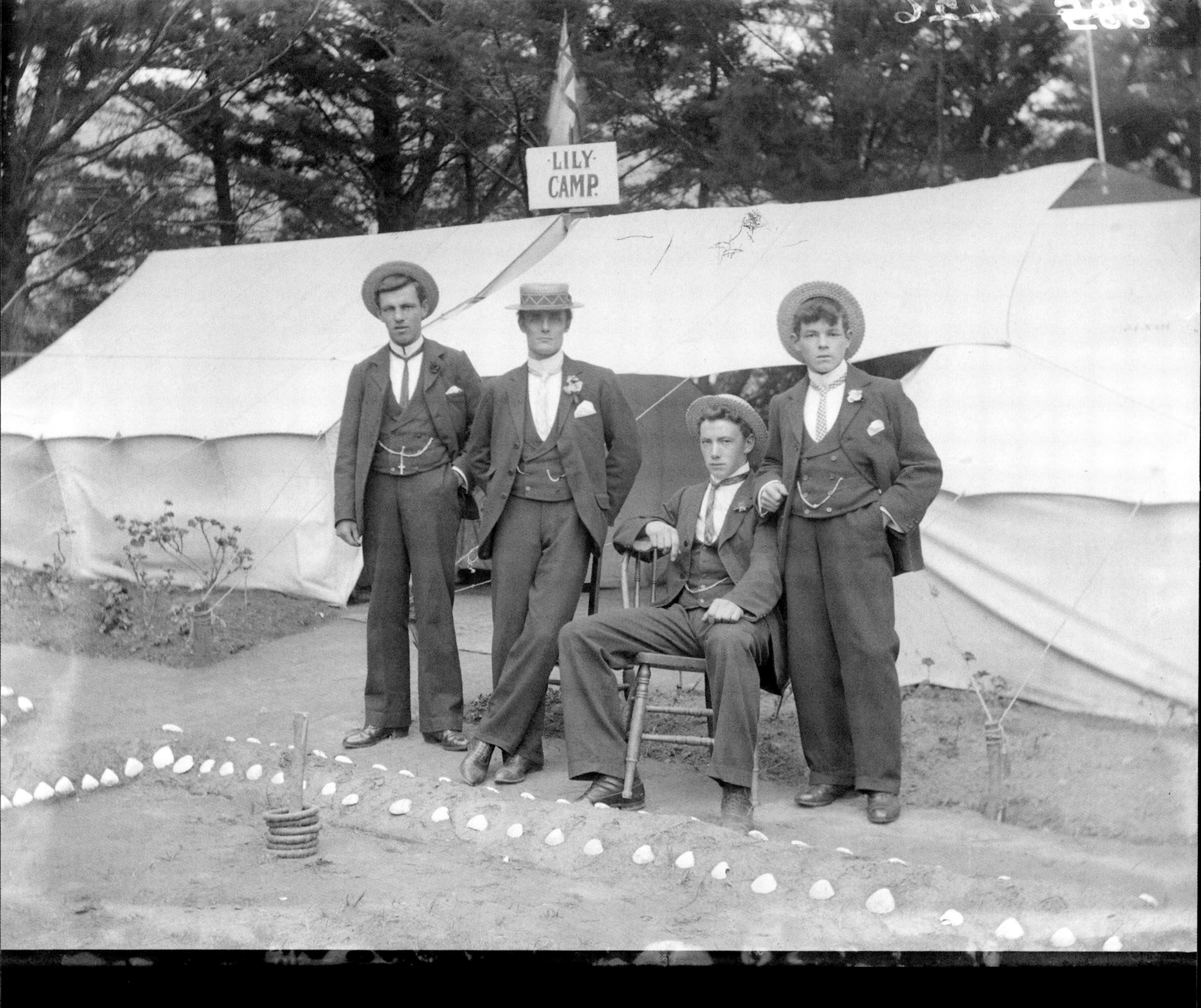

Adam Maclay took numerous portraits of young men posed alongside their camps at Sumner and New Brighton. Some, like this one, emphasised the urbanity of the campers; others played up the work associated with sustaining a camp.

Ref: 1/1-023733-G, Adam Henry Pearson Maclay: Negatives, Alexander Turnbull Library, Wellington, New Zealand

30

On Holiday, At Home

Christchurch's Seaside Tent 'Camps', c. 1892–c. 1910

Kerry Hines

Lily Camp. At first glance, it resembles a theatrical setting – curtains drawn back on an elaborately arranged stage, an atmosphere of expectancy and scene-readiness – or perhaps a canvas B&B, open for inspection, a guest register ready for signature next to the flowers on the table.[1] Lily Camp headquarters, tents linked by awnings, everything well turned out: the neatly formed path with its decorative edges; the 'garden' border around the tents; and the young men, possibly guests, but with an air about them that is distinctly proprietorial.

Looking through images taken by Adam Henry Pearson Maclay, a professional photographer who worked in Christchurch in the late nineteenth and early twentieth centuries, it quickly becomes apparent that Lily Camp is not a one-off. Of the more than 6700 Maclay negatives digitised by the Alexander Turnbull Library, some 250 relate to 'camps', many of them unidentified but others bearing names such as Flora, Red Rose, Bluebell, Tivoli, Keora and Tui.[2]

By the time these photographs were taken, tents had long been part of the New Zealand landscape as a form of temporary accommodation used during colonisation and settlement. They were in widespread contemporary use in military camps, survey camps and public work camps, as well as in recreational pursuits such as tramping and hunting and on family camping trips. Some organisations, such as the Seventh-Day Adventists and the Salvation Army, held tent-based gatherings that brought several hundred members together.[3] Maclay's images, however, with their unexpected juxtaposition of urbane youths, beachy surroundings and ornamented domesticity, suggest a different kind of life under canvas.

In the late 1880s, aided by the extension of tram services that reduced travel times to and from Christchurch, Sumner and New Brighton became increasingly popular as resorts on the Canterbury coast.[4] Christchurch's 'toilers and moilers' could now take excursion trips to the seaside for a day or an evening; they could enjoy bathing and promenading on the long, fine beaches, and at Sumner they could take advantage of such attractions as donkey rides, merry-go-rounds, swing-boats and fireworks displays.[5]

The new proximity of the beach settlements also meant that young people working in the city could establish a form of summer quarters, positioned somewhere between seaside resort and workaday urban world and allowing them to partake of each.[6] In December 1892 the Christchurch *Star* reported that young men had set up tents at Sumner and given some of them names such as the Sunflower Camp and the Daisy Camp, noting that these camps could 'entertain their visitors pleasantly', with 'quite a rivalry in respect to hospitality'.[7] The Christchurch Tramway Company put on additional services for commuters in Sumner the following season, and by early January 1894 more than 100 people were living in around 40 camps there, including two 'suitably chaperoned' young women.[8] By the summer of 1895–96 up to 80 tents could be seen in Sumner; in New Brighton, 200 campers were reported in the final week of January 1895.[9] Although some camps were up for as little as three weeks, others were in place for as long as five months.[10]

Some of those living under canvas enjoyed what one report in the *Star* referred to as the 'primitive style of camping', but others went to great lengths in setting up their tents – this, along with catering for visitors, being a source of pride. The article highlighted three such camps at Sumner in early January 1894: the Daisy Camp, a bell tent occupied by six campers; the Geranium Camp, whose four inhabitants had two large tents (one a substantial dining room with 'cheffonier, mirrors, ornaments, &c', the other a bedroom with Liberty muslin curtains) connected by 'a covered way' that served as their kitchen; and the Lily Camp, which had one principal tent (8.5 x 4.3 metres, with sides 2.1 metres tall) housing separate areas for eating and sleeping, and a subsidiary tent in which the five campers shared the cooking. 'The furnishings and decorations are all arranged with great taste,' the reporter noted, 'and the emblematic flower is worked on most of the articles used.' Visitor numbers were not insubstantial. Daisy Camp had done least well, with just under 200 visitors in the month since they had set up, but Geranium Camp's visitors' book had accumulated about 1100 signatures in just over two months, and Lily Camp had recorded 850 visitors in some six weeks.[11]

The identity of a camp could be promoted in a number of ways. Most had a sign or banner over the tents. Some, like the Lily, had decorations that prominently referred to the camp's name; some spelled out their names in shells around the border of their tents; and a number displayed photographs of their tents and members taken in earlier seasons.[12] Some members wore identifying items: Daisy Camp members had caps decorated with daisy motifs, and Myrtle and Flora Camp members wore tie or lapel pins bearing their camps' initials.[13] A camp's identity could be reinforced out of season via its 'annual social', typically held in town in a suitably decorated hall, where the campers and their friends might enjoy musical and theatrical performances, refreshments and dancing.[14]

In addition to these specific affinities, a camp member was more generically a 'camper', who might participate in social events such as the 'annual campers' sports', and activities with Sumner and New Brighton residents such as the Sumner Moonlight Festival, sports events, cribbage matches and public

Some campers took great care in furnishing and decorating their sleeping quarters, equipping them with items such as dressers, floor coverings, pot plants and framed prints. Here, the Bluebell Camp members' efforts have extended to adorning the tent supports.

Ref: 1/1-028827-G, Adam Henry Pearson Maclay: Negatives, Alexander Turnbull Library, Wellington, New Zealand

This interior view of Myrtle Camp's 'bedroom' includes framed photographs taken of the camp by Maclay on an earlier occasion – a feature of several camps that operated over multiple seasons. Other decorations here include advertising posters, banners with messages such as 'Happy New Year' and 'Home Sweet Home' and a hand-drawn 'Myrtle Camp' sign.

Ref: 1/1-028441-G, Adam Henry Pearson Maclay: Negatives, Alexander Turnbull Library, Wellington, New Zealand

The hospitality extended by the camps to visitors is a recurring theme in contemporary newspaper items and Maclay's photographs. It took a variety of forms, including offering refreshments to casual visitors, hosting evening entertainments and inviting lady friends to tea on Sundays (using the kind of fine dining ware on display here).

Ref: 1/1-029346-G, Adam Henry Pearson Maclay: Negatives, Alexander Turnbull Library, Wellington, New Zealand

Gaiety Camp members create a tableau in which they enact some of their daily chores for the camera. Photographs of campers in this vein highlighted the 'work' of camping and presented the camp as a team in which every member made a contribution.

Ref: 1/1-026436-G [Detail], Adam Henry Pearson Maclay: Negatives, Alexander Turnbull Library, Wellington, New Zealand

concerts.[15] Some of these activities, too, extended into the off season, as in the September 1894 'Sumner Campers v. Residents' football match.[16]

Apart from these social dimensions, what other drawcards might the camps have held for their participants? Presumably, spending time by the sea was as appealing to them as it was to those Britons who flocked to their coastal resorts in the Victorian and Edwardian eras, taking advantage of similar attractions and similar opportunities for greater freedom, flexibility and sensual pleasure.[17] The seaside was a recognised site for the enjoyment of leisure, which by this period was widely acknowledged to be a legitimate undertaking, of value in its own right.[18] In addition, sea air and bathing were viewed as health-enhancing, and the campers' participation in team sports would have been considered good for both their physical wellbeing and their character.[19] The increasing number of men who worked and lived in the city were considered to be at risk from spending too much time indoors, not doing enough physical work and experiencing an unhealthy degree of comfort; fresh air and exercise at the coast went at least some way towards compensating for this.[20]

Tent living seems to have been a particular factor. When it was suggested, in Sumner in 1896, that campers might rent cottages instead, the *Star* pointed out that 'the life under canvas is one of the principal attractions which camping has for them'.[21] The lower cost of living may also have been part of the appeal: one estimate put it at around one-fifth of the outlay required in the city.[22] Campers could also determine how long they wanted to stay, cater for themselves, furnish and arrange their space as they liked and, within the constraints of being in a semi-urban area and of having to commute during the working week, organise their activities as they wished. Tent living offered shelter while providing a greater sense of proximity to the outdoors than a hut or house; it allowed the campers to get away from the city, but also to socialise and meet new people; and it allowed for a pleasurable combination of simplicity and comfort. It gave campers the possibility of being both urbane men of the world and self-sufficient outdoors men, free from the confines of town (which some campers emphasised by having photographs of themselves taken in both modes).[23]

Born in 1873, Maclay was about 20, and presumably in the early phase of his career, when he began photographing the camps. What first drew them to his attention is uncertain, but he clearly photographed them on multiple occasions and over many years. The way in which his photographs feature within later images of the camps indicates that campers were happy to acquire them, and they may have had a wider appeal to visitors and friends too, possibly giving Maclay avenues for making links and building up custom. His connection with the camps may also have been personal: his composite image of the Primrose Club includes a photograph of 'A. Maclay', who resembles a camper in some images of the Waterloo Camp, and who may be the photographer.[24] If so, this association may have increased some campers' readiness to be photographed by him, and may partly account for the longevity of his interest in the camps as subjects.

To date, Maclay's photographs and contemporary newspaper reports have supplied the names of some 65 camps in the period between 1892 and 1910, some of them appearing over several years, others for a single season. There will undoubtedly have been many more, particularly as Maclay's images suggest that some names, including Myrtle, Lily and Lilac, were used by different campers at different times. The majority of newspaper references to the camps relate to the mid-to late 1890s, but it is unclear whether this was the peak of the camps' activity or that they were less of a novelty and therefore less remarked on subsequently.

One factor that may have affected camp numbers was council regulation. Many Sumner businesses and residents welcomed the campers' custom and the way in which they 'enlivened' the borough, and were happy with their comportment, but others were less enthusiastic, connecting recreational camping with such problems as poor sanitation and unclad bathers.[25] Interestingly, some of their concerns were echoed in coastal centres further afield: many British seaside resorts were troubled by sewage disposal and naked bathing during the nineteenth century, and difficulties over sanitation contributed to the demise of beach camps at Vancouver, where 'well-to-do families' holidayed in 'well-appointed' tents between 1894 and 1908.[26] In late 1896 the Sumner Borough Council introduced by-laws intended to regulate tent usage, including provision for a controversial tent licence fee, with the result that just 15 camps were in evidence in Sumner the following January.[27] Initially there was a corresponding increase in the number of campers at New Brighton, but once it acquired a borough council it, too, began to emphasise the need for 'neck to knee costume', 'proper sanitary arrangements' and prior permission to put up tents.[28] By November 1907 Sumner required all camps to have sewer connections; a year later, some businesses were complaining about the absence of camps, holding meetings and lobbying council to draw more visitors to the borough.[29]

As Bill Garner has suggested in relation to Australia, another settler society with a long history of tent usage, camping in its various forms has played an ongoing role in 'a process of cultural and social formation'.[30] The seaside camps of Christchurch did this in a distinctive way, providing campers with the opportunity to take up singular identities and social roles, including those of hosts offering hospitality to friends and strangers alike, 'campers' contributing to the social and cultural activities of a wider community, and practical men of taste who could use and adapt tents creatively for their own ends.

31

An Art Nouveau Jug Collected by Walter Cook

Michael Fitzgerald

Part of a tea and coffee set in Art Nouveau style designed for Liberty & Co. in 1903 by Archibald Knox, this pewter hot water jug was manufactured by the Birmingham firm of W.H. Haseler & Co. from 1904 to 1926. The jug is also an entrée into the world of an extraordinary collector, and his fascination with the history of colonial taste. It is part of the Walter C. Cook Decorative Arts Collection, about 750 items of ceramics, glass and metalware, wallpaper and tiles, gifted to the National Museum, now the Museum of New Zealand Te Papa Tongarewa, in 1992. Cook's collection documents the history of taste and the marketing of modern domestic design in this country, and provides evidence for a strong aesthetic sensibility and colonial awareness of British and European design trends over a century. This awareness derived from strong family links to Britain, and familiarity with art and design publications, exhibitions and strong retail networks.

Archibald Knox's popular designs featured 'bold interpretation of continental Art Nouveau' combined with the use, as on this jug, of interlaced Celtic motifs.[1] The set's marketing name, Tudric, alludes to the supposedly 'Olde English' associations of pewter utensils. In Britain Tudric ware was usually sold by Liberty. It was also popular on the Continent and was widely marketed throughout the British Empire. This jug, however, bears the stamp of the Dunedin firm of Dawsons Ltd, agents for Liberty in Otago and Southland.[2] Several other New Zealand retailers, including Fanny Wimperis and Eleanor Joachim, also in Dunedin, and specialists such as the celebrated Alcorn sisters in Wellington, as well as department stores, imported Liberty's varied wares – textiles, ceramics, glass and metalware – well into the 1920s. Dawsons won a gold medal for their display of 'pewter ware' at the 1925–26 New Zealand and South Seas Exhibition in Dunedin, which suggests that the popularity of these items in New Zealand was long-lived.[3]

The Tudric jug is part of what Walter Cook calls the 'first serious purchase' of his nearly 30 years of collecting.[4] He bought it in 1965 when, for the sum of £15, he acquired a nearly complete Tudric ware tea and coffee set from a curio shop called Odds & Ends in Wellington's Willis Street. Walter was only 24 years old at the time, yet his reasons for the purchase epitomise his already-formed collecting philosophy and his developing ambition to

Hot water jug, Tudric ware, in pewter and cane. Designed by Archibald Knox (1864–1933) and made by W.H. Haseler & Co., England (in production 1904–26).

Ref: GH004265, Walter C. Cook Decorative Arts Collection, Gift of Walter Cook, 1992, Courtesy of the Museum of New Zealand Te Papa Tongarewa

document through objects what he saw as 'half-forgotten facets of the cultural development of New Zealand'. In this purchase, and the other acquisitions he would go on to make over three decades, he traced this cultural development in 'the conscious or unconscious decisions made by New Zealanders when they purchased items and constructed their personal environments'.[5]

Although Tudric or Liberty ware was little regarded in New Zealand in the early 1960s, for Walter its significance lay in its anticipation of the Scandinavian modernism that was then the hallmark of progressive taste in interior design and furnishings. As he wrote later, 'For me, beginning to collect Liberty's art nouveau pewter, this point of view meant that the basic clean-lined modernity of Archibald Knox's designs made them significant. They had a functional simplicity comparable to contemporary Swedish designs for stainless steel – except for their idiosyncratic ornamentation. These artefacts, it seemed to me, were definitely precursors to modernism.'[6] In investigating what had equipped Walter to make this connection and set about collecting such unfashionable items, we need to turn to his upbringing and education.

Walter was born in 1941, in Wellington. His mother was a talented artist who had trained in Wellington, Paris and London.[7] His father was a clergyman, in poor health in later life, an autodidact imbued with the aesthetic values and ideals of late Victorian and Edwardian Britain. Because the family moved around parishes in the lower North Island, Walter's father essentially home-schooled him during his teenage years. This was not, from Walter's point of view, a particularly happy experience, but as a result by the time he was a young man he had acquired a deep knowledge of British culture of that era, especially the writings of William Morris and John Ruskin, and a fascination with the ideals and products of the Arts and Crafts movement.

At the age of 19, in 1960, Walter moved to Wellington to train as an apprentice gardener at the Botanic Garden. Living in an Anglican hostel for young men in the central city, he was close to some of Wellington's intriguing and well-stocked curio and antique shops. He was the right person at the right time and in the right place to begin building a collection of British and European decorative arts that would aim to document New Zealanders' tastes in domestic furnishings from the late nineteenth to the mid-twentieth centuries.

Despite his father's rather oppressive attempts to force him into the mould of a 'great man' and cultural leader like William Morris or Matthew Arnold, Walter continued to develop a deep knowledge and appreciation of Victorian and Edwardian cultural values. He read widely, and from second-hand bookshops built a reference collection of old exhibition catalogues and early twentieth-century periodicals such as *The Studio* and *Decorative Art*, which had kept their readers abreast of exhibitions and design developments in Britain and the Continent.

Two books were crucial. First, Walter purchased a copy of the 1960 Penguin edition of Nikolaus Pevsner's *Pioneers of Modern Design*. Pevsner contextualised Art

Left: *Walter Cook, 2012.*

Ref: MA–1.352870. Photograph by Kate Whitley, Courtesy of the Museum of New Zealand Te Papa Tongarewa

Below: *Krenit bowls, cold-pressed enamelled steel, 1953. Designed by Herbert Krenchel (born 1922) and made by Torben Orskov & Co., Denmark (in production 1953–66).*

Ref: CG001945/1-8, Walter C. Cook Decorative Arts Collection, Gift of Walter Cook, 1992, Courtesy of the Museum of New Zealand Te Papa Tongarewa

Nouveau for him, linking the movement to Morris and the English Arts and Crafts movement, and inspiring him to appreciate it as a precursor of modernism. The second, Isidore Spielmann's catalogue of *The British Government Exhibit at the New Zealand International Exhibition (1906–1907)*, included illustrations of the Arts and Crafts section. These exhibits in the British Court showcased a stunning assemblage, selected by artist and illustrator Walter Crane, of ceramics, metalwork, textiles, woodwork and glass.[8] Through this volume in particular, Walter became aware of the crucial role of the major exhibitions of the early twentieth century, especially the New Zealand International Exhibition, held in Christchurch over the summer of 1906–07, as moulders of New Zealanders' tastes. Walter's interest in British ceramics of the era was aroused. Through Pevsner, he also came to appreciate the wares of Liberty & Co., which had been excluded from representation in the British Court because they were mechanical productions rather than the handwork of individual artisans.[9]

The British government's exhibit was not the only vehicle for promoting current British decorative art productions at the 1906–07 and later exhibitions. The products of ceramics manufacturers such as Doulton and Pilkington were heavily promoted, most famously by the Christchurch-based emporium of John Bates & Co., and contemporary press comment extolled the colourful displays. The *Star*, for example, noted that the 'large cases of "Pilkington", "Ruskin" and other pottery in the British Court are a feast of colour and grace, and should prove of great service in the education of public taste'.[10]

Walter Cook was also living in Wellington, a city that was still, as it was to remain for 20 years or so, essentially late Victorian and Edwardian in its built environment. But more specifically, the capital's diverse range of antique, curio, second-hand and junk shops offered rich, affordable pickings for an informed collector. The generation who had purchased new, or been given, Art Nouveau objects was dying off, and heirs were often inclined, in Walter's words, 'to discard inherited objects associated with the gloomy past'.[11] In the popular taste of the early 1960s, modernity was 'in', but it was Walter's genius to begin collecting 'against the grain' of current taste.

'*Pioneers of Modern Design*,' he wrote later, 'also had an influence on how I began to shape my collection in the beginning. Central to Pevsner's argument is a sort of social Darwinism applied to art history. Implicitly things were struggling towards the millennium of the triumph of modernism – survival of the fittest meant functionalism in architecture and product design.'[12] Walter saw a continuum, and a focus for his collecting, in the history of modernism and functional design from the work of Christopher Dresser in the 1870s and 1880s, forward into the 'art deco and Scandinavian modernism of my youth'.[13]

The last key dimension of Walter's collecting practice and philosophy is that, as he had with the Tudric jug, he obtained almost all his objects from New Zealand sources. He saw the objects not only as direct evidence of the well-informed tastes of New Zealanders, but also as artefacts of a kind of nationhood or national self-fashioning, as 'relating to the political and social structures we devised as a

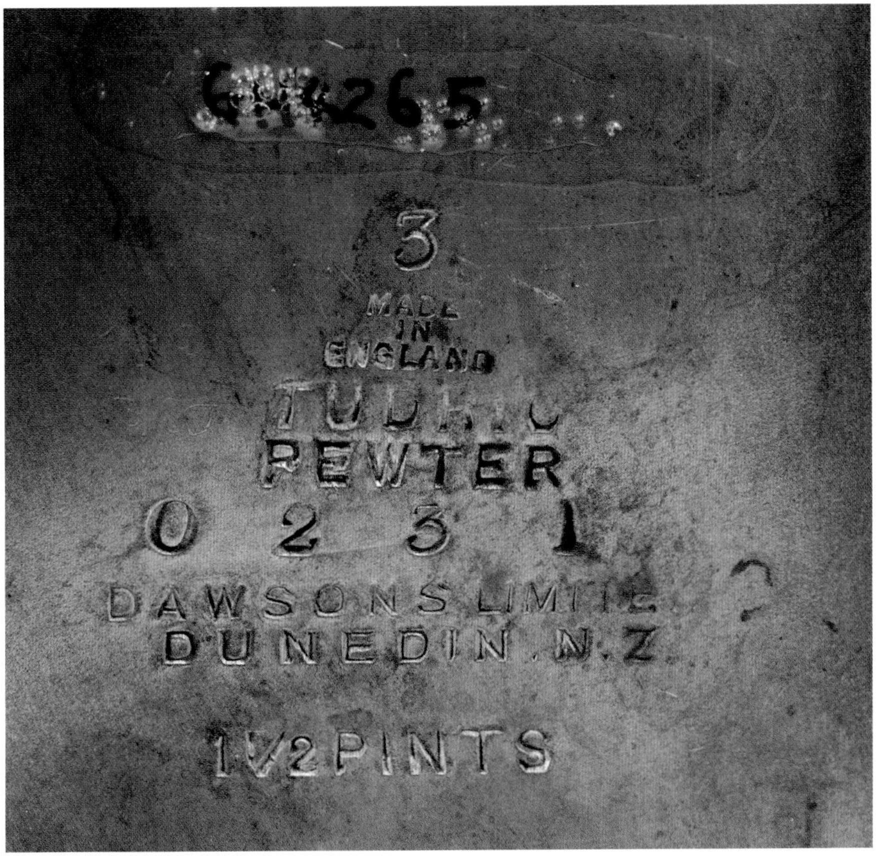

Retailer's mark of Dawsons, Ltd, Dunedin, stamped on the base of the Tudric ware jug.

Ref: GH004265, Walter C. Cook Decorative Arts Collection, Gift of Walter Cook, 1992, Courtesy of the Museum of New Zealand Te Papa Tongarewa

framework for our lives. There was a brave new world envisioned before the rise of modernism and neo-liberalism. William Morris, John Ruskin, the Fabians, the Welfare State and the values that went with all of these, were also embodied in Liberty pewter, art pottery, arts & crafts houses and the state house garden suburb.'[14]

These comments help us to place the Tudric jug in context, as tangible evidence of the influence of these broadly socialist late nineteenth-century ideals in this country. It was one of the objects that enabled him 'to touch the reality of Morris and the pre-Raphaelites in far off New Zealand'.[15] His comments also help to articulate the dual impetus of his apparently quixotic decision, in the early 1990s, to donate the collection to the then National Museum. One imperative was historical. As he wrote to the director, 'I am a New Zealander of European descent and I believe that a collection like mine is relevant to our social and cultural history most of which is under-represented and unsystematically represented in our Museum collections.'[16] But his other imperative, illustrated in the explicit connections he makes between the 'brave new world' of the political and artistic sensibilities of the Arts and Crafts movement and his own collecting, was political. This very conscious connection helps to make sense of the gift in terms of Walter's defiance of prevailing trends, at a time of rampant neo-liberalism and self-interest, in gifting his collection to the people of New Zealand.

32
Katherine Mansfield's Hei Tiki
Jane Stafford

On 12 October 1907 Mrs Annie Beauchamp gave a party at her home at 47 Fitzherbert Terrace, Wellington. In the manner of society journalism of the time, the *Free Lance* newspaper's column, 'Social Gossip by Christabel', gave extensive space to what the hostess and her (female) guests were wearing, describing them in a vocabulary that is now curious and arcane. The report is a welter of chiffon taffetas, Valenciennes lace, rose pink Louisiennes and sequin lace berthe. But the detail that is now the most interesting is the description of 'Miss K. Beauchamp', 'in a black crepe-de-chine dress, her sole ornament being a large ivory tiki'.[1]

There is a hei tiki in the Katherine Mansfield Birthplace collection. It was displayed in their 2008 *Material Mansfield* exhibition and pictured in the accompanying publication of the same title, with an account of its provenance. In a section headed 'A Sense of Home', it is referred to as 'the whalebone tiki that she once wore to a ball, in defiance of the conventional tastes of colonial Wellington'; it 'now resonates with her strong sense of her New Zealand identity'.[2] The hei tiki was donated to the birthplace by Janet, Lady Wild in 1997. Mansfield's eldest sister Vera had given it to her more than 20 years before with a note:

> This maori tiki was shared and worn by me and my sister K.M. when as school girls, in LONDON, we wished to be identified as New Zealanders.
>
> March 20th 1972.[3]

The Material Mansfield quotes part of a letter written on 14 October 1907 by Mansfield's sister Chaddie to her cousin Sylvia Payne describing Mansfield's nineteenth birthday and the presents she had been given, including greenstone earrings from her mother, 'two sweet Liberty broaches' from her father, and a jewel case, comb, writing case and bag from her sisters and brother. 'Oh, one was a fascinating old Tiki which I'm sure you will love. It is a Maori God to keep away the Evil Spirit and is made of carved bone.'[4]

The Material Mansfield concludes this section with a passage from Joanna Woods' *Katerina: The Russian World of Katherine Mansfield*: 'For her dance, Katherine eschewed girlish pastels and dressed entirely in black … the metamorphosis from wealthy banker's daughter to artist had begun.'[5]

This hei tiki was, according to Mansfield's sister Vera, worn by the sisters when they were at school in London as a mark of their New Zealand identities. Mansfield was given a second hei tiki for her nineteenth birthday and wore it with a black crêpe-de-chine dress to a party at the family home in Thorndon, Wellington.

Ref: 0855. Courtesy of the Katherine Mansfield Birthplace Society, Wellington, New Zealand

Mansfield studies are riddled with narratives of what we desire her to be. There are narratives of rebelliousness. There are narratives of affiliation to New Zealand, a belief in her abiding wish to return after her final departure in 1908. And there are narratives of biographical exceptionalism, where all details of her Wellington existence are unique to her and point exclusively to her future genius. The hei tiki described in the *Free Lance* and the actual object in the birthplace collection seem to endorse all three of these.

I would like to complicate this. First, since the sisters' education at Queen's College, London, began in April 1903 and ended in July 1906, there were obviously two hei tiki: one that they wore 'as school girls, in LONDON' between 1903 and 1906, and one that was given to Mansfield for her birthday in Wellington in October 1907.

Second, what evidence is there that the birthday hei tiki was worn 'in defiance of the conventional tastes of colonial Wellington' and, in more general terms, how unusual was Mansfield's appearance at that party? Although today we might be struck by the dramatic image in the *Free Lance*, black was then a common and fashionable colour for young women. In the same issue Miss Stafford is described as wearing black chiffon taffetas and crimson roses, Miss Simpson black chiffon taffetas with reveres of Irish lace and pink roses and Miss Eileen Ward is 'graceful' in black spotted net. In fact, with one exception, an 'all white dance', every social occasion reported in all three Wellington papers in 1907 include young women dressed in black.

The significance of the hei tiki is more difficult to gauge. Pounamu hei tiki were common in both private and museum collections at the turn of the century. Significant hei tiki date from an earlier period, have specific whakapapa central to their significance, and demonstrate a particular aesthetic. New Zealand ethnologist H.D. Skinner writes: 'The old authorities are agreed that the major part of [the hei tiki's] *mana* ... derives from contact with the great people who have worn it, and not from a magic meaning or from size or beauty.'[6] In the colonial period, the hei tiki was 'quickly identified as a unique marker of tangata whenua' and was part of their conventional representation in colonial portraiture and photography.[7] But commodified versions of the hei tiki also permeated Pākehā costume codes. The fact that Mansfield was given hers as a birthday present suggests that it was in no way a defiant statement on her part; that it was paired with the gift of greenstone earrings points to her family's participation in 'Maoriland' culture of late colonial New Zealand, where indigenous objects were shifted from their original context to become the decorative markers of a mild form of settler nationalism.

This nationalist use of Māori culture was not completely divorced from indigenous reality. Upper-class Edwardian Wellington society admitted prominent Māori. Mansfield went to school with Maata Mahupuku, the Ngāti Kahungunu heiress described by the *Free Lance* as 'the charming half-caste young lady who is known as the "Wairarapa princess"'.[8] James Carroll, Ngāti Kahungunu, Minister for Native Affairs from 1899 to 1912, and Āpirana Ngata, Ngāti Porou, who was elected to the Eastern Māori seat in

Miria Pōmare, the wife of Sir Māui Pōmare, was a feature of the Wellington social scene in the early decades of the twentieth century. Her costume here blends Māori tradition – huia feathers, heru and hei tiki – with a fashionable European ostrich feather fan and beaded evening dress.

Ref: 1/2-043506-F, S.P. Andrew Ltd: Portrait Negatives, Alexander Turnbull Library, Wellington, New Zealand

1905, appear regularly in newspaper social pages at club dinners, receptions, sporting events and musical evenings. In September 1907 Carroll attended the same 'Brilliant Ball' at Government House as did 'Mr. and Mrs. Beauchamp and the Misses Beauchamp'.[9] Carroll's wife Hēni usually remained at their home in Poverty Bay, as did Ngata's wife Arihia. But Mīria Pōmare, wife of Ngata's associate and fellow Te Aute old boy, Māui Pōmare, was a favourite of the society pages from the time of her engagement in 1902, reported in the same column of the *Free Lance* as a wedding at which Edith Bendall, later Mansfield's lover, was bridesmaid.[10]

Born Mildred Amelia Woodbine Johnson in 1870 in Poverty Bay, Mīria Pōmare was the daughter of a wealthy Cambridge-educated Pākehā sheep farmer and Mere Hape, of Rongowhakaata and Te Aitanga-a-Mahaki descent. A photograph in the Alexander Turnbull Library's collection shows her in hei tiki and evening dress. The photograph is undated but may have been taken in 1918 when she was awarded the OBE, which she is wearing.[11] Pōmare's adornment mimics the traditional representations of Māori women, with huia feathers and hei tiki, but here the customary mere is replaced by an ostrich feather fan and the korowai by an elaborate evening dress. Her hair is arranged in a fashionable style but fixed with a heru. The juxtapositions, and the medal, demonstrate her easy inhabiting of both worlds and her mana in each. This is a formal portrait and does not necessarily mean that Pōmare wore her hei tiki to social functions. But she may have, and she was certainly a sufficiently striking figure to have been a fashion influence.

In November 1907, a month after her birthday, Mansfield went on a camping trip to the Urewera, and her notebooks and letters record the collision of traditional and modern she observed there. When, on her return, she was given permission to use the General Assembly Library, one of the books she read was Augustus Hamilton's *The Art of Workmanship of the Maori Race*, which she refers to by its popular title, *Maori Art*.[12] The seriousness with which Hamilton situates the Māori objects he discusses in his book in the context of traditional culture and international ethnographic scholarship, but also as art, may have impressed Mansfield, and may have suggested she reconsider her birthday hei tiki.

But back in October 1907 her choice of jewellery for her mother's party may have been more a response to a fashionable fad. Earlier that year the *Evening Post*'s 'Anglo-Colonial Notes' column had quoted a London newspaper article with the title, 'The Lucky Pig gives place to Hei Tiki— the God of the Maoris':

> A year or two ago the lucky pig, or the lucky bean, was worn more for fun than anything else; nowadays women are wearing more charms and amulets than ever, but they are all in the design of some mystic sign, and their owners have implicit faith in their efficacy. Perhaps the favourite amulet is 'Hei Tiki,' the sacred God of the Maoris. Thousands of representations of him are sold in green jade, the New Zealand lucky greenstone, at prices ranging from half-a-crown for small ones about ¾ in high, to £20 or £30 for large ones decorated with jewels. One London firm that deals in greenstone ornaments said yesterday that they have sold nearly 1000 of these charms this Christmas. 'Many people firmly believe in them,' declared the dealer.'[13]

This suggests another, though not mutually exclusive context, within which to view Mansfield's combination of crêpe-de-chine and hei tiki – as part of a fashion for the primitive and the exotic which, at least in part, sourced its symbolic objects from empire. Fin de siècle orientalism and the aesthetic movement were both registered in late colonial Wellington. Indeed the society columns' descriptions of furnishings, fabrics and flowers are positively Wildean, as is their frequent use of the word 'artistic' as a term of approval. This is a commodified version of aestheticism, exemplified by the London department store of Liberty & Co. and signalled in what the Wellington newspapers call Miss Vera Beauchamp's 'most artistic liberty frock',[14] or by Harold Beauchamp's present to his daughter of two Liberty brooches. 'Liberty's,' said a women's magazine of the time, 'is the chosen resort of the artistic shopper.'[15]

In this context individual objects are stripped of meaning – or convey multiple and casual meanings. An advertisement in the *Weekly Graphic and New Zealand Mail* in February 1909 shows Wellington jeweller Stewart Dawson's stock of 'Fashionable Pendants': alongside flowers, stars, bluebirds, thistles, hearts and crucifixes, there is a 'Greenstone Tiki'.[16] Far from the elaborate whakapapa and narrative accretions of traditional hei tiki, or even the appropriative but informed use of such decorative motifs in Māoriland culture, Mansfield's hei tiki is costume. It is worn in a similar manner to the 'more or less Maori fashion' she dressed in at a musical party in London in 1909,[17] or the necklace of Native American design she wears in a 1917 photograph.[18] Here, in a confused and essentially meaningless mixture of exotic and imperial sources, she is also wearing a paisley-patterned kimono-shaped jacket. The hei tiki (or necklace, paisley or kimono) signals both primitivism and commodification, authenticity and dressing up – not the careful signposts of Mīria Pōmare's costume, but a knowingly inauthentic bricolage.

All the women at Mrs Beauchamp's party, in their overload of decorative accoutrements, each minutely recorded for the consumption of the newspaper-reading public, are in costume, enacting the wealth of their husbands and fathers. In Mansfield's draft novel 'Juliet', written at this time, the father asks, 'What have I got for my money. Come along – deck yourself out, show the world that you are expensive …'[19] The *Free Lance*'s rival, the *Dominion*, makes no mention of Mansfield in its report of the party but does describe a guest, 'Miss Butts', wearing 'a black dress and quaint Indian jewels'.[20] Eva Butts was Mansfield's teacher at Miss Swainson's school where she would arrive, according to Antony Alpers, 'magnificently mounted on a horse, in purple tweed'. It was her that Mansfield asked about 'free love', says Alpers, 'in those days a scandalously daring topic even for adults'.[21] Mansfield studies would like to see the young KM as scandalously daring. But was it Eva Butts, one of a number of progressive, flamboyant women teachers in late colonial New Zealand, who was the daring one, the one who invited such an enquiry? Was it Miss Butts' style that Mansfield was imitating? Miss Beauchamp and Miss Butts, side by side at Mrs Beauchamp's dance, both in black, both with fashionably exotic jewellery.

It is perhaps an odd exercise to argue for Mansfield's unexceptionality rather than focusing on her uniqueness. But in her black crêpe-de-chine and ivory tiki, Mansfield may have been at least as normal a part of Wellington colonial high society as Vera in her 'artistic liberty dress' or Miss Butts in her 'quaint Indian jewels'.

Mansfield enjoyed dressing up – as a gypsy, as a Māori, and here, in a mixture of Native American, Japanese, Russian and Indian styles. 'How can one look the part and not be the part? Or be the part and not look it? Isn't looking – being? Or being – looking?' says a character from one of her stories.

Ref: MSX-4147-65, John Middleton Murry: Diaries and Notebooks, Alexander Turnbull Library, Wellington, New Zealand

33

Te Pai o Ngā Āhua

The Visitors' Books at the Lindauer Art Gallery

Roger Blackley

Tastefully bound in shiny green leather, the two imposing ledgers sat side by side in the gallery of Māori portraits that opened on Auckland's Queen Street in 1901.[1] Embossed on one was the title, *Pukapuka Mo Nga Manuhiri Tangata Matakit[a]ki*; today it is informally known as the 'Māori Visitors' Book'. The other, which carried the title, *Visitors Book Lindauer Art Gallery*, is now referred to as the 'Pākehā Visitors' Book'. In fact Māori visitors contributed their names to the very first page of the Pākehā book and, when it was filled completely in 1908, everyone then wrote in the Māori book. These hundreds of inscriptions, from Māori and Pākehā visitors, foreign tourists and sundry anonymous graffitists, document the bicultural context of an extraordinary national portrait gallery of Māori celebrities.

On the very first page of the Māori book appears the shaky name of Ruka Aratapu, the fifth recorded visitor to the gallery and the subject of a portrait on display, who came with a group from Poverty Bay on 3 June 1901. Most of the Māori visitors belonged to the succeeding generations: the sons and daughters, nieces and nephews. Sometimes characterising themselves as the mōrehu, or remnant, they saluted their now-departed elders who were arrayed before them in the gallery. And following the messages of greeting and farewell came fulsome accolades to the 'tohunga', Gottfried Lindauer, and to the generous patron and curator, Henry Partridge, whose initiative in forming the gallery was commended by so many of the Māori visitors.

This rich documentation of Māori involvement with the collection reveals a reception of ancestral depictions distinct from European notions of art and ethnography. Portrait paintings had long served important roles within the Māori world, displayed within meeting houses and deployed at tangihanga, but such collections emphasised the genealogical connections between portrayed individuals. The collection of Lindauer portraits formed by Partridge was quite different, encompassing a multiplicity of tribes, both 'rebels' and 'friendlies'. Hence the oblique comment on the nature of the collection made by Tūpōtahi Tukorehu of Kihikihi (No. 147 in the book): 'The caretaker of these paintings was right to display them at the same place.'

By the 1890s Partridge's fast-growing collection had achieved considerable fame in both the Māori and Pākehā worlds. Descendants and relatives were

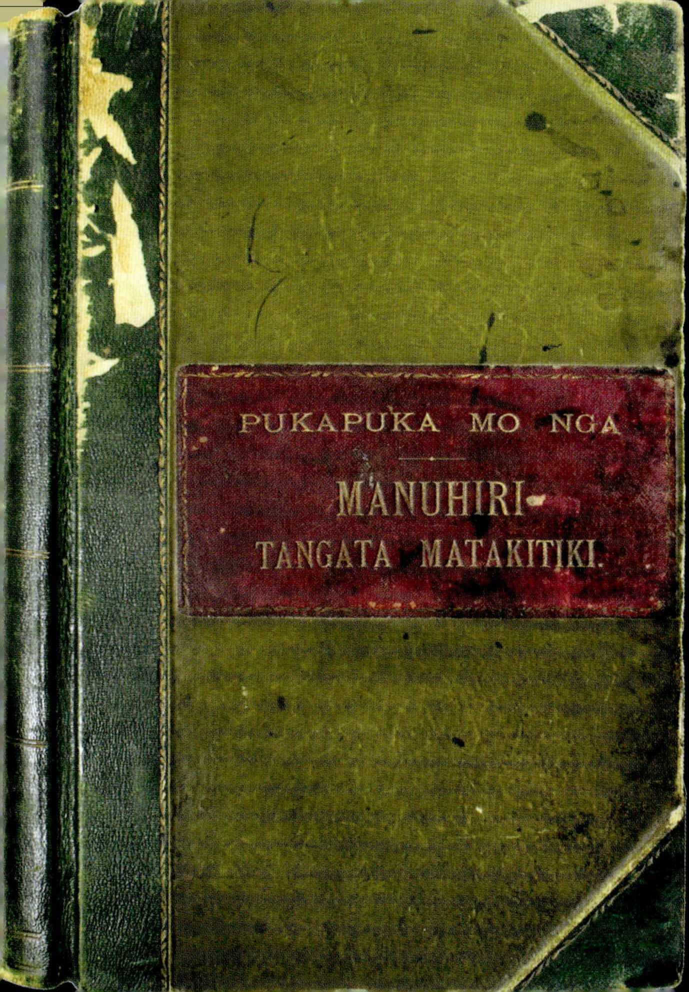
PUKAPUKA MO NGA
MANUHIRI
TANGATA MATAKITIKI.

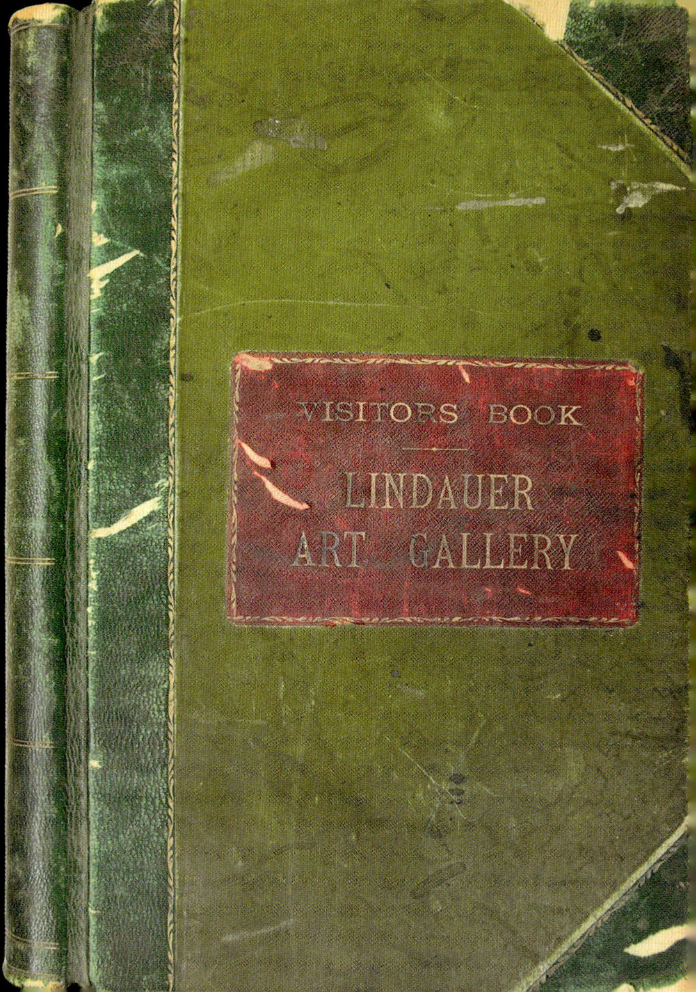
VISITORS BOOK
LINDAUER
ART GALLERY

No. NAMA.	DATE. TE RA	NAME. INGOA
78	June 24 · 1901	Hemana Te Pokiha

regularly welcomed at the Partridge residence in Grafton Road, and it is likely that the facilitation of such visits was a significant motive behind the 1901 opening of the Lindauer Art Gallery. The very existence of the Māori book, in which a printed message in te reo invites viewers to contribute, is evidence that Māori access to the collection was central to the gallery's planning. This need not have excluded other motives, such as the provision of more secure housing for a uniquely valuable collection of national significance.

Certainly many of the visitors thought that Partridge's initiative was made on behalf of Māori. Rameka Poi of Waiapu (No. 124) considered it 'a noble gesture', while Te Kei Paehua of Ngāti Raukawa (No. 145) paid homage 'to the Pākehā who fashioned you in this way to be admired by your future descendants'. Hone Mima Tiuakauamate of Ngāti Porou (No. 157) wrote that 'to my knowledge it is an act of kindness to us from the Pākehā, to take care of things like this so that we will remember our loved ones who have departed from us'.

Mita K. Ngatipare of Raglan visited the gallery on at least three occasions, when he inscribed fulsome messages in the book (Nos 125, 154 and 164). He shows his awareness that Partridge had created something distinctively new in bringing together individuals of disparate tribes but, like many Māori visitors, he invokes the gallery as a profoundly Māori space: 'Farewell to you, the noble people of New Zealand, in your house that is remembered as Aotearoa.'

Over and over, the Māori visitors wrote of the 'whakamīharo'– surprise or amazement – provoked by the life-like quality of the portraits, and of how they could sense the spiritual presence of the depicted ancestors. The Rev. Hone Peri Paerata of Ngāti Tūwharetoa (No. 108) writes of Te Heuheu Tūkino's 'amazement in relation to the spiritual chiefs [rangatira wairua] present in physical form in this house'. According to Rere Te Kowha of Ngāpuhi (No. 146), 'they are happy living here in the presence of my Pākehā friend, who has done a great job'.

In an evocative phrase, Āpirana Ngata (No. 84) referred to Lindauer's paintings as 'shadow carvings of the European artist' (te ata whakairo a te tohunga Pakeha), thereby incorporating them within a Māori aesthetic. In 1903 Meretini Kipa Te Whatanui and Heeni Kipa Te Whatanui of Otaki (Nos 189 and 190) wrote, 'We the Māori do not know how to make these images of our ancestors, so greetings to you'. Five years later, on 12 June 1908, Kuīni Wī Rangipūpū of Ngāti Ruanui and Rangitopeora of Te Āti Awa expressed their 'great admiration for the Pākehā expert', but also the prospect that Māori might take up portrait painting for themselves: 'We sincerely hope the day will come when Māori will acquire this skill as it seems very much akin to the carving work of the Māori.'

It is impossible to quantify the number of early Māori visitors to the Partridge collection with any precision, partly because it is likely that not all of them signed the book. Individual entries were given consecutive numbers until mid-1907 when the Māori book took on a more chaotic aspect, following the completion of the Pākehā book with its 7039 numbered visitors over six years. Nevertheless, of the 332 numbered entries in the Māori book over this same period, the vast majority were made by Māori visitors.

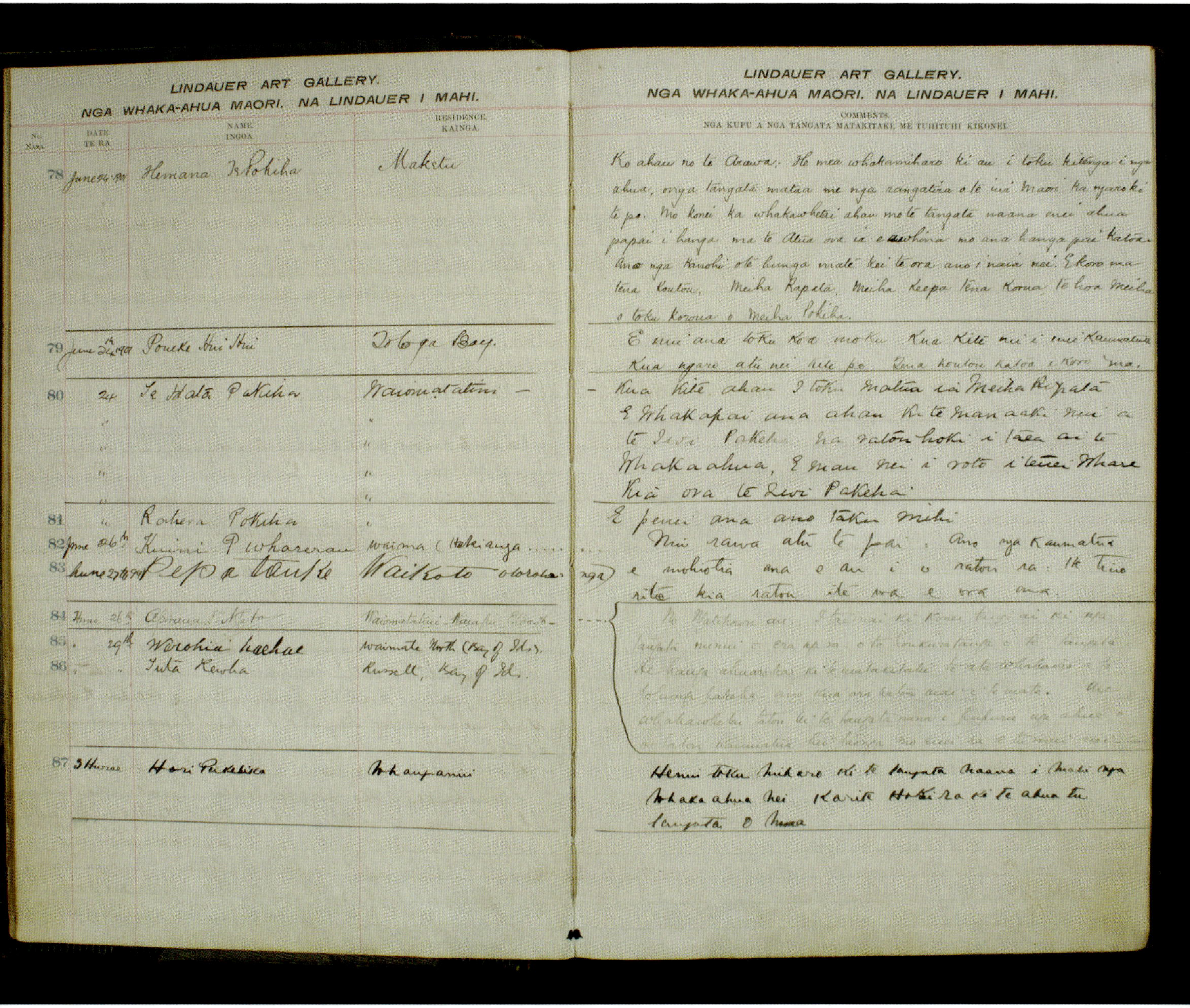

Entry No. 78, by Hemana Pokiha of Maketū on 24 June 1901 (Māori Visitors' Book, page 10). 'I am from Te Arawa. It is amazing for me seeing the images of important people and chiefs of the Māori people who have now passed on. For this, I am ever so thankful to the artist who painted these excellent images; may God bless him for the wonderful work. It is as if those who have passed on still live today. To my elders, I greet you. Major Rāpata, Major Keepa: greetings to you both, colleagues of my grandfather, Major Pokiha.' (Translation: Te Taura Whiri i Te Reo Māori – The Māori Language Commission.) E.H. McCormick Research Library, Auckland Art Gallery Toi o Tāmaki

James Cowan published a selection of visitors' comments in an appendix to his *Pictures of Early New Zealand*, the 1930 book that documented the entire Partridge collection.[2] Although these excerpts have been known to New Zealand art historians, until 2003 the ledgers themselves remained hidden in a basement storeroom of the Auckland Art Gallery Toi o Tāmaki. As it turns out, they are much more than a catalogue of famous names, recording their visits to Auckland's latest attraction. Instead, they reveal astonishingly intense and intimate comments from a wide range of relatives and descendants, who speak to and sometimes hear from the portraits, and provide compelling evidence of the spiritual presence that Māori visitors sensed in the collection. This same presence was felt by successive generations, who continued to pay such visits after the collection became available at the Auckland Art Gallery in 1913. Perhaps the greatest occasion in their subsequent history was when the great-great-grandchildren assembled before the entire collection of portraits in 1987, at the opening of *Te Maori: Te Hokinga Mai* at the gallery.

Although it is not yet digitally accessible, the Pākehā Visitors' Book is also a crucial source for the reception of the Lindauer Art Gallery. One of the earliest visitors, William Simpson of Sydney (No. 6), remarked on 31 May 1901 that Partridge's collection was 'more interesting than the public Art Gallery; it is to be hoped that this will never be lost to the public of New Zealand', while an Auckland visitor on 2 July 1901 felt 'bound to say that they are the best I have seen outside the National Gallery, London'. A more measured judgement came from J.A. Baker of London (No. 185), the special artist and correspondent accompanying the Duke and Duchess of Cornwall and York in 1901: 'Fine example of disinterested work in interest of education, than which no subject is more important. Kia ora, Mr. Partridge. When New Zealand wakes to a proper interest in its traditions, it will owe you much.' Another informed foreign visitor was Allen Hutchinson (No. 163), a British-born sculptor who produced a bust of Lindauer for Partridge's gallery. Hutchinson characteristically stressed the ethnological importance of the collection: 'The value of Mr Lindauer's work can hardly be estimated by this generation. The time when such types can be procured is rapidly passing. It will be the generations to come who will understand the full value of such a collection.'

As with the Māori book, where it is easy to imagine one person reading out texts for the benefit of others in the group, visitors undoubtedly perused previous comments. For example, on 6 August 1901 Alice Pilkington of Auckland (No. 573) wrote 'Ought to belong to the city'; shortly afterwards, S. Wordsworth of Waverley (No. 578) countered with: 'Very interesting shd be sent Home.' Pilkington and Wordsworth are in turn responding to the comment made on 3 August by John L. Wilson of Auckland (No. 562): 'Too good for private ownership'. While numerous writers in the Māori book hailed Partridge as the patron of Lindauer, not a single Māori commentator contested his ownership of the resulting collection.

The category of 'tourist' included ethnic Polynesians such as John Kaukahale of 'Hawaiian

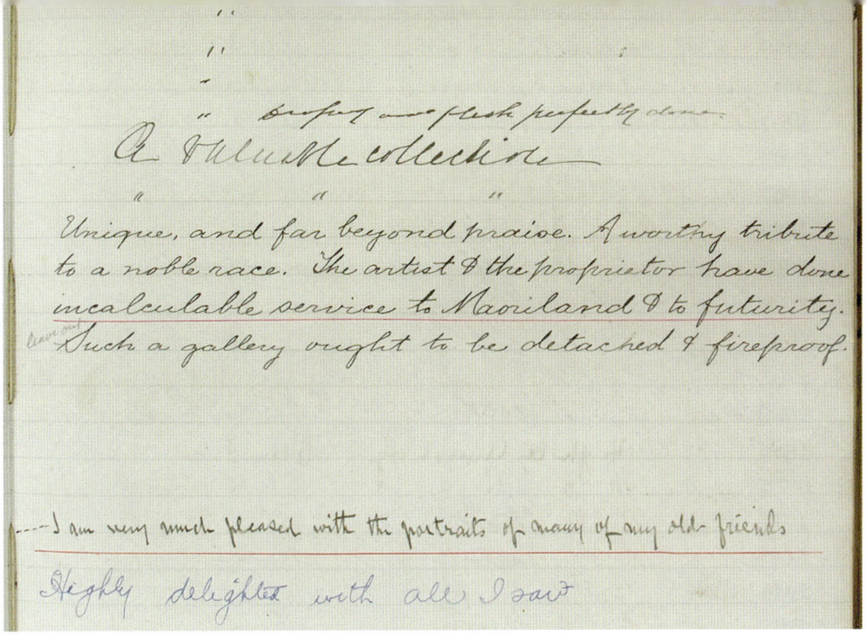
A valuable collection

Unique, and far beyond praise. A worthy tribute to a noble race. The artist & the proprietor have done incalculable service to Maoriland & to futurity.

leave out Such a gallery ought to be detached & fireproof.

I am very much pleased with the portraits of many of my old friends

Highly delighted with all I saw

Entry No. 1038, by Wilhelmina Sherriff Bain on 5 November 1901 (Pākehā Visitors' Book, page 72). Her final sentence, 'Such a gallery ought to be detached & fireproof', is preceded by 'leave out' in pencil, probably added by James Cowan while collecting accolades for an appendix to Pictures of Old New Zealand.

E.H. McCormick Research Library, Auckland Art Gallery Toi o Tāmaki

Island' (No. 763), who wrote 'Wonderful', and Fatu of Samoa (No. 692), who visited with Alfred Exshaw of London on 28 August 1901. But it also included the likes of Sarah E. Jolliffe of Upolu and Annie E. Ffrench of Tutuila (Nos 1220 and 1221, 4 January 1902), the former flaunting her palagi status with a Samoan-language inscription: 'Ua tele lo`u fiafia aua ua ou mafai ona matamata i ata nei. Ua matagofia lava!' (It gave me so much pleasure to see these paintings. They are truly beautiful!) The most exotic would have to be the visitors (Nos 1623–28) who on 9 June 1902 inscribed their names in Chinese characters.

Of equal or greater interest is the roll call of eminent New Zealanders, beginning with two judges of the Native Land Court, who signed two days before the Māori book was first inscribed. Among the earliest signatories were leading politicians such as the Native Minister, James Carroll of Gisborne (No. 13), who on 3 June 1901 wrote, 'Charming group of pictures representing our most celebrated Maori chiefs who figured prominently in the history of the colony'. Hēni Carroll (No. 19) used te reo to reinforce her husband's comment: 'Nui atu te pai o nga ahua' (the images are exquisite). MPs Māui Pōmare (No. 67) and W.H. Field (No. 68) attended together on 10 June, when the latter announced his personal acquaintance with a number of the portrait subjects and vouched for the works as 'excellent speaking likenesses of these chiefs'. Stephenson Percy Smith of New Plymouth (No. 592), Secretary for Crown Lands, Surveyor-General of New Zealand and leading apostle of the Polynesian Society, also highlighted his first-hand connection with the subjects: 'I am very pleased to have had the opportunity of seeing such an excellent colln of pictures. Many of them were old personal friends of myself, which renders the sight of their faces all the more pleasant.' Other Pākehā commentators, such as 'Settler, 1840', spoke of seeing 'familiar faces', proclaiming the verisimilitude of the portraits in tandem with asserting their own long-standing residence in the colony.

Henry Partridge would have been the keenest reader of both visitors' books, undoubtedly gratified both by the elevated status of his guests and by their flattering comments. Perhaps the most subtle was written on 2 September 1901 by T.E. Donne of Wellington (No. 706), the secretary of the newly established Department of Tourist and Health Resorts, who later borrowed a group of Partridge's Lindauer portraits for inclusion in the New Zealand display at the 1904 St Louis Exposition: 'I break the tenth commandment each visit to this charming gallery.'

34

Toko Toru Tapu

A Tale of Four Churches

Damian Skinner

Interior, Toko Toru Tapu, 1889.

Photograph by William Crawford. Ref: WFC A294, Tairāwhiti Museum, Te Whare Taonga o Te Tairāwhiti. Reproduced with the permission of the trustees of Toko Toru Tapu

Below: *Carving, Toko Toru Tapu, 2010.*

Photograph by Studio La Gonda. Reproduced with the permission of the trustees of Toko Toru Tapu

On 16 January 1912, under the heading 'A picturesque church', the *Poverty Bay Herald* announced to its readers that 'The new Anglican Church at Manutuke is nearing completion, and promises to be the most picturesque throughout the entire district.' Designed by Gisborne-based architects Graham & Brown, and built by John Colley & Co., the church, named Toko Toru Tapu (or Holy Trinity), was built on the site of a previous church that had burnt down a couple of years earlier. Like its predecessor, the new church promised to be 'one of the show-places of the district'.[1]

A high-pitched roof of red asbestos slates, wide eaves and projecting buttresses and walls of rough-cast plaster made the exterior a pleasing sight. Inside, an 'artistic porch, and a pair of handsome swing doors' opened onto an interior of brick walls finished with white cement and a lofty roof, rising 5 metres, with oiled rimu ceiling timbers, and windows of the 'choicest lead lights, which are decidedly in keeping with the general picturesque design'. Most dramatically, the newspaper wrote with approval of 'a massive carved dado', almost 5 metres tall, which would cover the lower walls of the church: 'Forty-two totara trees will be required for this work, and thirteen of these have already been procured. It is stated that the work of carving the ancient designs will occupy at least eight months.'[2] When the church was formally opened on 9 March 1913, the *Poverty Bay Herald* reported that 'The building cost about £2000, and the carvings are stated to have run into about £500.'[3]

There is no doubt that the substantial carvings gracing the interior walls of the church, with the exception of the chancel, are the most striking feature of Toko Toru Tapu. The combination of European architecture and Māori art links this building to other Māori churches built in the first half of the twentieth century, such as St Mary's at Tikitiki on the East Coast, and St Paul's Church at Pūtiki, near Whanganui. It was certainly something that people celebrated about Toko Toru Tapu at the time. 'To the handiwork of the white man we have added the art of our forefathers,' proclaimed the Rev. R.T. Kōhere in his address during the five-day hui that accompanied the opening, suggesting that 'By this happy combination we hope to enhance the beauty of this sacred building'.[4]

There are many reasons why Toko Toru Tapu deserves its wāhi tapu status with Heritage New Zealand. But, as is often the case with historic buildings,

Interior triptych, Toko Toru Tapu, 2010.

Photograph by Studio La Gonda. Reproduced with the permission of the trustees of Toko Toru Tapu

it is not only the current church that makes this a place of great importance. Toko Toru Tapu is like a palimpsest, a parchment page from a manuscript that was scraped clean and reused. Traces of the old remain under the new, which explains why the term is used in architecture to describe clues to old buildings that no longer exist. Toko Toru Tapu, the church that currently stands at Manutuke, carries with it evidence of the churches that preceded it, and especially of the carvings, 'claimed to be the most exquisite Maori carvings extant', which were lost in the fire of 1910.[5] As newspapers around the country reported, 'Modern Maori carvers have been called in from Rotorua and elsewhere, and an earnest endeavour has been made to "reincarnate" the old carvings.'[6] The idea of reincarnation is very suggestive, and to understand why the writer might have chosen this term – and to understand how Toko Toru Tapu is an architectural palimpsest – it is necessary to go back further in time.

This is the story of four churches, and it begins with the arrival of Anglican missionaries from the Church Missionary Society in 1835. The first mission station in Poverty Bay was built at Kaupapa, next to the now-vanished Umukapua pā, in January 1840. This was the site of the first church in the area, a whare-style building of raupō and timber slabs. After the church was destroyed by a storm on 22 November 1842 services were held at the Ōrākaiapu marae, in a large meeting house called Hāmokorau, located where the Latter Day Saints Church at Manutuke now stands.[7]

The second church stood on the south side of the urupā (cemetery) beside the current church. This was also a whare-style church, following the layout of the Māori meeting house, with large poutokomanawa (pillars) running down the centre. As Richard A. Sundt points out, this church was actually a result of two building campaigns.[8] In 1849 several panels were carved for the church featuring stylised images of the human figure, similar to the carvings created for Te Hau-ki-Tūranga, a meeting house in Manutuke that was started in 1842. Missionary William Williams' objection to these panels led to a temporary abandonment of work on the church, before the Māori artists decided on a different approach. The editor of the *Church Missionary Intelligencer* summarised the situation in 1852:

Exterior, Toko Toru Tapu, 1891. Photograph by William Crawford. Ref: WFC 341-10, Tairāwhiti Museum, Te Whare Taonga o Te Tairāwhiti, Reproduced with the permission of the trustees of Toko Toru Tapu.

The carving was commenced, during Archdeacon Williams' absence from the Station, in the old native style, in which grotesque and hideous figures are conspicuous, as in much of the church architecture of our own country, executed during the usurpation of the Papal power. To this the Archdeacon strongly objected, as being improper for a Christian place of worship. Some of the Chiefs took offence, the carving of their tribe being famous throughout the island; but Archdeacon Williams remaining firm, and suggesting that they should adopt some other mode of carving, these disciples of the old school gave way. On going to the workshop, the Archdeacon found a man chalking out a new pattern upon a plain piece of timber, in which the character of native carving remained, without the devices to which he had objected.[9]

The solution was the manaia,[10] a versatile design from Māori art that is not obviously a representation of the human figure – Williams described it as 'a new pattern that is quite non descript exhibiting neither man beast or creeping thing but giving a very good specimen of native carving'. As a departure from the carved human figures in Te Hau-ki-Tūranga, it was acceptable to both Williams and the Māori artists working on the second church.[11] Stimulated by the artistic challenge, the carvings and kōwhaiwhai for the church were completed in about a year and the building's framework was erected in 1851. A series of delays, including a lack of funds to pay for the weatherboard exterior, meant that the walls and roof were not added until over a decade later, in time for

the church's opening on 19 April 1863.

It is almost impossible to exaggerate the importance of this second church. It was one of the most impressive early Māori churches, rivalled only by Rangiātea at Ōtaki, yet the church at Manutuke was fully carved in a way that other Māori churches of the time were not. (Rangiātea is decorated with tukutuku weaving and kōwhaiwhai.) As Sundt puts it, 'It was the locals' insistence on employing sculptural decoration that makes this church so significant for the history of Maori art.'[12]

The carvings were done by a number of skilled Tūranga (Gisborne) artists, including Raharuhi Rukupō, one of the most important Māori carvers of the nineteenth century, whose legacy includes Te Hau-ki-Tūranga, the earliest surviving whare whakairo and an important model for subsequent Māori art.[13] In choosing the manaia, which 'Williams deemed to be a simple decorative "device" devoid of human characteristics, Rukupō and his group of carvers considerably expanded the scope of Māori art by handling the manaia in new ways.'[14] The carvings and kōwhaiwhai for the church at Manutuke did something that had never been seen before, and that changed the possibilities of Māori art.[15]

Eventually the church fell into disrepair and was dismantled in 1881. Construction on a new, third church began in 1888. This was located in the same spot as the present church, and about 300 metres north of where its predecessor had stood. Built of timber, it followed European ideas of church architecture and was designed in the Gothic Revival style and dedicated on 2 March 1890.[16] The third church reused the carvings from the second church, although since it was smaller, these had to be trimmed and rearranged to fit their new home.

'What was undoubtedly one of the most regrettable fires that have occurred in Poverty Bay for a long time took place at Te Arai between 1.30 and 2 o'clock this morning,' reported the *Poverty Bay Herald* on 28 January 1910, 'when the historic little church of Whakato was reduced to ashes, together with all the furnishings and magnificent carvings which have been a centre of very great attraction.'

Exterior triptych, showing location of second church, Toko Toru Tapu, 2010.

Photograph by Studio La Gonda. Reproduced with the permission of the trustees of Toko Toru Tapu

> Throughout to-day little groups, especially of the older natives, were to be seen wending their way to the scene, and it was pitiful to hear the wailings of the women and the sobs of the men as they gave vent to their feelings of great sorrow over the remains of an edifice that was extremely dear to them … The carvings were very rare, there being few like them in New Zealand. 'In fact,' said one of the natives, 'we shall never again have another church like that.'[17]

With the carvings used in the second and third churches either destroyed or out of reach, new carvings were made for Toko Toru Tapu. The carvers were Te Ngaru Ranapia and Te Ipu, from Te Arawa, and Te Tuhi from Tūhoe, and their work was completed by 22 January 1913, when the *Poverty Bay Herald* reported that 'a waggon-load of Maori carvings for the handsome new church at Manutuke was being carted into Te Arai yesterday'.[18] A comparison of William Crawford's excellent photographs of the third church with the current building reveals that both the architect and the carvers looked closely at the model that was lost in the fire, and worked hard to ensure that the spirit of the church – and its legacy reaching back to the middle of the nineteenth century and the art of Rukupō and others – was 'reincarnated' in the new building.

In his formal opening address on 9 March 1913 the *Poverty Bay Herald* recorded Archdeacon William Leonard Williams as saying that 'Whilst the carving of the new building was good, he considered it was not equal to the old slabs destroyed in the fire … [but] that the real greatness of a church was not in the building or its ornamentation, but in the soundness of the worship which was conducted in that church, and in the lives its worshippers led outside.'[19] From an architectural or heritage point of view, we could paraphrase this sentiment: the real greatness of a church is not always in the existing building or its art works, but in the history that these represent, and the way in which the traces of the past continue to exist, like a shadow or an echo, available to us if we know how to look.

35
A Gentleman's Slippers
Chanel Clarke and Catherine Smith

Detail, heel of tāniko slipper.

To walk a mile in someone else's shoes is to experience the same things that they do. But what if the person has long since died and one of the few material things remaining are their shoes – what can we then say about their life?

When the owner of these tāniko shoes, the celebrated Muaūpoko leader Te Keepa Te Rangihiwinui, or Major Kemp as he was commonly known, died in 1898, it was declared that his tangi would be one of the largest ever known in the colony.[1] Indeed the town heaved as over 1500 Māori and the local townspeople, reported as numbering upwards of 10,000,[2] lined the street as he was carried on a gun carriage specially sent by the Defence Department. A joint committee of influential Māori and Europeans made the funeral arrangements, an indication of the two worlds in which this man confidently strode. What had Major Kemp done to warrant such ceremony and to have politicians and leading statesmen act as his pallbearers?[3]

His obituaries provide clues to the multiple worlds Major Kemp negotiated and the high regard in which all held him. The *New Zealand Herald*, for example, described him as 'a chief of great mana, a gallant soldier, and a faithful subject'.[4] The first title derived from his inherited leadership but was also an indication of the mana he achieved and the power base he built during his distinguished military service. Kemp's military career began early when he joined the Armed Police Force, probably in the late 1840s. By the early 1860s he was regarded as one of the leading pro-government Māori and joined early campaigns against the Hauhau along the Whanganui River, and later campaigns against Te Kooti and Tītokowaru. Kemp gained a formidable reputation and when his volunteer flying column was dispatched in pursuit of Tītokowaru, European officers and rank and file soldiers chose, for the first time, to serve under a Māori leader.[5] Kemp won universal praise from the government, and Sir George Whitmore believed he was 'personally worth any 200 ordinary men in the field'.[6] He was rewarded for his gallantry and loyalty by being presented with Queen Victoria's Sword of Honour in 1870, the New Zealand Cross in 1874 and the New Zealand War Medal in 1876.[7]

Kemp's history, as a faithful subject of Queen Victoria, reveals the larger context in which many Māori leaders operated in colonial New Zealand.

Tāniko slippers owned by Te Keepa Te Rangihiwinui (Major Kemp).

Accession no. 2002.78.1, donated by B. Angland, Auckland War Memorial Museum – Tāmaki Paenga Hira

Major Kemp in his military uniform including his sword and medals. *Ref: PH-CNEG-C3557, Auckland War Memorial Museum – Tāmaki Paenga Hira*

Wikitōria (Victoria) Kemp, daughter of Major Kemp, 1866. *Ref: PH-CNEG-C18556, Danbury Album, Auckland War Memorial Museum – Tāmaki Paenga Hira*

He clearly had personal motivations for aligning himself with the monarch, and with her military and government representatives. With increasing pressure placed on Māori communities by European settlement, fighting on the side of the British militia ensured that tribal lands were protected and their people were looked after and prospered,[8] or so it was thought. In later years, however, Kemp became increasingly disillusioned with the continued alienation of Māori land and helped to establish the Kotahitanga movement, becoming a key player in encouraging tribal cohesion and solidarity.[9]

Considering this life story it is easy to see how tāniko shoes would have appealed to Major Kemp. The slipper uppers are made with muka, woven using a traditional Māori tāniko technique: full and half twist weft-twining using a number of colours, highly fashionable for decorative borders on cloaks at the time of European contact. The design features conventional chevrons and triangular shapes (known as aramoana, or pathway to the sea), and the muted tones and colour palette suggest that traditional dyes were used. The tāniko uppers have been machine stitched to the leather lining and additional pieces of leather have also been added into the heel for reinforcement. The stitched soles, the insoles and the nailed heels are leather and have been welted by hand. The leather itself is likely cow or goat hide, and a cord for reinforcement acts as a binding underneath the leather, which creates a piped effect at the top line of the shoes. A pattern iron has been used along the outer top edge of the built-up heel to create further design interest befitting a bespoke finish.

The slight heel, plain leather sole and worked tāniko uppers make the slippers very similar in style and construction to Prince Albert slippers. To avoid marking expensive rugs and hardwood floors after being outdoors on rough Victorian roads, English gentlemen would exchange their shoes at the door for more comfortable house slippers. Prince Albert, who was a fan, elevated the status of this footwear with the addition of velvet uppers and quilted linings, and the slip-on shoes were thereafter referred to by his name. They were usually reserved for receiving guests at home or hosting formal dinner parties.[10]

Major Kemp's slippers are similar to examples in Berlin wool work, which was popular during the mid-nineteenth century. Mrs Cremer, whose shop was located on Victoria Avenue in Whanganui, was a direct importer of 'Art Needlework and Fancy Goods' and advertised regularly in the local *Wanganui Chronicle*. She always kept a well-assorted stock of needlework patterns, and slippers – 'both canvas and traced cloth' – were listed among her goods for sale. She also stocked a good supply of Brigg's patent transfer papers, which included a variety of designs for use on cushions, slippers and other fancy needlework.[11]

The uppers of Major Kemp's shoes were probably crafted first, possibly from a pattern bought from Mrs Cremer's store, or one like it. Perhaps a family member, maybe his daughter Wikitōria, did the work. Alternatively, and judging by the uniquely Māori designs, the maker may have used a standard slipper pattern as a template to create the tāniko upper. It is evident that much care has been taken in placing the tāniko patterns on specific areas to produce an aesthetically pleasing design. The designs on each slipper are almost identical, which makes the use of a transfer pattern more than likely. After the uppers were made they would have been taken to a local shoemaker for crafting into slippers that would have been considerably more expensive than their ready-made counterparts. Dress slippers were the epitome of Victorian dandyism. Major Kemp's military achievements and service to his tribe belie the dandy label, but these fashionable slippers mark him as someone of taste and style, a consumer of fine luxury goods and a true gentleman of his time.

Kemp left his entire estate to his only daughter, Wikitōria, with the exception of his military accoutrements and swords, left to his son, and his decorations, which he bequeathed to his nephew.[12] Wikitōria gave the slippers to her father's good friend, John Roderick McDonald, who was one of the largest landholders in the Horowhenua district, where he established Heatherlea, the family estate and homestead, in the 1890s.[13] As this relationship shows, Kemp and Wikitōria mixed in well-to-do upper-class circles locally and nationally. McDonald spoke fluent Māori and, according to the *Horowhenua Chronicle*, was helpful 'in every movement taken to uplift the Maori race',[14] though, as the following essay shows, he was also a keen purchaser of Māori land. The Auckland War Memorial Museum recently acquired the tāniko slippers, and another pair of slippers, also with uppers made using customary Māori weaving techniques, from McDonald's granddaughters. These tāniko slippers reflect both Major Kemp's Māori heritage, and the European world in which he sought to be recognised. They are tangible evidence of his self-fashioning and his use of dress and adornment to express two identities: as a Māori leader, and one who was also successful in the European world.

The combining of European and Māori elements in dress had been occurring in New Zealand since the first tentative contacts between the two peoples. Māori quickly incorporated novel European materials into their customary dress and later, particularly with missionary encouragement, adopted European dress. At the same time European dress forms were combined with Māori materials or decoration as they were in these tāniko slippers.

In 1871 Mr Healey's boot and shoe warehouse, in Bridge Street, Nelson, had exhibited in its window a pair of shoes made 30 years before of woven New Zealand flax fibre. 'The soles and lining are leather and the woven fibre has received a black coating, to resist the destructive action of the sea water, as well as to make them water-tight.'[15] Shoes, as well as other interesting articles including a smoking cap, tea cosy and watch pockets all made from harakeke, were displayed at the New Zealand International Exhibition in Hagley Park, Christchurch in 1882.[16] The 1906–07 International Exhibition in Christchurch also included Māori slippers, although it is not known whether these were based on earlier customary Māori footwear or were a combination of leather and harakeke to emulate European shoes.[17] Major Kemp's tāniko slippers have a number inscribed on the insole, which perhaps indicate that they themselves were exhibited at some time.

Major Kemp's typewriter.

Accession no. 1899.183.2, donated by Wikitōria Kemp, Whanganui Regional Museum Collection

Several other objects belonging to Kemp survive in museum collections, and, like the slippers, they are not traditional Māori heirlooms but objects that offer material evidence of a man who straddled two different worlds with ease. The surviving objects also encapsulate how Kemp wished to be remembered. He bequeathed to the town of Whanganui a life-sized portrait painted by Gottfried Lindauer, requesting it be kept in the museum or similar public institution for posterity.[18] Kemp is pictured with his European tokens of loyalty including his sword of honour, which now also resides in the museum, as does his typewriter, donated by Wikitōria.[19] It is symbolic of the roles Kemp played in the machinery of European government in his early life as a Native Land Court assessor and a land purchase officer. In later years when Kemp become disillusioned with the government and the continued alienation of Māori land, the typewriter provided a method of gaining support for his causes through the use of words and political influence.[20]

Major Kemp had all the insignia of a solid British gentleman. He also gained the respect of Māori through his earlier military endeavours and, in later life, through his efforts towards Māori development. Although his vision of a biracial urban community living harmoniously together never eventuated in his lifetime,[21] his slippers remain as a symbol of the way he effortlessly blended the two worlds in his own life.

36

Māori Monument or Pākehā Propaganda?

The Memorial to Keepa Te Rangihiwinui, Whanganui

Ewan Morris

In Moutoa Gardens or Pākaitore, Whanganui, stands what is surely New Zealand's wordiest memorial: a marble statue of a man in military uniform on a stepped granite plinth, with four panels of dense text carved into the polished stone at the top, then four bronze panels depicting battles from the New Zealand Wars and four more with detailed descriptions of those battles.[1]

The memorial commemorates Te Keepa Te Rangihiwinui, also known as Taitoko, a rangatira of the Whanganui iwi Te Āti Haunui a Pāpārangi and of Muaūpoko from the Horowhenua district.[2] Known to Pākehā as Major Kemp, Te Keepa was one of the most famous leaders of the Māori who fought on the Crown side in the New Zealand Wars. His monument is one of several significant memorials in Pākaitore, a site that came to national attention when it was occupied by Māori in 1995.[3] The occupiers articulated a view of Whanganui's colonial history that emphasised Māori independence and challenged the message of loyalty to the Crown they saw represented in the town's memorials.[4] At first glance, the Keepa memorial appears to be another instance of Pākehā domination of the symbolic landscape, yet an investigation of its history, like that of Te Keepa himself, reveals a more complex picture.

The 2007 documentary film, *Te Whiringa Taura o Whanganui*, states that the memorial to Te Keepa 'was erected by the Whanganui settlers to honour his part in protecting the town'. Whanganui iwi spokesperson Gerrard Albert then describes the memorial as 'he mahi pōhēhē nā te Pākehā', undertaken by Pākehā in the mistaken belief that Te Keepa was fighting for them rather than for his own people's interests.[5] Looking at the memorial, it is easy to understand the assumption that it was erected by local Pākehā.

Based on Gottfried Lindauer's portrait, the statue shows Te Keepa as a soldier in the service of the Crown. Dressed in full military uniform, he wears his military decorations and holds the sword of honour awarded to him by Queen Victoria for 'unfailing loyalty and valour'.[6] The front panel declares that the memorial was 'raised by a grateful country', in conjunction with Te Keepa's sister. It describes Major Kemp as a 'high-born Maori chief, brave soldier & staunch ally of the N.Z. Government during the troublous times of the Maori rebellion against British authority'. Two further panels consist of extracts from Walter Gudgeon's *Defenders of New Zealand* (1887),[7] including tributes from Colonel George Whitmore and Sir Walter Buller. There is also a fourth panel

OPPOSITE: *Memorial to Taitoko Keepa Te Rangihiwinui, Pākaitore/Moutoa Gardens, Whanganui.*

Photograph by Andy Palmer, Manatū Taonga/ Ministry for Culture and Heritage

OPPOSITE, BELOW: *Bronze panel depicting the battle of Moturoa (1868). Photograph by Andy Palmer*

Right: *Portrait of Taitoko Keepa Te Rangihiwinui by Gottfried Lindauer. The statue of Te Keepa on the memorial was based on this portrait.*

Ref: 1899.224, Whanganui Regional Museum Collection, Reproduced with permission of the portrait's kaitiaki

in te reo Māori, to which I will return. On the panels below are pictures and descriptions of four battles: Pungarehu, Moturoa, Te Pōrere and Maraetahi. The viewpoint is unashamedly Pākehā: 'our' men face 'the enemy', described as 'rebels' or 'Hauhaus'.

The memorial was not, however, initiated by Pākehā. A month after Te Keepa's death in 1898, Premier and Native Minister Richard Seddon and MP James Carroll met Māori assembled at Pūtiki pā, Whanganui. Māori speakers talked of Māori home rule and quoted Te Keepa's reported last words, which urged the retention of the remaining Māori land. In this context Porokoru Patapu requested 'that the Government should erect a suitable memorial to Major Kemp'. Seddon responded enthusiastically and called on Te Keepa's family to choose an appropriate memorial.[8] The Wanganui Borough Council approved a design in December 1899, but progress was then delayed by uncertainty about government funding.[9]

Not until 1911 was the memorial project taken up again, by Te Keepa's sister Rora Hakaraia, who signed a contract with monumental masons Frank Harris & Co. for the construction of a statue and monument. After Carroll, now native minister, promised up to £300 for the memorial from the government, Rora was persuaded to add the bronze panels depicting battle scenes. A commercial traveller for Frank Harris & Co., Walter Grace, researched the battle scenes, reading written sources and interviewing several veterans. Auckland sculptor W.H. Feldon did the initial work on the statue and the bronze relief panels.[10]

The memorial was erected at Moutoa Gardens in September 1912. Preparations were begun 'on an extensive scale' for its unveiling,[11] but when Rora saw the memorial she objected that the statue bore no resemblance to Te Keepa. A meeting of Māori at Pūtiki also refused to accept the memorial unless the statue was replaced, and consequently no unveiling ceremony was ever held.

Rora's agent, and Te Keepa's friend, John Roderick McDonald, had paid £550 to Frank Harris & Co. on her behalf, but the company still claimed £600 and sued for the balance. Rora counter-claimed for the £550 already paid, alleging that the statue was not a likeness of her brother and that the work on the memorial was badly done. When the case was heard in May 1913 in the Palmerston North Supreme Court the jury found in favour of the company, but Rora's lawyers then moved for a new trial. Justice Chapman agreed, setting aside the verdict. The statue, he concluded, was not 'a work of art within the category to which the defendant is entitled'.[12] This decision was appealed, but the Court of Appeal not only upheld Justice Chapman's judgement but found in favour of Rora in Frank Harris's claim against her. This decision left open the question of Rora's counter-claim, but in January 1915 she died and the case lapsed.[13]

During the trial, stonemasons, sculptors and art experts gave evidence that the statue was 'out of proportion', anatomically incorrect and looked like a Guy Fawkes dummy. It had a 'grotesque' back 'like a sack on two posts', legs 'like drain pipes' or 'like the funnels of a ship', and a 'stiff and artificial' pose.[14] The bronze panels depicting battle scenes looked to one witness like 'a lot of flies crawling up a piece of zinc', and to Justice Hosking in the Court of Appeal 'like pictures of extinct birds' feet in sand'.[15]

Above: *Portrait of Rora Hakaraia, probably by Gottfried Lindauer, from a painting formerly in the possession of Rod A. McDonald of Levin. The current location of the painting is unknown. Ref: PA1-q-002-111, Adkin Album 13, G.L. Adkin Collection, Alexander Turnbull Library, Wellington, New Zealand*

Rora and other Whanganui Māori objected simply that the statue did not look like its subject. The Māori who met at Pūtiki in 1912 to discuss the memorial would have preferred a statue of Te Keepa as an older man.[16] There was also some discussion at the trial about whether the statue looked too Pākehā.[17] One witness said the only objection of Māori was to the marble statue's colour: 'It would look more Maori if it were black.'[18] A lawyer's suggestion that the statue might be painted brown provoked John McDonald into a revealing conflation of colour and character: 'Kemp was one of the greatest generals who had lived, and … was almost as white as himself.'[19]

McDonald, who belonged to a prominent Horowhenua settler family, told the court that he had helped Rora 'in business matters for some time past'.[20] But McDonald was also an assiduous acquirer of Māori land.[21] Rora sold him land for £2000 to fund construction of the statue, a sad irony given Te Keepa's reported last words warning against the continued sale of land.[22] Rora testified that she had signed the memorial contract believing that the government would pay half of the cost. No government contribution was ever made.

Furthermore, Rora's understanding of the proposals for the monument is in doubt. She apparently spoke little English, and an interpreter attended the meeting where she signed the contract that added the battle scenes. Rora testified that Walter Grace and the interpreter 'were speaking among themselves about battle pictures in English', and the interpreter admitted under cross-examination that 'We gave her very little detail of what she was going to get for the extra £350'.[23] Rora signed contracts with no Māori translation attached,[24] and there is no evidence that the lengthy battle descriptions were translated for her in full.

Panel in Māori showing the whakapapa of Te Keepa and Rora.

Photograph by Andy Palmer

On one part of the memorial, however, Rora seemingly speaks in her own voice: the panel in Māori, which has no equivalent text in English. It emphasises Te Keepa's loyalty and service to the Crown as strongly as the English texts, but mentions his work as a policeman, mail-carrier and court assessor alongside his military career. In contrast to the focus elsewhere on Te Keepa's gallantry and bravery, the Māori text describes him as 'he tangata kaha, rangimārie, hohourongo' – a strong, quiet or peaceful person, a peacemaker.[25] Uniquely, the Māori text gives a prominent place to the whakapapa of Te Keepa and Rora. By the late nineteenth century it had become common for Māori newspapers to publish whakapapa of prominent Māori following their deaths,[26] but I know of no other public memorial that does so. The whakapapa demonstrates that Te Keepa and Rora are 'he momo ariki, he uri rangatira, he uri toa' – the descendants of chiefs and warriors. While displaying Te Keepa's and Rora's links with iwi elsewhere in the country, it also connects them, through their mother Rere ō Maki, to the land and waters of Whanganui. The Māori panel faces the Whanganui River, a stretch of which is named Rere ō Maki.[27] The panel also upholds the mana of Rora, who appears with Te Keepa in each of the whakapapa lines and is described elsewhere on the memorial as 'a chieftainess of several tribes'.

The Māori panel is the only place where a distinct Māori identity and tradition is represented; there are no Māori motifs on the memorial, for example. Moreover, the trial's focus on whether the statue was a realistic representation raises an intriguing question. Why did Rora Hakaraia want a European-style statue when Māori had their own artistic and commemorative traditions? By the early twentieth century Māori had, as Roger Blackley has shown, assimilated European portraiture into their own culture and customs, but few Pākehā understood the language of Māori art.[28] If the Keepa memorial, standing in a public park in a predominantly Pākehā town, was to speak to both Pākehā and Māori, it needed to employ Pākehā representational conventions. Similarly, if Te Keepa was to be recognised as the equal of Pākehā leaders, such as former Premier John Ballance, whose statue stood nearby, he needed to be represented similarly.

The appeal to a Pākehā audience may also help to explain the memorial's focus on Te Keepa's military career. After the wars, Te Keepa turned to defending his people's land. He established a land trust in Whanganui, marking out over 800,000 hectares for protection from land sales. In Horowhenua he sought to advance Muaūpoko land interests against the claims of other iwi. Although he never repudiated his loyalty to the Crown, in the 1890s Te Keepa became a leader of the Kotahitanga movement, which established a Māori Parliament and called for the retention of Māori land.[29] None of this appears on the memorial.

Perhaps, given the eventual failure of many of his later projects, it seemed better to Rora and other Whanganui Māori to focus on Te Keepa's undoubted military success. A military memorial might also appeal more to Pākehā and potential government funders than one that dealt with Te Keepa's later endeavours. It seems clear, too, that cultural and language barriers prevented Rora from truly exercising control over the memorial. Only on the panel in Māori does she appear to speak for herself.

The Keepa monument is a significant and unusual public tribute to an important Māori leader that not only proclaims Te Keepa's skill and daring as a warrior but also shows his strong ancestral ties to the land on which the statue stands. The 1995 dispute over Pākaitore saw the toppling of the Ballance statue and the defacing of the memorial to Māori who fought on the Crown side in the Battle of Moutoa. It is surely no accident that Te Keepa came through the occupation unscathed. The monument to him is, in a sense, bicultural: Māori in its origins, subject and the prominent place of whakapapa; Pākehā in form and prevailing messages. Like Te Keepa's own life, it embodies the contradictions, ambiguities, cultural misunderstandings and shifting power relations of its colonial context.

37

Naturalising Nightingale in the Ashburton Domain

The Florence Nightingale Memorial Tree and Tablet

Katie Pickles

The Florence Nightingale memorial tree and tablet, photographed in 2014, dominate the central lawn of the Ashburton Domain.

Photograph by Michael Hall

In the central lawn of the Ashburton Domain, beneath a voluptuous English beech tree that has grown tall, wide and glorious, there is a stone tablet, a little worn with the years. The history of both tablet and tree is a component of New Zealand's colonial past, where imperial connections loomed large and where local initiative led to these relic markers in the Ashburton landscape. They are symbolic of a colonial attachment that naturalised local imaginations of a distant English woman in the soil of Ashburton.

On 13 August 1910 Florence Nightingale, famous for her nursing work during the Crimean War and as the founder of the modern Protestant nursing profession, died in her sleep at the age of 90 in London. It took only two weeks for Ashburton to spring into commemorative action: the memorial tree was planted on 1 September at 2.30 pm. School children formed a circle in the domain and the Mayor Henry Davis opened formal proceedings with an address that 'dwelt on some of the things Florence Nightingale had done for humanity', especially her work in saving lives of soldiers during the Crimean War by lowering mortality rates through improved sanitation. The mayoress planted the tree, 'hoping that it would flourish for all time, and commemorate the work of Florence Nightingale'. The Rev. H.E. Bellhouse then addressed the children, emphasising Nightingale's sense of duty as an heroic example that each of them might reflect upon and emulate.[1]

The species chosen was not an indigenous tōtara or a cabbage tree but a quintessentially European beech. Planting the tree was an organic act of 'ecological imperialism', of introducing old world flora to the colonies. And just as Florence Nightingale was considered fine 'British stock', so the beech was chosen as a fitting tree to spread its roots and flourish in a colonial setting.

Creating parks and domains in colonial New Zealand was an imported idea that was a part of taming the landscape to resemble Britain. Ashburton, laid out as a planned Canterbury Association town in 1861, created a scenic new world partly by setting aside land for an extensive, central domain. In 1894 William Walter Smith was appointed caretaker. His work was influenced by his training and experience on estates in Scotland and the Lake District, and on the Burghley estate in England. Accordingly 'the major design elements of the domain were accomplished using familiar European species along with

ABOVE: *This 1982 postcard depicts Florence Nightingale's grave at St Margaret's Church, Wellow, England.*

Author's Collection

LEFT: *The continuation of commemorating and naturalising imperial women in the landscape: The Diana, Princess of Wales memorial tree and plaque, planted in September 1997 by Ashburton Mayoress Annette Anderson.*

Photograph by Michael Hall

Opposite: *The tablet at the foot of the memorial tree bears a verse from Longfellow's 1857 poem, 'Saint Philomena'. Signalling a female settler elite, the tablet also prominently names the Ashburton mayoress who planted the tree.*

Photograph by Michael Hall

other novel North American ones and included formal flower gardens, specimen trees, lakes, panoramas, and scenic vistas'.[2]

As the Florence Nightingale tree and tablet testify, the domain was a site where the imperial connection was explicitly cultivated. In November 1912, for example, seeds from the king's London gardens were planted in the domain, some close to the Nightingale memorial.[3] There are many commemorative trees in the Ashburton Domain, and most of them are for members of the British royal family. That Florence Nightingale was memorialised attests to the respect in which she was held: locally and throughout the empire she was literally 'well thought of'.

Beyond the domain, as a town with clear British colonial origins, Ashburton was a stronghold for commemorating a range of local and imperial citizens, including early settler John Grigg and the local men who lost their lives fighting for the British Empire during the Great War.[4] Commemorating Nightingale fitted with this patriotic era of imperial unity. But in an age where it was rare to commemorate women, the objects also signal the important status of women in Mid-Canterbury, where nurses and matrons occupied an influential position in society.[5]

It is significant that it was the mayoress who planted the tree. Her name features prominently on the tablet. Strong British womanhood was a fundamental part of settler colonialism. 'Female imperialists' had taken on the mantle of Queen Victoria herself, with elite women such as Davis enjoying a position as promoters of empire unity and good citizenship, especially to children.[6] In this context, Florence Nightingale was an important colonial symbol, representative of women's noble nursing role in the imperial and colonial enterprise, and revered as a role model for women and children.

Although Florence Nightingale never set foot in New Zealand, she was clearly part of the settler consciousness, a colonial household name. When she received the Order of Merit in 1907, the first woman to do so, the *Ashburton Guardian*, like newspapers throughout the country, reported on the honour, and on the flowers that were sent by the Kaiser a few days later.[7] Newspaper coverage was invariably celebratory: the news of her ninetieth birthday on 18 May 1910 advanced her as 'one of the ablest women that ever breathed'.[8] Her death made front-page news in the *Ashburton Guardian*.[9]

Florence Nightingale appeared as part of an 'imperial curriculum' well into the twentieth century.[10] She occupied a legendary status as a female 'lifesaver', the archetypal nineteenth-century ministering angel – 'the lady with the lamp' who had selflessly nursed men in the Crimea. Canterbury's Provincial Chambers included a carved stone mask of her on its wall, and she appears in the stained glass window of the Great Hall at the original University of Canterbury in Worcester Street, completed in the interwar years.[11]

In London the main memorial service for Florence Nightingale took place in St Paul's Cathedral. Her relatives refused an offer of burial in Westminster Abbey and she was interred on 20 August in the family plot at East Wellow, Hampshire. Meanwhile, in Ashburton, a stone tablet was commissioned, and at the beginning of 1911 it was placed at the foot of the tree in the domain.[12] Made from the local Mt Somers stone and mounted on a concrete base, it so resembled a tombstone that an Ashburton Borough Council meeting recommended the Domain Board inspect it as a few members had 'raised an objection to turning any part of the Domain into the semblance of a cemetery'.[13]

Claiming her, and naturalising her memory in the domain, the tablet's inscription lists her birth and death dates and uses the words 'benefactress to suffering humanity', which were written by Queen Alexandra on a card sent with her floral tribute to Nightingale's funeral.[14] The tablet also contains a passage from Longfellow's 1857 poem 'Saint Philomena':

> A Lady with a Lamp shall stand
> In the great history of the land
> A noble life of good,
> Heroic womanhood.

Longfellow's poem was instrumental in securing Nightingale's status as an icon: 'It brought together all the strands relevant to his public, in essence the notion of a Christian lady walking alone at night among the mass of common soldiery, bringing hope, through the light from the lamp.'[15] The choice of verse captures the maternal value attached to British women, and assumes colonial women, including the mayoress and the women of Ashburton, as subjects of 'the land' and part of a tradition of 'heroic womanhood'.

In the years following the planting of the tree in the domain, attitudes towards Florence Nightingale went through a series of reinventions. In 1913 the beech came to the attention of peace activists conscious of Nightingale's complicity in militarism. At what a newspaper report desribed as a 'rowdy meeting', English Quaker John P. Fletcher, in New Zealand to head the campaign against the conscription provisions of the Defence Act, said, 'In your Domain I saw a tablet erected in memory of that noble woman Florence Nightingale. If there had been no war between Russia and England, there would have been no need for that lady to have gone to the Crimea … She would have been needed in the slums of London.'[16] This perspective was shouted down at the meeting: there was an enduring reverence for Nightingale's role in the Crimea.

Unsurprisingly, leading up to and during World War I, Nightingale's memory was enlisted to promote patriotism. In February 1914 two Crimean War veterans, William Choat, aged 78, and John Connors, 70, were present at the inspection of senior cadets at the Ashburton parade ground. Choat recalled being nursed in Scutari by Florence Nightingale, who 'paid the utmost attention to all the wounded'.[17] And at the 1916 A & P show the Red Cross Society ran a 'very nicely got up' Florence Nightingale sweet stall to raise funds for wounded soldiers.[18] When Miss E. McKee, who had been the hardworking secretary of the local Red Cross throughout the war, moved to Christchurch in 1919, one of those speaking at her farewell described her as 'the Florence Nightingale of the County'.[19]

Asburton may have had its own Nightingale memorial, but there was still keen local interest in commemorative efforts at the heart of the empire. Ashburtonians were keen to view the 1915 unveiling of Arthur Walker's Florence Nightingale Memorial in

The Florence Nightingale memorial tree and tablet are unnamed, yet central, in this photograph used on the Ashburton District Council's publicity website for the Ashburton Domain in 2013. Would viewers assume a tombstone?

Courtesy of Experience Mid Canterbury

Waterloo Place, London as part of the *Pathe Gazette* screened by Hayward's Pictures in the town in May of the following year.[20]

Nurses, who followed Nightingale's example during both world wars, have continued to claim her. In the early twenty-first century nurses striking for better conditions took their campaign to the tree in the domain: as one retired Ashburton nurse said, 'they went to see our Florrie'.[21] The memorial had transformed into a place where nurses could gather for strength and energy, a legacy of the enduring importance of female imperialism.

A pragmatic way of 'keeping alive the memory of Florence Nightingale' was an annual essay competition for the district's schoolchildren, which started in 1911. The prize was a framed portrait of Nightingale, which was hung in the winning student's school for a year.[22] Around New Zealand, and in Britain, Canada and Australia, there were also widespread Florence Nightingale memorial nursing prizes and scholarships.[23]

What do the tree and plaque mean today? Mayoress Davis planted the tree as a progressive conservative act. The intention was for colonial society to grow and flourish through the remembrance and emulation of past worthy examples, acts and deeds, such as those of Florence Nightingale. Paradoxically, as the tree grew, the colonial attachment waned. Its broad roots and branches remain to mark the colonial underpinnings of the everyday present. In 2013 the tree and tablet's neutral, unnamed appearance in a picture of the domain on the Ashburton District Council's website raises the question of whether historical attachments are now surplanted, irrelevant and unnoticed, or whether in naturalising Nightingale so effectively and confidently into the landscape the imperial past lives on in the present, firmly rooted, tall and strong. The answer perhaps lies in the Diana, Princess of Wales memorial tree and plaque, planted in September 1997, off to the side of the Nightingale memorial. As with the Nightingale memorial, the mayoress, Annette Anderson, planted the tree. At the close of the twentieth century the Ashburton Domain continued to proudly commemorate and naturalise imperial women in the local landscape.

38

A Bottle of Mineral Water from Te Aroha

Peter Hodder

Glass bottle containing water from Te Aroha thermal springs. This particular bottle dates from the 1930s, but the water is thousands of years old.

Courtesy of Te Aroha Museum

This bottle contains water from Te Aroha, but also a story characteristic of New Zealand's colonial past: the identification of a naturally occurring resource – in this case geothermal water – and its harvesting for profit with the assistance of technology,[1] perhaps with unexpected social consequences. The water, now known to be thousands of years old, is from Spring No. 8 in the Te Aroha Domain. It contains sodium bicarbonate ($NaHCO_3$) and 'free carbonic acid', in effect carbon dioxide (CO_2), which imparts a fizzy character. In the 1870s water from a nearby spring (No. 15) was recommended for drinking by those suffering from dyspepsia and was also claimed to 'confine the bowels', while that from Spring No. 8 was said to 'relax them'.[2] In fact there is no obvious difference in the chemical composition of these waters, but by 1963 chemical analysis had revealed that the water contained significant amounts of boron and a sign was erected advising against drinking it.[3]

Māori recognised the thermal springs of the North Island as taonga, and used them for cooking, bathing, medicinal and therapeutic purposes.[4] They were also quick to capitalise on the springs' commercial potential, charging to guide tourists through the scenery of the thermal areas. The visit in 1870 of Prince Albert, the Duke of Edinburgh, further popularised New Zealand's most important tourist attraction, the Pink and White Terraces, and bathing in their silica-laden waters. In Canterbury, Hanmer's first bathhouse was built in 1883; in the Waikato there were seven bathhouses at Te Aroha by 1886, and a hotel. Rotorua's Duchess Bath opened in 1901 and the well-known main bathhouse in 1908.[5] However, it was the 1902 appointment of a government balneologist (an expert in the therapeutic use of mineral waters), Dr Arthur Stanley Wohlmann, that truly initiated the prospect of spa towns in New Zealand which would mimic those of Europe.[6] Wohlmann travelled throughout the country, visiting and classifying springs, initially publishing pamphlets about Te Aroha, Hanmer and Rotorua and later combining his data into a single book, *The Mineral Waters and Spas of New Zealand*, which also described alleged therapeutic benefits.[7] He claimed that the chemical compositions of the New Zealand waters compared favourably with those of the famous European spas. Wohlmann noted that the water at Te Aroha contained 'a very

No. 8
Spring
in the
OVERNMENT SPA
TeAroha
RAL MINERAL WATE
INVALUABLE FOR
of the stomach and intestines, disorders of
and pharyngeal catarrh, rheumatism and
after certain internal operations.
OF INDUSTRIES & COMMERCE, TOURIST &

much larger proportion of sodium-bicarbonate' than France's well-known Vichy water and ranked as 'one of the strongest, probably the actual strongest, alkaline thermal waters of the world'.[8] Such observations provided the foundation for adding 'taking the waters' to New Zealand's geothermal tourism. A model geyserland, complete with cold-water geysers and plaster casts of silica mounds, was displayed at the 1906–07 New Zealand International Exhibition in Christchurch.[9]

Depending on its chemical composition, drinking or bathing in geothermal water was considered to be good for the health. The bicarbonate-rich water from the Te Aroha springs was sold for drinking to the bathing patrons of the Rotorua spa. It appears, however, to have been a minority taste: 196 bottles were sold in 1926, but sales decreased through the late 1920s to about 40 in the 1930s.[10] It would nevertheless have tasted better than the highly acidic water in Rotorua, which dissolved the lime plaster of the bathhouse's interior walls, and accordingly was used for bathing rather than drinking.

Most of the patients undergoing treatment at Rotorua under Wohlmann's stewardship were seeking relief from 'rheumatic' complaints; the next most popular problem was diseases of the nervous system.[11] Moreover, most visitors reportedly left 'very much better' than when they arrived. Nevertheless, the emphasis on the alleged medical benefits of the chemicals in the waters slowly faded, though immersion in their warmth was still considered beneficial for rheumatism and similar disorders.

At the elegant Edwardian spa and its extensive gardens in Te Aroha, there was increased use of public pools in preference to private baths in the early twentieth century, indicating a shift in perception of the water's value from therapy to recreation. Even so, patronage of facilities declined from nearly 40,000 in 1904 to less than 24,000 in 1924.[12]

In Rotorua the 1930s saw the opening of the Ward Baths and the Blue Baths, the latter clearly aimed at the leisure rather than the health market.[13] However, the balneological heritage of the Rotorua spa was not yet abandoned. A 1932 poster showing a montage of illustrations of activities and facilities available at Rotorua includes a view of the swimming baths, and patients being treated by Schnee multipolar electric bath (a massage therapy), high-frequency valve and Aix massage douche.[14] The Publicity Branch of the New Zealand Railways promoted both health and holiday at Rotorua in the 1930s – 'Nature's own'.[15]

Of these two establishments, the Ward Baths are the most famous. This elegant neo-classical building, which opened in 1932 next to the main Rotorua bathhouse and sanatorium, offered both a large male-only pool with nude bathing, and private pools that couples could hire. From the beginning locals and visitors made the most of the 'opacity of the water, tinged asprin-grey by its minerals', which 'facilitated approaches and the tentative touching of feet and the other bathers rarely noticed what was going on'.[16]

By the end of the colonial era, even recreational use of the waters was in decline, possibly hastened by the behaviour of some patrons, particularly at the Ward Baths, and much later by the highly publicised fatal cases of amoebic meningitis caused by bathing

LEFT: *Octagon shelter for drinking water from the No. 8 Spring, with the No. 1 Bath to its right, Te Aroha Domain.*

Courtesy of Te Aroha Museum

BELOW: *A group of men enjoy a hot bath at Rotorua.*

Ref: PA1-f-051-32-3, Railways Album 2, Alexander Turnbull Library, Wellington, New Zealand

in geothermal waters.[17] The locations of the waters containing the amoeba were not specified, giving rise to the public belief that all hot springs were implicated. In fact, no cases were reported from the springs at Te Aroha or Rotorua.

After 1950 geothermal waters continued to be exploited and technologically confined – not in bottles, but in pipes and equipment for electricity generation. A power station was built at Wairakei, a location which was considered to be a 'typical section' of the thermal region stretching from Ruapehu to the Bay of Plenty[18] using steam separated from the high-pressure water from deep wells. This led to dramatic reductions in the periodicity and height of eruption of geysers in the area and significant changes in the temperature and composition of the water,[19] destroying forever the springs' value as a recreational resource. The pipes confining the geothermal water spread across the landscape through the 1950s and 1960s,[20] and exploitation of the resource for electricity generation, albeit on a smaller scale, continues.

This apparently simple object – a bottle of geothermal water – is embedded in a much wider cultural context, impinging on technological themes of science, energy and medicine, and social themes of tourism, leisure and lifestyle, related to the changing value and use of the geothermal resource during the colonial period and beyond.[21]

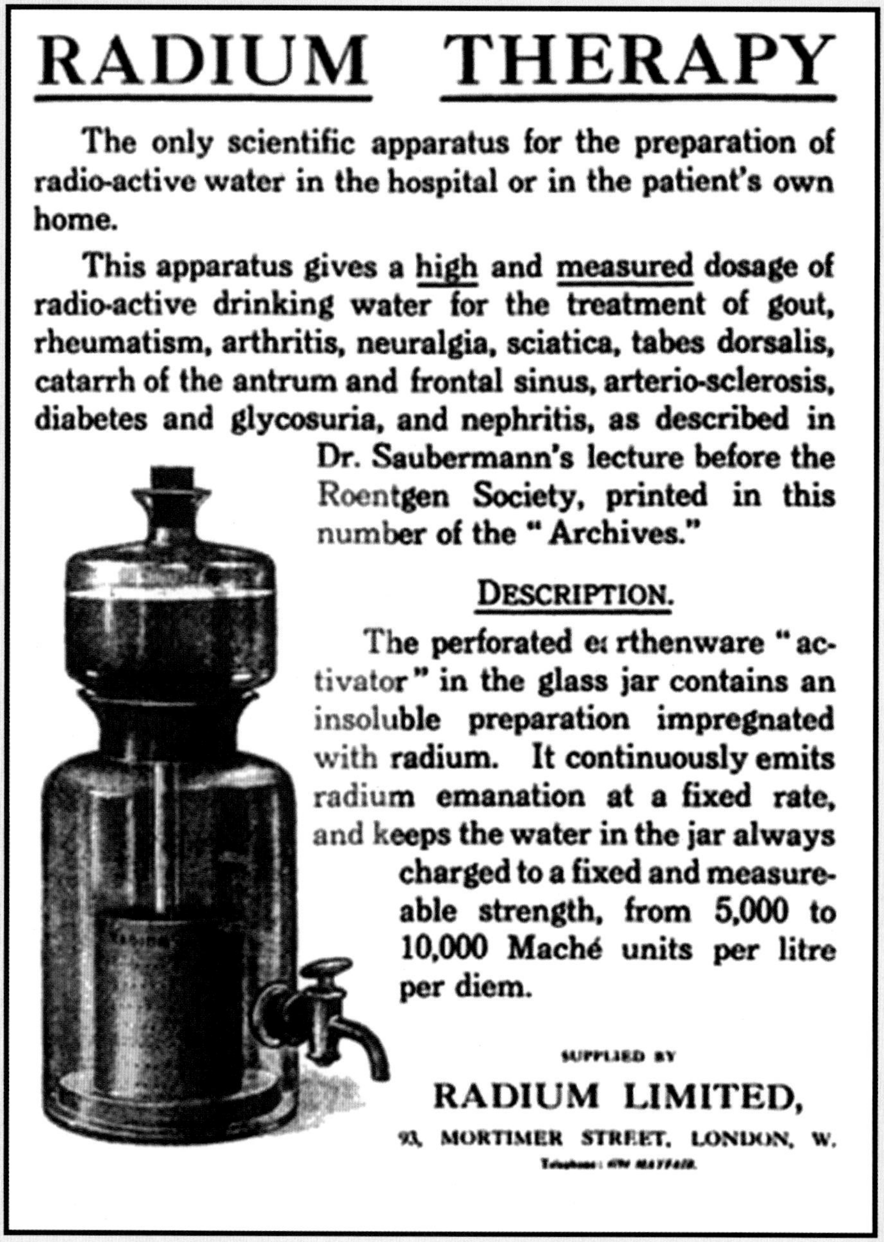

In the northern hemisphere radium activators, which infused water with radioactive radon gas, were promoted for home as well as hospital use. This 1913 advertisement shows a device made by the same London firm that made the Rotorua Bathhouse's radium activator.

Courtesy of www.en.wikipedia.org/wiki/File:Radium_therapy_-_1913.jpg

39

The Rotorua Bathhouse Radium Activator

From Therapeutic Device to Quack Curiosity

Rebecca Priestley

The device that arrived at the Rotorua Bathhouse in 1914 looked much like a regular ceramic water filter – there was a lid for pouring in water at the top and a spigot for draining off water at the side – but it was special. Inside the jug was a second ceramic container holding a small amount of a radioactive compound; it was probably radium sulphate. Any water stored in the jug would be irradiated with radon gas, a radioactive decay product of radium. Dr Arthur Wohlmann ordered the 'radium activator' after a 1913 trip to Europe, during which he visited several spas offering radioactive water therapy and met Dr Sigmund Saubermann, a Berlin-based doctor who had designed a radium activator that was widely used on the Continent. Like similar devices used in health spas and private homes throughout Europe and North America, the Rotorua Bathhouse radium activator was used to produce irradiated drinking water that doctors, patients and domestic consumers believed was a therapeutic tonic. But changes in scientific and medical knowledge would see an evolution of attitudes towards such a device: today it would be seen as an instrument of quackery with an inner chamber containing a dangerous carcinogen.

Wohlmann, an Englishman who had trained as a medical doctor in London, was appointed as New Zealand's first government balneologist in 1902. As an Englishman in a colonial position, Dr Wohlmann naturally looked back to Europe for the latest therapeutic treatments and therapies. As well as keeping up to date with medical literature, he made several journeys to visit European spas, including the 1913 tour on which he made a 'prolonged and close investigation of the principal English spas', conferred with many leading British and continental balneologists and met Saubermann.[1] On his return Wohlmann convinced the government to invest in a radium activator, which was designed to irradiate water with radon gas. In making his case to the general manager of the Department of Tourist and Health Resorts, Wohlmann described radon therapy as a treatment that had 'come to stay' and offered assurances that the apparatus would soon pay for itself, as the New Zealand public was already 'mad on radium', which was then widely used as a cancer treatment.[2] The manager was convinced, as was the Cabinet: in June 1914 they approved expenditure of £250 – equivalent to more than $20,000 in today's money – on a radium activator. One was immediately ordered from Radium

The enterprising idea of adding radioactive water to the Rotorua Bathhouse's list of treatments came from government balneologist Arthur Wohlmann, who said the New Zealand public was 'mad on radium' and the radium activator was well worth the £250 investment.

Ref: 1/2-037890-F, Alexander Turnbull Library, Wellington, New Zealand

Ltd in London, who made it to Saubermann's design and shipped it to New Zealand on the SS *Pakeha*. The carefully packaged device, which stood 65 centimetres tall and weighed 27 kilograms, arrived in Auckland in September 1914 and was in use at the Rotorua Bathhouse by late October.

In his 1914 book, *The Mineral Waters and Spas of New Zealand*, Wohlmann described the portals by which radium emanation, or radon, could enter the body. The most important, he said, were the lungs, the skin and the mouth, though radon could also be administered by injection, by vaginal or rectal douches, or by insertion into tooth cavities. But Wohlmann, perhaps to the relief of his patients, had decided that the preferred way was orally, in a glass of drinking water: 'Not only is the dosage easy to determine and the method of administration simple, but the period of retention in the body is markedly longer than in the case of inhalation.'[3]

When the radon water went on sale at the Rotorua Bathhouse in October 1914, Wohlmann advised each patient to take four to six glasses of radon water a day, at threepence (about a dollar) per glass. Because radon-222 has a half-life of only four days – after four days only half of the radon would remain – patients were advised to drink the water while it was still 'fresh' and before the radon gas had decayed away. Wohlmann recommended that they linger over each glass, sipping rather than gulping the tonic. 'Taking sips at frequent intervals,' he said, helped to 'maintain the charge in the blood.'[4]

Wohlmann recommended the new treatment for a range of chronic conditions, particularly gout and diabetes. Radium water 'looks and tastes exactly like pure water,' said the *Rotorua Times*, 'but it has very different properties. The emanations which it contains have been proved valuable in the treatment of diseases affecting the joints, especially gout, and of diabetes. They are also useful as a nerve soother, and they also have the singular property of tightening loose teeth.'[5]

Today it seems like the worst kind of quackery to prescribe radioactive water as a 'treatment' for chronic illness, but Wohlmann was no charlatan. A colonial doctor and a government employee who got no personal financial gain from prescribing radon water, he was striving to keep up to date, or ahead of, England and continental Europe when it came to the application of his science. In giving radioactive water to his patients, he was acting according to scientific beliefs based on work by Marie Curie and others that suggested moderate doses of radioactivity could invigorate healthy cells and kill cancerous cells.

Radium, though discovered by Curie only in 1898, was by 1914 used widely as a treatment for cancer. A small quantity of radium, or an amount of radon gas sealed in a small capsule, could be placed in close proximity to an external tumour or inserted into an internal tumour. It was known that exposure to radium could cause burns, but the properties of this new element were still being investigated and radon, its daughter gas, was considered relatively benign and therefore suitable for spa treatment of the chronically rather than the acutely ill. What's more, mineral water from hot springs had been used for many centuries and was generally believed to have a curative effect. When radon was discovered in a German hot spring

HAVE A RADIUM WITH ME

SOMETHING NEW IN DRINKS.

(Per Independent Cable Service.)
LONDON, May 12.

The request "Give me a brandy with a dash of radium water," or "I'll have a radium highball," may soon be a common call for a drink. According to an expert radium water has a direct infusion of radium salts, and is kept sparkling by the infiltration of ultra-violet rays and the addition of carbonic acid gas.

A new preparation is being patented and will be shortly issued in syphons for public consumption. The inventors claim that it will be gratifying and also health-giving.

ABOVE: *In 1914, a new therapy arrived at the Rotorua Bathhouse: patients with such chronic conditions as gout, diabetes or constipation were offered glasses of radioactive drinking water produced by a radium activator. This image shows the Bath House, Rotorua, c. 1909, photographed by C.P. Parkerson.*

Ref: OP-2489, Rotorua Museum Te Whare Taonga o Te Arawa

LEFT: *Radium highball anyone? Radioactive water was seen as fashionable and sophisticated and not just for therapeutic use. When added to a soda siphon, radium could deliver a cocktail with a blast of radon-infused carbonated water.*

Grey River Argus, *21 May 1914, p. 8, Courtesy of the National Library of New Zealand*

long believed to have curative powers, the theory emerged that radon was responsible for the tonic effects of bathing in or drinking those waters. Some of the principles of homeopathy were involved here: even if radium was potentially harmful, the much diluted version, the radon gas in water, would have an invigorating effect.

In his justification of radon therapy, Wohlmann referenced the published research of German physicians Saubermann and Paul Lazarus who claimed that:

> 1 … radium emanation in moderate doses promotes the multiplication and growth of healthy cells and the decay of morbid ones.
> 2 Emanation increases the output of urine.
> 3 Emanation increases the activity of the digestive tract, and especially the excretory activity of the bowels.
> 4 It increases the excretion of uric acid …
> 5 It dilates the blood vessels.
> 6 It diminishes the viscosity of the blood …
> 7 It lowers the blood pressure.
> 8 It increases metabolism …
> 9 It has a profound nerve-soothing effect.
> 10 It increases sexual activity.
> 11 It modifies the constitution of the blood, causing first hyper-leucocytosis, then leucopenia and increase in the number of red corpuscles.[6]

Whatever its actual efficacy, the therapy was popular. As word spread, patients flocked to the Rotorua Bathhouse for a course of treatment. Sales of radon water peaked in 1916, when 8500 glasses were sold. To 'save cripples the constant journey to the baths', Wohlmann also arranged for the water to be dispensed in glass-stoppered bottles that each held six glasses of radioactive water.[7]

Sales of radon water declined after 1916. Wohlmann, who had changed his Germanic surname to Herbert during the war, returned to Britain in 1919 and was replaced by Dr Campbell Duncan. In 1923 only 300 glasses of radon water were sold. This was partly because radon water was a fad – there was no credible evidence that it did any of the things that were originally claimed. Despite this lack of therapeutic evidence, an American-made radium-activator called the Revigator was now available to domestic consumers. This product, distributed by a Wellington business calling itself the Radium Ore Revigator Agency, irradiated water via a jar lining of radium ore, and produced water of a much lower radioactivity than the Rotorua Bathhouse device. As one American doctor put it, such devices included 'a few cents worth of crude ore, having a low grade of radioactivity, and possessing no more therapeutic value than do the luminous figures on the dial of a two dollar watch'.[8] Radon water remained popular with domestic consumers until the widely publicised 1932 death of American golfer and industrialist Eben Byers from cancer linked to drinking radioactive water. Radithor, the water Byers drank, contained minute amounts of radium, so was much more potent than the Rotorua radon water or that from domestic devices like the Revigator.

Wohlmann's successors, however, displayed a startling ignorance of the nature and potency of the Rotorua Bathhouse radium activator. In a 1922 memo, Duncan said that the public rarely asked for radon water, and he now rarely prescribed it. 'I would not

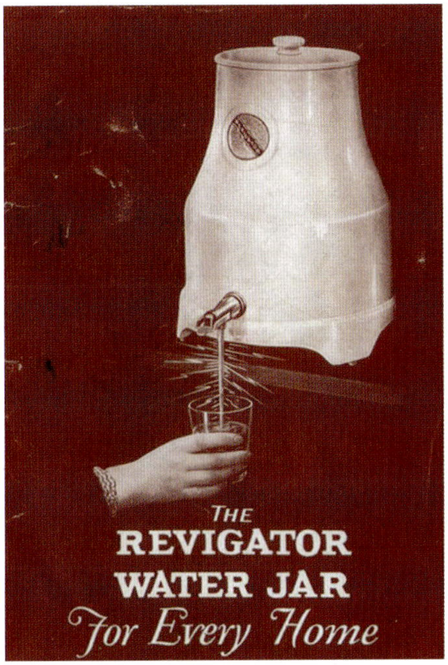

The Revigator Water Jar, sold throughout the United States in the 1920s and 1930s, was promoted as being suitable 'for every home'.

Courtesy of www.en.wikipedia.org/wiki/ File:Revigator_for_every_home.jpg

be prepared to say that the water now possesses any radium properties,' he added.[9] In 1925 the tourist agent at Rotorua described the activator, which was now chipped and broken and sitting in a storeroom, as having 'what appears to be a kind of earth' inside the porcelain cylinder. 'Whatever efficacy this may have had has long ago been expended,' he added, stating that the device was now 'quite valueless'.[10] This showed a total ignorance of the properties of radium and how the radium activator worked. With a half-life of 1620 years, radium would go on releasing radon gas almost indefinitely – as Wohlmann had promised when making the case for the expensive purchase: 'the initial cost is high owing to the price of radium, but the upkeep is nil and the material is to all intents and purposes everlasting'.[11]

The ultimate fate of the Rotorua Bathhouse radium activator is unknown. Rotorua's acidic mineral waters damaged the furnishings and fittings of the bathhouse, necessitating costly repairs and contributing to the business's poor financial performance. By the 1940s the bathhouse was extremely run down and the baths were eventually closed in 1966. The radium activator, with the radium sulphate in its inner chamber continuing to irradiate the air or water surrounding it, probably ended up in a dump somewhere.

The Rotorua Bathhouse radium activator arrived in New Zealand as a piece of scientific equipment, a medical device that issued radon, a substance capable of curing or relieving people of symptoms of chronic ailments like depression, arthritis and constipation. By 1925 it was surplus to requirements, perhaps a bit of an embarrassment to the medical staff, an example of a past fad, an oddity that no one quite knew what to do with. Today we would see an intact radium activator as something sinister and dangerous. With all traces of the radium removed, we could see this as a curiosity, a relic of a time when we were ignorant of the potentially harmful effects of radioactivity. Such items have now become collectibles. A hundred years ago the radium activator purchased by the Rotorua Bathhouse was regarded as a sophisticated medical device; now we are most likely to find one in a museum of quack curiosities.

40

'Pōua's Cloak'

The Haberfield Family Kahu Kiwi

Michael J. Stevens

Kākahu, handwoven cloaks, are prestigious objects within Māori culture. Taking many months or even years to complete, they are high-status items synonymous with leaders and leadership. Because they embody mana, kākahu are referred to in oral compositions and feature in Māori myth templates. Like their owners, kākahu were traditionally tapu. Unauthorised handling of one could therefore lead to punishment by death or even trigger internecine warfare. Both things happened within Kāi Tahu in 1826–27 after Murihaka, a woman living at Waikākahi, a village located at the Horomaka end of Kaitōrete Spit, tried on a dog-skin cloak belonging to the upoko ariki (paramount chief), Te Maiharanui.[1]

European explorers and traders who visited New Zealand from the late eighteenth century, and misleadingly referred to kākahu as mats, actively sought this type of Māori curio. This interest was sustained throughout the colonial period from 1840, buttressed no doubt by a belief that Māori material culture was 'dying out'. Consequently, private collectors and public institutions, many of them in the northern hemisphere, now hold large numbers of antique kākahu. Notwithstanding, some continue to be kept by Māori families as treasured heirlooms passed down from previous generations – tangible links with key ancestors.

European contact and British colonisation influenced kākahu in other ways too, most notably the materials used in their construction. Exotic bird feathers were introduced, and threads of wool and cotton partially displaced those made from whītau (also known as muka), laboriously dressed harakeke fibre. Just as kākahu are woven with a twining technique that requires two types of threads – vertical whenu and horizontal aho – this essay describes one antique kākahu, and traces its history within one southern Kāi Tahu family over the last 100 or so years.

There are many different types of kākahu and specific names for them. As mentioned, some feature feathers and some are adorned with tāniko – geometrically designed, often colourful, borders. Both feature in the kākahu discussed here, a kahu huruhuru – a cloak completely covered with feathers. Because these are kiwi feathers it is specifically referred to as a kahu kiwi. Feather cloaks were apparently rare in the 1700s but became more common

Page 252: *Close-up detail from the centre of the kahu kiwi that shows a small tuft of dark feathers, which may be the 'signature feathers' of the maker(s).* Photographs by Michael Hall

Previous page, (top): *The top rows of feathers are worked into the cloak in such a way that they lift, which is called whakaararaara. This detail shows the transition between these upper feathers and the lower ones that sit flatter.* (Bottom): *This close-up view of the underside of the kahu kiwi clearly shows the woollen threads of the vertical whenu, crossed by the horizontal aho of traditional whitau, dressed fibre extracted from harakeke (New Zealand flax).*

from the mid-1800s.[2] Accordingly, of the 300 kākahu held by the Museum of New Zealand Te Papa Tongarewa, more than 100 contain feathers and 52 of these feature kiwi feathers.[3] The predominance of kiwi feathers is generally attributed to the bird's once greater numbers, but some weavers also assert that kiwi feathers were prized because they neither attract nor are affected by mites.[4]

With its tight, imbricated rows of kiwi feathers and striking, earth brown and yellow-gold tāniko running along its remu or hem, this cloak looks like something that a sailor or trader might have acquired in pre-colonial New Zealand. However, it was born out of the colonial encounter. It is a colonial object. It bears the mark of literacy: part of the tāniko, which mainly consists of an Aonui pattern, is bookended by the phrase 'ROKA O TAUPO' (which may or may not indicate the cloak's origins). Moreover, a view of the underside of the kaupapa, the main body of the cloak, reveals that though the aho are made from whītau, the whenu are made from fine wool.

The kahu kiwi measures 110 centimetres long by 86 centimetres high, including the 6-centimetre-wide tāniko. The amount of work that went into making the cloak is clear to see: there are about six whenu per 10 millimetres and only about that distance between each row of aho. Four feathers are worked into every third or fourth aho, meaning that the cloak probably contains more than 10,000 of them.[5]

As well as being closely woven, the kahu kiwi has shaping lines so that it follows the body and hangs well. It is also tied in a certain place so that in a gentle breeze several top rows of feathers, which are worked in so that they lift, 'sort of stand up and dance'. This technique is called whakaararaara.[6] Less obvious is a small tuft of very soft and dark feathers, probably from another species of bird (possibly huia),[7] which is quietly woven into the centre of the kahu kiwi. It has been speculated that these so-called 'signature feathers' might be a weaver's mark or contain a coded message for the intended wearer.

This kahu kiwi belonged to William Isaac Haberfield (1874–1936), a great-grandson of Piki – a sister of Te Maiharanui. William is my great-great-grandfather. We, his descendants, refer to him as Pōua. Born at or near the small coastal kaik of Omaui, Pōua was baptised at Bluff in 1875 by the Rev. J.F.H. Wohlers of the Ruapuke mission. Both his parents were, in the parlance of the time, 'halfcastes'. His mother, Noki (1839–1914), was born on Whenua Hou, an island west of Rakiura (Stewart Island) that was home to one of New Zealand's earliest bicultural communities.[8] His father, John (1845–1902), was born at Moeraki on the North Otago coast, where his Pākehā father, William Isaac Haberfield (1815–1907), helped to establish a whaling station in 1836. As with his parents, where and how Pōua lived consistently owed something to both persisting pre-European Māori practices and the opportunities and constraints of colonial society. We do not know when or under what circumstances Pōua acquired the kahu kiwi. In 1891 he reportedly found a 9-ounce nugget while working a gold claim with his father in South Westland and it is possible that he bought the kahu kiwi with some of the money that this generated. However, there is no family tradition of this. For most of his working life Pōua was a shearer

RIGHT: *Frances Mercy Haberfield (née Bailey, formerly Spencer), 'Big Nana', and her husband William Isaac Haberfield, 'Pōua', at Greenhills in the late 1920s.* *Mouru Haberfield Collection*

ABOVE: *John Kerle Tipaho ('Boy') Haberfield, Koa Gladys Haberfield, Taura Hemera and 'Buku' Hemera in fancy dress, probably for a Greenhills School fête in the late 1920s. The costumes declare the ease with which the children situate themselves in a colonial world: Boy and Buku are respectively dressed as a cowboy and 'Red Indian' while Taura wears an 'Oriental'-inspired costume. Koa wears the kahu kiwi as the pièce de résistance of her 'Māori Princess' look.* *Mouru Haberfield Collection*

RIGHT: *Michael Stevens wears the kahu kiwi as he and Dr Emma Wyeth proceed to his PhD graduation, University of Otago, May 2010.*

and a wharfie: he variously removed wool from sheep and loaded bales of wool onto ships. The wool that features in the kahu kiwi therefore seems highly appropriate. As a shearer Pōua worked up the east coast of both the South and North islands. Through this he met Aritaku Maaka, of Ngāti Kahungunu, who became his best friend and, from 1903, his brother-in-law, when Aritaku married Pōua's sister, Ani, in Takapau.[9] Perhaps, as a token of appreciation for his matchmaking efforts, this branch of Ngāti Kahungunu presented Pōua with a kahu kiwi? Again, this is pure conjecture. Pōua was also known to enjoy a flutter on the horses. Perhaps one came in for him and he bought the kahu kiwi with the winnings? This, too, is speculative.

In 1906 Pōua married Ritea/Ruby Rehu, a cousin from Moeraki, and in 1907 he moved to Port Chalmers to work on the new graving dock: a job so horrible that locals would not do it.[10] While waiting for appropriate accommodation the couple rented part of a dilapidated wooden two-storey house on George Street, the port's main thoroughfare. On 6 July Pōua worked crushing stone until 9 pm and then returned to the family's first-floor lodgings. Ruby, her son from an earlier relationship, Jacob Tahupūriri Te Aika, and her 11-year-old sister, Hineawhitia Kathleen Rehu, who was visiting from Moeraki, had already gone to bed. By daybreak Ruby and Jacob were dead and Pōua and Kathleen seriously injured: victims of an intense fire.

Kathleen died in Dunedin Hospital a few days after the fire in what was described as a 'merciful release'. The *Otago Witness* also quoted Pōua from his hospital bed as saying that at least '[t]he wife and boy will not be feeling the pain I am in; that's one good thing.' 'She came from Moeraki, poor girl,' he explained, 'and she and the boy will go back there to be buried.' A tangi was indeed held at Moeraki and Ruby, Jacob and Kathleen were interred there together.[11] A large, impressive marble headstone marks their grave. Part of me wonders if Pōua was presented with a kahu kiwi in connection with this sad chapter of his life, which would perhaps explain why we, descendants of his second marriage, do not know about its origins.

Following his return south to his parents at Greenhills, a small railway siding settlement situated at the top of Bluff Harbour, Pōua met and eventually married Frances Mercy Spencer (née Bailey) (1885–1966), a Bluff widow and mother of two young sons. She and Pōua went on to have three more children together and also raised a brother and sister whose parents died in the 1918 influenza epidemic. Times were tight and the family consistently relied on muttonbirding to help pay the mortgage. When Aritaku died in 1936 Pōua's eldest child, my great-grandmother, Mouru (1911–1999), sold medals that she had won in her youth for Highland dancing to raise money so that family members could attend the tangi. The kahu kiwi, however, remained within the family, and this continued to be the case when Pōua died a few months after his friend.

Pōua's memory is kept alive in a number of material objects, including pounamu fobs from his pocket-watch and a few pairs of his hand shears. Nothing is as large or as striking, however, as his kahu kiwi, which hung on a shaded wall in the sitting room of the family home at Greenhills. Its occasional use during his lifetime largely amounted to his daughters wearing it to school concerts where an appropriately attired 'Māori Princess' mingled with siblings dressed as cowboys and 'Red Indians'. By and large, though, the kahu kiwi just hung on the wall, simply part of the furniture. Recollecting his 1930s and 1940s childhood, my grandfather recalls that 'Pōua's cloak' was joined in the sitting room by a fine kete huruhuru (a basket, also covered in kiwi feathers) that had seemingly belonged to Noki, and a large model of a sailing ship in a glass case that had been made by the 'ship's chippie with a pocket-knife and bradawl'. This model ship is also still held within the family. These items were joined by a dozen or so little elephants carved out of ebony, small porcelain rabbits 'of the sort given as a sideshow prize', and later, a stuffed baby crocodile from a family friend who managed a silver dredge in Malaya before World War II.

In the 1950s the kahu kiwi was occasionally lent to husband and wife team Norman and Ngawara Bradshaw (née Kereti) for the likes of Southland's 1956 centenary. Ngawara, who at the age of 16 had played the lead female part in the feature film *Hei Tiki – A Saga of the Maoris*, shot by controversial American filmmaker Alexander Markey near Lake Taupō in 1930, was a key teacher of kapa haka in Bluff.[12] The contribution that she and her family made to this aspect of Māori culture in the port was significant, especially as te reo Māori was probably functionally dead there before the end of the colonial era in 1907. My great-grandmother possessed the kahu kiwi by the time parliament passed the notorious Maori Affairs Amendment Act 1967, referred to by Māori as the 'last land grab'. Her younger sister inherited the kete huruhuru. As perhaps suited the spirit of the time Nana folded the cloak up and placed it in a drawer out of sight, but never totally out of mind. When she died in 1999, immediately before muttonbirding and just after I moved to Dunedin to attend university, Nana was called onto Bluff's Te Rau Aroha marae by our whanauka (relation) Hana Morgan, a daughter of Ngawara and Norman's. We then draped Nana's tūpapaku with her father's kahu kiwi. A decade later, immediately after muttonbirding, I wore the kahu kiwi in a University of Otago graduation procession. Although I spared a thought for Nana, my mind really went back to Pōua, who convalesced from his burns more than a century earlier in a building right next to where the procession began.

Pōua's cloak is a fine example of an iconic item of Māori material culture, but is also deeply affected by the colonial world in which it was created and through which it moved before settling in southern New Zealand. However, this kahu kiwi is significant for us, his descendants, not because of its genus and genius, as significant as they are, but because it was his and because of the way it links us to him. It also connects us to more recently departed family members as well as significant family events beyond tangi and hura kōhatu, such as weddings and university graduations. This cloak then, this colonial object, has remained within our whānau because of a lived sensibility of whakapapa, which it helps to illuminate.

Spectacular ostrich feathers were fashionable from the 1880s. That they were harvested from live, farmed birds rather than from wild ones killed for the purpose, accounted for their longevity as special occasion wear. Martha Cranstoun trimmed her velvet wedding hat with feathers sent by her fiancé from South Africa in 1916.

Ref: GH017583, Museum of New Zealand Te Papa Tongarewa

41
Feathers for a Wartime Bride
Kate Hunter

The Great War, if not a colonial conflict, was an imperial one. For the approximately 100,000 men who served overseas with the New Zealand Expeditionary Force, their voyages transformed the geography of the British Empire from one shaped by the pages of the *School Journal* and the newspapers, to a tangible world of actual ports and people. From the beginning of British settlement in New Zealand, intercolonial trade routes were well established, and goods from across the empire had been present in shop windows and homes. But with the Great War came mass travel and the chance for thousands to see the world for themselves and send home souvenirs from far-off places. All but the earliest recruits had at least some idea, through casualty lists and letters from family and friends already serving, of what awaited them as soldiers fighting overseas. Although in no way minimising the discomforts, fears and terrors of war, this essay focuses on a lesser known aspect of the war experience: the objects the men bought while they were away.

For most soldiers the journey to war took in the Australian ports, and then turned northwest to Colombo and Suez, Cairo and Port Said. For Southland farm labourer Percy Heenan, his route from Wellington to England was via Durban and Cape Town, where he had shore leave. Many of the troops treated the voyage and the ports of call as a tourist adventure and shore leave was an opportunity to write home, send postcards and buy souvenirs. In Durban Percy and his friends had their photo taken with the Zulu 'ricksha' driver, resplendent in his feathered and horned headdress, with beadwork over the calico 'kitchen suit' insisted upon by the colonial government.[1]

The buying of souvenirs was one way in which enlisted men could share with their families and friends the delights and exotic nature of overseas travel. New Zealand soldiers, like those of the other dominions, were well paid in comparison with the British, and because going home was not possible, they spent their leave in foreign towns and cities. Soldiers shopped for lace, embroidered handkerchiefs and postcards in France, as well as textiles and silver in Egypt. Soldier-author Fred Waite recorded that New Zealanders purchased 'precious stones and expensive silks down to cocoanut wood elephants and little green-backed beetles'.[2] That soldiers were keen shoppers was also reflected in George Bollinger's reporting of a rumour in his diary:

In a Great War 'happy ending', Percy and Martha married early in 1918, just weeks after Percy's repatriation. In addition to letters, objects had sustained their connection while they were separated for 20 months.

Courtesy of Robert Heenan and Family

'Word has been received that New Zealanders are to receive only half pay in the future. This is owing to the extravagant way they have been spending money here. One would think they are all tourists.'[3]

In Cape Town Percy Heenan bought six pale, naturally coloured ostrich plumes, one for his sister, Grace, the other five for his fiancée, Martha Cranstoun. That the plumes Percy sent to Martha were undyed could be interpreted as patriotic: by 1900 the centre of the world's chemical dyeing industry was in Germany. Indeed, the outbreak of war not only cut off the dominions' fashionable milliners from German imports, but caused an immediate shortage of dyestuffs in the British industry as the necessary chemicals were diverted to explosives manufacture.[4]

Sending the feathers home to Martha, Percy wrote, 'It's the best present I could dig up and I think you will like them.' Martha clearly did like them, and they came to mean more to her than a simple present because of the circumstances of their purchase. Percy was not a young, naïve enthusiast for the war: he enlisted in May 1916 at the age of 29. Both he and Martha would have been aware of the risks his enlistment posed for their future. Percy's brother Walter had enlisted in October 1915 and was already in Egypt when Percy joined up, further suggesting that Percy would have had few illusions about his decision. The plumes, then, may have acted as a talisman for Martha: perhaps they remained carefully wrapped up, awaiting Percy's return and a suitable occasion to wear them.

Ostrich plumes were an important and long-standing South African export. Since the 1880s they had become increasingly popular as trimmings for hats, fans and boas; the value of feathers had trebled by 1910. Elaborate trading routes, involving many groups of indigenous people, had developed through North Africa and into Europe in order to export animal products, including ivory, horns, hides and plumes, and a market in farmed ostrich feathers was conducted through South African ports.[5] By the early 1900s the volume of ostrich plumes being traded was enormous: in 1912 just over 450,000 kilograms of ostrich feathers, valued at £2.6 million, was exported from the Cape.[6] The trade grew in part as a result of the establishment of ostrich farms. With the right climate, ostriches could be plucked every eight months, making farms in certain districts very wealthy.[7] In addition, governments around the world were beginning to restrict the hunting of wild birds of all kinds for feathers for the fashion trade. In South Africa, Australia, North America and New Zealand, conservationists were targeting the 'vanity of woman' as the chief cause for the depletion of populations. The numbers of birds killed for the millinery and garment industry *was* enormous, but at the same time fashion was an easy target in comparison with introduced predators and the clearing of forests for agriculture.

By 1916 the more austere wartime fashions, and the strength of the conservationist lobby, meant that even ostrich feathers had largely fallen out of favour with the upper classes in Britain and the United States. They remained popular in New Zealand, perhaps because the birds were farmed and not hunted, though they were certainly worn with more restraint than before 1914. Feathers still trimmed hats worn by New Zealand brides in the war years, though their outfits were generally less ornate.

Encounters with diverse populations and cultures were recorded in photographs and postcards, bringing the empire to life both for those at home and those travelling. Percy Heenan (left) and friend had their picture taken with an unnamed Zulu rickshaw driver in Durban, while en route to England. *Ref: PS003304, Gift of the McCredie Family, Museum of New Zealand Te Papa Tongarewa*

Wartime weddings diverged from tradition for reasons ranging from fabric shortages to the urgency injected into relationships by a man's enlistment. The description of a wedding in a newspaper as 'quiet' indicated that the groom was shortly leaving for the front, and there was a rise in the numbers of going-away outfits made of khaki in addition to the more usual dove grey and navy blue. Whether the preference for khaki reflected a shortage of other fabrics or a patriotic impulse is difficult to tell, but the former could certainly be passed off as the latter.

Martha Cranstoun and Percy Heenan enjoyed a quiet wedding after his repatriation early in 1918. Martha's brother William was still a prisoner of war and in deference to the anxiety her family was still experiencing, Martha wore a sober navy blue suit, but her navy velvet hat was fashionably trimmed with ostrich plumes.

42
'Badness Personified'
Nola Pratt's Photograph Album
Chris Brickell

Nola Pratt's high school photograph album, personalised with the school crest and well loved.

Ref: PA1-o-883-Cover-01, Alexander Turnbull Library, Wellington, New Zealand

One scorching hot day in 1912 a group of four young women and three young men drape themselves over the beach at Waimārama. They are not immodestly clad – the women wear hats and the men singlets – but all have bare arms. Their pose is informal, a little haphazard; they are spaced unevenly, and two of the party ignore the camera. In the words of the caption writer, the subjects of this photograph are 'Badness Personified'.

This memento of an idyllic afternoon is one of many images in a small blue photograph album 14 centimetres high and 17 wide, its front cover embossed with the word 'Sketches' in gold foil and adorned with a small Wanganui Girls' College crest.[1] The self-adhesive sticker was not invented until the 1930s, so the crest was probably glued onto the album cover. Inside, silver gelatin prints are pasted onto the cream card pages. Now tucked away in the collections of the Alexander Turnbull Library, it used to belong to Nola Pratt, then in her final year at Wanganui Girls'. Nola was born in 1895 in Hunterville, a small settlement in the Manawatu. Her upbringing was solidly middle-class; her father bought and resold retail businesses for a profit, and moved the family around the North Island.[2] By 1912 Hawke's Bay had become their home and the beach at Waimārama their summer holiday spot. Nola's album is a record of Pākehā adolescent lives in the year before the outbreak of World War I, telling a story of young people's schooling and leisure. As is usual in a photograph album, the selection, arrangement and captioning of the images reflect the owner's preoccupations, desires and points of view. 'Badness Personified'– and many other photographs in the album – evoke a range of transitions: between land and sea, childhood and adulthood, seriousness and amusement.

'Badness', of course, is meaningful only in relation to its corollary. If the pleasurable spell on the beach was 'bad'– lax and enjoyable with bared flesh on display – a group of young men in uniform were 'Goodness Personified' (p. 265). Although these lads, school pupils, are also out of doors, the pleasures of the beach elude them. The grass out the back of the schoolhouse is their setting, and they sit on hard wooden forms or stand regimentally, as they have been told to. While Nola's beachgoers embrace the sun, the chaps in 'Goodness' squint and tolerate the heat in their serge waistcoats, jackets and shorts. Only one of them, fifth from the left in the middle row, manages

'Badness Personified', in which a beach becomes the setting for gender, leisure and display.

Ref: PA1-o-883-031-1, Wanganui Girls' College Album, No. 1, Nola Luxford: Photographs, Alexander Turnbull Library, Wellington, New Zealand

anything resembling a smile. They are fully clothed, orderly, posing under the watchful eye of the teacher standing second from the right in the back row. Nola's juxtaposition of two images – 'Goodness' and 'Badness' – offers a commentary on pre-war social expectations. In 'Goodness', the subjects of institutional authority, confined and obedient, stand (and sit) in marked contrast to the young people enjoying the beach. 'Badness' suggests a 'sensuous geography', to use Paul Rodaway's term[3] – a response to warm, salty air on the body, the pleasure of an unencumbered stretch on the sand, the freedom of movement in a space of leisure. The gentle transgressions of 'Badness Personified' lie partly in the image's gender mixing: both men and women enjoy an intimate closeness in a public space where anyone might see them. Young people's social worlds had changed rapidly in the preceding decades: chaperonage declined during the 1880s, by the end of the nineteenth century the newspapers told of young men and women freely associating in public, and the beach became 'a new frontier for self-expression' as the century turned.[4] Members of the older generation promenaded at the seaside while the younger ones lounged. As Nola compiled the album, she suggested her female friends led the charge towards freedom. In 'Badness', the girls occupy centre stage, while the boys chip in from the sidelines. In 'Goodness', the boys do their duty in sulky compliance. Such an assertive move was typical of Nola. According to her biographer, her friends accepted her as a leader. Her old chums remembered her as 'an individualist', even 'a tearaway', who 'always had a knack for getting what she wanted'.[5]

Young women challenge social expectations on the other pages of Nola's album. One blurry and faded image shows two young women leaning against a tree in a back yard, a corrugated iron fence behind. Nola, on our left, looks confidently towards the camera, while Thelma grasps a tennis racquet and glares at the photographer, actively asserting her presence. The two captions interpret this picture rather differently. The first inscription reads: 'Hair-washing day. Don't we look sweet?' In contrast, the second caption suggests that 'Nola looks sleepy' but 'Thel. looks dangerous. Them's me sentiments.' Sweetness, a trait publicly expected of young women, gives way to something rather less delicate. Indeed, a demure demeanour does not necessarily prove compliance.

Another photograph shows an adolescent girl in a chair on the lawn, a book in her lap, looking earnestly towards the camera. The caption suggests that appearances may be deceiving: 'Nancy swotting French. I don't think.' The viewer cannot tell whether Nancy's volume is indeed a French primer or something racier.

If the early twentieth century provided fresh opportunities for young women's relaxation and self-expression, it also gave rise to a new character: the flapper. She made an early appearance in 1905, in the pages of Christchurch's *Star*, as a 'young girl who delays putting up her hair and wearing long skirts. She is so-called because her hair hangs down her back and "flaps" in the gentle breeze. She may be of any age from 16 to 28, and she is to be seen at her best at the seaside in summer time.'[6] The beach provided one natural habitat for the flapper, the office another. In 1914 Wellington's *Evening Post* insisted the flapper

'Goodness Personified', in which nobody has any fun.

Ref: PA1-o-883-031-3, Alexander Turnbull Library, Wellington, New Zealand

Below: *Nola and Thelma: sweet or dangerous?*

Ref: PA1-o-883-03, Alexander Turnbull Library, Wellington, New Zealand

'ran about offices at the most critical time of her life'.[7] She was a product of the early-twentieth-century typewriter revolution that created a great many office jobs for young women.

Nola Pratt and the flapper style were made for each other. Not only did Nola love the seaside, but her commercial college course in bookkeeping and typing trained her for office work. A year later, in 1913, she would become an office assistant for her father. In one photograph Nola poses against a tree – seriously, mostly, with just a trace of a smile playing on her lips. She wears a long dress, a large silver belt buckle and a jaunty tie. The caption reads 'Flapper!'. In another picture, she and friend Grace pose at the seaside, clad from head-to-toe, wide-brimmed hats keeping the sun at bay. This time, the caption is more descriptive: 'The Heavenly Twins at Waimarama Picnic: Flappers.' A handy annotation, added at a later date, points out who is who, though Nola's biography reveals that these two were not sisters. Nothing in these captions hints at the flapper's significance in terms of freedom and social change, but the term was securely in place and the prevailing discourse did the rest. Here is a writer in the *Grey River Argus* in 1914:

> The rising generation are drunk with the new wine of liberty. They are born free, and they laugh when any Rip van Winkle offers them a pretty little set of chains to wear in a dainty little doll's house ... the Flapper has turned childhood inside out. She has changed the meaning of juvenility. For her childhood means the time when you go everywhere and do everything ... Indeed, the younger she is the more intractable and untamable she is apt to be.[8]

Freedom was the flapper's passion, and not everybody was happy about it. In 1908 the *Otago Witness* pined for 'that pretty, demure, dove-like creature with sloping shoulders, dancing ringlets, and big, baby eyes. She has gone so utterly that it must seem one can kill a type as utterly as one can kill a fashion.'[9]

This was a world of literal and symbolic connections. Nola Pratt's photograph album is a discrete object, but it incorporates, evokes and sits alongside a range of other interwoven objects: photographs of partly and fully-clothed bodies at the seaside, in fields and under trees; captions that give meaning to the images; newspapers reminding readers of appropriate adolescent behaviour. Nola's images hint at the gendered ways Pākehā adolescents occupied public space in the early years of the twentieth century, in the wake of first-wave feminist exhortations for greater freedom and mobility for women. Nola's captions suggest a gentle repudiation of expected behaviour, and spur us to look carefully at the pre-war gender order. Is a look 'sweet' or is it 'dangerous'?

Nola's life was not without its own ambiguities. Upward mobility was important to her: encouraged by her mother, for a time she aspired to join the privileged Hawke's Bay pastoralist set, and possibly even to marry into it.[10] At the same time, she had little patience for the *Witness*'s doe-eyed ideals. In 1919, with her new husband, a jobless returned soldier called Maurie Luxford, 23-year-old Nola left New Zealand for the United States. She starred in a number of silent Hollywood films before moving

Grace and Nola, at their best at the seaside in the summer time. Underneath the caption, a drawn-in smiley face accentuates the happiness of the occasion.

Ref: PA1-o-883-027-2, Alexander Turnbull Library, Wellington, New Zealand

to New York and taking on a role in radio. Having a career suited her. Nola was the prime mover in the Anzac Club, an organisation for Australian and New Zealand servicemen in New York during World War II, and the antipodean visitors adored her. Nevertheless, Nola's biographer theatrically describes a personal life of 'rapture and thrill … abandonment, betrayal, madness and despair': Nola Luxford survived an intense, and sometimes perilous, friendship with author Zane Gray, along with three difficult marriages.[11]

Later photographs echo aspects of the life pictured in the small blue album. Her portraits from the 1940s, 1950s and 1960s, many of them in the Alexander Turnbull Library, maintain the pride and self-possession of those early images, even though they are tinged with a little sadness: the legacy of a roller-coaster life.

43
Hiding and Revealing
The Emotional History of a Travel Diary
Genevieve de Pont

On the northern side of Remuera/Mt Hobson stands a house that surveys, broadly, the grand homes on the slopes below, slipping away down to the edge of the Waitematā Harbour. Evelyn Weir Bond and her husband Elon, the owner of the Bond & Bond chain of stores and of Choysa Tea, built this house in the 1920s. Eve named it Pukerānui (sunny hill), and when the driveway that reached up from Remuera Road became a paved street, she was asked by the council to name that too: she chose Pere (Bell) Street, perhaps because of the nearness of several churches with bells in their steeples.[1] When the Bonds' son (Elon) Bryce was young, the family approached the house by car up Pere Street and parked it at a green garage some distance down the slope from the house. After walking past a deep, stone-walled fishpond, they ascended to the house via some wide, flat steps, decorated in mosaic tiles. One read 'E ♥ E'; another 'EB'. When I knew the place, the driveway continued above the old garage, cutting a grand swath past a huge copper beech up to the house and its large attached garage, which Bryce, my grandfather, had built when he returned to live in this home after his parents' deaths in 1968. The fishpond and the mosaic staircase remained, but hidden, no longer part of daily life for the inhabitants of Pukerānui.

If you had stepped through the dark green front door in the last three decades of the twentieth century, on the right-hand side on the hallway you would have found a small, beautiful room: my grandfather's den. Where walls were not wood-panelled, they were papered in gold printed with Chinese figures; the light fitting was shaped like a copper barrel, and the back wall was covered in a built-in bookshelf, with lead-light sliding covers, which were always detached and leaned against the wall.[2] Many of the books were leather-bound – there was a collected set of Dickens – and the smell was rich.[3] As a child, I was sure that this room contained mysteries. If only I moved the right book, then the wall would swing away to reveal a secret passage or space. Across the hall from the den was my mother's former bedroom. The little bookshelf in this room was more accessible to me than the high shelves of the den. It was here that I discovered five small volumes, travel diaries handwritten in a loopy script I initially found quite impenetrable. Their stiff, navy buckram covers creaked a little as they opened, and they were full of small, hole-

Evelyn Weir Bond, Travel Diary, 16 March–18 October 1937. This diary measures 12.5 by 17.1 cm; the monogram was applied to the formerly plain cover.

Private Collection. Photograph by Michael Hall

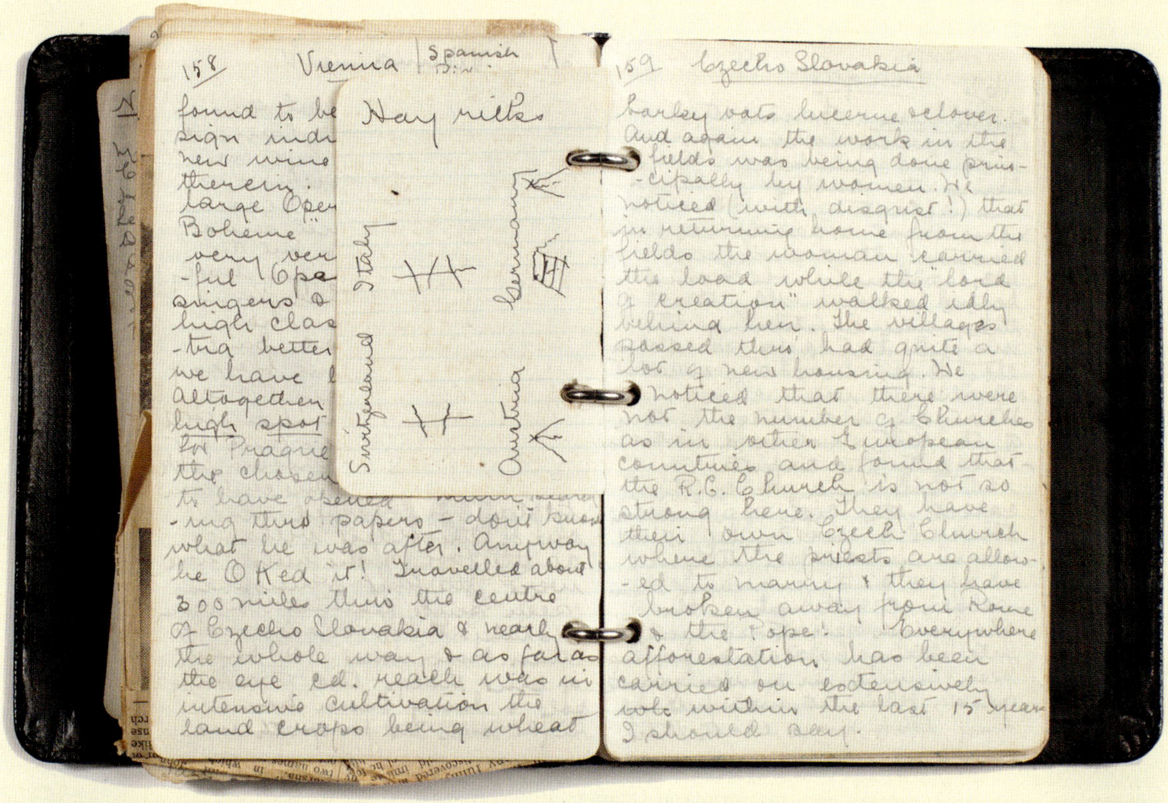
158 Vienna
Spanish
Hay ricks
Switzerland
Italy
Germany
Austria
-ing thro' papers - don't know
what he was after. Anyway
he O.K.ed it! Travelled about
300 miles thro the centre
of Czecho Slovakia & nearly
the whole way & as far as
the eye cd. reach was in
intensive cultivation the
land crops being wheat
159 Czecho Slovakia
barley oats lucerne & clover.
And again the work in the
fields was being done prin-
-cipally by women. We
noticed (with disgust!) that
in returning home from the
fields the woman carried
the load while the "lord
of creation" walked idly
behind her. The villages
passed thru' had quite a
lot of new housing. We
noticed that there were
not the number of Churches
as in other European
countries and found that
the R.C. Church is not so
strong here. They have
their own Czech Church
where the priests are allow-
-ed to marry & they have
broken away from Rome
& the Pope. Everywhere
afforestation has been
carried on extensively
within the last 15 years
I should say.

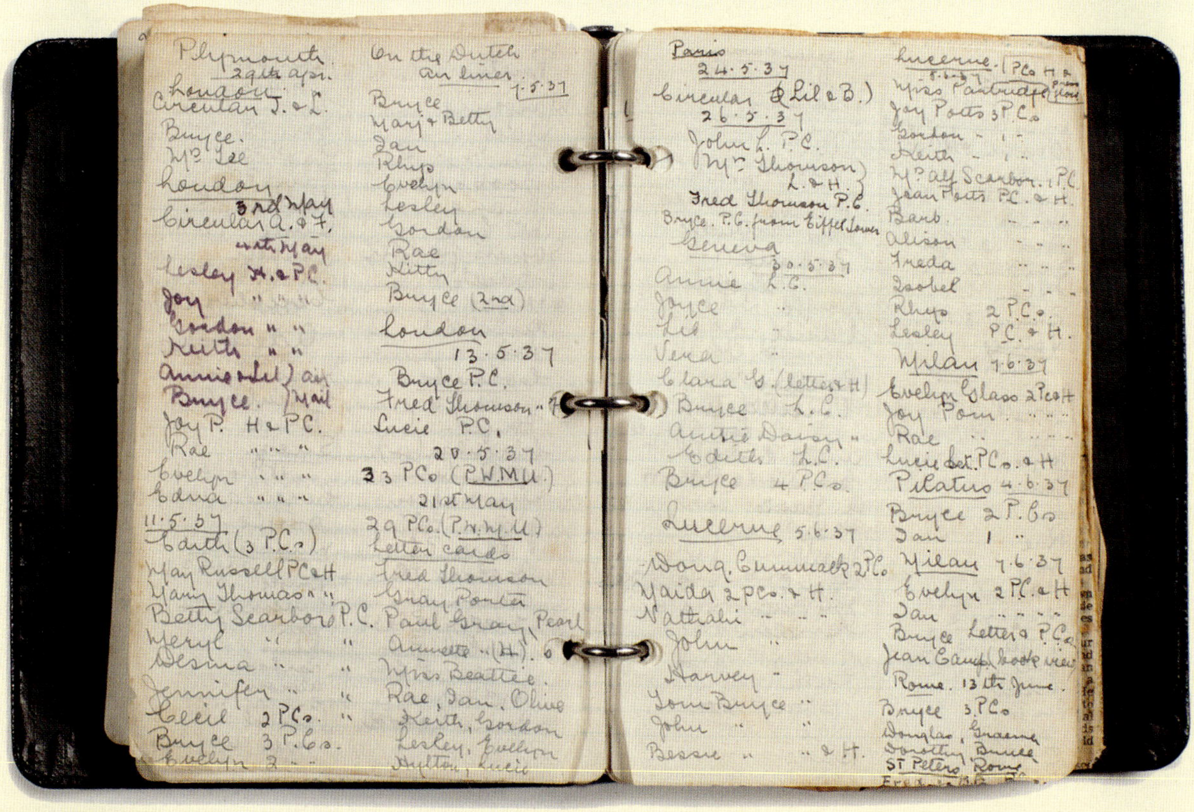
Plymouth
London
On the Dutch air liner 7.5.37
London 13.5.37
Paris 24.5.37
Geneva 30.5.37
Lucerne 5.6.37
Milan 7.6.37
Lucerne
Milan 7.6.37
Rome. 13th June.

Opposite, top: *Between pages 158 and 159 Eve inserted a kind of legend into the binding, schematising the shape of hay ricks in various European countries.*

Photograph by Michael Hall

Opposite, bottom: *On these pages Eve listed the letters she sent over the course of six weeks of her travel. As we can see, on a short flight between London and Amsterdam she produced 10 letters or postcards to send home.*

Photograph by Michael Hall

punched pages, densely filled. The places I could make out, written on the top of each page, intrigued me: Colombo, Aden, Paris, Geneva, Santa Fe, Hawai`i. I was sure, once again, that inside those books were secrets – or at least, the answers that only people who were no longer living could give. This time I was right.

And so, when my grandmother was preparing to move from the place that had housed members of my family for 80 years, I asked if I could keep these diaries, with their stories about the house and its dispersed former contents, many of which had been purchased abroad. They also revealed a personality: they showed something of my great-grandmother, Eve, as a woman in her energetic prime. She had driven the building of this house I knew so well, and there she was, speaking, making jokes, quoting poetry, expressing her amusement, her emotions and her irritations, and maintaining apparently boundless enthusiasm during long continuous periods of travel. Yet just as the diaries revealed Eve Bond's idiosyncrasies, they also reflected shared contemporary cultural practices – much like the Chinoiserie in her house, and her use of Māori words for Pākehā experiences of place while covering over Māori experience – and represented one example of a common form of self-expression: the travel diary.[4]

This essay concentrates on the first volume, that for 1937, when, between 16 March and 29 October, the Bonds travelled from New Zealand around the Australian ports, headed west through the Indian Ocean with stops in Colombo and Bombay, then went on to Aden, Port Sudan, Cairo, Malta and Marseilles before disembarking in London. They toured the British Isles and Ireland, the Netherlands, France, Switzerland, Italy, Austria, Germany, Czechoslovakia and Belgium, before leaping aboard another ocean liner and making for Montreal. After spending time in New York and Illinois, they took the Santa Fe Railway through the American West, toured around California and then headed for home via Hawai`i.

Even the material form of such diaries reflects how rich they are as sources of information about travel and ways of remembering it. These hardy books were made to be used. The covers, only slightly flexible, and the firm ring-binding kept them protected from knocks and weather – and allowed Eve to insert material with ease – and their small size made them portable. Unlike other travel diarists, who sometimes posted their diary home in sections, in small notebooks or on loose sheets of paper, Eve kept hers with her throughout her journeys.[5] They functioned as repositories for both information and memories of personal experiences. She recorded in the diaries data she could refer back to: the current exchange rates, the population figures of certain places, addresses of those she met abroad,[6] and she added material – mainly newspaper articles – after she returned to New Zealand, tucked inside the front cover, or taped into the relevant spots. Eve also formatted her diary pages so she could easily revisit particular parts. Each page was headed with a place name and numbered in the top outer corner. She also put numbers on the spines. Unlike many other travel diaries of the same period, Eve's were elegantly personalised with her monogram in gold on the covers.

Travel diaries are also home to varied and complex

emotional experiences and connections. Eve's contained lists of letters received and sent: during the six months she kept her 1937 diary, she wrote around 640 letters and postcards – more than three a day on average.[7] She described the fervour with which she greeted a packet of letters arriving from New Zealand.[8] She made new friends, too, while travelling: personal handwritten poems kept in the front bore witness to the creation of friendships with other steamship passengers. A poem titled 'Legend of Bond' was kept in an envelope with some limericks in Eve's handwriting, composed for, and about, Sir Norman Nock, Lord Mayor of Sydney,[9] with whom the Bonds seem to have shared a fairly intimate friendship. After a stanza that wished him good health on his birthday, and another full of insider jokes about his experience playing deck sports (Eve rhymed 'Sir Norman' with 'dashing games scoreman'), she and Elon capped off their poem with a stanza explaining their accompanying gift:

> Sir Norman wears fine nylon sundries
> So light and so clean are those undies
> They're almost as airy
> and light as a fairy
> May this sachet enclosed scent those undies?
> E & E.B.

While abroad Eve also located members of her community, both living and dead. For instance, in France she visited the grave of Rhys Perkins, a family friend who was killed on the Somme during World War I, reflecting that it seemed he was spiritually present at his gravesite and at peace. Using her words and her presence as a conduit, she tried to bring together this dead young man and his family in New Zealand: 'peace seemed to brood there and how we wished all the relatives of those dear lads who slept there, could just visit the place once. It would be such a comfort. It almost seemed that Rhys knew we were there trying to make contact between him and his Mother and sisters.'[10] As the diaries often record, while travelling she constantly kept in touch with friends and family about occasions such as birthdays, weddings and more serious matters, entertaining or comforting them.

Travel diaries like Eve's are invaluable for historians. Both their appearance and content give us a sense of the ways in which New Zealanders travelled in the interwar period: the things they noticed, the ideas they had about the world, and the ways in which they elected to describe it. Comparison of Eve's diary with others written around the same time indicates that her dedication to community connections and the forging of new relationships abroad was typical (though her letter output was exceptional). The kinds of material she recorded, too, were conventional. Travel diaries have been drawn on fairly sparely in New Zealand history writing about this period, but they can add considerably to our knowledge of travel and of New Zealanders' mental and emotional worlds.[11]

But this essay has focused on a single diary by a particular traveller, with her specific itinerary, interests and experiences. It, and its four companions, found in the place where my great-grandmother kept them, served as an anchor to home while she was travelling, and then as a reminder of her journeys once she had returned home. For me, the 1937 diary in particular

Above: *This hand coloured and written card, from 'Maida' to 'Auntie Eva', was kept inside the front cover of Eve Bond's 1937 travel diary. The inside message is a poem, printed carefully in a neat script: 'Just a wish however simple,/Just a greeting ever true,/Just a heartfelt kind remembrance,/Just from me to you.'* Photograph by Michael Hall

Left: *Eve preserved in an album a postcard of the Bond party produced in Sydney. From left to right, the travellers are Eve, Elon, Elon's mother Catherine, and Kitty, the eldest daughter of Elon's brother Percy.* Private Collection

is indelibly linked with a house that was both literally and figuratively inscribed with my family's relationships. It is, among other things, a mnemonic device, and one that crosses generations, though the memories it evokes have shifted as the years have passed. Just as Eve's chosen name for her street endures, as perhaps the mosaic tiles asserting her love for husband and son remain, this diary is an object with continuing significance, one that both represents and bears witness to fragments of colonial history.

INTER DISTRICT POLO
SILCHAR
1919~1920
Won-by
ROSEKANDI POLO CLUB
SECOND TEAM
E.G.PETERS (Capt.)
A.G.McARTHUR
A.G.CUTLER
A.D.FARLIE

44

From Polo to Poultry

A Planter's Legacy

Jane McCabe

> I shall never forget the experience of going over it and of seeing Birdie in the midst of her work. She is the undoubted leader. Takes it with a laughing face, with kilted frock and gumboots. She introduced me to a family of 300 little chicks which had come out of the incubator the day before … The older fowls she leaves to her father and husband. Mr Peters takes them to market in a van. It is remarkable to see him who used to be a great polo player in Cachar in the midst of it all.[1]

Egerton Peters was born in Nova Scotia, Canada, in 1875 of English parents. His life was to be truly one of empire. His grandfather had a career with the East India Company, and his father, a lieutenant in the Royal Engineers, transferred from Nova Scotia to Burma, then to Afghanistan and finally to India. Like other British children in India, young Egerton was sent 'home' to be educated, at St Paul's College in London, where he lived with his Aunt Caroline. As a teenager he was again sent away, this time to California 'to learn fruit farming'.[2] From there he made his way back to India, where he would spend 30 years as a tea planter in the Cachar district of Assam. In 1926 he retired to Pine Hill, then a rural area on the outskirts of Dunedin, where he lived on a small farm with his daughter and her family until he died.

Egerton Peters' polo trophy.

Peters Family Archive. Photograph by Michael Hall

Egerton Peters was my great-grandfather. His daughter, my grandmother, was Lorna Birdie Peters. She and her two siblings were the offspring of Egerton's relationship with a Nepali tea worker. As a child, I knew about the Indian ancestry because my grandmother had noticeably brown skin, as did my father and brothers. The other visible reminders of the Indian background were the objects on permanent display in the sitting room of the small Pine Hill cottage Lorna continued to occupy long after her father's death – two large sets of antlers, a set of war medals and a polo trophy. Those things told us not only of a different place, but of a very different kind of life. The information they conveyed was accompanied and enhanced by various other items that seemed out of place in these very modest surroundings, such as fine porcelain teacups. There was a strong sense of disjuncture between the objects and the way in which they were used in this very practical rural setting. Out in the sheds on the farm more discoveries awaited and were used in adventurous childhood re-enactments of life in an exotic place.

The polo trophy was, and still is, a permanent fixture on the Pine Hill mantelpiece. Noticeably heavy, tarnished but in good condition, it has a distinctive handle on the back with 'PINT' engraved close to it. The front of the trophy is inscribed as follows:

Inter District Polo
Silchar
1919–1920
Won by
Rosekandi Polo Club
SECOND TEAM
E.G. Peters (Capt.)
A.G. McArthur
A.G. Cutler
A.D. Farlie

Lorna died when I was five years old, having never spoken about her upbringing in India or how she and her siblings arrived in Dunedin some five years before their father. As I grew up the Indian heritage became more than mere curiosity: I wanted to know how the three siblings had come to New Zealand, and particularly to Dunedin? Why had their father followed several years later? What of their mother? The polo trophy was an enticing lead because it named a specific location in India, but in effect it merely kept the Indian heritage to the forefront of my thinking when I visited my grandfather and uncle, Lorna's husband and her eldest son, both named Bill.

As the years went on the sense of disjuncture grew. It seemed the whole place had been outfitted by Egerton Peters in 1926 and then left to age. Everything about the cottage was dark and cramped. The tiny kitchen was attached to a dining room of sorts that I remember mostly for the flies that traced squares around bare light bulbs. The bedrooms, only big enough for a bed, were crammed with dark, imposing, once-grand furniture. The wallpaper, white with a black pattern, was so covered in soot that the design was no longer visible. Bright red enamel paint had been plastered over mantelpieces and doorframes in a brief Uncle-Bill effort to brighten the place up. Like him, the place was charming and strange and a big part of our lives. We made the 40-minute trip to Pine Hill every Sunday afternoon. Tea and scones were served in the sitting room from a tea trolley that rattled ungraciously as it navigated the uneven floors and worn floral carpets. We drank from those fine teacups, which afterwards sat for days on the dining room table marked with my uncle's large thumbprints.

The questions about the Indian background, therefore, were as much about this seemingly drastic reduction in circumstances as the silence over their ancestry and what had brought them to Dunedin. The thought that Egerton Peters, owner of all of these treasures, lived here, at Pine Hill, in this cottage, was scarcely believable. Had it changed so much between his death in 1945 and our childhood visits in the 1970s? What had happened to all the money? How was it that he went from owning what we imagined as a large plantation in India to a very modest poultry farm at Pine Hill? The reminders of that background were all around us, part of the present-day circumstances that saw the family on the social as well as the geographical margins of this southern city.

There is some wonderful scholarship about this kind of familial engagement with memorabilia. Martha Langford, in *Suspended Conversations*, has written of the relationship between photographs and silence, in childhood and beyond, when we begin to fill in political and historical circumstances.[3] Marianne Hirsh, also on photography but applicable to the kind of imaginative investment in objects described above, uses the term 'post-memory' to describe the process where the next generation 'gives narrative shape to the surviving fragments of an irretrievable past'.[4] Equally pertinent is the work of Annette Kuhn and Kirsten McAllister, who write of the capacity of objects to 'disturb the present moment' when associated information is lost, and of such objects taking on a more familiar and less haunted quality when details are recovered.[5] This is certainly an apt way to describe the transformation in my understanding of the Peters family history that resulted from my trip to Kalimpong in 2007.

Kalimpong is a small town in Northeast India, the site of an institution known as Dr Graham's Homes. I was led there by a photograph found among Lorna's things with the caption 'Kalimpong school'. There, all the questions I had about my grandmother's upbringing and emigration were answered. The homes were established by a Scottish Presbyterian missionary named Dr John Graham, to educate and house mixed-race children of British tea planters and local women, who, on reaching working age, would be sent to settler colonies for a new beginning in the belief that they would escape discrimination against Anglo-Indians in India and Britain. Information from the Dr Graham's Homes archive transformed my understanding of the Pine Hill artefacts, and was the impetus for my doctoral research looking at the migration scheme that brought some 130 people to New Zealand from Kalimpong.[6] Contact with descendants of these emigrants has revealed remarkable similarities in the impact of this Indian heritage on the next generation, and the crucial role of colonial objects in sparking curiosity about a subject that was otherwise pervaded by stubborn silences. Many descendants have cited the very physical, persistent presence of these objects over many years as the catalyst for research and travel to India to counter those silences.

Egerton Peters' polo trophy did indeed evidence the comfortable lifestyles of tea planters in India. Living in substantial bungalows, they were waited on by numerous servants, enjoyed pursuits such as hunting and polo and socialised with other planters at clubs and large picnics.[7] The Peters family archive includes a photograph of Egerton in Assam (see over) that attests to this lifestyle. He is posing with many of the objects that can now be found at Pine Hill. Unless one could afford to invest in tea, however, the financial rewards for working in the industry were not great. Egerton, like most of the fathers of the Kalimpong emigrants, did not own a tea plantation; he was employed by a tea agency first as an assistant, then as a manager. In letters to his Aunt Caroline in London, he often grumbled about the high risks involved in a tea planter's life for scant financial reward.[8] Sending photographs of polo trophies home to England was a positive way of showing inclusion in social life and local British networks. Unlike his interracial family,

Egerton Peters in Assam, c. 1920. The polo trophy can be glimpsed behind the rifle.

Peters Family Archive

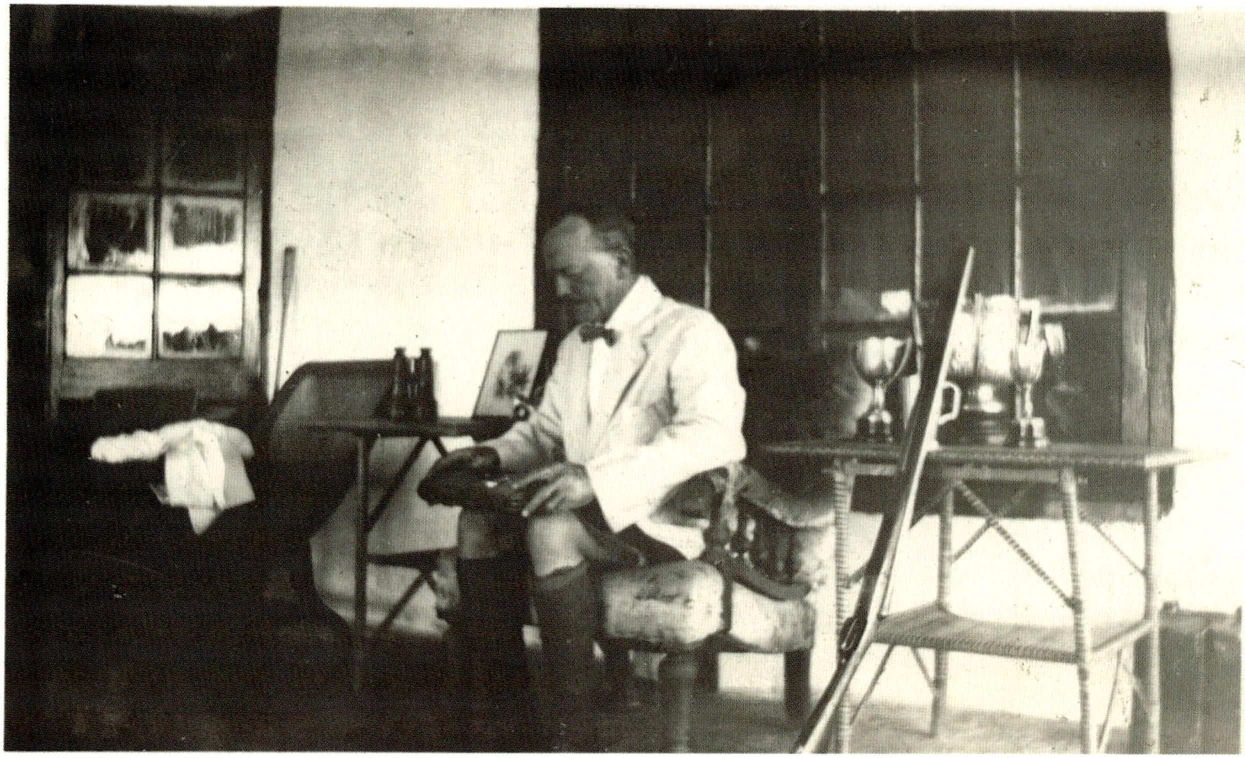

success in sporting pursuits was something to be publicly shared.

In New Zealand, too, these reminders of the Raj were, and continued to be, the publicly acceptable legacy of life in British India. Egerton was certainly not alone in leaving India with a high degree of nostalgia,[9] but it was his daughter, Lorna, who was responsible for the continued presence of the Indian plantation artefacts in the Pine Hill cottage. Anthropologist and historian Laura Bear has written evocatively of the uncanny and ghostly place of colonial relics in Anglo-Indian households in India, where such memorabilia is displayed as evidence of European ancestry.[10] The Kalimpong emigrants were perhaps creating a similar display. But this has, I suggest, changed significantly in subsequent generations. Whereas in India these relics continue to speak of a British heritage, in New Zealand their 'Indianness' has taken priority. Egerton's trophy

Egerton Peters at Pine Hill, c. 1930.

Peters Family Archive

was of interest because it spoke of polo in India, of a planter's lifestyle. A polo trophy from England would have had an entirely different meaning. In just one generation this colonial object came to communicate precisely the opposite of what Lorna had likely intended.

Reflecting on the place of this polo trophy in different colonial settings allows the move from a plantation in Assam to a poultry farm in Pine Hill to be viewed as a transition rather than a fall from grace. A number of the tea planting fathers of the Kalimpong emigrants chose retirement in the colonies over Britain, as did many ex-India careerists who struggled to find a place at 'home'.[11] When Graham, the founder of the homes in Kalimpong, visited New Zealand in 1937, he was most pleased with Lorna's new life in the colony. As his diary entry at the beginning of this essay suggests, he was a little surprised to find her father 'in the midst of it all'. His words support Egerton's letters to his aunt in London, which told of long working days in a bracing climate. As he had done on the plantation in Assam, he immersed himself in the quintessential colonial experience, for meagre financial reward but substantial personal satisfaction. Those contrasting but comparable fortunes are neatly captured in the only surviving photograph of Egerton at Pine Hill, in which he stands in a casual pose, in working attire, sleeves rolled up and hammer in hand, constructing one of several sheds that still stand today.

Pate (cricket bat) gifted to Walter Crowther by the Avele Cricket Team in Sāmoa, 1936.

Ref: FE007823, Museum of New Zealand Te Papa Tongarewa

45

Reconfiguring Cricket Culture in Colonial Sāmoa

Safua Akeli

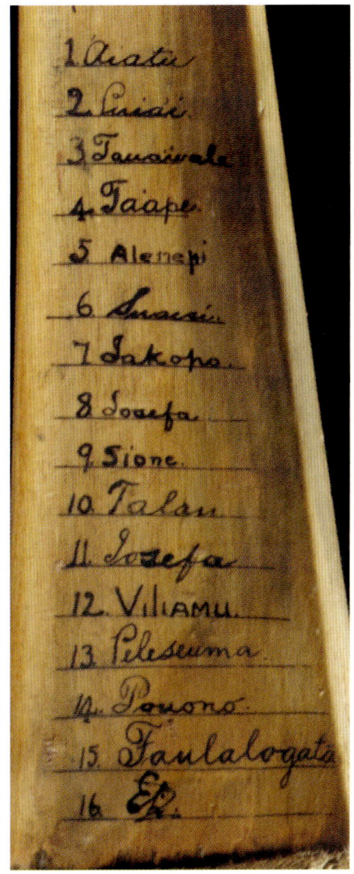

In July 1983 A.J. Crowther gifted a pate (cricket bat) to the National Museum, now the Museum of New Zealand Te Papa Tongarewa.[1] It had been presented in 1936 to his father, Walter James Crowther (1897–1983), on his departure from Apia, where he had held the post of treasurer and collector of customs in Sāmoa since October 1933. During that time Crowther, his wife Doris and their two sons lived in the village of Vaiala, in the Vaimauga district. At their farewell ceremony, the Crowthers were 'presented gifts made of local wood, together with a Samoan cricket bat from the Avele team, which Mr Crowther had captained last season. The bat was autographed by members of the team.'[2] Inscribed on the bat's face is: 'Avele Cricket Team, 1935–36, Aiatiu, Liua`i, Taua`ivale, Ta`ape, Alenepi, Suaesi, Iakopo, Iosefa, Sione, Talau, Iosefa, Viliamu, Peleseuma, Pouono, Faulalogata, Eti.'

Crowther had captained a team playing 'English' cricket, but Samoan pate were often given as gifts, most probably for perceived 'exotic' representation of a game reconfigured by Samoans since its introduction to the islands in the late nineteenth century. For instance, during his 1939 visit to several Pacific islands, including Sāmoa, New Zealand Governor-General Viscount Galway was given a pate by the Leulumoega-Fou London Missionary Society Boys' High School. Te Papa acquired this pate in 1980 through Galway's daughter, Lady Celia Rowley.[3]

Crowther's well-used pate symbolises Sāmoa's complex cricketing culture: it is an example of both the indigenising of English cricket by Samoans, and the persistence of that form of the game in the face of attempts to control it. Compared with the customary English cricket bat, the pate has an unusual shape. It measures about a metre in length, and has a long handle that extends towards a three-sided triangular face. For a tight grip, the handle is bound with `afa (plaited coconut sennit fibre). It is one of several objects from Crowther's time in Sāmoa donated by his family to the museum, including models of `ato (baskets) and a fale (house), which were made for him by students of Malifa School. Before Crowther went to Sāmoa in 1933, Samoans had been playing the English and Samoan forms of cricket for almost 60 years. In the 1870s the British consul, William Churchward, recorded that English residents were playing cricket two or three times a week in the evening on 'a rough grass road'.[4] Surprisingly, Churchward observed the interest of Tongan residents, but noted initial Samoan reluctance. This, however, did not last long: 'One by one, innovations of their own and Tongan manufacture crept into the game, until soon nothing remained of cricket, *pur et simple*, but the practice of one man bowling a ball to another man trying to hit it. All the rest of the proceedings were purely of their own manufacture'.[5] The new Samoan game became known as kilikiti, and for the sake of clarity this essay will use this term to refer to the indigenous form of the game.

Throughout the later part of the nineteenth century, when Britain, the United States and Germany all claimed parts of Sāmoa, kilikiti became the subject of much public discussion and was widely reported on by journalists. Debate focused on the number of people involved, ranging from 100 to 200 in a team, and the duration of matches, which could last up to two weeks, and how this affected work productivity and village resources.[6] During his five years in Sāmoa, Scottish writer Robert Louis Stevenson observed that 'cricket matches, where a hundred played upon a side, endured at times for weeks, and ate up the country like the presence of an army'.[7] The indigenous refashioning of the game led to government restrictions on kilikiti from the 1880s, in response to European settlers' complaints that the duration of matches led to Samoans abandoning work and placed an enormous economic burden on villages hosting such events. One of the first legislative interventions on kilikiti came from Samoan high chief Tamasese Titimaea in 1888, partly in an attempt to prevent people from forming political alliances.[8] In an 1890 proclamation issued by Malietoa Laupepa, who had been appointed 'king' under the Berlin Treaty of 1889, which settled the ruling rights between Britain, Germany and the United States, 'The Law Regarding Cricket' prohibited intervillage and village competitions. For those who disobeyed, the penalty was a fine or imprisonment with three months' hard labour.[9] Although English cricket was played and encouraged by the colonial elite, German authorities had issued an ordinance to curb the frequency of kilikiti, permitting it to be played only on Wednesday and Saturday afternoons.[10] When Major-General George Richardson took up his position as New Zealand administrator of Sāmoa in 1923 – New Zealand had a mandate to administer Sāmoa from 1919 until 1946 – village kilikiti was on his target list of games to be controlled.[11] Despite these challenges, both forms of cricket continued to thrive.

From the early part of the New Zealand administration of Sāmoa through to the 1930s, English cricket was emphasised as the primary game. From 1914, which marked both the start of World War I and also the beginning of the occupation of German-held Sāmoa by the New Zealand Expeditionary Forces, English-style cricket matches were a regular event, advertised almost weekly in the local *Samoa Times*. Matches were played between several clubs, including the Apia Cricket Club (established in 1881), the Nomad Cricket Club, the Sāmoa Toea`ina Cricket Club, the Young Men's Cricket Club and the Catholic Men's Cricket Club. Matches often took place between the navy, military and with crews from visiting ships such as the USS *Fortune* from Pago Pago.[12]

For their membership teams drew on both the Samoan and colonial elite, and players often switched from club to club. Among them was New Zealand administrator Lieutenant-Colonel Robert Logan (1863–1935), an avid cricketer who often captained the military teams. On one occasion in 1915, the military played the civilians at Matautu Point, and a garden party was organised around the match to collect donations for the New Zealand Hospital Ship Fund. This included a performance by the Blue Hungarian Band and Tamasese's Band, as well as siva (dances) by various groups. The amount raised was over £100.[13] In another match that year, Samoan high chief and fautua (adviser) Malietoa Tanumafili I (1879–1939) captained the Matautu Club against Logan's army team: Malietoa's men lost by 68 runs.[14] Such was the popularity of the game among the military that when the forces in Sāmoa were replaced in 1915 an appeal was made to the New Zealand public for donations of 'discarded cricket material' such as hats and pads for the new troops' recreation.[15]

The English style of cricket was played regularly at the pilot station, the Matautu Malae, the cricket ground in the village of Vaimoso, the wireless station and the Catholic mission. The pilot station was described as 'a fine, breezy point with a wide *malae* (grassy space), and the sea lapping the shore on three sides'.[16] Apart from the competitive nature of the game, cricket-associated events provided entertainment, social mixing and fundraising opportunities. For example, in October 1915, the Sāmoa Toe`aina Cricket Club organised a Monster Samoan Festival at the Matautu Malae, which included a performance by the popular Togoula Band and the sale of fruits, tea, cocoa and coffee to raise funds for a hall for the club. A month later the Catholic Young Men's Cricket Club organised a concert at the Catholic Hall in Saleufi, which involved siva afi (fire dancing), dance performances and a boxing match.[17] Not only a cricket ground, the Matautu Malae was also a venue for several festivities, including the welcome for returned soldier Albert Fruean in April 1917, while the Vaimoso cricket ground was the location of the office building of the Mau resistance movement that emerged in the 1920s. Cricket, politics and Samoan culture were always intertwined.[18]

English cricket was strongly encouraged in school and played by senior students during the period of the New Zealand administration. The first school to organise a cricket team was Malifa in 1921, during the time of the New Zealander Donald Rutherford (fondly known as Latafoti), who was superintendent of schools in Sāmoa from 1919 to 1936. School cricket competitions were hotly contested in the 1920s: in 1926 Avele, an agricultural school that had opened two years before, won the cricket league under the directorship of Percy Williams. By the 1930s there appears to have been a decline in English cricket competitions in general, largely due to the lack of grounds and sports equipment. Annual matches with visiting ships revitalised the competitions, however, and schools like Avele performed very well.[19]

By the time Crowther and his family left Sāmoa for New Zealand in 1936, cricket culture in Sāmoa had undergone several changes. The English cricket game, which had been especially popular in the first two decades of the twentieth century, was in decline and there were fewer clubs – sometimes, as with the

First Malifa cricket team, 1921.

Ref: PA1-o-445-006, Alexander M. Rutherford: Photographs of Samoa, Alexander Turnbull Library, Wellington, New Zealand

Toe`aina Cricket Club, as a result of political and financial problems.[20] Moreover it appears English cricket was played primarily by the Samoan and colonial elite, whereas kilikiti maintained its currency within village and church activities. By 1936, too, rugby, also introduced in the 1920s, was reportedly at its peak.[21]

Little is known about Walter Crowther after his return to New Zealand, although we do know he joined the Wellington 2nd Battalion Military Reserve in 1941. He was laid to rest at the age of 86, in the capital's Karori Cemetery in October 1983. His time in Sāmoa coincided with the final decade of New Zealand's interwar administration of the islands, during which the game of English cricket was being transformed and reconfigured by Samoans. In this way, Crowther's pate complicates the story of Sāmoa's colonial history. It is true that the British

Avele School cricket team 1926, Apia, Sāmoa, photographed by Alfred J. Tattersall. Back row: Neli, Iosefa, Masiki, Fiti, Mautu, Sele/Seve/Sene [?], Ta`aga. Middle row: Puipui, Mr Wild, Percy Williams, Vailepa. Front row: Pouono, Pose.

Ref: O.039485, Gift of Barbara Williams, 1986, Museum of New Zealand Te Papa Tongarewa

carried cricket to various parts of its empire, not just as a cultural practice from home, but also as a means of implanting British cultural practices among indigenous peoples. New Zealanders followed this practice within their own Pacific sub-empire: Crowther captained a team of Samoans who played the English game. However his Samoan team-mates gave him a kilikiti pate, a hybrid product that emerged out of their colonial experience, but one that also reflected fa`asāmoa, their Samoan pride and culture. This is a reminder that Crowther's pate is not only a story about colonialism, because although cricket was a part of the colonial process, it was not entirely defined by it. In fact there was a genuine enjoyment of the game, demonstrated both by its rapid reconfiguration and its persistence among Samoans. Crowther's pate draws attention to the complex history of kilikiti, which he had encouraged students to play in 'the game of life'.

46

'A "Lucky" Snap'

Reframing Colonial Culture Through a Pictorialist Lens

Felicity Barnes

In May 1930 the Wellington Camera Club held an exhibition of 'photographic art'. Among the prints on display was 'The Team', taken by club member Harry Moult. With its horses in motion and rising clouds of dust, it seems to be, as one reviewer described it, 'a lucky "snap"'.[1] But apart from that split second of serendipity as the shutter closed, luck had little part to play in the production of this image. It was a studied, not a spontaneous shot: its subject, composition and reproduction all reflected the disciplines of a particular photographic aesthetic known as pictorialism.

Developed in Britain at the end of the nineteenth century, pictorialism was the first international movement to champion photography as an art form, rather than a mechanical process for recording reality. Pictorialists wanted to make, rather than simply take, pictures. To do so they drew upon such fine arts conventions as the picturesque to compose their images, and played with light and focus to privilege the beauty of the shot over the reality of the scene. Sometimes nature itself could provide the requisite romantic atmosphere by furnishing clouds, mist or steam: accordingly local pictorialists found that 'rather misty spring or autumn weather' produced the best results.[2] When natural effects were found wanting, processing could take their place. Underlining the crafted nature of their art, pictorialists spent considerable time working on images before they were printed, manipulating textures, tones, shades and even content to enhance their artistic expression. As another Wellington pictorialist claimed, through processing a 'photographer can impress his own individuality upon his pictures as surely as can an artist'.[3]

'The Team' was a product of these pictorial conventions. Its rustic subject matter was suitably, even routinely, picturesque. Moult himself had taken several other similar shots of horse and bullock teams, and he was not alone.[4] George Chance, New Zealand's most prolific pictorialist, had made similar studies, the best known being 'Labourers of the Field', created in 1925. Further, the composition of 'The Team' was marked by the landscape conventions of fine art, notably in the S-shaped 'line of beauty' formed by the road. The road also lent some typically pictorialist detail, its dust rising up to form a softening mist-like effect. The increasing technical capabilities of cameras meant some desirable effects could be created with the shot, but Moult seems

Harry Moult, 'The Team'.

Camera Pictures of New Zealand, Ref: O.032243, Museum of New Zealand Te Papa Tongarewa

to have enhanced the atmosphere of his picture at the processing stage too, balancing the foreground's flying dust with the addition of some fluffy white background clouds. Two versions of this picture exist, and they feature distinctly different sets of clouds.[5] Finally, Moult then printed both versions, enhanced or not, carefully controlling tones and shades through the technically demanding and consummately artistic carbon process.

'The Team', then, was no lucky snap but a premeditated and highly crafted example of pictorial conventions at work. Indeed the conventionality – even cliché – of pictorialist practice has been a factor in its relative neglect by historians. In photographic histories, which are often structured as stories of technical and stylistic progress, pictorialists occupy a cultural no-man's-land. They fall between the doughty 'pioneers' of mid-nineteenth-century photography like the Burton Brothers, and 'nationalist' or 'modernist' styles of the mid-twentieth century. Lodged between pioneers and modernity, between colony and nation, pictorialism is a cultural caesura, its dependence on imported conventions and its preference for an imagined English ruralism making it seem an obstacle to a more authentic local vision. Pictorialism is cast as a stifling legacy of the colonial past, a nasty case of 'cosy national narcoplesy'.[6]

Yet by identifying this work simply as derivative, sentimental or nostalgic, we ignore 'the ideological use of [such] conventions in their specific place and time'.[7] Photography's colonising role has been recognised in other genres, but its powerful presence in amateur art photography has been overlooked. There are three reasons for this. First, photography's role as handmaiden in the production of 'objective' forms of colonial knowledge, often anthropological, topographical, botanical or geographical, has been emphasised, rather than its role in the production and deployment of subjectivities.[8] Yet as work with fine art has shown, aesthetics can construct a settled landscape as surely as the science of a survey does. Second, colonial knowledge has been confined conceptually to understanding the relationship between colonial subjects and their colonisers.[9] However, the business of 'rendering indigenous landscapes legible and suitable for settlement by whites' was not always carried out by such direct means.[10] As Moult's photographs demonstrate, settler colonial cultural links to Britain were part of this process, though pictorialism's reliance on borrowed conventions – its 'cringing colonialism' – makes it easy to dismiss, distracting our attention from the work it performs at home. Finally, art photography is a twentieth-century cultural form, whereas in New Zealand's historiography 'being colonial' remains, with some exceptions, a distinctly Victorian activity.[11] This essay argues instead for its colonising power, first by overturning the idea of pictorialism as colonial relic and then by reconsidering it instead as an active and contemporary form of colonial culture.

Pictorialism's introduction was certainly not outdated. In 1896, just four years after British pictorialists had founded their Brotherhood of the Linked Ring, to promote the concept of photography as fine art, local enthusiasts had arranged for the first collection of their art to tour New Zealand.[12] By this time the locals were already practising: the collection offered photographers an 'inestimable service … in helping them improve their own work'.[13] Another 'improving' collection arrived in 1899, when more than 600 photographs were exhibited in Wellington, including works by Henry Peach Robinson, claimed as the movement's founding father, fellow luminary Alfred Horsley Hinton and other noted British photographers.[14] A Royal Photographic Society collection came to New Zealand in 1905.[15] Shortly afterwards the local pictorial scene was invigorated by the migration of a few metropolitan practitioners. George Chance, who had worked with Horsley Hinton – with what must have been an impressive sense of intimacy, since he referred to him as 'our dear old Horsley Hinton' – arrived in 1909, while English photographers E.T. Robson and J.W. Johnson came to Wellington around 1917, re-energising pictorial practice in the capital and setting standards that were 'the equal of any'.[16]

Aspiring pictorialists could stay up to date with the latest in those standards in a variety of ways. Local booksellers carried key texts, including Horsley Hinton's *Handbook of Illustrations*.[17] Key journals such as *Amateur Photographer* and *Photograms of the Year* circulated throughout New Zealand, carrying reproductions of pictorial work from around the world. However, perhaps the most influential early print advocate of pictorialism was local. *Sharland's New Zealand Photographer* (1899–1911) was a canny marketing initiative by pharmaceutical distribution agency Sharland and Company, to capture some of the growing market for photographic supplies. Although the journal served a local market, it remained tied into a wider world. Many of its articles were cribbed from overseas publications like the *Amateur Photographer*, and though the publication had a New Zealand editor, it was published in London.[18]

All these sources created dynamic and contemporary connections with the prevailing artistic trends. They were colonial versions of what Elizabeth Edwards has described as a 'massive system of dissemination of ideas and images', which helped to establish pictorialism internationally as the dominant photographic aesthetic, a role it maintained in amateur circles into the late twentieth century.[19] At the heart of this system, camera clubs worked to substantiate pictorial practice, channelling its lofty principles into practical camera work, through regular programmes of lectures, seminars and competitions. Once taught, pictorialism's conventions – its particular way of seeing – would then be tested. Most clubs ran regular monthly competitions, with subjects and marking criteria that reinforced and codified the pictorialist aesthetic. New Zealand's first camera club was formed in Wellington in 1882,[20] and in 1899 *Sharland's* listed 13 clubs, not only in major centres but also in places like Denniston and Hokitika.[21] It has been suggested that clubs began to decline around 1910 as technological advances, such as the Kodak, demystified the business of taking pictures.[22] However, the development of art photography gave them a new lease of life: interclub competitions began in 1919,

The romance of pictorialism: Harry Moult's 'Morning Mist, Milford Sound'.

Camera Pictures of New Zealand, Ref: O.032255, Museum of New Zealand Te Papa Tongarewa

Recreating the old world: Harry Moult, 'The Pensioner's Hut'.

Camera Pictures of New Zealand, Ref: O.032246, Museum of New Zealand Te Papa Tongarewa

and clubs from Timaru, Masterton and Hamilton now competed alongside such venerable clubs as Dunedin and Auckland.[23]

Like older nineteenth-century improving movements, clubs performed a colonising role, helping to weave the fabric of local community. But photography was an internationally expanding pastime and clubs were always part of a much wider community. They strengthened ties with Britain, especially through affiliations with the Royal Photographic Society. When the Gisborne photographic club was formed in 1934, they 'arranged immediately to be affiliated',[24] while Wellington affiliated twice, once in 1901 and again, as the club structure changed, in 1926.[25] Belonging marked them as active participants in, not passive recipients of, metropolitan culture, and this sense of participation was made clear in other ways. New Zealand photographers contributed material to the prestigious English journals: two featured in *Photograms of the Year* as early as 1902.[26] Others, like Una Garlick, went on to be exhibited at the Royal Photographic Society. The local press regularly reported on such 'success overseas', noting awards, exhibitions and the occasional nomination of a New Zealand photographer as fellow or associate of the society.[27]

Pictorial practice led to the construction of a new set of cultural relationships with the old metropolis. But pictorialism's colonising power was not confined to the creation of new links with the old world. As is obvious in Moult's wider collection of photographs, exhibited in 1930, its conventions constructed a distinct version of New Zealand.[28] His pictorial New Zealand was British, white, rural and empty. 'The Team' evoked an imagined English ruralism, which required some effort: as *Sharland's* journal advised readers, 'Farmhouses in the dominion suffer from the fault of being too modern. We have no abbey farms with gnarled trees and the stone homestead hoary with age and weight of ivy around its walls … there is ample

Part of the past: Harry Moult, 'Look-out Tower and Whare, Native Village, Rotorua'.

Record Pictures of New Zealand, Ref: O.032189, Museum of New Zealand Te Papa Tongarewa

London, New Zealand's urban centre: Harry Moult, 'Winter Sunshine'.

Photograph Album – London, Ref: O.031868, Museum of New Zealand Te Papa

scope for careful reflection in order to give the correct emotional value to the photograph.'[29] However, by carefully selecting such subjects as 'The Team' and 'The Pensioner's Hut', some semblance of England's history could be recreated here.[30]

Pictorialism's borrowed old world neatly replaced New Zealand's actual colonial past. In a collection of more than 200 photographs, Māori feature in only four, a notable absence given contemporary tourist fascination with asserting a mythic Māori past in places like Rotorua. When Māori do appear, they have their own 'correct emotional value'. The buildings in 'Look-out Tower and Whare, Native Village' are deserted: even the hills behind have been cleared.[31] That these photographs should function as symbols of a disappearing way of life is underlined in their categorisation by Moult as 'Record Pictures', a term used by the British photographic survey movement. The movement took such pictures as a way of preserving, if only on film, older forms of architecture that were no longer in use, before they disappeared entirely.[32]

Moult's images reshaped the present as much as the past. Many created New Zealand as a reservation for the picturesque, all wild alps and tamed rural spaces. Accordingly, no urban New Zealand appeared. Street scenes, crowds, monumental buildings – in short, urban life – were all contained within his work on London.[33] This was not necessarily the product of pictorial convention which, despite its preference for the picturesque, could still embrace the cityscape. Rather, this division reflects the changing colonial form of which his work was both part and product. Against the grain of nationalist narratives, pictorial practice helped to draw New Zealand closer to London. That new relationship was echoed in Moult's images, which created New Zealand as a rural hinterland, neither old colony or new nation. The essence of this was captured in 'The Team' – it was, after all, a lucky snap.

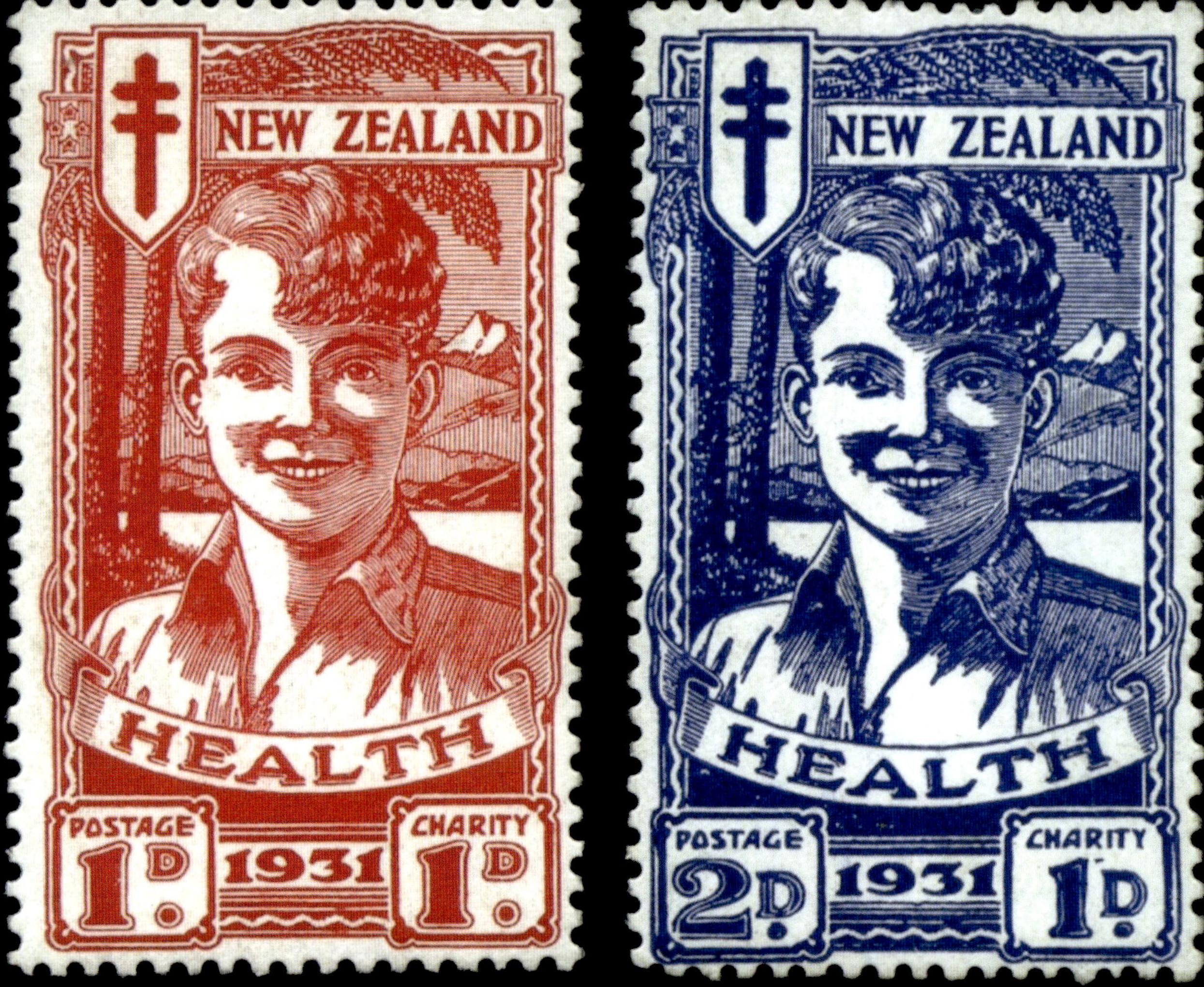

Leonard Cornwall Mitchell, 1d and 1d and 2d and 1d Charity Issue (aka the 'Smiling Boys'), 1931.

Author's Collection

47

The 'Smiling Boys'

The New Zealand Health Stamps of 1931

Mark Stocker

Stamps are like paper ambassadors, functioning both as miniature art works and as government-issued propaganda. What, then, does the pair of stamps issued in 1931, the so-called 'Smiling Boys', tell us about New Zealand and its official self-image? That, several years before the first Labour government, the country was a humanitarian social democracy, which cared about the wellbeing of its children, especially during hard economic times; that its people were generous, prepared to fork out a penny premium on top of the standard postage if this assisted a good cause; and that, both artistically and temperamentally, there was a straightforwardness, candour and cheerfulness about New Zealand and young New Zealanders.

New Zealand issued its first health stamps in 1929. Their introduction is traditionally credited to Danish immigrant Kirstine Nielsen (1873–1937), whose country of origin had first produced official charity seals as part of the fight against tuberculosis in 1904. The first three annual issues (the 'Smiling Boys' were the third) were all officially known as 'Charity' rather than 'Health' stamps. This was consistent with the Cabinet's decision that sales underwrote the tuberculosis prevention campaign, although Health Minister A.J. Stallworthy stated that funds raised would benefit 'primarily the establishment of children's health camps'.[1] The two causes were allied: 'by the later 1920s health camps were seen as the major weapons against tuberculosis. Most particularly, they were promoted as a means of building up childhood resistance to the disease.'[2]

The rather unremarkable 1929 charity stamp and its near-identical successor of 1930 both depict a young registered nurse. Their designs incorporate traditional Māori border motifs – in this case generic kōwhaiwhai patterning. The double-barred cross, later adopted by the Free French in World War II, symbolises the International Union Against Tuberculosis, while the bottom corner panels denote the dual postage and charity functions. The punning slogan, 'Help stamp out tuberculosis', was approvingly quoted by Opposition politician and future Labour prime minister Peter Fraser. The timing of the issue, two weeks before Christmas, capitalised on seasonal sales and goodwill. Thereafter equivalent stamps would be launched in October for overseas Christmas mail.

Stanley Davis, 1d and 1d Charity Issues, 1929 and 1930.

Author's Collection

Perkins, Bacon & Co. (attributed) after Leonard Cornwall Mitchell, 1d and 1d trial proof.

Robin Gwynn, Collecting New Zealand Stamps, *Reproduced with permission of the author.*

The New Zealand Post Office originally planned to issue a 'Smiling Boys' charity stamp in 1930, envisaging this entirely new design as a grander replacement, almost 50 per cent larger than the 'Nurses'. The Wellington-based artist Leonard Cornwall Mitchell (1901–1971), embarking on his notable 40-year career as a stamp designer, provided the original drawings. But owing to problems experienced by the London-based printers Perkins, Bacon & Co., a stopgap plate had to be prepared by the Government Printer in Wellington, and the 1929 image was reissued.

The Royal Mint inherited the postponed commission and made numerous refinements to the design. The boy's smile becomes less shark-like, while his face, neck and shirt are shaded, providing greater uniformity with the mountain backcloth. The wavy lines of the border, no longer Māori-inspired, are better defined. An additional stamp was hurriedly prepared when the government, desperate to raise revenue, doubled the postage rate for standard letters to twopence. As there was no time to make a plate in London, veteran local engraver W.R. Bock inserted the new value in the left-hand panel, altering its right-hand counterpart to provide visual uniformity. The Post Office received his proofs on 22 October 1931; nine days later the new scarlet and blue stamps were on sale.

Iconographically, the 'Smiling Boys' occupy a transitional position between charity and health, prefiguring the annual health stamps synonymous with New Zealand's philatelic distinctiveness and heritage since 1932. In Mitchell's design, 'Health' is dominant, brandished on a mini-banner wrapping around the frame, while at the bottom right, 'Charity' makes a final appearance. 'Charity stamps' remained their official appellation until at least late 1932, and the promotional poster for the 'Smiling Boys' used that term four times. However, 'charity' provoked 'a good deal of objection'.[3] In the grip of the Depression, it carried demeaning Victorian connotations, incompatible with New Zealand's cherished image as 'God's Own Country'. The newly appointed Health Minister, James Young, referred to 'Christmas Stamps' at the October launch, while the *Auckland Star* stressed that 'the object is to give the children not charity but a chance'.[4]

The catchy slogan, 'Buy Health Stamps for Health Camps', emerged at this point so that, as Margaret Tennant notes, 'the link was never broken'.[5] In 1931 the health camp movement was new: barely a handful of camps existed, running heroically on a diet of sunshine, fresh air, canvas, the smell of an oily rag and now the modest proceeds of stamp sales. Raukawa, later the Otaki Children's Health Camp, was the first permanent, year-round operation. Opening in February 1932, shortly before the 'Smiling Boys' were withdrawn, its success marked the graduation of health camps from 'rugged individualism' to part of the more sophisticated, government-funded and regulated welfare state apparatus. Exponential growth of health camps and their populations followed, with a concomitant upsurge in health stamp popularity. The 186,731 'Smiling Boys' were swamped by the 1,449,980 'Lifebuoy' or 'Smiling Girl' stamps of 1936, a bonanza inconceivable in 1931.

Department of Health official Edwin Myers was given the task of promoting the campaign in November 1931, just days after the 'Smiling Boys' were launched. 'A slump [was] at the front door,' he later recalled, and the Newspaper Proprietors Association's policy of 'no pay; no puff' precluded any complimentary publicity. Armed with a minuscule advertising budget of £88 3s 4d, Myers undertook a national whistle-stop publicity campaign that inspired several new health camp associations. Realising the low public recognition of charity stamps and their raison d'être, Myers publicised the camps, then the stamps as their means of support, deploying 'variations in the attack … including the use of a few original "wheezes"'.[6] In 1931 the legendary racehorse Phar Lap 'mark[ed] his approval' of the sale of stamps, his hoof 'stamp' auctioned at a community sing-a-long at Wellington Town Hall.[7]

Despite there being 'no puff', the campaign received conscientious and positive press coverage. A charming *Evening Post* photograph shows the Kirkcaldie & Stains' department store Father Christmas sending his parcels to England, naturally using the 'health charity' stamps.[8] The message was repeated and reaffirmed. Young put the case simply, even movingly: 'Children's health camps deserve Dominion-wide support. Many sickly children are made well and happy by them.' Postmaster-General Adam Hamilton stressed that 'only a little was asked, but that little was asked of everyone'.[9] The 'little' proved too much for many; fortune did not smile on the 'Smiling Boys'. Their sales yielded £778 0s 11d, compared with almost £900 for the 1930 stamp and £2470 for that of 1929. According to the philatelic historian R.J.G. Collins, the explanation was straightforward: this was the nadir of the Depression.[10]

Did their unusual design also count against them? Certainly the stamps did not enjoy instant classic status, and though they were scarce and therefore more valuable than their peers, in 1942 *Scott's Monthly Magazine* valued them at a still modest $US2.50 apiece.[11] There is only one lengthy, but particularly damning, newspaper review of the design, in the specialist *Australian Stamp Monthly*. It was republished verbatim in the *Evening Post* 10 days before Christmas 1931, probably too late for a response from Myers. The article's invective was probably triggered by an element of the 'shock of the new'. There was no obvious philatelic precedent for the 'Smiling Boys', and while a Swiss Pro Juventute (child welfare) stamp depicting a smiling girl was issued in 1933, there has been little or nothing like them since. Although more polite than the *Australian Stamp Monthly* reviewer, philatelic author Robin Gwynn could still assert in 1988: 'No one would call the "Smiling Boys" the most attractive of

Publicity photograph for 'Health Charity' stamps, 1931. Gordon Burt, Santa Claus, with a parcel for England and assorted toys. Ref: 1/1-015745-F, Alexander Turnbull Library, Wellington, New Zealand

New Zealand's Health stamps.'[12] Not conventionally attractive, perhaps; but their smile is a peculiarly potent and memorable synecdoche for happiness, health and youth. If nothing else, the 1931 stamps helped to 'bolster New Zealand's image as a supposedly healthy, humanitarian country, with a concern for its future citizens'.[13] The 'Smiling Boys', far more than the penny plain 'Nurses', were the first such stamps to achieve this and therefore rank as pioneers of their genre.

'Glowing with health', 'brown and bonny', 'bubbling with enthusiasm': these were how children on health camps were expected to look, feel and be. Above all, the camps and their residents were meant to exude 'cheerfulness'. In the documentary film, *Health Stamps for Health Camps*, made at the apogee of the movement in 1949, the viewer is introduced to a joyful real-life boy – the son, perhaps, of the 'Smiling Boy' – munching his daily apple at Campbells Bay Children's Health Camp, whereas two less fortunate urchins, left behind in tumbledown Auckland, glower at us. Narrator, poet A.R.D. Fairburn, observes: 'Some are healthy in spite of lack of places to play. Some are not. Buying stamps gives kids happy days.'[14]

Perhaps most obviously, the 'Smiling Boys' reveal the benefits of dental care, an important aspect of health camp culture ever since the first camp at

Turakina in 1919, which included innovations such as 'toothbrush drill', where children were lined up, given a mug of water, their own toothbrush and toothpaste, and then proceeded to dip, brush and rinse in cheerful unison. Few such children, however assiduous their brushing, could hope to brandish teeth comparable with those of the 'Smiling Boys'. Mitchell's image is necessarily idealised; gap-toothed ultra-realism would have looked inappropriate and undignified. Perfect teeth such as these reflect both the healthiness and the happiness central to the stamps' message. David Scott has remarked on how the largest symbolic sign on each stamp, 'Health', echoes the shape of the boy's smile. Still subtler is the placing of the postage and charity panels that approximate to the level of the boy's hands – or outstretched palms? Scott posits a plausibly ingratiating message: 'Give me a penny, sir, and I will be healthy and smiling.'[15]

The 'Smiling Boys'' meaning, and viewers' appropriate response, then, are plain. These stamps have the courage of their convictions: wholesomeness, candour, even innocence are manifest. The 'Smiling Boys' could date only from a particular moment in history. In his *A Brief History of the Smile*, Angus Trumble notes its comparative rarity in art before the introduction of motion pictures, which 'revolutionised the way people looked at the world and at each other in the twentieth century'.[16]

Who, then, is the 'Smiling Boy'? Perhaps a future All Black, a war hero, or both? Like Michelangelo's *David*, he almost certainly existed purely in the artist's mind and visual databank. Although several other charity and health stamps – notably the 1935 'Key to Health' and the 1937 'Rock-climber' – are based on photographs of individuals, this is not so here. Frank and Allan Mitchell do not believe that the boy was an identifiable individual, although they maintain that having three small sons around him subliminally influenced their father Leonard's creation.[17] Whatever and whoever he may be, the 'Smiling Boy' is not a portrait. Portraiture presupposes a sense of personality and characterisation as well as likeness. His attractive, symmetrical features instead make the 'Smiling Boy' a 'type'; a composite, construct and ideal.

The criticism of the *Australian Stamp Monthly* notwithstanding, Allan Mitchell, himself a stamp designer, admires the soft, rounded and modelled features of the 'Smiling Boy', conveying the lines of Leonard's pen drawing. Like this author, he considers the stamps more successful than has traditionally been maintained. Nowhere is this more evident than in their semiotic efficiency. Typographical and iconic components, the latter emblematic of national identity, are effectively synchronised to exude a 'concentrated ideological density' within their necessarily small frames.[18] A design crammed with icons and symbols (the Southern Cross, the double-barred cross, postage, charity and health), a miniature New Zealand landscape tableau of mountains, lake and ponga trees, framing the pièce de résistance of the 'Smiling Boy' himself, placed close to the picture plane and engaging in eye contact with the viewer: all this courts thematic confusion and visual disaster. To his credit, Leonard Mitchell treads the tightrope precariously but successfully.[19] The 'Smiling Boys' smile on, and the spectator smiles back at them.

Rin Tin Tin plaque (front and rear), crafted by Minoru Matsuyama, c. 1942.

Private Collection. Photograph by Pete Nikolaison

48

The Rin Tin Tin Plaque

A Man, His Dog and a Japanese Prisoner of War

Kristyn Harman

When New Zealand agreed to house more than 800 predominantly Japanese prisoners of war captured by United States Marines in World War II, it became necessary to find meaningful tasks to occupy their time. Placed at a camp just outside of Featherston in the Wairarapa in 1942, more than 500 of those captured were labourers who had been conscripted into the military. Their peacetime occupations ranged from farming, fishing and rice selling to carpentry and stonemasonry. Less than half were soldiers or sailors.[1]

The daily routine for many prisoners included labour 'of direct benefit' to New Zealand.[2] From November 1942 this involved a party under guard working between 2790 and 10,428 man-hours per month in market gardens at nearby Greytown. Between February 1943 and April 1944 work was phased in at an onsite concrete works and a nearby piggery. Some men also wound jute. The greatest time commitment was to labouring in the camp's furniture factory, where prisoners worked a combined total of up to 13,950 hours per month.[3] The furniture produced was of sufficiently high quality to be used in Bellamy's at Parliament House, Wellington.[4]

Outside working hours, the prisoners were 'encouraged to employ their spare time in making carvings and mementoes from pieces of wood which are refuse from the furniture factory'.[5] This trench art included elaborate mah jong sets, ornate walking sticks, gettas (sandals), boxes, letter openers, animals such as elephants, snakes, tortoises and camels, and a range of wall plaques. The output was sufficiently extensive for a formal procedure to be introduced to regulate its sale. The works officer valued each object in New Zealand pounds and the items were then displayed by the padre at the Featherston camp to be sold. Since POWs were not allowed New Zealand currency – they were issued with metal tokens – the proceeds were handed to the pay office and recorded on prisoners' pay cards.[6] The largest collection of trench art is displayed at the Featherston Heritage Museum.

Because many of the men involved have since died, the items themselves remain as repositories of stories, some of which have been handed down through the families of those associated with the camp. The Rin Tin Tin plaque is one such item. Parts of its story have been handed down through my family, along with the artefact itself, while recent archival research has filled in a crucial gap in its provenance.

Interior of the furniture factory at the Japanese prisoner of war camp near Featherston, 1943.

Ref: 1/4-000783-F, Alexander Turnbull Library, Wellington, New Zealand

The Rin Tin Tin plaque was carved with a 6-inch (15 cm) nail from a rimu offcut and stands 19 centimetres tall and 14.5 centimetres wide. The dog's compelling image is coated in shellac, a non-toxic substance derived from South East Asian insect resin and mixed with turpentine before being applied to wood to give it a glossy finish.[7] Although it could be viewed simply as an expression of one man's creativity, when considered in the context of its production, the Rin Tin Tin plaque stands both as testament to the friendship that grew between a Japanese POW and a New Zealand camp guard, and as a symbol of the strong bond that existed between a man and his German Shepherd dog.

On 28 April 1942 my grandfather, Greytown orchardist Ronald Noel Farmer, was called up for the Territorials.[8] After undergoing basic military training at Dannevirke and Trentham, he was sent as a guard to the Featherston camp in his home valley. Ron's views about the Japanese prisoners were expressed in his letters home to Sheila, my grandmother, in nearby Greytown. Soon after the arrival of 475 prisoners to the Featherston camp in 1943, he wrote to his young wife that the prisoners were 'not Japanese soldiers, just working men' like himself.[9] Ron noted their comparative youthfulness, and described how 'the poor thing [*sic*] look done out they will do anything for you they have no hope of getting out'. He felt a measure of compassion for these young men who arrived at the camp with nothing more than the clothes on their backs and little hope of returning home in the near future, if at all.[10]

His propensity for occasionally slipping away from camp under the cover of darkness to spend an illicit night at home, returning before dawn so that he would not be missed, earned my grandfather the army nickname of 'The Fox'. Ron artfully shed his uniform before crossing several rivers that lay between his home and the camp, carrying it above water level to avoid any signs of dampness that might otherwise give him away. He was concerned to ensure that his wife and young family were getting on all right without him, and he also had a deep bond with his champion show dog, Rin Tin Tin, who had been left in his parents' care for the duration of the war.[11]

Shared concerns for loved ones at home, both human and animal, as well as a sense of class camaraderie, meant that Ron, like many other camp guards, formed friendships with some of the POWs, who were roughly the same age. It was a Japanese prisoner he had befriended, known to our family by his Kiwi nickname 'Joe', who carved the plaque depicting Ron's faithful canine companion, Rin Tin Tin. Such friendships were not unusual: the guards were generally quite relaxed, particularly around those of their charges who were civilian conscripts rather than career military men. As Greytown resident Molly Mahupuku later recalled, 'the guards would put their guns against the walls and didn't seem too worried about the prisoners' when they were overseeing labourers in the local market gardens. Despite the initial alarm felt by many of the town's residents, social bonds were forged between civilians and prisoners. For example, Mahupuku's younger brother, Ian, learned

some Japanese language through interacting with the labourers.[12]

As an informal social network flourished at and beyond the Featherston camp, an informal system of barter developed. This operated alongside the formal processes through which the prisoners' carved items were ostensibly to be sold. Decades after the war ended, Featherston resident Norman Grenfell discussed the acquisition of his numerous objects of Japanese trench art from the camp with writer Cathy Casey. He was keen to emphasise how 'the various items were not bought from the prisoners but bartered for from colleagues at the camp'.[13] Some of Grenfell's camp colleagues used barter to obtain wooden carvings. Former Japanese POW Soichi Kawai, who later wrote a memoir about his time at the Featherston camp, recalled how he had swapped wooden items he had made, including 'Go and Chinese chess boards, mah jong tables, and mah jong pieces', for cigarettes, a prized commodity that functioned as the main currency within the camp. He also carved a walking stick decorated with dragon and frog designs and presented it as a gift to a camp interpreter and pastor, Lieutenant Keith Robertson, who was teaching Kawai some English language.[14]

The Rin Tin Tin plaque is one of several pieces of trench art acquired by my grandfather and still held by my family. We do not know whether Ron bought the elephant, gettas and Wellington West Coast Mounted Rifles wall plaque through the camp padre or traded the items for cigarettes, but the Rin Tin Tin plaque is an altogether more personal item. It was probably either carved by 'Joe' as a gift or possibly as a specially commissioned piece. Named after the canine film star of the eponymous 1926 classic, Rin Tin Tin was one in a long line of Ron's German Shepherds. In carving the dog's image, it is possible that 'Joe' worked from one of several amateur photographs taken in the 1940s, which remain in the family's collection.

Numerous plaques carved at the camp are said to have been worked simply with pieces of broken glass or large nails. Grenfell recalled the making of these 'rudimentary carving tools':[15] they were simply sharpened pieces of metal inserted into roughly made yet utilitarian wooden handles. A collection of them is now on display at the Featherston Heritage Museum.

Some of the wooden carvings produced by the POWs are inscribed in pencil. The rear of the Rin Tin Tin plaque states that it was carved in 1942 by a maker from Japan (represented by the inscription JYAPN) named M. Matsuyama. My archival research has revealed a match between this pencilled inscription and one of the names on the list of prisoners held at the Featherston camp, Minoru Matsuyama. This was the man my grandfather warmly recalled as 'Joe'. Allocated the prisoner number 39, Matsuyama was aged 26 when taken into captivity. In civilian life, he had been a metal worker, an occupation with skills easily adapted to wood carving.[16]

The following summer the camp hit world headlines when, on 25 February 1943, after rising tensions between the Japanese officers and some guards came to a head, what has since become known as the 'Featherston Incident' took place.[17] As some of the guards opened fire on prisoners involved in the insurrection, gunshots from the camp were heard

LEFT: *Private Ronald Noel Farmer.*

Private Collection

BELOW: *Rin Tin Tin, c. 1942.*

Private Collection

from as far away as Greytown. Ron survived the riot that ultimately saw 48 prisoners and one guard die from their wounds, but the conflict clearly troubled him. Decades later, when he was interviewed by Mike Nicolaidi for a book about the incident, my grandfather explained how 'at nights, for a long time, I had bad dreams, nightmares about it'. In the aftermath, those who had been on guard duty were granted leave.[18]

Rin Tin Tin himself did not long survive the war. My grandfather was devastated, when he retrieved his beloved dog from his parents, to find that the animal was suffering from severe malnutrition. Despite his careful ministrations, Rinty died not long after Ron's return home from the Featherston camp. The carving of Rin Tin Tin has survived for more than 70 years, first as a memento for Ron of his much-loved dog, then handed down as a cherished family object.

49

The Final Link in the Empire Route

New Zealand and the TEAL Short Solent Flying Boat

Michael Findlay and Gerry Barton

The Royal Mail Airliner *Aranui*, one of the last tangible reminders of the Empire Air Mail Scheme (EAMS), rests in a hangar at the Auckland Museum of Transport and Technology (MOTAT) in Western Springs. The Short Solent Mk IV was the largest and most powerful commercial aircraft of its type in the world when purchased by the New Zealand government for Tasman Empire Airways Ltd (TEAL) in 1949.[1] This was the last country to base its international civil aviation on new flying boats, and the purchase of the Solents marks the closing of a period when the politics of empire confronted the new technological and commercial imperatives of a changed post-war world. The EAMS was an initiative of the British government and Imperial Airways to maintain a global stake in the civil aviation sector by undertaking to deliver all first-class mail within the empire by air. It spurred several airlines – Imperial Airways, Qantas and TEAL – to develop extensive new routes, connecting mail routes from England to Cape Town, India, Singapore, Hong Kong, Australia and eventually New Zealand.

The Empire series of Solent boasted an advanced design featuring an all-metal aluminium structure and four powerful radial engines. Safety was assured as they could fly on two engines and land safely in open sea. Although freight carrying was the flying boats' primary role, they did carry passengers and Imperial marketed the service as safe, comfortable but, more importantly, 100 per cent British.[2] The cabins were luxuriously appointed: early craft had a promenade deck where passengers could view the scenery en route. Auckland-born architect Brian O'Rorke (1901–1974) designed the modern passenger cabin after coming to the notice of aircraft manufacturers, Short Brothers, through his work on the Orient Line passenger ships.[3] Early publicity showed a proud English family with their terrier joining the children for a game on the wide internal gangway. The planes, which could carry 44 passengers, flew the Tasman from Auckland to Sydney and later to Fiji, Western Sāmoa, Aitutaki and Tahiti on the Coral Route.

The core aim of the EAMS, however, was to increase the efficiency of commercial air services by carrying far greater freight loads than ever before. The EAMS was seen as an important way to solidify trade and communication links in the face of growing economic competition from other national airlines.

OPPOSITE: *Aotearoa, Tasman Empire Airways Limited's first EAMS carrier, on Waitemata Harbour, Auckland in 1940. The colour-tinted photograph would have originally hung, suitably framed, in a travel agent's office.*

Private Collection

TOP LEFT: *A commemorative envelope sent on 26 July 1938 from Christchurch to the Malay state of Johore on the first EAMS service to Great Britain. Master Tony Barton posted it to his aunt, Babs Hamilton, asking that she send it back, which she did. It took about 14 days to reach Sydney at which point it went airmail to Singapore. Barton's uncle, H.W. Hamilton, was a New Zealand surveyor employed by the Johore government.*

Private Collection

TOP RIGHT: *The EAMS at last reaching New Zealand by air: a commemorative envelope sent on 26 April 1940 to Sydney and turned around on 1 May, a five-day return service.*

Private Collection

EMPIRE AIR SERVICE
Master Tony Barton
60 Murray Place
Christchurch
New Zealand
JOHORE
INAUGURATION OF REGULAR AIR SERVICE CARRYING ALL FIRST CLASS MAIL TO GREAT BRITAIN

EMPIRE AIRMAIL
NEW ZEALAND
AUSTRALIA
ENGLAND
THROUGH AIR MAIL SERVICE
INAUGURAL FLIGHT.
1940
NEW ZEALAND POSTAGE & REVENUE
Mr.A.W.Barton,
60 Murray Place
St Albans
Christchurch
New Zealand
AUSTRALIA
NEW ZEALAND
CAMMERAY
NEW SOUTH WALES
R
No 1140

AOTEAROA

It also came with strong appeals to empire loyalty, belief in technological progress and the importance of 'buying British'.[4] The greater weight of seaplanes, as well as their design for large volume air freight, eroded the main competitive advantage of commercial air travel, which favoured the higher air speed of land-based aircraft. The great flight distances proposed in the route favoured flying boats: no land-based aircraft could cross the oceans without refuelling and there were no airports at which to land.

The plan for the airmail service was unveiled to the British Parliament in 1934. Its main feature was an 'all up' service that would carry first-class mail to the empire at a standard cost of 1½d per quarter-ounce. The estimated cost of the first year of operation was £2.65 million. The great expense involved in this ambitious programme required subsidies from the dominion countries of £287,000 per year and participating nations were expected to provide their own ground facilities and waive any fees or charges.[5] Imperial Airways sought a competitive advantage on the international civil routes in the face of growing competition from North America with Pan American Airways, Europe with German, French and Dutch airlines, and within the empire itself.

Many senior aviation industry figures, particularly in Australia, opposed the flying boat option. Until his death in 1935 famed colonial aviator Sir Charles Kingsford Smith advocated the purchase of American land-based aircraft for any future service, asserting that it was not 'un-British' to do so.[6] The Australian government was divided on the issue and its investigation of the EAMS proposal judged it fatally flawed. The load calculations supplied from Royal Mail fell well short of the Australian's expectations and made no allowance for the Christmas peak period. The budgets were questionable but, worse still, the British authorities provided no accurate survey of the route. Despite these misgivings, the British government persuaded the Australian Parliament to ignore the advice of its aviation experts and a deal was signed for Australia to join the EAMS early in 1937.[7]

New Zealand papers carried regular progress reports on the expansion of the EAMS service. In 1936 5 million letters were dispatched along the approximately 43,500 kilometres of air routes radiating from Southampton at a rate of just under 6 tonnes per day. The extent and efficiency of the service recalled the revolution of the penny post in the previous century, where a letter could be delivered at the standard rate anywhere in the empire. New Zealand was anxious to be included in this scheme and the crew of the first Empire flying boat enjoyed a tumultuous welcome from the citizens of Auckland when *Centaurus* alighted on Waitemata Harbour on its survey flight on 27 December 1937. It arrived shortly after the Pan American craft *Samoan Clipper* and for a brief time both flying boats were moored in the harbour, attracting thousands of spectators.

The service had hardly begun when the end was in sight for EAMS: cracks in the system soon appeared, with lengthy delays and disruptions over the 1938 season. The scheme proved unworkable and its failings were part of a major overhaul of British civil aviation in 1939, resulting in the creation of the British Overseas Airways Corporation (BOAC) from

A very Britain-in-the-Pacific TEAL advertisement in White's monthly aviation news magazine, December 1948.

Private Collection

the amalgamation of Imperial Airways and British Airways. World War II was the death knell for large flying boats, and it was clear by 1943 that the future of aviation was going to be land-based planes.

So how did the post-1945 New Zealand government become committed to purchasing more flying boats? In just the way that events had earlier unfolded in Australia over the EAMS debacle, imperial loyalty came to the fore. Curiously, the only other country to continue building giant flying boats after the war was France, similarly in thrall to old colonial fantasies. No other countries entertained the idea.

TEAL was formed in 1940 as a partnership between the Union Steamship Company, the New Zealand government, Imperial Airways and Qantas. Although the seaplane service during the war was safe and reliable, the New Zealand government and its advisers regarded land-based planes as the best for the future. Yet when the government was faced with the choice of replacing its ageing flying boat

OPPOSITE: Aotearoa II, *one of* Aranui*'s three sister ships, in a Short & Harland Ltd publicity shot for the new Solent IVs, 1949. Launched by Princess Elizabeth in Belfast, it ended its life a hulk hauled up on a mud bank on the Tagus River, Portugal and was finally scrapped in 1971.*

Private Collection

fleet after the war, it decided in 1946 to purchase four Sandringhams, optimistically described in Short's advertising as 'the most popular flying boat in the world'.[8] TEAL officials had wanted to buy American land-based planes and join the rest of the aviation world, but New Zealand bowed to the influence of a Britain acting in the interests of its own struggling civil aviation industry. The Short S.25 Sandringham IV 'Tasman Class' proved unexpectedly troublesome – the planes overheated and required extensive modification – and they were quietly retired after only two years when discussions began again on their replacement.

In a world of DC-4s, DC-6s, Boeing Stratocruisers and Lockheed Constellations, TEAL went back to Short & Harland Ltd in Belfast and purchased four new Solents. New Zealand could justify the purchase because of its commitments to the South Pacific, and its lack of ground-based airport infrastructure, but TEAL's commitment to 'buying British' reflected the political and economic realities of a period when civil aviation throughout the old empire had passed from commercial to state control. Governments could apply pressure to control services but also to protect the industries that served aviation. The decision was made easier for TEAL as Walter Nash's Labour government was reluctant to spend on ground aviation infrastructure, despite subsidising TEAL's trans-Tasman operation to make it appear profitable.[9]

When BOAC dispensed with its flying boats in 1950 the game was up. American aircraft would dominate the skies and the giant flying boats ended up, as all aged civil aircraft must, in the backwaters of small nations or at scrap-metal yards. TEAL replaced most of its fleet in 1954, leaving just two flying boats, *Aranui* and *Aparima*, in the twilight zone of the money-losing Coral Route. Only four Royal Mail Airliner flying boats have survived the wrecker's yard. The last Solent Mk 4, RMA *Aranui*, was mothballed at Whenuapai Air Base, Auckland, when the Coral Route service ceased in 1960. Sir Geoffrey Roberts, then deputy chairman of TEAL, was adamant that such an important piece of aviation heritage be saved from destruction. In 1966 it was floated across the upper Waitemata Harbour to become part of the MOTAT aviation collection. Volunteer work teams inaugurated a number of attempts to restore *Aranui* in the 1960s and 1970s, none of them successful. In 1982 a group of ex-Solent crew members and former TEAL staff, concerned at the flying boat's continuing degradation at the museum, formed the Solent Preservation Society. The members indefatigably raised funds to return RMA *Aranui* to its former glory and then, once the refurbishment was complete, gathered more money to contribute to a hangar large enough to house the flying boat. By 1990 the task was complete. The society's display, which included showcases of TEAL history and Coral Route memorabilia, quickly made *Aranui* one of the museum's drawcards.

In 2009, however, the flying boat was put outside once more as the hangar was extended. For more than three years *Aranui* remained without protective tarpaulins to stop rainwater seeping into the cabins and flight deck. The interior fittings of timber and fabric rotted, metal fittings and fixtures corroded, fabric ceilings sagged with pooled water and the

ABOVE: *RMA* Aranui *at Aitutaki Lagoon, 1958.*

Solent Preservation Society

LEFT: *Passengers in the upper deck cabin of a TEAL Solent flying boat en route to Auckland, 1949.*

Solent Preservation Society

seating upholstery was bleached by sunlight coming through the windows.

The new display hangar opened in July 2011 and in December 2012, some 18 months after the installation of other aircraft in the collection, the flying boat was towed on its beaching gear into the new building. In the meantime a new conservation plan had been drawn up to deal with the degraded condition of the vessel. This proposed a three-year work schedule to return the airliner to its 1951 appearance, the era selected as the best to represent TEAL's flying boat glory days. Commencing in August 2012 when the flying boat was still outside, the project has involved up to five specialist contractors under the guidance of the museum conservator. By mid-2014 much of the hull requiring attention had been repaired, the entire interior structure sanitised, and half of the six passenger cabins, the lower deck corridor, and stairwell to the upper deck refurbished to their original appearance. At time of writing *Aranui* remains incomplete. It also awaits a display context that represents its rarity as a remarkable piece of aviation heritage and an artefact of great significance to New Zealand and the South Pacific.

Mataatua wharenui, after its return to Ngāti Awa in 1996, restored and erected at Whakatāne as part of a tribal cultural centre. *Courtesy of Te Rūnanga o Ngāti Awa.*

50

Afterword

The Wharenui Mataatua, and some Thoughts about Things

Conal McCarthy and Jonathan Mané-Wheoki

On 17 September 2011 the splendidly refurbished meeting house Mataatua, the pride of Ngāti Awa, was opened with due ceremony on a site adjacent to the Wairaka marae in Whakatāne. Serving as a whare rūnanga, a parliament, for Ngāti Awa, Mataatua is the centrepiece of an impressive architectural complex that functions as a cultural, conference and visitor centre. The facility symbolises the resurgence of Ngāti Awa in expectation of the settlement of long-standing grievances with the Crown. The return of the whare to its people in 1996, 117 years after it had been lent to the colonial government for exhibition in Australia, constituted one part of a bundle of claims lodged with the Waitangi Tribunal. Before its return, Mataatua had become one of the most travelled and most widely exhibited Māori buildings in history. It was displayed six times – in Sydney, Melbourne, London (twice) and Dunedin (twice) – and its exhibition history spans more than a century of absence from Whakatāne.[1]

Mataatua was originally carved in 1875 by Wēpiha Apanui and a team of artists, in part as a gesture of reconciliation with the Crown after the devastation of recent wars.[2] The house was acquired by the government, a subject of much later debate, and in 1879 sent to the Sydney International Exhibition, where it was displayed inside out. After travelling to Melbourne and then London, it was stored in the basement of the South Kensington Museum (later the Victoria and Albert Museum). During World War I the house was 'rediscovered' and, after being displayed at Wembley as part of the New Zealand court in the British Empire Exhibition of 1924–25, it returned to Aotearoa to be re-erected at the 1925–26 New Zealand and South Seas Exhibition in Dunedin.[3] Finally it was installed in the Otago Museum, where it served as the entrance to the Māori exhibits arranged by ethnologist H.D. Skinner.[4] After decades of relative obscurity, it came into greater prominence in 1986–87 during *Te Maori*, when it served as a venue for pōwhiri to welcome the huge crowds that attended the popular exhibition in Dunedin. This ground-breaking exhibit ushered in sweeping changes in museum practice in terms of Māori involvement in the collecting and display of taonga Māori, leading ultimately to calls for consultation, co-management and even repatriation of several prominent houses, carvings and other ancestral treasures.[5]

The carved meeting house Mataatua at the Sydney exhibition in 1879, displayed inside out.

MU 14, 5 (13/27/127), Museum New Zealand Te Papa Tongarewa

Mataatua wharenui interior. *Courtesy of Te Rūnanga o Ngāti Awa.*

Mataatua's sibling, the whare Hotunui, carved by Ngāti Awa for Ngāti Maru in Thames, had fallen out of use by the 1920s and was gifted to the Auckland War Memorial Museum, where today it is displayed in the Māori court.[6] It is reasonable to assume that Mataatua, had it remained on its original site, would eventually have arrived at a comparable level of deterioration. But its conservation within the protective environment of a museum has prevented this and prolonged its life. Although Otago Museum had been a most conscientious steward of this precious taonga over the years, a process began that, alongside the settlement of Ngāti Awa's claim to the Waitangi Tribunal, demanded the return of this taonga to its iwi.

When one of the authors visited the wharenui at Whakatāne in January 2013, the house was several times referred to as 'living and breathing'. The personhood of a whare tupuna is a key element in Māori thinking: the building is conceptualised, not only as a being, with many of its components named after parts of the body, but as the embodiment of the ancestor. When the iwi or hapū enters the whare, it enters the protective body of its ancestor.[7] In early wharenui the illusion or impression of being inside a living, breathing being must have been palpable.

Forget the printed page you are reading for a moment, and embrace the sensory experience of being in a physical place. Close your eyes and imagine that you are in the darkened interior of a large whare. Smell the earth floor, the body of Papatūānuku, the earth mother; sniff the smoke from the firewood, pick up the scent of the plant fibres used in the woven mats, the fish oil used to bind the pigments in the painted designs, the odours and fragrances of human bodies. See the glint of the pāua shell eyes on the carved faces of the ancestral poupou. Feel them watching. Listen: hear the murmur of voices and other human sounds. Hear the rustling of the wind through the fibres of the roof and wall cladding. Hear the creaking of the timbers.

Discussing Mataatua as an 'object', however limited that is in cultural terms, given its physical embodiment of ancestral power, usefully opens up the themes addressed in this book. The book embraces two key Māori concepts: taonga, or cultural treasures, and kōrero, or stories. According to Hirini Moko Mead, when Māori see and respond to taonga, these object-beings are animated by the kōrero, the story, talk or language that surrounds and 'clothes' them, giving them meaning and value for the people interacting with them.[8]

The life story of Mataatua and its travels throws light on colonial history in general and on the history of colonial New Zealand in particular. It speaks of the art of carving, the history of museum display, the conflicts of the New Zealand Wars and the development of contemporary Māori society after the settlement of Treaty of Waitangi claims. Like many other Māori possessions in the colonial period, the house passed out of tribal ownership, but in recent times has returned to iwi control, adding a post-colonial coda to its complex story. From captivity to repatriation, it is an example of the ways in which culture and history are being reclaimed so that the past can be kept alive in the present.

Like the other objects in this book, the house was made, used and exchanged. It travelled around the

world, was exhibited, moved in and out of museums, its meanings changing as it was framed and reframed by a succession of display conventions, discourses, audiences and policies – seen, at various times, as a taonga, trophy, specimen, artefact and symbol of regeneration. This trajectory of construction, conflict, travel, alienation and return reflect the colonial experience. Now Mataatua has returned to its home in Whakatāne, and by forming an afterword to the legacy of colonisation, it also becomes a fitting taonga with which to conclude this book.

The lives of this object, along with others in these pages, bring the past down into the present in concrete form, linking us through sight and touch to an outpost of the British Empire in the South Pacific. What do the lives of objects tell about our colonial past? In their introduction, the editors describe the great variety of objects presented in this volume and in the conference that led to it, all brought together to tell the history of colonial New Zealand 'through things'. In Tony Ballantyne's study of the 'webs of empire', he advocates 'relocating' colonial history, through more attention to capitalism, nation and archive.[9] To this list we would add objects and material culture. In this afterword, therefore, we offer some thoughts about things that refine the analysis of colonial culture.

Together the essays in *The Lives of Colonial Objects* demonstrate the power of objects as witnesses to the colonial past. The range of things is extraordinary: large (buildings, monuments and whales), small (stamps and jewellery), natural and cultural (rocks, trees, mineral water and art and craft), crafted (shoes and textiles), and manufactured items and machines (billies, presses, harpoons, stereopticons and radium activators). Some move (flying boats, tents) but most remain still. There are objects that unfold in the landscapes (roads), and objects that perform, resonating in space and time (pianos, pūtōrino). Some objects have immense power (cannons), and some are light and seemingly insignificant (feathers).

We have chosen just a handful in order to reflect on the things and thoughts of colonial New Zealand. In the very first essay, Lucy Mackintosh follows a pūtōrino from Aotearoa to Salem, Massachusetts, as it 'weaves through space and time', examining the 'glimpses of lived experience amidst the archival silence surrounding these epic voyages and early encounters'. We were struck by how the writer was drawn to this taonga, and in turn how it drew her into its own history, just as the music played by such an instrument ensnares listeners by 'connecting distant places, ancestors and gods with the present'.

But for other objects, such as William Colenso's composing stick, the archives are not silent. In Sydney Shep's skilful telling of its story the reader learns about the extraordinary birth of print culture in these islands and its interaction with Māori oral practices. A humble and ordinary artefact, rescued from the dirt floor where it had lain for many years, it was an instrument in the creation of powerful documents that shaped New Zealand, namely the Māori Bible and the Treaty of Waitangi. 'Now too fragile to touch or hold,' writes Shep, the stick remains a 'potent witness to the power of print and its role as agent of colonisation and conversion, instrument of literacy and preserver of language'.

Print, books and language are key features of this collection and of our colonial culture, an empire of words that linked New Zealand to the British world. But sometimes they were tools wielded by other hands, and directed against empire as well as its enemies – as demonstrated in Lachy Paterson's essay on the printing presses for Māori newspapers that were caught up in the Waikato 'cold war' of the 1860s. And they were not the *only* instruments of empire. Roads were a far more prosaic way of transporting colonisation, as Annabel Cooper shows with her analysis of a contested route cut into Te Urewera. Cricket bats in colonial Sāmoa may have started as an essentially 'English' symbol but were soon indigenised into the local cricket culture, as Safua Akeli shows. In Lynette Townsend's essay on the Crowther family's Noah's Ark, we have an example of 'colonising through play'. Yet Townsend's research also reveals the personal associations and memories of the children who played with it, a private world of memory and emotion. Like other essayists, she also opens up a new area of New Zealand's colonial history, that of children's recreation, imagination and creativity.

Images and visual culture are another form of connecting tissue in empires and colonisation. In Charlotte Macdonald's meticulous reconstruction of the provenance of John Singleton Copley's *Mrs Humphrey Devereux*, we see how this wonderful painting, a sober realist depiction of a loved mother 'with old age creeping upon her', was at the same time an object, an art work and family. Painted in Boston in 1770, it travelled across the Atlantic to England and then halfway around the globe to Wellington in the nineteenth century where it was rediscovered in the 1950s and moved from the walls of a family home to the National Art Gallery. The elderly woman is 'an American face in our midst', a reminder of the cosmopolitan nature of colonial society, which troubles the conventional notion of an English 'there' paired with a colonial or New Zealand 'here'.

A domestic colonial space emerges, too, from the essay by Kirstine Moffat, with its evocative opening in which, describing the Broadwood grand piano at The Elms, she recalls walking into the house, sitting at the instrument and playing it. As she plays, she is haunted by stories of 'heartbreak, courage and romance'. We were also moved by the account of the piano's owner Euphenia Maxwell and her travails and travels from Scotland to Wadestown to Tauranga, the piano accompanying her and her family. The way that Moffat connects the object and the owner/player speaks not only of the use of things, but of their embodied, emotional and gendered nature, in rooms full of music and dancing. The photographs of the time should not give us the impression that our ancestors were Puritan killjoys. 'Colonial music making,' she reminds us, 'could be both improving and fun.'

A party in Thorndon, Wellington, in 1907 is described in a newspaper report that mentions a young woman in a black crêpe-de-chine dress who was wearing a large bone hei tiki. The woman was none other than Miss K. Beauchamp, or Katherine Mansfield. From this intriguing incident Jane Stafford begins a fascinating meditation on narratives of desire, and the ways in which we make the Mansfield we want KM to be: artist, bicultural, New Zealander.

Sometimes objects lie, or at least, are yoked to different versions of history, the past as we would like it to be. Contextualising the object in the Māoriland of late colonial New Zealand, Stafford points out that indigenous things became 'decorative markers of a mild form of settler nationalism' while at the same time prominent Māori women such as Mīria Pōmare were pictured in the society press wearing a mixture of European fashion and Māori clothing. Maybe KM was not so exceptional after all. And perhaps the same may be said for other examples of colonial material culture that are not progenitors of a nationalist future. The variety of objects – from health stamps, tents, flying boats and diaries, to mineral water, embroideries and memorials – suggests that the colonial period, and therefore colonial history, was one of breadth and cosmopolitan diversity, moving, not static, and in colour rather than in black and white.

These are just some of the thoughts that come to mind on reading particular essays in this volume, but we could equally have chosen many others. Overall there are some strong impressions of life in colonial New Zealand and consequently useful ways we might think of using objects to construct colonial history. Three groups of objects stand out. There are many photographs: this visual technology, invented in the nineteenth century, captures its quotidian existence in unparalleled detail. There are many books in various forms – diaries, registers, scrapbooks, albums, ledgers, minute books, visitors' books – suggesting that the Victorian period was saturated with print (the printing press is another reminder of this). And there are the Māori decorated heirlooms we now call taonga – kākahu, tauihu, tokotoko, hei tiki – which make this diverse collection, the stories it tells and the history of interaction it illuminates – what Judith Binney called a 'bi-history' – a very distinctive one in the global context.[10]

The essays lead us naturally to consider the value of object histories and books of museum collections like Neil MacGregor's *History of the World in 100 Objects*.[11] The study of objects as an integral part of colonial history enriches our understanding of the past. However, despite the obvious success of McGregor's book and radio series drawn from the collections of the British Museum, the range of objects in these kinds of studies is naturally limited by what is preserved in museums or by families. Books like *The Lives of Colonial Objects* cannot reveal a complete picture of everyday colonial life – textiles and clothing often do not survive, whereas wood, bone or steel are more common – and whole areas of social life are difficult to represent: here we find childhood, religion and leisure, but not old age, sexuality or war, at least not as much as we might expect in a period characterised by conflict. Other aspects of colonial life are illuminated in interesting ways in the essays: the ties to the land, whether for settlers or indigenous people; the central importance of family whether extended or nuclear; and what Tony Ballantyne refers to as the second-hand or recycled nature of colonial material culture, a phenomenon far more significant than the twentieth-century myth of DIY Kiwiana. These material things provide us with valuable glimpses of life in New Zealand that texts, on their own, could not give us (at least not with such clarity).

The study of objects has much to offer colonial historians but there is much left to do. Many studies are preoccupied with representation, with showing, which tends to reduce objects to illustrations of events, processes and people. There is a tendency either to focus on the *history*, so that the object is overwhelmed by detail (usually drawn from textual sources), or to focus on the *object*, at the expense of its social context, so that the wider social arena fades from view. We get the object, or the colonial history, but not always both. The essays here do not focus too much on either *colonial* or *object* but try to keep them connected. This acknowledges, in anthropologist Nicholas Thomas's memorable phrase, that they are 'entangled objects'.[12] When the balance is struck between the two, as happens so often in these pages, then the results are rich and revealing. Material thinking, plus historical analysis, is a powerful method that adds immeasurably to the discipline of history and our knowledge of the colonial past.

Object biographies naturally celebrate the beauty of material things and can at times neglect the darker aspects of their histories, such as the violence of colonial conflict. There is a tendency to look at the soft and decorative, rather than the hard and mechanical – more cushions and curtains than ploughs and bullets. Despite attempts to broaden them, the range and variety of objects remains relatively narrow, and scholarship has perhaps not grasped the everyday as well as the rare and the beautiful, the low as well as the high. Objects are often seen in isolation, fixed in space and time. Accounting for the movement of objects, and rehearsing well-worn scholarly paradigms – reading, representation or aesthetics – can be enhanced by referring to recent literature on museum studies, material culture studies and cultural history.

Although some of the objects in *The Lives of Colonial Objects* are not held by institutions, and have never been 'colonised', or removed from their 'natural' locales or social relationships, many, as might be expected, are from museum, gallery or archive collections. These repositories are both essential and problematic. Collecting colonial objects preserves them for posterity but also takes them out of life circulation and deposits them in a museum – the quintessential colonial institution – which uses them to construct nations, histories, peoples and their identities. It can be difficult, too, given the professional classification systems of museums, to look at these objects and reconnect them with their historical contexts, to 'reassemble the social', as Bruno Latour put it.[13] Sometimes this means rethinking the lives of objects before they entered a collections store and received a label and accession number.

Museums are not, moreover, neutral containers of objects. Museums and collecting practices have many limitations. They themselves, of course, are the product of history, and generally ossify conventional concepts about society and culture, whether it is taste, gender, sexuality or myths about colonial history, from the pioneer work ethic, and female domesticity or nascent 'national identity'. At the very least, there are gaps in collections, and thus absences in our knowledge, due to the subjectivities of collecting, changing intellectual fashions or lack of space or resources. Museums are always already compromised as representations of the material world, a world which, after all, can never be captured in all its limitless plenitude. Museums are useful, but we cannot rely on them as a record of the colonial past.

On the other hand, museums are sometimes unfairly singled out in critical accounts of colonialism's culture, treated as crude instruments of empire, which regard the collections they hold as passive products of big historical processes: colonisation, nationalism and modernity.[14] Recent studies have balanced this with micro histories, material histories and history from below – working up from the objects rather than down from the theory.[15] New work on colonial museums figures them as relational entities interconnected with other institutions and processes, and objects as active things that speak, act and move around – that is, they have agency.[16] Scholars talk not just of collectors acquiring objects, but of objects collecting people. This greater attention to social and material agency shifts the focus away from language and meaning towards performance, feelings and embodiment.[17] The literature of 'new' material culture studies with its object-centred approach to 'stuff', allows for an understanding of things as well as words.[18]

A fruitful confluence of material culture studies and history can be found in the work of scholars such as Thomas Schlereth, who see objects as concrete survivors of the past that can be experienced emotionally through the senses.[19] Other useful texts also show how historians can unlock people's past lives by using both objects and written sources.[20] Alongside *The Lives of Colonial Objects* there are other exciting new developments in New Zealand that sit at the intersection of history and material culture studies.[21] Bronwyn Labrum, a historian with experience in museums, has developed the idea of 'material histories' in the New Zealand context, making a persuasive case for bringing together the material and the social in a single frame.[22] She calls for more research that is driven by objects and accounts for how they are used. 'By bringing together the material and the social,' she argues, 'and examining how things are done, as well as how things are possessed and consumed, fresh perspectives and innovative histories will be created that uncover and explain past worlds and quotidian experiences.'[23]

Much can be gained from scholars working in museum studies, such as Sandra Dudley, who has successfully foregrounded 'the thingness of things'.[24] She describes how she walked into an art gallery one day and was literally stopped in her tracks by the power of an object: a Chinese sculpture of a bronze horse from the Han dynasty made in the fourth century. Her response was a 'fundamental, emotional, sensory, even visceral one to its form, materials, colour, scale and texture'.[25] But Dudley is not advocating a return to some unreconstructed notion of concrete reality. She calls for an approach to material culture that balances the thing, its context and the social relations around it.[26]

Even the seemingly self-evident word 'object' is problematic, Dudley reminds us.[27] It refers to something visible, tangible and bounded – a pot, for example – but this overlooks things that are extended, such as landscapes, dams and railroads, which are of course central to colonisation, as demonstrated by some essays in this collection.[28] Sometimes overlooked, too, is the immateriality of objects. We forget that the intangible, the virtual and the performed are equally 'objects'. The same might be said about the way that common sense understandings of 'object' exclude the natural world – but are not natural things equally objects? Tim Ingold, for example, breaks down the western division of nature/culture and social/material, and treats artefacts and organisms equally – he talks about things that are made and things that grow.[29] We can see this relationship most clearly in Katie Pickles' essay, where she traces how the imperial figure of Florence Nightingale has become naturalised into the colonial landscape of the Ashburton Domain, while Peter Hodder's essay also draws attention to the natural world, reminding us of the significance and value of water to colonial science, to leisure and to industry.

Whereas too much attention to the object obscures and even effaces the social and historical, we would point to good examples of research, particularly in anthropology, which analyse the intersection of the two. In their book *Collecting Colonialism*, Chris Gosden and Chantel Knowles successfully explore the connections between people, objects and colonial relations.[30] Taking the example of a piece of bark cloth from Melanesia sitting in the Pitt Rivers Museum at Oxford, they warn us not to regard it as a direct representation of the past. Rather we are encouraged to see it as the 'nexus of a tangle of ongoing historical connections', such as the child whose head was bound with it, the collector who did the fieldwork, the colonial administrator and missionary for whom it is a sign of progress in acculturation, the academic to whom it represents a stage in the history of anthropology, and the museum/private collection where it is kept, catalogued and displayed. The point is, they stress, that the object is a *process*. 'The apparent singularity of objects when sitting in a glass case or museum store room should not mislead us,' they write, because the 'physical circumstances of the object change continuously, but so also do its sets of significances as it accumulates a history (i.e. a history of individuals, of colonialism, of museology)'.[31]

Other theories of objects conceive them in different ways: to Arjun Appadurai they have 'social lives', to Igor Kopytoff they have 'biographies', to Alfred Gell they are 'actants' or agents mediating social relations.[32] Bill Brown talks about 'thing theory'.[33] Some regard objects as 'assemblages', interconnected aggregates with no inside/outside, which are continually in a state of forming, breaking apart and reforming.[34] This concept has been usefully applied to the 'materialities of colonial government,' explored through the interconnections of museums, anthropology and indigenous people, including examples from New Zealand.[35]

Indigenous and other non-western understandings of being are increasingly drawn on in an effort to break down the distinction between subject and object.[36] With this in mind we can better appreciate how tribal people might view sacred object-beings as alive. In Aotearoa New Zealand the things that Māori people call taonga tuku iho (treasures handed down) are not just precious heirlooms, but, as Paul Tapsell and Amiria Henare show, ancestors who move across time and space, connecting descendants to their ancestral landscapes and life-worlds.[37] In their essays, Lucy Mackintosh, Pāora Tapsell, Migoto Eria, Megan Pōtiki and Paerau Warbrick all draw attention to the varied ways in which objects can be understood as ancestors, or possessing mana deriving from their contact with tūpuna.

This brings us back to where we began, to Mataatua, the ancestor house that has travelled the world and come home again. The story of Mataatua, and its contemporary postscript, is a sober reminder that the effects of colonisation are still with us, and that object stories are about power, loss and reconciliation. Āpirana Ngata, who himself did so much to foster Māori carving through the School of Māori Arts and Crafts, declared in the 1940s that he would never wish a taonga to be 'a dead exhibit in a museum' but, rather, to remain 'a living force in the community'.[38] That is why the repatriation of Mataatua to its people in Whakatāne is so momentous for Ngāti Awa. Like many Māori objects in museum collections, and some in this book, which changed hands in the colonial period, it has been decolonised and become once more a 'living force in the community'. It resumes its central place in the maintenance of tribal whakapapa, and in the construction of iwi identity. Mataatua is witness to, and participant in, Ngāti Awa life cycles. It will live out its life among them and, perhaps, even die in due season. Mataatua never really belonged to Ngāti Awa. They belonged to it. It was, in the words of Hirini Moko Mead, not theirs to sell or give. No longer 'a captive museum exhibit', it looks overjoyed to be back among its people. As Mead puts it, 'It looks liberated.'

Contributors

Safua Akeli is of Samoan heritage. She was Curator Pacific Cultures at the Museum of New Zealand Te Papa Tongarewa from 2008 to 2013. Safua holds graduate and postgraduate qualifications in history from the universities of Otago, Victoria and Canterbury. Her research interests include Sāmoa's colonial history and Pacific material culture.

Steve Austin studied Chinese history at Canterbury University. He has a BA (Byzantine and medieval art history), and BA (Hons) (First Class) in Chinese history. Steve started researching early Chinese settlers in New Zealand in 2004, and was appointed Chief Executive of Marlborough Museum in 2006.

Tony Ballantyne is a professor of history and head of the Department of History and Art History at the University of Otago. He also serves as the director of Otago's Centre for Research on Colonial Culture. He has published widely on the history of the modern British empire, especially on colonial knowledge, print cultures and cultural mobility.

Felicity Barnes is a history lecturer at the University of Auckland and has a particular interest in imperial connections and settler cultures. She is the author of *New Zealand's London: A colony and its metropolis*, and is now working on a project examining the issue of culture and identity in New Zealand, Australia and Canada.

Gerry Barton is conservator at the Museum of Transport and Technology, Auckland. He was appointed conservator at Auckland War Memorial Museum in 1981 and worked as a freelance conservator before taking up the position at MOTAT. He is co-author, with Stefan Dietrich, of *This Ingenious and Singular Apparatus: Fishing kites of the Indo-Pacific* (2009) and is presently conserving MOTAT's Short Solent flying boat and working on a monograph about it.

Catherine Bishop graduated with a PhD from Australian National University in 2012. She currently works at the University of Western Sydney and the Australian Catholic University. Her eclectic research interests include New Zealand and Australian colonial history, gender and heritage, twentieth-century Australian missionaries and post-war internationalist peace education.

Roger Blackley teaches in the art history programme at Victoria University. Formerly a curator at the Auckland Art Gallery, he organised exhibitions of the 62 portraits from the Partridge Collection in conjunction with *Te Maori* (1987) and *Goldie* (1997). His current project is *The Galleries of Maoriland*, exploring Māori depictions in colonial New Zealand.

Chris Brickell is an associate professor in gender studies at the University of Otago. He has published extensively on gay history, masculinity, theories of gender and sexuality, and visual history. His next book project is *Teenagers: A New Zealand history*, under contract with Auckland University Press.

Barbara Brookes is a professor of history at the University of Otago. Her research concentrates on areas where the history of women and the history of medicine intersect. She is currently completing a history of women in New Zealand.

Alison Clarke has written a history of childbirth and other publications on New Zealand's nineteenth-century social and religious history. She works at the Hocken Collections and as a Research Fellow at the University of Otago, where she is researching and writing a 150th anniversary history of the university.

Chanel Clarke (Ngāpuhi, Te Rarawa, Ngāti Porou and Waikato-Tainui) is Curator Māori at the Auckland War Memorial Museum Tāmaki Paenga Hira. Previously she was Ethnology Curator at the Waikato Museum of Art and History, Hamilton. Her specific collection interests include the social and cultural aspects of Māori dress in both traditional and contemporary contexts.

Annabel Cooper is an associate professor in gender studies at the University of Otago. Her research has ranged across gender, place, memory, media and colonial culture, and she is currently working on screen media and cultural memory of the New Zealand Wars.

Rosi Crane's doctoral research at the University of Otago, Department of History and Art History, is on the academic career of zoologist T.J. Parker FRS (1850–1897). The biographical approach aims to reclaim his place in the colonial culture of the late nineteenth century and reflects her broad interest in history of science.

Kelvin Day is Tumuaki Director of Puke Ariki, the integrated museum, library and visitor information centre in New Plymouth. His research interests are centred on the archaeology and Māori material culture of the Taranaki region. He is currently researching the history of several Taranaki collectors of Māori artefacts.

Genevieve de Pont completed her PhD in history at the University of Auckland in 2014. Her thesis centred on travel diaries written by New Zealanders travelling internationally during the mid-twentieth century, and analysed these as both material and textual objects.

Migoto Eria (Ngāti Pāhauwera, Ngāti Kahungunu, Ngāi Tuhoe, Japan) is Curator Māori at Otago Museum. Previously Migoto was Curator Taonga Māori at Museum Theatre Gallery Hawke's Bay and an editor for Māori medium publishing at Learning Media Ltd. Before this she was project co-ordinator of lexicography at Te Taura Whiri i te Reo Māori, Māori Language Commission. Particular areas of research include the interpretation of Māori history to ensure appropriate and relevant accessibility by hapū and iwi.

Michael Findlay joined the University of Otago following a curatorial career in New Zealand museums. He was assistant curator of decorative arts at the Auckland War Memorial Museum Tāmaki Paenga Hira and collections curator at Toitū Otago Settlers Museum, where he developed exhibitions on music, film, architecture and product design. He joined the Department of Design Studies in 2000. He is currently working on a PhD on the effect of travel on New Zealand architecture from 1880 to 1950.

Michael Fitzgerald is Curator Colonial New Zealand at the Museum of New Zealand Te Papa Tongarewa. Decorative arts come within his curatorial portfolio and he has worked closely with Walter Cook for over 20 years on exhibition and research projects.

David Haines is an historian of whaling interested in issues of cultural contact, gender and colonialism. He is the author of several articles on Māori participation in the New Zealand whaling industry, including 'In Search of the "Whaheen": Ngai Tahu Women, Shore Whalers, and the Meaning of Sex in Early New Zealand' in Tony Ballantyne and Antoinette Burton (eds), *Moving Subjects: Gender, intimacy and mobility in an age of global empire* (University of Illinois Press, 2009).

Jill Haley was the archivist at Toitū Otago Settlers Museum until 2014 and is now a PhD candidate in the Department of History and Art History, University of Otago. She earned her MA through the Winterthur Program in Early American Culture at the University of Delaware. Her research interests are nineteenth-century photography and material culture.

Kristyn Harman is a social historian and a lecturer in the Faculty of Arts at the University of Tasmania. She is the author of *Aboriginal Convicts: Australian, Khoisan, and Maori exiles* (University of New South Wales Press, 2012). Kristyn researches and writes histories of captivity, domesticity and cross-cultural encounters, with a particular focus on the former British Empire.

Ruth Harvey is Manager Programmes and Experiences at Puke Ariki, a combined museum, library and visitor information centre in New Plymouth, New Zealand. She is particularly interested in both historical and contemporary photography, as well as art history and audience involvement in museums.

Kerry Hines is a Wellington-based poet, writer and researcher with an interest in photographic histories. Her PhD in creative writing, awarded by Victoria University in 2012, examines and responds to the work of nineteenth-century New Zealand photographer William Williams.

Peter Hodder's current research interests are in the history of science, its management, and its communication and dissemination in the public sphere, building on a background of research and teaching in geochemistry and earth sciences, and experience in science centres and museums. He works at Victoria University of Wellington.

Kate Hunter teaches in the History programme at Victoria University of Wellington. She is the author of *Hunting: A New Zealand history* (Random House, 2009) and, with Kirstie Ross, *Holding onto Home: New Zealand objects and stories of the First World War* (Te Papa Press, 2014).

Helen Leach is emeritus professor in the Department of Anthropology and Archaeology, University of Otago. She has a special interest in the evolution of human diet, and the history of food production and cookery. Among her recent books are *The Pavlova Story*, *The Twelve Cakes of Christmas* and *From Kai to Kiwi Kitchen*.

Charlotte Macdonald is a professor of history at Victoria University of Wellington. Her research focuses on nineteenth-century British empire and gender, and the cultural history of bodies and sport in the interwar decades. Her recent work, *Strong, Beautiful and Modern* (Bridget Williams Books, 2011), won the Ian Wards and Australian Society for Sports History book prizes.

Lucy Mackintosh is a doctoral student at the University of Auckland. She has worked as a public historian for over 15 years on historic places, cultural landscapes and material culture. She lived in the United States from 2010 to 2012, where she researched taonga Māori in the Peabody Essex Museum.

Jane McCabe is a teaching fellow in the Department of History and Art History at the University of Otago. She has published several articles from her recently completed doctoral thesis, which examined the lives and labours of 130 Anglo-Indian adolescents resettled in New Zealand between 1908 and 1938.

Conal McCarthy is Director of the Museum and Heritage Studies programme at Victoria University of Wellington, New Zealand. Conal has degrees in English, art history, Māori language and museum studies and has worked in galleries and museums in a variety of professional roles. He has published on museum history, theory and practice, and in particular the indigenous engagement with collecting and display, including the book *Museums and Māori: Heritage professionals, indigenous collections, current practice* (Te Papa Press, 2011). His next book is *Museum Practice: The contemporary museum at work* (Wiley, 2015).

Jonathan Mané-Wheoki (Ngāpuhi, Te Aupouri, Ngāti Kuri) (1943–2014) was an art historian, architectural historian, cultural historian and curator. A pioneer in the development of contemporary Māori and Pacific art and art history, Jonathan held academic positions at the University of Canterbury and Elam School of Fine Arts at the University of Auckland, as well as leadership positions at the Museum of New Zealand Te Papa Tongarewa.

Kirstine Moffat is a senior lecturer in English at the University of Waikato, where her research focuses on New Zealand settlement writing. Music is also one of Kirstine's passions; she started to learn the piano when she was five and is the author of *Piano Forte: Stories and soundscapes from colonial New Zealand.*

Ewan Morris is a Wellington-based historian. He is researching memorials at Pākaitore/Moutoa Gardens as part of a larger project looking at what debates over flags, anthems, memorials, place names and holidays can tell us about relations between Māori and non-Māori.

Lachy Paterson teaches Māori language and Māori history in Te Tumu: School of Māori, Pacific and Indigenous Studies at the University of Otago. He researches Māori and New Zealand colonial history, with a special interest in Māori newspapers and print culture.

Katie Pickles teaches history at the University of Canterbury. Her research covers aspects of gender, empire and colonisation in New Zealand and the British world. She has forthcoming books on 'New Zealand's Empire' (edited with Catharine Coleborne), and a text on Christchurch's history in the wake of the Canterbury earthquakes.

Megan Pōtiki is a lecturer at Te Tumu: School of Māori, Pacific and Indigenous Studies at the University of Otago. Her research interests focus on local Kāi Tahu history and Māori language archives.

Rebecca Priestley is a senior lecturer in the Science in Context group, in the School of Chemical and Physical Sciences at Victoria University of Wellington. She teaches history of science, science communication and creative science writing, and conducts research into twentieth-century New Zealand science history and science communication.

Claire Regnault is Senior Curator History (Creative Industries) at the Museum of New Zealand Te Papa Tongarewa. Her research interests lie primarily in New Zealand's fashion, textile and craft histories. She is the co-author of *The Dress Circle: New Zealand fashion design since 1940* (Godwit, 2010), which was a finalist in the 2010 New Zealand Post Book awards.

Rebecca Rice is Curator Historical New Zealand Art at the Museum of New Zealand Te Papa Tongarewa. She was formerly a part-time lecturer in art history at Victoria

University of Wellington where she also managed the art collection. Rebecca has written for the collection publications of Te Papa and Auckland Art Gallery and has published on New Zealand's colonial art and exhibition culture in local and international journals.

Sydney J. Shep is Reader in Book History and The Printer, Wai-te-ata Press, Te Whare Ta o Wai-te-ata, at Victoria University of Wellington. She specialises in topics on New Zealand printing and publishing history as well as typography and design and directs a digital history collaborative research hub.

Damian Skinner is an art historian and Curator of Applied Art and Design at the Auckland War Memorial Museum Tāmaki Paenga Hira. He is currently working on a project about the role of art in settler colonial societies.

Catherine Smith is a senior lecturer in the Department of Applied Sciences – Clothing and Textile Sciences (CLTE), University of Otago, where she teaches social and historical aspects of dress and manages the CLTE Teaching Collection of dress artefacts. Catherine has research interests in material culture, in particular the analysis of pre-contact Māori textiles. She is also a conservator who has worked throughout Australia and New Zealand, developing ethics and practice in regards to conservation of objects from indigenous and world cultures.

Jane Stafford teaches in the English programme of Victoria University of Wellington. She is the co-author of *Maoriland: New Zealand literature, 1872–1914* (Victoria University Press, 2006), the co-editor of *The Auckland University Press Anthology of New Zealand Literature* (Auckland University Press, 2012) and co-editor of volume 9 of *The Oxford History of the Novel in English: The world novel to 1950* (forthcoming).

Kate Stevens has a PhD in Pacific history from the University of Cambridge. She researches at the intersections of criminal justice, race and gender in the British and French empires, specifically in Fiji, New Caledonia and the New Hebrides/Vanuatu. Her previous work focused on interracial marriage and intimacy in nineteeth-century southern New Zealand.

Michael J. Stevens (Kāi Tahu) is a lecturer in Māori history based in the Department of History and Art History, University of Otago. His research focuses mainly on nineteenth-century southern New Zealand, increasingly with a maritime focus, and in 2013 he was awarded a Marsden Fast-Start grant by the Royal Society of New Zealand to undertake a three-year study of his home town entitled 'A World History of Bluff'.

Mark Stocker is Curator, Historical and International Art, at the Museum of New Zealand Te Papa Tongarewa. From 2003 to 2014 he taught at the Department of History and Art History, University of Otago. He has published extensively in the areas of Victorian and modern British art and New Zealand art, focusing particularly on sculpture, public monuments and numismatics. He edited 10 issues of the *Journal of New Zealand Art History* (2002–11) and regularly contributes book and exhibition reviews to the *Burlington Magazine*.

Pāora Tapsell is Chair of Māori Studies, University of Otago. His specialties include museums/heritage sector, Pacific navigation, Indigenous entrepreneurial leadership and Maorimaps.com. In between research, teaching and whānau, Pāora contributes his governance expertise to his tribe of Ngāti Whakaue as well as to wider national and international indigenous-aligned organisations.

F. Jane Teal has an MA in anthropology from the University of Otago. For most of her working life she has been employed as an archivist, currently for the Anglican Diocese of Christchurch and Christ's College. Her research interests include ecclesiastical, culinary and family history and she has published in all these areas.

Lynette Townsend is a history curator at the Museum of New Zealand Te Papa Tongarewa with an interest in New Zealand's cultural and social diversity. Her exhibition-based research has focused on the Italians and Scots in New Zealand and, in 2013, the Aztecs. Her current research explores the personal stories and history associated with the material culture of childhood.

Angela Wanhalla lectures in the Department of History and Art History, University of Otago and researches the relationship between race, gender and colonialism. Her most recent book, *Matters of the Heart: A history of interracial marriage in New Zealand* (Auckland University Press, 2013), won the Ernest Scott Prize in 2014.

Paerau Warbrick comes from a history, law and Māori studies background. Since 2005 he has been a lecturer in Te Tumu: School of Māori, Pacific and Indigenous Studies at the University of Otago, where he lectures on the Treaty of Waitangi, Waitangi Tribunal and Māori customary law. Paerau also practises part time as a barrister with expertise in the work of the Māori Land Court, Māori Appellate Court and the Waitangi Tribunal.

Megan Wells is currently the assistant curator in charge of social history and accoutrements at the National Army Museum in Waiouru. Her research focuses on material culture and object theory and she has a strong grounding in the Nelson region.

Jonathan West came late to history, when writing a PhD on the environmental history of the Otago Peninsula; his interests are still primarily in histories of New Zealand, especially its early, maritime, Māori and environmental aspects. He works at the Waitangi Tribunal in Wellington.

Endnotes

List of Abbreviations

AJHR *Appendices to the Journal of the House of Representatives*
ANZ Archives New Zealand, Wellington
ATL Alexander Turnbull Library, Wellington
HC Hocken Collections – Uare Taoka o Hākena, Dunedin
TOSM Toitū Otago Settlers Museum, Dunedin
TPA Archives and Collections of the Museum of New Zealand Te Papa Tongarewa, Wellington

Introduction: A Scheme of Things

1 Neil MacGregor, *A History of the World in 100 Objects*, London, 2010, p. xiii. MacGregor's collection discusses objects held in the British Museum. Testimony to the rising interest in object histories are the several volumes based on New Zealand museum, library and archive collections published in recent years: Andrew Moffat, *Flashback: Tales and treasures of Taranaki*, Wellington, 2011; Chris Jones and Bronwyn Matthews with Jennifer Clement, eds, *Treasures of the University of Canterbury Library*, Christchurch, 2012; Ray Waru, *Secrets and Treasures: Our stories told through the objects at Archives New Zealand*, Auckland, 2012; Fiona McKergow and Kerry Taylor, eds, *Te Hao Nui/The Great Catch: Object stories from Te Manawa*, Auckland, 2013.

1. Intimate Immensity: A pūtōrino in the Peabody Essex Museum

1 I am grateful to Alexander Nemerov, Amiria Salmond, Jolisa Gracewood, Gillian Forrester, Rhys Richards and Chanel Clarke for their insightful comments on earlier versions of this paper. I would also like to thank Annabel Cooper, Lachy Paterson and Angela Wanhalla for their helpful suggestions. Thanks also to Professor Ned Cooke and the members of the Yale Material Culture Study Group for their feedback on a paper I delivered there in 2012. Finally, thanks to staff of the Peabody Essex Museum and the Yale University Library for their help with accessing archival material. Longer versions of this article appear in *Material Culture Review*, 74/75 (Spring 2013), and as a chapter in Alexander Nemerov, ed., *Experience and American Visual Culture* (forthcoming, 2016).

2 C. Copeland, 'To the farthest port of the rich east', *American Heritage Magazine*, 6, 2 (1955); J. Phillips, *Salem and the Indies*, Cambridge, 1947, pp. 31, 46.

3 E.S. Dodge, *New England and the South Seas*, Cambridge, MA, 1965, pp. 24–25, 60–61; Rhys Richards and Margaret Richards, 'Pacific artifacts brought home by American whalemen', A report for the New Bedford Whaling Museum 2000, p. 2.

4 *Sydney Gazette and New South Wales Advertiser* (*SG*), 29 December 1805, p. 2; *SG*, 5 January 1806, p. 1; *SG*, 2 March 1806, p. 2; Philip Payn Pinel 'Logbook of the *Eliza* 1805–7', M 656 1805E, Peabody Essex Museum (PEM); Rhys Richards, 'A "lost galleon?" The Spanish wreck at Taumako', *Journal of Pacific History*, 34, 1 (1999), 123–28, p. 124.

5 *Salem Gazette* (*SalG*), 28 April 1807, p. 2; *SalG*, 9 June 1807.

6 A. Salmond, *Between Worlds: Early exchanges between Māori and Europeans, 1773–1815*, Auckland, 1997, pp. 321–32. Maritime historian Rhys Richards has researched the provenance of a number of early Māori artefacts in the PEM, including Richardson's collection, and will document his findings in a forthcoming publication (personal communication, February 2011).

7 *SG*, 9 March 1806, p. 1; *SG*, 29 December 1805, p. 2; *SG*, 5 January 1806, p. 1.

8 Salmond, *Between Worlds*, p. 321; B. Flintoff, *Taonga Pūoro. Singing Treasures: The musical instruments of the Māori*, Nelson, 2004, p. 17; S. Hooper, *Pacific Encounters: Art & divinity in Polynesia, 1760–1860*, Wellington, 2006, p. 61; Richards and Richards, 'Pacific artifacts brought home by American whalemen', p. 17.

9 D. Brown, *Northland Māori Wood Carving, Tai Tokerau Whakairo Rākau*, Auckland, 2003, pp. 71, 123; E.S.

Dodge, *The New Zealand Maori Collection in the Peabody Museum of Salem*, Salem, 1941, p. 7.
10 J.C. Andersen, *Maori Music with its Polynesian Background*, Wellington, 1934, p. 275.
11 Flintoff, *Taonga Pūoro*, pp. 74, 101; R. Nunns and A. Thomas, 'The search for the sound of the pūtōrino: "Me te wai e utuutu ana"', *Yearbook for Traditional Music*, 37 (2005), 69–79, p. 73.
12 There are early European accounts of Māori singing or reciting into a pūtōrino, but scholars have varying opinions about whether Māori actually used the pūtōrino in this way. See Nunns and Thomas 'The search for the sound' and M. McLean, *Maori Music*, Auckland, 1996 for further discussion.
13 Andersen, *Maori Music*, pp. 283–84; R. Gabel, 'Pīpīwharauroa!', *Mai Review 1* Intern Research Report 4 (2009), Nga Pāe o te Māramatanga, University of Auckland, p. 1.
14 H. Hakopa, 'The paepae: Spatial information technologies and the geography of narratives', PhD thesis, University of Otago, 2011, p. 149.
15 See Salmond, *Between Worlds*, pp. 170–72, for a more detailed discussion of Māori and European views of time and space; Matt K. Matsuda, 'The Pacific', *The American Historical Review*, 111, 3 (2006), 758–80, p. 763.
16 Flintoff, *Taonga Pūoro*, pp. 16, 22.
17 Ibid., p. 20.
18 Brown, *Northland Māori Wood Carving*, p. 35; Hooper, *Pacific Encounters*, p. 44.
19 Brown, *Northland Māori Wood Carving*, p. 35; A. Henare, 'Taonga Māori: Encompassing Rights and Property in New Zealand', in A. Henare, M. Holbraad and S. Wastell, eds, *Thinking through Things: Theorising artefacts ethnographically*, New York, 2007, 47–67, p. 60; Nicholas Thomas, *Entangled Objects: Exchange, material culture, and colonialism in the Pacific*, Cambridge, MA, 1991, p. 4.
20 *Salem Directory and City Register*, Salem, 1843, p. 119.
21 J.R. Grimes, *Uncommon Legacies: Native American Art from the Peabody Essex Museum*, New York, 2002, pp. 17–18.
22 J.M. Lindgren, '"That every mariner may possess the history of the world": A cabinet for the East India Marine Society of Salem', *The New England Quarterly*, 68, 2 (1995), 179–205, p. 184; Salmond, *Between Worlds*, p. 32; Nathaniel Hawthorne, quoted in D.A. Morrison, 'Salem as citizen of the world', in D.A. Morrison and N.L. Schultz, eds., *Salem: Place, myth, and memory*, Lebanon, NH, 2005, 107–28, pp. 113–14.
23 Lindgren, '"That every mariner may possess the history of the world"', p. 184.
24 *SalG*, 11 December 1807, p. 3.
25 *Notebook of Donations 1799–1820*, Series V11 Collection Catalogs MH-88, East India Marine Society, PEM; Hooper, *Pacific Encounters*, p. 67.
26 Lindgren, '"That every mariner may possess the history of the world"', p. 194.
27 Ibid., p. 198; Melani McAlister, *Epic Encounters: Culture, media, and U.S. interests in the Middle East, 1945–2000*, Berkeley, 2001, pp. 16–17; Jennifer Wagelie, 'Māori Art in America: The display and collection history of Māori art in the United States, 1802–2006', PhD thesis, City University of New York, 2007, p. 29.
28 P. Beatson, 'Richard Nunns: The renaissance of traditional Māori music', *Music in the Air*, 16 (2003), 117–133, p. 126; Flintoff, *Taonga Pūoro*, p. 17.
29 A.J.M. Henare, *Museums, Anthropology and Imperial Exchange*, New York, 2005; Linda Tuhiwai Smith, *Decolonizing Methodologies: Research and indigenous peoples*, London, 2012, p. 87.
30 E.S. Dodge and E.T. Brewster, 'The acoustics of three Maori flutes', *Journal of the Polynesian Society*, 54, 1 (1945), 39–64, p. 45.
31 To hear music clips of these instruments being played, visit www.richardnunns.net.nz/a/instruments/ Flintoff, *Taonga Pūoro*, p. 7; C. Royal, 'Mōteatea: Traditional Maori song poetry', Conference paper, *Oceania, World Music Days, International Symposium and Festival Dialogue in Music*, Beijing, China, 3 November 2009.
32 F.W. Veys, 'Awakening sleeping objects' in A. Salmond and R. Raymond, eds, *Pasifika Styles: Artists inside the museum*, Dunedin, 2006, 121–23, p. 123.
33 Paul Tapsell, quoted in A. Henare, 'Taonga Māori: Encompassing rights and property in New Zealand' in Henare, Holbraad and Wastell, eds, *Thinking Through Things*, 47–67, pp. 57–58; Georgina Born, 'Music and the materialization of identities', *Journal of Material Culture*, 16, 4 (2011), 376–88, p. 378.

2. Te Haupapa

1 This essay began life as an oral presentation in November 2001 at the Stout Research Centre conference titled 'Loaded cannons'. In 2004 aspects materialised in written form in the Whānau-a-Tapihana Reunion 1830–2004 booklet as a short essay titled 'Tapsell's cannons'. This mōteatea, *Takiri mai ko te ata*, was composed

by Haerehuka in 1836 and is still sung today by Ngāti Whakaue in memory of the death of Te Haupapa. This chapter concludes with an English translation (by the author).

2 Taonga is any object, item or thing, tangible or intangible, that has been passed through the generations and is recognised as being of ancestral importance. See Pāora Tapsell, *Pukaki: A comet returns,* Auckland, 2000, pp. 13–16.

3 See W.T. Parham, 'Tapsell, Phillip', from the Dictionary of New Zealand Biography: www.TeAra.govt.nz/en/biographies/1t11/tapsell-phillip

4 E.M. Tapsell, *Historic Maketu*, Rotorua, 1940, pp. 41–42.

5 Iwi included, among others, Ngāti Pikiao, Tapuika, Tūhourangi, Tūwharetoa, Ngāti Rangiwewehi, Ngā Pōtiki, Ngāti Tawhao, Ngāti Pūkenga, Whakahemo, Ngāi te Rangi, Ngā Hapū and Patuwai, each taking up residence around the Kaituna Harbour and over 10 kilometres up the river.

6 Cited in Tapsell, *Historic Maketu*, p. 43.

7 Over a five-year period many shiploads of guns, powder, shot and tobacco were traded for hundreds of tonnes of dressed flax, which were shuttled back to the Bay of Islands. From there the flax was delivered to the Sydney trading firm, Jones and Walker, who were contracted to supply unlimited hemp to the Royal Navy over Te Tapihana's initial Maketū years, 1830–35.

8 The *Valcona* or *Falcon* – named after Tapsell's Danish name, Falk or Falcon – was not wrecked until 1840 and there is no record of it carrying any cannons or of any associated with its salvage: see A. Matheson, *Historical Review* (Journal of the Whakatane and District Historical Society), 37, 1 (May 1989), pp. 1–11, for a full account of 'Tapsell's big guns'.

9 Edited excerpts from Pāora Tapsell and Q. Tapsell, *Whānau-a-Tapihana Reunion 1830–2004*, Tauranga, 2004, pp. 16–17.

10 See Pāora Tapsell, *Ko Tawa – Maori Ancestral Treasures,* Auckland, 2000, pp. 119–23, for further narrative and images of this pātiti, named Te Hunga.

11 Pāora Tapsell, *Pukaki*, pp. 68–73.

12 Phillip Tapsell, Reminiscences, MS-Group-1890, ATL.

13 This wāhi tapu – place of spiritual restriction – also hosted a number of graves up to the 1900s, including the carved tomb of Ahukata Kiharoa that now rests in Canterbury Museum, Christchurch.

14 E.M. Tapsell, *Historic Maketu*, p. 64.

3. Voyaging Taonga: The Kīngi Tauihi

1 Quoted in A. Moffat, *Flashback: Tales and treasures of Taranaki*, Wellington, 2012, p. 211.

2 W.C. Carkeek, *The Kapiti Coast Maori Tribal History and Place Names of the Paekakariki–Otaki District*, Wellington, 1966, p. 25.

3 Paul Tapsell, 'The flight of Pareraututu: An investigation of *Taonga* from a tribal perspective', *Journal of the Polynesian Society*, 106 (1997), 323–74, p. 337.

4 See Carkeek, *The Kapiti Coast,* pp. 25–26; H. Collins, *Ka Mate Ka Ora! The spirit of Te Rauparaha*, Wellington, 2010, p. 86.

5 Carkeek, *The Kapiti Coast,* pp. 86–87; B. Wells, *The History of Taranaki*, New Plymouth, 1878, pp. 145–46.

6 For consistency the name *Kaupahanui* is used as the name of Kīngi's canoe.

7 The names of four of the waka are recorded in Carkeek, *The Kapiti Coast,* p. 25.

8 *Taranaki Herald*, 16 April 1883, p. 2.

9 *Taranaki Herald*, 23 November 1880, p. 2.

10 9 November 1882, W.H. Skinner Diary, ARC2001-165, Puke Ariki.

11 A William Craig Lawrence, who is presumed to be the donor of the tauihu, died on 27 July 1922 aged 75 and is buried in Waitara.

12 C. McCarthy, *Exhibiting Māori: A history of colonial cultures of display*, Wellington, 2007, p. 13.

13 The full title of the exhibition was *Te Ahi Kā Roa, Te Ahi Kātoro Taranaki War 1860–2010: Our legacy – our challenge.*

14 Tapsell, 'The flight of Pareraututu', p. 335.

4. William Colenso's Composing Stick

1 Colenso's will and codicil, reproduced in *eColenso* newsletter (April 2011), p. 36; and in Stuart Webster, *Sainsbury, Logan and Williams, Lawyers since 1875*, 2011, p. 368. Available at: www.slw.co.nz/content/167/defualt.aspx

2 The composing stick was often termed the printer's rifle. In Colenso's time there were 13 letters in the Māori alphabet, so his type cases were built to suit.

3 Martin K. Speckter, *Disquisition on the Composing Stick*, New York, 1971, p. 101.

4 Bracken's poem is printed in full in the No. 6 (August 1876) issue of the *New Zealand Press News and Typographical Circular* (*NZPN*), p. 3, as part of the announcement of a 'Prize for the best air for a national hymn'.

5 MacKellar's poem is reprinted in full without an author named but with *American Printer* referenced in the *NZPN*, 4 (June 1876), p. 8.

6 *Scottish Typographical Circular* (*STC*), XI, 304 (1 December 1886), pp. 427–29. Ten years earlier, *NZPN* ran 'Typo's New Year's Address to his Auld-Stick' written by a Glasgow compositor (No. 6 (August 1876), p. 8). The same organ ran 'The Setting Machine', 6 (July 1876), p. 8 by Mr James Kelly from the firm of Aird and Coghill, printers, Glasgow, undoubtedly also gleaned from the Scottish press. See also 'The Type-Setter's Song', *NZPN*, 14 (April 1877), p. 7 clipped from the *Printers' Circular*, Philadelphia, and 'The Old Compositor' by Oscar H. Harpel, Cincinnati in No. 19 (September 1877), p. 8. *STC*, XIII, 416 (1 April 1896), p. 528: reprint of poem 'The Song of the Setting Stick' from *Australasian Typographical Journal*, 26 (December 1895), pp. 2614–15.

7 A.G. Bagnall and G.C. Petersen, *William Colenso: His life and journeys*, ed. Ian St George, Dunedin, 2012, p. 39.

8 *NZPN*, 36 (1 February 1879), p. 2.

9 *Old Bailey Online*, Reference Number: t18661022-906, www.oldbaileyonline.org

10 William Colenso, *Fifty Years Ago in New Zealand*, Napier, 1888, p. 6.

11 David Mackay, 'Colenso, William', from the Dictionary of New Zealand Biography: www.TeAra.govt.nz/en/biographies/1c23/colenso-william

12 Robert Coupland Harding, 'Relics of the first New Zealand press', *Transactions of the New Zealand Institute*, 32 (1899), 400–04, p. 401.

5. The Harpoon's Head

1 Sincere thanks to Associate Professor Ian Smith of the University of Otago who, with Nigel Prickett, discovered the harpoon, for access to the artefact and for advice in the writing of this essay. For more on the Oashore excavation see Jaden Harris and Ian Smith, 'Artefacts from the Oashore shore whaling station', Otago Archaeological Laboratory Report, 1 (November 2005), www.otago.ac.nz/anthropology/archaeology/reports, p. 61.

2 Gordon Ogilvie, *Banks Peninsula: Cradle of Canterbury*, Wellington, 1990, pp. 214–16.

3 Harry Morton, *The Whale's Wake*, Dunedin, 1982, p. 237.

4 Frances Steel, 'Uncharted waters? Cultures of sea transport and mobility in New Zealand colonial history', *Journal of New Zealand Studies*, 12 (2011), pp. 137–54.

5 I am grateful to Dr Emma Carroll for sharing her research. See also C. Scott Baker and Phillip J. Clapham, 'Modeling the past and future of whales and whaling', *TRENDS in Ecology and Evolution* 19, 7 (2004), pp. 365–371; and Dennis p. Gordon, Jennifer Beaumont, Alison MacDiarmid, Donald A. Robertson and Shane T. Ahyong, 'Marine biodiversity of Aotearoa New Zealand', *PLoS ONE* 5, 8 (2010), pp. 11–12.

6 For the dangers of the whale chase see Morton, *The Whale's Wake*, pp. 32–50.

7 James Belich, *Making Peoples: A history of the New Zealanders from Polynesian settlement to the end of the nineteenth century*, Auckland, 1996, pp. 131–32.

8 Nicholas Thomas, *Entangled Objects: Exchange, material culture, and colonialism in the Pacific*, Cambridge, MA, 1991, p. 4.

9 Geoffrey Sanborn concludes that the enigmatic harpooner Queequeg in *Moby-Dick* was inspired by George Craik's account of Ngāti Toa rangatira Te Pēhi Kupe in *The New Zealanders* (1830). Geoffrey Sanborn, *Whipscars and Tattoos: The last of the Mohicans, Moby-Dick, and the Maori*, New York, 2013, pp. 73–92.

10 For an overview of Māori participation in the business of shore whaling, see M.W. Cawthorn, *Maori, Whales and 'Whaling': An ongoing relationship*, Wellington, 2000, p. 8.

11 See Seán Brosnahan, *To Fame Undying: The Otago Settlers Association, 1898–2008*, Dunedin, 2008, p. 53.

12 Fiona Kidman, *The Captive Wife*, Auckland, 2005. See also Daphne De Jong, *Gather the Wind*, Auckland, 1999.

6. 'Keep the head cool, the feet warm, and the bowels open': Octavius Harwood and the Weller Brothers' Medicine Chest

1 Robert Fulton, *Medical Practice in Otago and Southland in the Early Days*, Dunedin, 1922, p. 8.

2 Handwritten notes by Octavius Harwood, DC-0096, TOSM; Mac Harwood, *Octavius Harwood, Titopu, Piro, Janet Robertson*, Nelson, 1989, p. 7.

3 See Arthur Viseltear, 'Looking back at tomorrow: Commencement address delivered at the Yale University School of Medicine, New Haven, Connecticut, May 24, 1981', *Yale Journal of Biology and Medicine*, 54 (1981), pp. 219–25.

4 Ian Church, *Opening the Manifest on Otago's Infant Years*, Dunedin, 2002, p. 43; Journal of Octavius Harwood, G.C. Thomson Papers, MS-0438/3, HC, 1–10 October 1839.

5 Journal of Octavius Harwood, 11 May 1839.

6 Booklet, biography & genealogy, by Lucy Ann Harwood, DC-1475, TOSM; Harwood, *Octavius Harwood,* p. 7. We do not know where Harwood acquired the surgical kit. One possibility, but it is no more than that, is that Crocome left it with him. Personal communication, Sean Brosnahan.
7 John Strachan, *Advertising and Satirical Culture in the Romantic Period*, Cambridge, 2007, p. 54.
8 Harwood also helped to disperse medical knowledge to others. For example, he sold medical books to the manager of the whaling station, C.W. Schultze. See Tony Ballantyne, *Webs of Empire: Locating New Zealand's colonial past*, Wellington, 2012, p. 322, citing Octavius Harwood, 'Miscellaneous accounts and lists of goods', 26 June 1842, MS-0438/026, HC.
9 Journal of Octavius Harwood, 11 May 1839.
10 Ibid., 1 April 1839, 19 May 1842.
11 Ibid., 23 March 1839, 29 March 1839, 1 April 1839.
12 G.C. Thomson Papers, MS-0438/005, HC.
13 On which, see generally Peter Entwisle, *Behold the Moon: The European occupation of the Dunedin district 1770–1848*, Dunedin, 2010, pp. 123–25, 134–35, 172–81; Jonathan West, 'An environmental history of the Otago Peninsula', PhD thesis, University of Otago, 2009, pp. 221–34.
14 Harwood, *Octavius Harwood*, p. 8.
15 Ian Church, 'French whalers at Otago 1838 to 1853,' in Glynnis M. Cropp, ed., *Pacific Journeys: Essays in honour of John Dunmore*, Wellington, 2005, 152–64, p. 158; Journal of Octavius Harwood, 19 May 1842.
16 Harwood, *Octavius Harwood*, p. 21.
17 Thomas Harwood to Octavius Harwood, 16 September 1857, cited in Harwood, *Octavius Harwood*, p. 71.

7. Colonising Through Play: The Crowthers' Noah's Ark

1 Philippa Mein Smith, *A Concise History of New Zealand,* Cambridge, 2005, p. 59.
2 Vicky Alexander, *Mary Crowther of 'Brookfield'*, Wainuiomata, 1993, p. 5.
3 *Wellington Independent*, 12 March 1872, p. 2.
4 Louis E. Ward, *Early Wellington,* Auckland, 1928, p. 390.
5 Helen May, *The Discovery of Early Childhood: The development of services for the care and education of very young children, mid-eighteenth century Europe to mid-twentieth century New Zealand*, Auckland, 1997, p. 19.
6 Mein Smith, *A Concise History of New Zealand*, p. 61.
7 Peggy Armstrong and Denise Jackson, *Toys of Early New Zealand*, Wellington, 1990, p. 59.
8 Mary Audrey Apple, 'The Noah's Arks of the Erzgebirge region of Germany', *The Magazine Antiques* (December 1991), 966–77, p. 969.
9 Ibid., p. 969.
10 See, for example, 22 June to 5 December 1885, Diary of Mary Ursula Crowther transcribed by Dawn Chambers, MSX-4114, ATL.
11 Helen May, *The Discovery of Early Childhood*, 2nd edn, Wellington, 2013, p. 143.
12 Apple, 'The Noah's Arks', p. 969.
13 Constance Eileen King, *The Encyclopedia of Toys*, New York, 1978, p. 63.
14 Apple, 'The Noah's Arks', p. 972.
15 Ibid., p. 975.

8. The Bishop's Register

1 H.J.C. Harper, *Official Acts of the First Bishop of Christchurch* (1856–1890), Christchurch Anglican Diocesan Archives (CADA). Bishop's register is the informal name for the official acts of each bishop and refers to the volume in which the record is kept.
2 During the period covered by the register the Anglican Church in New Zealand was officially known as The Branch of the United Church of England and Ireland in New Zealand (1849–74) and The Church of the Province of New Zealand (commonly known as the Church of England) (1874–1968).
3 A copy of the Deed of Consecration is in Harper, *Official Acts*, p. 10.
4 The Diocese of Christchurch was described as: 'All that portion of the Middle Island of New Zealand which lies to the Southward of a Geographical line drawn across the Middle Island at the northern boundary of the Territory set apart for the Canterbury Settlement under the provisions of an act passed for the purpose in the thirteenth and fourteenth years of Our Reign and which line is the forty third degree five minutes parallel of South Latitude (being about the latitude of Double Corner mentioned in the said Act) and also the Southern Island of New Zealand and the Auckland Islands and all adjacent islands lying to the southward of the forty third degree five minutes parallel of South Latitude, and should be styled and designated "the Bishopric of Christchurch".' *Letters Patent,* CADA.
5 Harper, *Official Acts*, p. 55; V. Matthews, *Official Acts of the Eighth Bishop of Christchurch* (2008–), p. 31, CADA.

6 Harper, *Official Acts*; C. Williams, *Bishop Harper's Journeys*, Archives Committee Diocese of Christchurch, 1997; H.T. Purchas, *Bishop Harper and the Canterbury Settlement*, Christchurch, 1909.

7 H.W. Harper, *Letters from New Zealand*, London, 1914, p. 49.

8 Ibid., pp. 97–98.

9 K.W. Orr-Nimmo, '"Whom am I that I should undertake this great work?" Bishop Harper's clergy', in C. Brown, M. Peters and J. Teal, eds, *Shaping a Colonial Church: Bishop Harper and the Anglican Diocese of Christchurch*, Christchurch, 2006, pp. 83–110.

10 J. Murray and P. Tremewan, 'Mutu and the Monita: An indigenous Maori church' in Brown, Peters and Teal, eds, *Shaping a Colonial Church*, pp. 161–87.

11 M.W. Blain, 'Who has the power in the Church? Testing the constitution' in Brown, Peters and Teal, eds, *Shaping a Colonial Church*, pp. 138–60. This cross was rescued from the river and given to Charles Coates, incumbent of Lyttelton. It is now Lyttelton's processional cross.

12 Proceedings of General Synod, 1859–2005, Church Papers online/Nga Pepa Hāhi ā Ipurāngi: www.kinderlibrary.outofprint.co.nz

13 H.J.C. Harper Inwards (BHIL) and Outwards (BHOLB) Correspondence, 1862–1893, CADA.

14 *Register of Baptisms Solemnized by the Bishop of Christchurch [and others] in Private Houses, throughout the Provinces of Canterbury, Otago and Southland, 1857–1876*, CADA (informally known as the Country Baptism Book).

15 H.J.C. Harper to L. Harper, 22 October 1888, BHOLB26, pp. 343–44, CADA.

9. The Face on the Wall: *Mrs Humphrey Devereux* as object, as art, as family

1. Paul Staiti, 'Copley, John Singleton (1738–1815), portrait and history painter', *Oxford Dictionary of National Biography*, Oxford, 2004: www.oxforddnb.com/view/article/6271.

2 John Singleton Copley, *Mrs Humphrey Devereux*, 1771, Reg 1965-0013-1, 1020 x 810 mm (1180 x 975 x 85 frame), TPA: www.collections.tepapa.govt.nz/objectdetails.aspx; Tony Mackle, 'Mrs Humphrey Devereux', in William McAloon, ed., *Art at Te Papa*, Wellington, 2009, pp. 42–43; Carrie Rebora and Paul Staiti, Erica E. Hirshler, Theodore L.E. Stebbins Jr., Carol Troyen, with contributions by Morrison H. Hecksher, Aileen Ribeiro, Marjorie Shelley, *John Singleton Copley in America*, New York, 1995; Papers relating to 'Mrs Humphrey Devereux', TPA. I am grateful to Tony Mackle for access to these papers and for generous assistance in the preparation of this article.

3 [Anon.], rev. Richard H. Saunders, 'Greenwood, John (1727–1792)', *Oxford Dictionary of National Biography*, Oxford, 2004: www.oxforddnb.com/view/article/11438

4 John Greenwood to J.S. Copley, 23 March 1770, *Letters and Papers of John Singleton Copley and Henry Pelham 1739–1776*, New York, 1970, pp. 81–83.

5 Laurel Thatcher Ulrich, *Good Wives: Image and reality in the lives of women in Northern New England 1650–1750*, New York and Toronto, 1980.

6 John Greenwood to J.S. Copley, 23 March 1770, *Letters and Papers of John Singleton Copley and Henry Pelham*, pp. 81–83.

7 T.H. Breen, 'The meaning of "likeness": Portrait-painting in an eighteenth-century consumer society', *Word and Image*, 6, 4 (1990), pp. 325–48.

8 Correspondence Captain R.G. Bruce, Benjamin West, J.S. Copley, 1766–1768, *Letters and Papers of John Singleton Copley and Henry Pelham*, pp. 41–73; Rebora and Staiti, *John Singleton Copley in America*; and Emily Ballew Neff, *John Singleton Copley in England*, London and Houston, 1995.

9 Mary Charnock (1710–1794) was married first in 1726 to the Boston merchant Samuel Greenwood (d. 1742), then to Joseph Prince, a Boston sea captain, and thirdly, in 1762, to farmer Humphrey Devereux: Rebora and Staiti, *John Singleton Copley in America*, p. 271, n. 2.

10 Rebora and Staiti, *John Singleton Copley in America*, pp. 246–49. The painting is in the Museum of Fine Arts, Boston: www.mfa.org/collections/object/paul-revere-32401

11 Benjamin West to Copley, 16 June 1771, also Copley to Henry Pelham, 9 September 1771, John Hancock to Copley, January 1772, *Letters and Papers of John Singleton Copley and Henry Pelham*, pp. 116, 151–54, 180–82.

12 Rebora and Staiti, *John Singleton Copley in America*, p. 271; Papers relating to 'Mrs Humphrey Devereux', TPA.

13 Neff, *John Singleton Copley in England.*

14 Janet Paul, 'Greenwood, Sarah', from the Dictionary of New Zealand Biography: www.TeAra.govt.nz/en/biographies/1g19/greenwood-sarah; Charlotte Macdonald, *Women Writing Home, 1700–1920: Female correspondence across the British Empire, Volume 5: New Zealand*, London, 2006, pp. 99–180.

15 Friends of the Turnbull Library, *Edward Gibbon Wakefield and the Colonial Dream: A reconsideration*, Wellington,

1997; Philip Temple, *A Sort of Conscience: The Wakefields*, Auckland, 2002.

16 The painting was gifted to the National Art Gallery in the will of Miss U.M. Greenwood and handed over by Mr A.R. Greenwood of Havelock North. The Greenwood family also gifted John Greenwood (1729–1792), *Landscape and Figures*, 1790, in 1967, and two further paintings in 2005: Lemuel F. Abbott (1760–1803), *Untitled (Portrait of John Greenwood, Snr, 1727–1792)*, c. 1790, and William Beechey (1753–1839), *Portrait of John Greenwood*, c. 1795. See McAloon, ed., *Art at Te Papa* and Mary Kisler, *Angels and Aristocrats: Early European art in New Zealand public collections*, Auckland, 2010.

17 P.J. Gibbons, 'The climate of opinion' and W.H. Oliver, 'The awakening imagination', in W.H. Oliver with B.R. Williams, eds, *Oxford History of New Zealand*, Oxford, 1981, pp. 302–30, 430–61.

18 *Mrs Humphrey Devereux* is included in Kisler's book, *Angels and Aristocrats*, without any comment on its American rather than European origins. McAloon, ed., *Art at Te Papa* uses categories of 'International Art' and 'New Zealand Art', with international and European often used synonymously.

10. Spinks Cottage: History, heritage and use

1 Gavin McLean, '"It's history, Jim, but not as we know it": Historians and the New Zealand heritage industry', in Bronwyn Dalley and Jock Phillips, eds, *Going Public: The changing face of New Zealand history,* Auckland, 2001, 158–74, p. 158.

2 A photograph of St John's Church in 1858 shows an almost obscured chimney top and gable end, suggesting Spinks Cottage was built by this year; See also Alison Dangerfield, *Spinks Cottage Willis Street Wellington*, Wellington, 2010, p. 4; *Wellington Independent*, 23 August 1859, p. 4.

3 *Wanganui Herald,* 9 May 1884, p. 2; *Evening Post* (*EP*), 3 July 1884, p. 2.

4 St John's Church (Spinks Cottage) 1974–1986, 00277:326:28/8/64, Wellington City Archives, Wellington.

5 Scott Thompson, *Church Standing Tall: A people's history of St John's in the City 1853–2003*, Wellington, 2003, p. 131.

6 Church staff, St John's in the City, email correspondence, 5 September 2012. I would like to thank the staff of St John's in the City for generously giving their time and assistance.

7 'Youth café clash', *Capital Times* (Wellington), 5 July 2006: www.capitaltimes.co.nz/article/800/YouthCaf233clash.html; Graham Redding, 'The youth café: An update', *The Messenger*, March 2005, pp. 4–5: www.stjohnsinthecity.org.nz.

8 Based on a visit in January 2013.

9 'Spinks Cottage', New Zealand Historic Places Trust, *New Zealand Historic Places Trust Register*: www.historic.org.nz/TheRegister/RegisterSearch/RegisterResults.aspx?RID=4704. Historic Places Trust is now known as Heritage New Zealand.

10 Based on a visit in January 2013.

11 Dangerfield, *Spinks Cottage Willis Street Wellington*, p. 10.

12 *EP*, 8 January 1885, p. 3.

13 Ibid., 8 December 1884, p. 3.

14 *Thames Star*, 16 December 1884, p. 2.

15 George Macmorran, *Some Schools and Schoolmasters of Early Wellington*, Wellington, 1900, p. 71.

16 *Explore Wellington Walk 3 Business District via Willis Street, Lambton Quay and Featherston Street,* Wellington, n.d. In fact the school was for both boys and girls.

17 7 June 1861–9 June 1862, Sarah Ellen Jane Anderson Diary, MSX-7831, ATL, passim.

18 For businesswomen before 1890 see Heidi Whiteside, '"We shall be respectable": Women and representations of respectability in Lyttelton 1851–1893', MA thesis, University of Canterbury, 2007; and Catherine Bishop, 'Commerce was a woman: Women in business in colonial Sydney and Wellington', PhD thesis, Australian National University, 2012.

19 See, for example, the Caversham Project: 'Class, gender and the opportunity structure in an emergent urban-industrial society, Dunedin's southern suburbs, 1881–1940': http://caversham.otago.ac.nz/index.php; Stephanie Wyse, 'Gender, wealth and margins of Empire: Women's economic opportunities in New Zealand cities c. 1890–1950', PhD thesis, King's College London, 2008; Caroline Daley, *Girls & Women, Men & Boys: Gender in Taradale 1886–1930*, Auckland, 1999.

20 Charlotte Macdonald, Frances Porter and Tui MacDonald, eds, *My Hand Will Write What My Heart Dictates: The unsettled lives of women in nineteenth-century New Zealand as revealed to sisters, family and friends*, Auckland, 1996, p. 114.

11. The Piano at The Elms

1 D.H. Maxwell, 'An old piano', *Journal of the Tauranga Historical Society*, (March 1981), p. 21.

2 Ibid., pp. 21–22.

3 Alice Maxwell, *Memories of a Mission House: Being reminiscences of the early days of Tauranga*, recorded by H. Bradney Williams, Tauranga, 1942, pp. 7–8.

4 Maxwell, 'An old piano', p. 22.
5 Maxwell, *Memories of a Mission House*, p. 8.
6 Euphemia Maxwell, Music Collection, The Elms Historic House Museum, Tauranga (EHHM).
7 Lady Martin, *Our Maoris*, Auckland, 1950, p. 28.
8 Maxwell, *Memories of a Mission House*, p. 7.
9 Charlotte Godley to her mother Sara Wynne, 29 August 1859, in Charlotte Godley, *Letters from Early New Zealand 1850–1853*, edited by John R. Godley, Christchurch, 1951, pp. 95–96; Daisy Collings, LD0010, tape 2, side A, Oral History Archives, Lakes District Museum (LDM); Elizabeth Caldwell, 1853 Journal, quoted by John Miller, *Early Victorian New Zealand: A study of racial tension and social attitudes, 1839–52*, Wellington, 1974, p. 174; Lel Luckie, LD0061, tape A, side 2, Oral History Archives, LDM; 'Motukaraka', *Northland Age* report of 1907 New Year's dance, sourced from Rudall Family Scrapbook, A152/1, p. 1, Far North Regional Museum, Kaitaia.
10 David Wainwright, *Broadwood by Appointment: A history*, Fakenham, 1982.
11 Sarah Selwyn, *Reminiscences*, quoted by John Mansfield Thompson, *The Oxford History of New Zealand Music*, Auckland, 1991, p. 29.
12 Information display, EHHM.
13 Stanley Bull, *The Historic Bay of Plenty: Te Papa C.M.S. mission station, 1835–1883*, Tauranga, 1983; Noeline Hall, *I Have Planted: A biography of Alfred Nesbit Brown*, Palmerston North, 1981; E. Maxwell, *Pioneering at Tauranga: The story of Archdeacon A.N. Brown and 'The Elms', past and present*, Dunedin, 1936; C.W. Venell, *Brown and The Elms*, Tauranga, 2012.
14 John Jolliffe, 'New Zealand journals', qMS-1073-1074, ATL.
15 Maxwell, *Memories of a Mission House*, p. 5.
16 E. Maxwell, *Recollections and Reflections of an Old New Zealander*, Dunedin, 1937, p. 181.

12. From 'Home Sweet Home' to the 'Kangaroo Hunt Polka': The colonial voyages of Marian Sargood's music album

1. I would like thank Bev Stevens for contributing invaluable time and knowledge of our family history, which helped to shape this essay. *Otago Daily Times*, 2 June 1914, p. 8.
2 'Sir Percy Sargood', video of 2011 Laureates of the Fairfax Media NZ Business Hall of Fame: www.businesshalloffame.co.nz/sir-percy-sargood. The survival of the piano is confirmed in the *Otago Daily Times* article referenced above.
3 Sir Frederick Thomas Sargood was a merchant and politician in Melbourne. See John Rickard, 'Sargood, Sir Frederick Thomas (1834–1903)', *Australian Dictionary of Biography*, www.adb.anu.edu.au/biography/sargood-sir-frederick-thomas-4538/text7435
4 The National Library of Australia holds another two volumes of sheet music collected by Marian Sargood. See 'Owner bound album of songs from the early 1850s [music] / originally owned by M.A. Sargood', 5077935; MUS N m 2011-401, and 'Owner bound album of dance music from the 1860s to 1870s [music] / originally owned by M.A. Sargood', 5077982; MUS N m 2011-404, National Library of Australia.
5 Carol Mills, 'Australian bookbinders and bookbinding in the 19th century', Conference Proceedings of AICCM Paper, Books and Photographic Special Interest Group Symposium, 2004, p. 69: www.aiccm.org.au/docs/BPG2004/Mills_BPG_2004.PDF
6 The varsoviana or varsovienne features numerous times in the collection. A slow dance in three-quarter time, the varsoviana, which combined elements of polka, waltz and mazurka, originated from Poland in the 1850s.
7 'Memoirs of Clara Webster (née Sargood)', unpublished manuscript, private collection, p. 12.
8 For background on Weinritter, see Graeme Skinner, 'WEINRITTER, George Mitchell (Michelle)': www.graemeskinner.id.au/biographicalregisterU-Z; and Graeme Skinner, 'Toward a general history of Australian musical composition: First national music, 1788–c. 1860', PhD thesis, University of Sydney, 2011, pp. 357, 524.
9 *The Illustrated Journal of Australasia*, 1857, II, p. 236. See also *Argus*, 21 February 1857, quoted in Skinner, 'Toward a general history of Australian musical composition', p. 327.
10 Like many early compositions, the 'Melbourne Varsovienne' was undated. Prue Neidorf, 'A guide to dating music published in Sydney and Melbourne, 1800–1899', MA (Hons) thesis, University of Wollongong, 1999, p. 82.
11 To date little information has been found on this composition or composer.
12 Neidorf, 'A guide to dating music published in Sydney and Melbourne', p. 82.
13 Skinner, 'Toward a general history of Australian musical composition', pp. 353–59. Singer, songwriter and composer Charles Thatcher (1830–1878) was also well known in New Zealand. See Robert H.B. Hoskins, 'Thatcher, Charles Robert', from the Dictionary of New Zealand Biography: www.TeAra.govt.nz/en/biographies/lt91/thatcher-charles-robert.

14 Neidorf, 'A guide to dating music published in Sydney and Melbourne', pp. 45–48; Harold Love, *The Golden Age of Australian Opera: W.S. Lyster and his companies 1861–1880*, Sydney, 1981.
15 Sargood married Julia Tomlin in England in 1880, and they returned with their child and the family to Australia in 1882.
16 Rickard, 'Sargood, Sir Frederick Thomas (1834–1903)'.
17 Richard Heathcote 'Solid joys and lasting treasure: Families and gardens': www.cv.vic.gov.au/stories/rippon-lea-estate/solid-joys-and-lasting-treasure. Rippon Lea is now a National Trust property.
18 'Memoirs of Clara Webster (née Sargood)', p. 10.
19 Ibid., p. 17.
20 Ibid., pp. 2, 17–19.
21 Ibid., p. 11.
22 Heathcote 'Solid joys and lasting treasure: Families and gardens'; 'Memoirs of Clara Webster (née Sargood)', p. 11.
23 'Memoirs of Clara Webster (née Sargood)', pp. 6, 9, 10.
24 Ibid., p. 9.
25 Ibid., p. 10.

13. Portrait of a Material Life: The photograph of Richard and Augusta Webb

1 Census returns of England and Wales, 1851.
2 Rollo Arnold, *The Farthest Promised Land: English villagers, New Zealand immigrants of the 1870s*, Wellington, 1981, p. 217; Philip Payton, *The Cornish Overseas: A history of Cornwall's 'Great Emigration'*, Dundurn, 2005, p. 131.
3 The Cahill Partnership and Cornwall Archaeological Unit, 'Cornwall industrial settlements initiative Redruth and Plain-an-Gwarry (Camborne/Redruth Area)', Cornwall, 2002, pp. 20–21, 37–38.
4 Census returns of England and Wales, 1851.
5 Webb file, DC-1842, TOSM.
6 Death notice for Richard Webb, *Tuapeka Times* (*TT*), 12 August 1899, p. 2. Death notice for Augusta Webb, *TT*, 2 September 1899, p. 2. Webb file, DC-1842, TOSM.
7 Modern cataloguing writing on the back of the photo is cropped, indicating that the museum has cut this photograph down at some time, probably to fit into a standard-sized frame for display.
8 The assumption that this photo was taken before the Webbs' first child was born is based on the presence of a pet cat and the absence of children.
9 Hardwicke Knight, *Joseph Weaver Allen Photographer*, Dunedin, 1997, p. 14.
10 Christine Whybrew, '"Reading" photographs: Burton Brothers and the photographic narrative', *Journal of New Zealand Studies*, 12 (2011), pp. 77–89.
11 Heather Bray, ed., *A Scottish Mother*, Dunedin, 2012. Teague advertised his photography business repeatedly in the *TT* between 12 December 1872 and 25 September 1873.
12 *Tuapeka Times Business Directory*, 3 July 1873, p. 3.
13 Webb file, DC-1842, TOSM.
14 Jeremy Salmond, *Old New Zealand Houses, 1800–1940*, Auckland, 1989, pp. 38–41.
15 Dr Jane Malthus, lecturer, Design Department, Otago Polytechnic, has examined the image and describes Augusta's appearance as 'well dressed' because of her neat hair tied possibly with a ribbon and the suggestion of a corset outline.
16 Nancy Swarbrick, *Creature Comforts: New Zealanders and their pets*, Dunedin, 2013, p. 59.
17 *Otago Witness* (*OW*), 23 May 1863, p. 5. The newspaper recounted a story from the West Coast about a child being attacked by a rat and the need for terriers and cats to be brought in to control the rodent problem: *OW*, 22 June 1867, p. 12. Other destructive behaviour included consuming anything edible, including candles, soap and hides: *OW*, 12 August 1864, p. 10.
18 Katherine C. Grier, *Pets in America: A history*, Chapel Hill, 2006, pp. 35–38.
19 *Letters from Settlers & Labouring Emigrants, in the New Zealand Company's Settlements of Wellington, Nelson & New Plymouth, from February, 1842 to January, 1843*, London, 1843, pp. 152–53.

14. A Photograph, a Feeding Bottle and the Tragedies of Colonial Family Life

1 Photographs of Rachel Stewart, MS-0985-057/075 and MS-0985-057/002, William Downie Stewart Papers, HC.
2 Clifford and Clifton advertisement, *Otago Daily Times*, 26 January 1870, p. 4. On cartes-de-visite, see Hardwicke Knight, *Photography in New Zealand: A social and technical history*, Dunedin, 1971, pp. 117–23; David Eggleton, *Into the Light: A history of New Zealand photography*, Nelson, 2006, p. 17; Mary Warner Marien, *Photography: A cultural history*, 3rd edn, New Jersey, 2011, p. 83.
3 D.B. Hutton, ed., *The Journal of George Hepburn*, Christchurch, 2010, pp. 28, 82; Jane Thomson, ed., *Southern People: A dictionary of Otago Southland biography*, Dunedin, 1998, pp. 483–84; Sean G. Brosnahan,

Women of Substance: The Otago women who wore 'fabulous frocks', Dunedin, 2008, pp. 43–46.
4 Album 66, TOSM.
5 Valerie A. Fildes, *Breasts, Bottles and Babies: A history of infant feeding*, Edinburgh, 1986, pp. 98–133.
6 Alison Clarke, *Born to a Changing World: Childbirth in nineteenth-century New Zealand*, Wellington, 2012, pp. 121–33.
7 Alexander Westwood Stewart death certificate, 2 February 1870, copy in author's possession.
8 Brosnahan, *Women of Substance*, p. 45.
9 George Hepburn to his sister Janet, 13 July 1883 and 4 October 1883, William Downie Stewart Papers, MS-0985-035/003, HC.
10 Hector Munro Hepburn death certificate, 27 September 1883, copy in author's possession.
11 Clarke, *Born to a Changing World*, pp. 173–77, 215–19.
12 Ibid., pp. 174–75; Hutton, *Journal of George Hepburn*, pp. 29, 80–81.

15. William Speer's Album: A scrapbook of colonial travel

1. William Henry Speer (creator), Speer Album, 1860–1867, E-395, ATL. The Speer Album was purchased in 1989 from Quilter's Bookshop, Wellington. It is not known when or how the album made its way back to New Zealand or how it reached Quilter's.
2 We do not know where and when Speer purchased his album. Commercial photograph albums designed for cartes-de-visite were sold in New Zealand from 1862, but little is known about the production and sale of albums of blank pages in this country. It is possible that Speer purchased the album before setting off on his journey with the express purpose of using it as a travel journal. On albums see Keith Giles, '*Cartes-de-visite* in New Zealand' in Michael Graham-Stewart, *Negative Kept: Maori and the carte de visite*, Auckland, 2013, pp. 7–15.
3 Alison Nordstrom, 'Making a journey: The Tupper Scrapbooks and the travel they describe' in Elizabeth Edwards and Janice Hart, eds, *Photographs, Objects, Histories: On the materiality of images*, London, 2004, 84–99, p. 85.
4 See Susan Tucker, Katherine Ott and Patricia P. Buckler, eds, *The Scrapbook in American Life*, Philadelphia, 2006.
5 The poem is annotated with Trinity College, Cambridge, 1857.
6 Henry Brett, *White Wings*, Vol. 1, Auckland, 1924, p. 199.
7 Geoffrey Batchen, *Forget Me Not: Photography and remembrance*, New York, 2004, p. 43.
8 *London Gazette*, 16 December 1862, p. 6386.
9 Ibid., 22 May 1868, p. 2952.
10 Ellen Gruber Garvey, *Writing With Scissors: American scrapbooks from the Civil War to the Harlem renaissance*, Oxford, 2013, p. 16.
11 Topi Patuki was a Ngāi Tahu leader, whaler, goldminer and storekeeper. See Atholl Anderson, 'Patuki, Topi', from the Dictionary of New Zealand Biography: www.TeAra.govt.nz/en/biographies/lp11/patuki-topi
12 An albumen print of John Clerke appears in the Speer Album.
13 Batchen, *Forget Me Not*, pp. 41, 65, 69.
14 Katie Day Good, 'From scrapbook to Facebook: A history of personal media assemblage and archives', *New Media and Society*, 15, 4 (2013), 557–73, p. 562.
15 Sumit K. Mandal, 'Popular sites of prayer, transoceanic migration, and cultural diversity: Exploring the significance of keramat in Southeast Asia', *Modern Asian Studies*, 46, 2 (2012), 355–72, pp. 356–58. My thanks to Samia Khatun for directing me to this source and for alerting me to the significance and meaning of *keramat* in the Indian Ocean world.
16 Garvey, *Writing With Scissors*, p. 3.
17 Ibid., p. 4.
18 Juliana M. Kuipers, 'Scrapbooks: Intrinsic value and material culture', *Journal of Archival Organization*, 2, 3 (2004), 83–91, p. 84.

16. Retrieved from Oblivion? Wiremu Kīngi Te Rangitaake and the photographic object

1 Martha A. Sandweiss, *Print the Legend: Photography and the American West*, New Haven, 2002, p. 7.
2 *Evening Post*, 31 March 1932, p. 13.
3 The full annotation on the rear of Puke Ariki's copy photograph can be viewed at: http://vernon.npdc.govt.nz/search.do?id=284874&db=object&page=1&view=detail
4 Ref: 1/2-045108-F, ATL.
5 For example, Matthew Wright, *Two Peoples, One Land: The New Zealand Wars*, Auckland, 2006, p. 85; Kelvin Day, ed., *Contested Ground Te Whenua i Tohea: The Taranaki Wars 1860–1881*, Wellington, 2010, p. 259.
6 For more on daguerreotypy, see Naomi Rosenblum, *A World History of Photography*, 3rd edn, New York, 1997, pp. 16–24, 47–48.
7 See Keith Giles, 'Is this a Polack daguerreotype?' in

A. Wanhalla and E. Wolf, eds, *Early New Zealand Photography: Images and essays*, Dunedin, 2011, pp. 28–32; R. Derek Wood, 'The voyage of Captain Lucas and the daguerreotype to Sydney', *Journal de la Société des Océanistes*, 102, 1 (1996), pp. 113–18.

8 For more on the carte-de-visite, see Rosenblum, *A World History of Photography*, pp. 56, 62–63, 341, 574, 656.

9 Personal correspondence via email with Geoffrey Batchen, 17 June 2011.

10 Letter from L.B. Inch to Rigby Allan, 20 June 1968. Copy in research files of Kelvin Day, director of Puke Ariki; location of original unknown.

11 It remains unclear who was operating the studio that produced these carte-de-visite portraits. There were at least five photographers operating in New Plymouth during the 1860s, including Hartley Webster, J.E. Bates, Oliver Hoby, Thomas Tuffin and George Jackson. However, Hoby seems to be the most likely candidate to have taken the photographs.

12 Keith Giles' unpublished paper '*Cartes-de-visite* in New Zealand' cites New Zealand's first published reference to the carte-de-visite format in the *Hawke's Bay Herald* on 2 January 1862.

13 *Taranaki Herald*, 24 February 1872, p. 2.

14 One possibility is Wiremu Kīngi Te Apaapa, a Ngāti Porou chief. Correspondence with Iain Sharp, Manuscripts Librarian, Auckland City Libraries, 11 January 2013.

15 Ref: 1/2-022668-F, ATL.

16 Sandweiss, *Print the Legend*, p. 9.

17. 'A Sparrow Alone Upon the House Top': The *Te Pihoihoi* press

1 James Moran, *Printing Presses: History and development from the fifteenth century to modern times*, Berkeley, 1978, p. 95.

2 See Philip Gaskell, *A New Introduction to Bibliography*, Oxford, 1974, p. 139.

3 See Helen M. Hogan, *Bravo, Neu Zeeland: Two Maori in Vienna 1859–1860*, Christchurch, 2003.

4 John Elson Gorst, *New Zealand Revisited: Recollections from the days of my youth*, London, 1908, p. 254.

5 *Te Pihoihoi Mokemoke* (*PM*), 2 February 1863, p. 2. 'Ki te he te tangi o te Hokioi, e taea ano te patu e tera mea iti e te Pihoihoi ina pono tona korihitanga.'

6 *PM*, 2 February 1863, pp. 2–3.

7 Gorst, *New Zealand Revisited*, p. 256.

8 *PM*, 10 February 1863, pp. 5–8.

9 *PM*, 9 March 1863, pp. 11–12.

10 *Te Hokioi e Rere atu na*, 12 February 1863, p. 2; 26 April 1863, p. 3.

11 *Te Karere Maori*, 25 February 1862, p. 4.

12 Gorst to Native Minister, 28 March 1863, MA 1 1863/394; Von Dadelzen, Memo, MA 1 1863/084, ANZ.

13 Gorst to Native Minister, 14 April 1863, MA 1 1863/434, ANZ.

14 John Eldon Gorst, *The Maori King*, Hamilton, 1959, pp. 228–29.

15 'The Hokioi Press', *Journal of the Te Awamutu Historical Society*, 6, 1 (1971), pp. 21–26.

16 W.J. Cameron, 'A printing press for the Maori people', *Journal of the Polynesian Society*, 67, 3 (1958), 204–10, p. 209.

17 Emails, Catherine Jehly (Collections Manager, Te Awamutu Museum), 7 October 2013, 6 March 2014.

18. He Rau Mahara: The *Te Wananga* ledger

1 *Te Wananga* Ledger, 1878, 32460, gifted by Mrs Gaisford, collection of the Hawke's Bay Museums Trust, Ruawharo Tā-ū-rangi.

2 *Te Wananga (TW)*, 5 August 1974, pp. 1–3.

3 *TW*, 5 August 1874, p. 1.

4 *TW*, 7 August 1875, p. 124.

19. Minute Books: An integral part of the Māori Land Court

1 The name 'Native Land Court' was changed to 'Māori Land Court' by operation of section 2 of the Māori Purposes Act 1947.

2 D.M. Loveridge, 'The origins of the Native Lands Acts and Native Land Court in New Zealand', unpublished report for the Crown Law Office, Waitangi Tribunal, Wellington, 2000.

3 See 'Further papers relative to the Taranaki Question', *AJHR*, 1861, E.2; James Belich, *The New Zealand Wars and the Victorian Interpretation of Racial Conflict*, Auckland, 1982, pp. 73–80, 305, 308.

4 An example of two sets of minutes in existence for a court hearing at Ohinemutu in Rotorua on 16 August 1883 are entries in the *Judge O'Brien Minute Book 5* (ANZ) at folios 140–48 and *Rotorua Minute Book 6* at folios 1–10, ANZ.

5 A number of judges' minute books exist for judges Brabant, Browne, Gudgeon, Johnson, MacCormick, Mair, O'Brien, Puckey, Scannell, Smith, Von Sturmer, Ward and Wilson.

6 Under section 12 of the Native Lands Act 1865 a decision of the court required concurrence of a judge and two assessors. But in practice the judges became the final arbiter for decisions of the court.
7 For instance, Friday 15 October 1886. The court opened at 10 am at the Native Court House, Kaiapoi, Present Alexander Mackay (judge), H.P. Tunuiarangi (assessor), H.S. Hadfield (interpreter), A.H. Mackay (clerk). *South Island Minute Book 2* at folio 110, ANZ.
8 *South Island Minute Book 2* at folios 1–4, 14, 24, 30.
9 Examples include part of the *Judge Gudgeon Minute Book 3*, nearly the whole set of assessor Hone Matenga's *Assessor's Minute Books* and the proceedings of various commissions such as in the *Urewera Minute Books*, ANZ.
10 Whangarei (8 March 1865) *Whangarei Minute Book 1* (ANZ); Tukapoto (26 June 1865) *Kaipara Minute Book 1* (ANZ); Ohinemutu (26 October 1865) *Rotorua Minute Book 1*, ANZ; *South Island Minute Book 1A*, ANZ.
11 'Duplicate copy of the Account of Collins Brothers & Company, 26 August 1911 [*sic*]', in From Registrar Native Land Court Wellington–Subject: As to rebinding old Minute Books of the Ikaroa and South Island Native Land Courts, MA1 1440, Record No. 1928/127, ANZ.
12 However, Judge Norman William Smith's entries in the *Whakatane* and *Rotorua Minute Books* of the 1950s and 1960s are in almost incomprehensible handwriting. These minute books are held at the Māori Land Court Registry, Rotorua.
13 Richard Boast, Andrew Erueti, Doug McPhail and Norman F. Smith, *Maori Land Law*, Wellington, 1999, pp. 42–45.
14 Evelyn Stokes, *The Individualisation of Maori Land Interests*, Hamilton, 2002, pp. 1–6.
15 See Ann Parsonson, 'Stories for land: Oral narratives in the Maori Land Court' in Bain Attwood and Fiona Magowan, eds, *Telling Stories: Indigenous history and memory in Australia and New Zealand*, Wellington, 2001, pp. 21–40.
16 *South Island Minute Book 14*, ANZ.
17 See Te Onehou Phillis, *Eruera Mānuera*, Whanganui a Tara [Wellington], 2002 and Don Stafford, *Te Arawa*, Auckland, 2005.
18 Janine Hayward and Nicola R. Wheen, *The Waitangi Tribunal*, Wellington, 2004.
19 Hirini Moko Mead, *Tikanga Māori: Living by Māori values*, Wellington, 2003.

20. A Road into Te Urewera

1 I am grateful to Pou Temara for discussing several matters with me as I wrote this essay, Koro Tihema for reading the draft for me, and Joanna Cooper for driving to Ruatāhuna with me.
2 James Cowan, 'Preece's Road', *Tales of the Maori Bush*, Wellington, 1934, pp. 37–42.
3 James Cowan, 'Maclean the roadmaker', *Sir Donald Maclean*, Wellington, 1940, pp. 105–08; p. 105.
4 Diary of George Augustus Preece, 1870–1872, MS 249, Auckland War Memorial Museum, 7 November 1871.
5 Ibid., 13 November 1871.
6 Ibid., 17–30 November 1871.
7 Ibid., 21 November 1871. Galatea was Fort Galatea in the Bay of Plenty, the departure point of the newly approved road.
8 Elsdon Best, *Tuhoe: The children of the mist*, Wellington, 1925; reprint 1972, pp. 404–78.
9 Cowan, 'Preece's Road', p. 37.
10 There is no space here to address this large matter, but the Waitangi Tribunal found that government breached the Treaty in confiscating large areas of Tūhoe land in the Bay of Plenty in 1866, and that its actions and failure to give redress were unjust. See Judith Binney, *Encircled Lands: Te Urewera, 1820–1921,* Wellington, 2009, pp. 99–100; Te Urewera Report, Part I, ch. 4, http://forms.justice.govt.nz/search/Documents/WT/wt_DOC_68004854/Te Urewera W.pdf; also Mere Whaanga, 'Te Kooti Whenua – Māori Land Court – 'Te kooti tango whenua', 1865–1873', Te Ara – the Encyclopedia of New Zealand: www.teara.govt.nz/en/te-kooti-whenua-maori-land-court
11 Binney, *Encircled Lands*, ch. 4, pp. 183–214.
12 Ibid., p. 190.
13 Ibid., ch. 4, pp. 183–214.
14 Ibid., pp. 183–214, 328–96.
15 For perception of Ngāi Tūhoe as 'wild', see the Te Urewera Report, Part I, 3.5.6.
16 James Cowan, 'Famous New Zealanders. No. 22. Captain G.A. Preece, N.Z.C.: A leader on the old bush war-path', *New Zealand Railways Magazine*, 10 (1 January 1935), pp. 17–20.
17 James Cowan, *The New Zealand Wars and the Pioneering Period*, Wellington, 1922–23, reprint 1983. Vol. II: The Hauhau Wars, 1864–72, p. 341.
18 For example, Preece to Te Whenuanui, Paerau, Te Minihera, Kereru, Te Kowhai, 11 May 1870, Preece's Diary.
19 Cowan, 'Preece's Road', p. 42.

20 Preece's Diary, 30 May 1871.
21 Letter from Te Whenuanui and Paerau to Captain Ferris, 2 October 1872, AGG-HB1 4, ANZ.
22 The best-known statement of this belief is in his conclusion to the official history of the wars: Cowan, *The New Zealand Wars*, Vol. II, p. 502. Cowan's views were never simple, however, and mostly alert to the complexity of colonialism.
23 Binney, *Encircled Lands*, pp. 373, 382.
24 'The Urewera Survey trouble', *Evening Post*, 21 May 1895, p. 2; 'Road-making dispute', *Auckland Star* (*AS*), 11 June 1895, p. 5; Binney, *Encircled Lands*, pp. 392–93 and more generally, ch. 10.
25 'Manuhiri' (James Cowan), 'Through Tuhoeland: The Urewera country and its people from Rotorua to Lake Waikaremoana: Part II', *AS*, 4 March 1899, p. 1; Binney, *Encircled Lands*, p. 403.
26 'The Native Bill debated in the House', *Poverty Bay Herald*, 9 October 1894, p. 3.
27 Judith Binney, Gillian Chaplin and Craig Wallace, *Mihaia: The Prophet Rua Kenana and his community at Maungapohatu*, Wellington, 1979, pp. 167–70.
28 Te Whenuanui to Apirana Ngata, Native Minister, 17 December 1928, MA1 1472, ANZ.
29 *Te Karere News*, TV1, 11 September 2013, http://tvnz.co.nz/te-karere-news/r-apa-11-mahuru-2013-5581056
30 See, for example, *Whakatane Beacon* 11 August 2009, p. 1; 10 August 2010, p. 1; 7 May 2013, p. 4; 17 May 2013, p. 1. Also Ben Schrader, 'Public protest: Pickets, blockades and boycotts', Te Ara – the Encyclopedia of New Zealand: www.teara.govt.nz/en/photograph/35097/omuriwaka-roadblock
31 Binney, Chaplin and Wallace, *Mihaia*, ch. 3; Danny Keenan, ed., *Terror in our Midst? Searching for terror in Aotearoa New Zealand*, Wellington, 2008.

21. Dunite: The adventures of a rock in colonial New Zealand

1 F. Hochstetter, *New Zealand: Its physical geography, geology, and natural history with special reference to the results of government exhibitions in the provinces of Auckland and Nelson,* Stuttgart, 1867, pp. 468, 474.
2 M. Johnston, 'Skin of a serpent' in I.J. Graham, ed., *A Continent on the Move: New Zealand geoscience into the 21st century,* Wellington, 2008, 86–87, p. 87.
3 H. Campbell and G. Hutching, *In Search of Ancient New Zealand*, Auckland, 2011, pp. 39–40.
4 J. MacKenzie, *Museums and the Empire: Natural history, human cultures and colonial identities,* Manchester, 2009; A. Shelton, 'Museums and museum displays' in Christopher Tilley, Webb Keane, Susanne Küchler, Michael Rowlands and Patricia Spyer, eds, *Handbook of Material Culture,* London, 2006, pp. 480–99; S. Sheets-Pyenson, *Cathedrals of Science: The development of colonial natural history museums during the late nineteenth century*, Kingston, Ontario, 1988.
5 M. Johnston and S. Nolden, *The Travels of Hochstetter and Haast in New Zealand, 1858–1860,* Nelson, 2012.
6 J.E. Bremer, *The History of Greenhills*, Invercargill, 1976, p. 25.
7 M. Johnston, *High Hopes: The history of the Nelson mineral belt and New Zealand's first railway*, Nelson, 1987, pp. 137–40. In 1966 the Mapua company, Lime and Marble Ltd, also began testing dunite, but nothing further developed.
8 Johnston, *High Hopes*, pp. 137–38.

22. Whale Tales

1 *Otago Witness* (*OW*), 18 August 1877, p. 7.
2 *Tuapeka Times*, 15 February 1882, p. 5.
3 William Jackson Barry, *Glimpses of the Australian Colonies and New Zealand: A thrilling narrative of the early days: embodying the life-history of Captain William Jackson Barry who arrived in New South Wales in 1829*, Auckland, 1903.
4 *Thames Advertiser*, 29 November 1880, p. 2.
5 *OW*, 4 August 1883, p. 22; *Star*, 19 October 1880, p. 2; *Thames Star*, 4 July 1882, p. 2.
6 *Thames Advertiser*, 24 February 1880, p. 3; *OW*, 2 October 1880, p. 21; *Akaroa Mail & Banks Peninsula Advertiser*, 1 October 1880, p. 3; *Star*, 13 October 1880, p. 3.
7 *Otago Daily Times*, 10 July 1883, p. 2.
8 *OW*, 14 July 1883, p. 11.
9 *Star*, 16 August 1883, p. 3.
10 T. Jeffery Parker to Julius von Haast, 22 August 1884, Haast Family Papers, MS-Papers-0037-126, ATL.
11 Lorraine Daston, 'On scientific observation', *Isis*, 99 (2008), pp. 97–110.
12 T. Jeffery Parker, 'Notes on the skeleton and baleen of a fin-whale recently acquired by the Otago University Museum', *Transactions and Proceedings of the New Zealand Institute* (*TPNZI*) 17 (1884), pp. 3–13, pl. 6.
13 H.G. Wells, 'Popularising science', *Nature*, 50, 26 (July 1894), pp. 300–01.
14 T. Jeffery Parker to W.H. Flower, 4 November 1886, William Flower Semi-Official Papers, Micro-MS-Coll-20-2843, ATL.

15 J.H. Scott and T. Jeffery Parker, 'On a specimen of *Ziphius* recently obtained near Dunedin', *Transactions of the Zoological Society*, 12, 1 (1890), pp. 241–48; pl. 48, 49, 50; *Los Angeles Times*, 17 October 1937, p. 13J.
16 Leonard Huxley, *Life and Letters of Thomas Henry Huxley*, 2 vols, London, 1900, vol. 1, p. 135.
17 Samuel J.M.M. Alberti, 'Placing nature: Natural history collections and their owners in nineteenth-century provincial England', *British Journal for the History of Science*, 35, 3 (2002), pp. 291–311.
18 W.H. Flower, *Essays on Museums and Other Subjects Connected with Natural History*, London, 1898, p. 41.
19 Stephen T. Asma, *Stuffed Animals & Pickled Heads: The culture and evolution of natural history museums*, Oxford, 2001, p. 154.
20 Juliana Adelman, 'Evolution on display: Promoting Irish natural history and Darwinism at the Dublin Science and Art Museum', *British Journal for the History of Science*, 38, 4 (2005), pp. 411–36.
21 T. Jeffery Parker, 'On an "Index–Collection" for small zoological museums, in the form of a genealogical tree of the animal kingdom', *TPNZI*, 18 (1885), pp. 73–78.

23. The Travelling Stereopticon

1 *Harpers' Weekly*, 16 July 1881: www.digital-periodical-images.net/MARCYS-SCIOPTICONS-LJ-Marcy-Chestnut-Street-Philadelphia-375929.htm
2 *Dayton Daily Empire*, 9 August 1864, image 3, *Chronicling America: Historic American newspapers*: www.chroniclingamerica.loc.gov/
3 Charles Musser, *The Emergence of Cinema: The American screen to 1907*, New York, 1990, p. 32.
4 *North Otago Times*, 27 November 1868, p. 1.
5 Elizabeth Hartrick, 'Consuming illusions: The magic lantern in Australia and Aotearoa/New Zealand, 1850–1910', PhD thesis, University of Melbourne, 2003, p. 34.
6 Lorenzo J. Marcy, *The Sciopticon Manual, explaining lantern projection in general, and the sciopticon apparatus in particular*, Philadelphia, 1877, p. 42: www.archive.org/stream/sciopticonmanual00marcrich/sciopticonmanual00marcrich_djvu.txt
7 Hartrick, 'Consuming illusions', pp. 18, 19.
8 'Two lecturers to-day', *Daily Pacific Commercial Advertiser* (*DCPA*), 3 November 1892.
9 'In the court', *DPCA*, 11 November 1892.
10 'Dr J. Chas. Harrison's first lecture', *DPCA*, 4 November 1892.
11 'A common nuisance', *Liberal*, 9 November 1892.
12 'In the court', *DPCA*, 11 November 1892.
13 'J. Charles Harrison, M.D., Lecture to men only', *Ashburton Guardian*, 11 July 1893, p. 3.
14 *New Zealand Herald*, 14 December 1892, p. 5.
15 *Age*, 9 May 1855, p. 6, quoted in Hartrick, 'Consuming illusions', p. 59.
16 *Observer*, 24 December 1892, p. 17.
17 *Marlborough Express*, 7 March 1893, p. 2.

24. Unanswered Prayers: The failure of W.F. Gordon's self-promotion

1 The initial announcement in the *Wanganui Chronicle* (*WC*) was, for example, reprinted in the *Star*, the *Oamaru Mail* and the *West Coast Times*. See 'Local and general', *WC*, 12 June 1879.
2 'Local and general', *WC*, 12 June 1879.
3 See, for example the illuminated address by Edward Touch, *Minister for Native Affairs, John Bryce, from the citizens of Waitara*, 1883, pen and ink, B-058-004; or that given to Edward Tregear on his retirement, *Edward Tregear: Illuminated address*, 1911, fMS-242, ATL. Interestingly, a framed illuminated address for Tregear features kōwhaiwhai and carved patterns on the frame, but not the address. See William Berry, photograph of an illuminated address for Edward Tregear, c. 1910, Ref: 1/2-038062-G, ATL.
4 Nicholas Thomas, *Possessions: Indigenous art/colonial culture*, London, 1999, p. 12.
5 Roger Blackley, *Stray Leaves: Colonial trompe l'oeil drawings*, Wellington, 2001, pp. 25–26.
6 Accounts of its display in shop windows in both Wanganui and Auckland also refer to the availability of photographs of *Te Inoi a te Ariki*: *WC*, 21 July 1879, p. 2; *Auckland Star (AS)*, 5 September 1879, p. 2.
7 *Otago Witness*, 12 July 1879, p. 7.
8 *AS*, 5 September 1879, p. 2.
9 The precedent was set by the entrepreneurial dealer and printmaker Ernest Gambart, whose London-based studio both revolutionised the Victorian art market and specialised in selling reproductions of artist's works. See Jeremy Maas, *Gambart: Prince of the Victorian art world*, London, 1975, and Pamela M. Fletcher 'Creating the French Gallery: Ernest Gambart and the rise of the commercial art gallery in mid-Victorian London', *Nineteenth-Century Art Worldwide*, 6, 1 (Spring 2007): www.19thc-artworldwide.org
10 MU1/6/1, TPA.

11 W.F. Gordon to James Allan Thomson, September 1917, MU1/6/1, TPA.
12 See, for example, the version available for sale through Webb's auction house in 2010: www.webbs.co.nz
13 Kay Sutton, 'Illuminated manuscripts' in Hugh Brigstocke, ed., *The Oxford Companion to Western Art*, from *Oxford Art Online*: www.oxfordartonline.com/subscriber/article.opr/t118/e1265

25. Embroidering the Whanganui

1 Letter from Messrs Atkinson, Dale, Ellingham and Jenkins, Barristers and Solicitors, to the Director, Dominion Museum, 6 September 1963, MU000002/070/0005, TPA.
2 Maud Brown was born in 1872 or 1873 in Crawley, England, to Benjamin and Mary Ann Brown. Ben Brown, a labourer, arrived in New Zealand in 1874. Mary Ann followed in 1875 with Maud, who died in 1941.
3 Letter from R.K. Dell, Acting Director, Dominion Museum, to Messrs Atkinson, Dale, Ellingham and Jenkins, Barristers and Solicitors, 23 September 1963, MU000002/070/0005, TPA.
4 Alice's older brother, Thomas Clapham, and his daughters gifted the embroidery, along with a range of family heirlooms, to the Dominion Museum.
5 Alice Clapham was born on 1 September 1866 in Ngāūranga to William and Mary Ann Clapham. She died in 1938.
6 *Evening Post* (*EP*), 24 February 1881, p. 2.
7 *Timaru Herald*, 8 December 1883, p. 3.
8 *Bruce Herald*, 22 December 1893, p. 3.
9 *Bruce Herald*, 11 July 1876, p. 3.
10 Mrs Swainson's Fitzherbert Terrace School later became Samuel Marsden Collegiate School. Alice Clapham's younger cousin, Edith Clapham (1872–1966), attended Mrs Swainson's, but there is no mention of Alice. Personal correspondence between Michael Fitzgerald, Te Papa, and Rosalba Finnerty, Librarian/Archivist, Samuel Marsden Collegiate School, 9 May 2006.
11 *New Zealand Herald*, 16 December 1884, p. 7.
12 Ann Calhoun, *The Arts & Crafts Movement in New Zealand, 1870–1940: Women make their mark*, Auckland, 2000, p. 26.
13 Alan Ward, *A Show of Justice: Racial 'amalgamation' in nineteenth century New Zealand,* Auckland, 1995, pp. 240–41.
14 David Young, *Woven by Water: Histories of the Whanganui River*, Wellington, 1998, p. 192.
15 'Tawhiao', New Zealand History Online, Ministry for Culture and Heritage: www.nzhistory.net.nz/people/tukaroto-potatau-matutaera-tawhiao
16 *The Official Record of the New Zealand Industrial Exhibition 1885*, Wellington, 1886, p. 150.
17 Tosti Murray, *Marsden: The history of a New Zealand school for girls*, Wellington, 1967, p. 49.
18 Michael King, *Maori: A photographic and social history*, Auckland, 1996, p. 26.
19 Young, *Woven by Water,* pp. 200–01, 205.
20 Christine Whybrew, 'The Burton Brothers studio: Commerce in photography and the marketing of New Zealand 1866–1898', PhD thesis, University of Otago, 2010, p. 191; *EP*, 3 August 1885, p. 4.
21 *The Official Record of the New Zealand Industrial Exhibition 1885*, p. 152.
22 Alfred Tyer, a tanner based in 'Ngahauranga [*sic*]', exhibited in the Leather and Skins section, and was awarded a number of prizes. Ibid., p. 55.
23 Ibid, p. 182.
24 Ibid., p. 148.
25 Rozsika Parker, *The Subversive Stitch: Embroidery and the making of the feminine*, London, 1996, p. 12.
26 *The Official Record of the New Zealand Industrial Exhibition 1885*, p. 21.
27 Whybrew, 'The Burton Brothers studio', p. 191.
28 Ibid.

26. Te Tokotoko

1 Poia Rewi, *Whaikōrero: The world of Māori oratory*, Auckland, 2010, p. 95.
2 Ibid.
3 Ibid, pp. 96–99.
4 Edward Shortland, *The Southern Districts of New Zealand*, London, 1851, p. 16.
5 John A.Williams, *Politics of the New Zealand Maori Protest and Cooperation, 1891–1909*, Auckland, 1969, p. 58.
6 *Press* (Christchurch), 13 August 1872, p. 3.
7 L.F. Head, 'Pita Te Hori's peacemaking with Waikato', *Te Karanga*, 2, 1 (1986), 3–7.

27. A Church Lectern Made by a Celestial of Industry and Ingenuity

1 George Fergusson, *Signs and Symbols in Christian Art*, London, 1954, pp. 13–14.
2 J.G. Furness, *A Century of Worship 1878–1978*, Blenheim, 1978, p. 11.

3 Quoted from the *Church Messenger* in Barry Loveridge, *Together in Faith*, Blenheim, 1973, p. 34.
4 Marriage Certificate Registration Number: 1871/8679.
5 'Haining-street', *Evening Post*, 12 May 1910, p. 2.
6 *Marlborough Express*, 7 April 1877, p. 4.
7 *AJHR*, Vol. II, 1871, 5.B, p. 4.
8 Manying Ip and David Pang, 'New Zealand Chinese identity: Sojourners, model minority and multiple identities' in James H. Liu, Tim McCreanor, Tracey McIntosh and Teresia Teaiwa, eds, *New Zealand Identities: Departures and destinations*, Wellington, 2005, 174–90, p. 177.
9 *Marlborough Express*, 25 July 1888.
10 *Poverty Bay Herald*, 9 October 1906, p. 4.
11 *Evening Post*, 12 May 1910, p. 2.

28. The Boyhood Diary of Herries Beattie

1 James Herries Beattie, 'A boy's diary', Beattie Papers, ARC-0162, MS-582/L/1, HC. Beattie's 'A reading book for spare moments' is not held in either the Hocken Collections or the Hokonui Heritage Centre in Gore.
2 Tony Ballantyne, 'Thinking local: Knowledge, sociability and community in Gore's intellectual life, 1875–1914', *New Zealand Journal of History*, 44, 2 (2010), pp. 138–56.
3 Tony Ballantyne, 'Reading the newspaper in colonial Otago', *Journal of New Zealand Studies*, 12 (2011), pp. 47–63.
4 Sydney Shep, 'Tobacco, matches and writing paper: Colonial survival strategies in rural New Zealand', *Bulletin of the Bibliographical Society of Australia & New Zealand*, 28, 1 & 2 (2004), pp. 148–60.
5 On these dynamics see Tony Ballantyne, 'Remaking the Empire from Newgate: Edward Gibbon Wakefield's *A Letter from Sydney*' in Isabel Hofmeyr and Antoinette Burton, eds, *Creating an Imperial Commons: Ten books that shaped the modern British Empire*, Durham NC, 2014, pp. 29–49.
6 Isabel Hofmeyr, *Gandhi's Printing Press: Experiments in slow reading*, Cambridge MA, 2013, chapter 1; also see Derek Peterson and Giacomo Macola, eds, *Recasting the Past: History writing and political work in modern Africa*, Athens, OH, 2009.

29. Billies in Colonial Australia and New Zealand

1 *Oxford English Dictionary Online* 2013: entries for billy, n.1–3, www.oed.com
2 Peter Buchan, *Ancient Ballads and Songs of the North of Scotland*, Vol. II, Edinburgh, 1828, pp. 179–80.
3 In 1922 a 1-quart billy could be purchased for 10d: *Auckland Star*, 3 June 1922, p. 14.
4 This aluminum billy is branded Hard Wear and was made by the Auto Machine Manufacturing Company Limited, whose products were sold in Australia and New Zealand in the 1950s–1960s: *Argus*, 13 December 1954, p. 3.
5 Entry for Tinware in Wikipedia: www.en.wikipedia.org/wiki/Tinware
6 For example William Hogarth's *A Harlot's Progress*, Plate 3, 1732; John Ireland, *Hogarth Illustrated*, vol. 1, 2nd edn, 1793, p. 10. Eighteenth Century Collections Online.
7 Watkin Tench, *A Complete Account of the Settlement at Port Jackson, in New South Wales*, London, 1793, p. 131.
8 For example, *Australian,* 20 September 1826, p. 2.
9 *Cornwall Chronicle* (Tasmania), 29 September 1847, p. 3; in May 1848 Elliott's soup and bouilli went on sale in Wellington in 6-pound tins: *New Zealander,* 20 May 1848, p. 4. Later in the same year bouilli beef preserves arrived in Wellington from the Camperdown factory of M. Joseph in Sydney: *New Zealander*, 19 July 1848, p. 4.
10 *Sydney Morning Herald*, 4 March 1833, p. 1; *New Zealand Gazette and Wellington Spectator,* 9 January 1841, p. 2.
11 W.S. Ransom, *The Australian National Dictionary*, Melbourne, 1988, p. 52.
12 George B. Wilkinson, *The Working Man's Handbook to South Australia with advice to the farmer, and detailed information for the several classes of labourers and artizans*, London, 1849, p. 79.
13 John Rochfort, *The Adventures of a Surveyor in New Zealand and the Australian Gold Diggings*, London, 1853, p. 63.
14 For example, *Sydney Morning Herald*, 13 October 1851, p. 2.
15 *Argus*, 28 May 1855, p. 7.
16 Thomson in Nancy Taylor, ed., *Early Travellers in New Zealand*, Oxford, 1959, p. 333.
17 One advertisement referred to both billies and quart pots implying some difference between them, and another referred to 'Bush pots, billies, camp kettles and ovens, tea kettles, saucepans': *Otago Daily Times*, 2 December 1861, p. 4.
18 Harry W. Orsman, *The Dictionary of New Zealand English*, Auckland, 1997, p. 51. The incorrectly dated 1839 quotation has yet to be corrected in the *Oxford English Dictionary* (2013).
19 *Daily News,* 12 January 1897, p. 2.
20 *Press*, 1 March 1913, p. 13.
21 For example, *Evening Post*, 22 November 1921, p. 4.

22 *Evening Post*, 20 June 1891, p. 1. An almost identical recipe was reproduced in a Perth newspaper in 1913: *Western Mail*, 8 August 1913, p. 43.
23 Orsman, *The Dictionary of New Zealand English*, p. 51.
24 For example, *Wanganui Chronicle*, 7 April 1916, p. 6.
25 For example, *Auckland Star*, 28 May 1935, p. 9.
26 Robert Baden-Powell, *Scouting for Boys*, facsimile of 1908 edn, Oxford, 2004, p. 145.
27 Philip Carrington, *The Boy Scouts' Camp Book*, new and revised edn, London, 1921, p. 62.
28 I am grateful to Jane Teal of Lyttelton for searching her collection of Scouting books for references to the billy.

30. On Holiday, At Home: Christchurch's seaside tent 'camps', c. 1892–c. 1910

1 Adam Henry Pearson Maclay, 'Inside a large camping tent decorated with single beds and table, carpet, Linwood Football Club picture, posters of films, other people and scenes, clothing hanging and "Lily Camp" sign, [Sumner?], Christchurch c. 1905–26', Ref: 1/1-028358-G, ATL.
2 Adam Maclay Collection, ATL. All Maclay images cited are from this collection, which comprises 6982 dry plate glass negatives by Maclay, with titles and dates assigned by ATL.
3 *Evening Post*, 24 November 1893, p. 2; *Star*, 12 February 1894, p. 1.
4 J.F. Menzies, *Sumner*, Christchurch, 1941, pp. 43–44; 'Trams, 'buses, and cabs', in *The Cyclopedia of New Zealand [Canterbury Provincial District]*, Christchurch, 1903, p. 63.
5 'Sumner', in *The Cyclopedia of New Zealand*, p. 405; *New Brighton, New Zealand: Canterbury's playground*, Christchurch, 1996, unpaginated; Walter De Thier, *Sumner to Ferrymead: A Christchurch history*, Christchurch, 1996, pp. 28, 62–63.
6 *Star*, 8 January 1894, p. 1.
7 *Star*, 23 December 1892, p. 4.
8 *Star*, 8 January 1894, p. 1. At the time of writing, I have been unable to uncover any further information relating to women's camps at either Sumner or New Brighton.
9 *Observer*, 26 January 1895, p. 11; *Press*, 12 September 1896, p. 5.
10 *Press*, 19 January 1897, p. 6.
11 *Star*, 8 January 1894, p. 1.
12 See, for example: Maclay, 'Interior of a large tent, furnished with beds, a table draped with a cloth, and decorated with prints hanging around tent and a flag inscribed "Lily", probably [Sumner, Christchurch district?] c. 1905–26', Ref: 1/1-029191-G, ATL; Maclay, 'Five unidentified young men in hats with wood burner stove and pot, accordion, broom, dog and axe, in front of two tents with awning and "Myrtle Camp" sign, trees beyond, [Sumner?], Christchurch
c. 1905–26', Ref: 1/1-028442-G, ATL; Maclay, 'Group of unidentified young men wearing straw boaters, sitting outside a tent, a sign behind them reads "Red Rose Camp", [New Brighton, Christchurch district?] c. 1905–26', Ref: 1/1-028937-G, ATL; Maclay, 'Interior of a tent, showing four beds and a dressing table, with paper decorations strung around walls, and printed reproductions of paintings attached to roof, possibly Christchurch district c. 1910', Ref: 1/1-028095-G, ATL.
13 Maclay, 'Six unidentified men at the campsite, possibly Christchurch district, showing three men sitting on stools with three men standing behind them in front of the tent and a flag in the tree above them c. 1902–3', Ref: 1/1-028811-G, ATL; Maclay, 'Group of five young men at a campsite, sitting alongside tents, with sign reading "Myrtle Camp" behind, and a sign reading "Please Keep Off The Grass" in front, possibly Christchurch district 191–?', Ref: 1/1-028174-G, ATL; Maclay, 'Four unidentified smartly dressed men, sitting with a cockatoo in a birdcage, beside tents, including a sign, which reads "Flora Camp, 1901-02", and a boy at left of image, location unidentified, between 1901 and 1902', Ref: 1/1-021713-G, ATL.
14 *Star*, 19 May 1892, p. 1; *Press*, 5 May 1893, p. 4; *Star*, 24 May 1893, p. 3; *Press*, 24 May 1894, p. 6; *Press*, 7 July 1894, p. 9; *Press*, 31 August 1894, p. 5; *Star*, 9 July 1897, p. 4; *Press*, 12 July 1899, p. 1. Some of these socials featured photographs of the camps among the decorations.
15 *Star*, 8 February 1894, p. 3; *Star*, 8 January 1895, p. 3; *Press*, 20 December 1895, p. 5; *Press*, 25 January 1896, p. 7; *Star*, 29 January 1896, p. 1; *Press*, 28 November 1896, p. 9.
16 *Star*, 25 September 1894, p. 3.
17 Janice Anderson, *The Victorian and Edwardian Seaside*, London, 1978, pp. 10, 37–40.
18 Caroline Daley, 'Modernity, consumption, and leisure' in Giselle Byrnes, ed., *The New Oxford History of New Zealand*, South Melbourne, 2009, 423–45, p. 424; Richard White, *On Holidays: A history of getting away in Australia*, North Melbourne, 2005, p. 55.
19 John F. Travis, *The Rise of the Devon Seaside Resorts 1750–1900*, Exeter, 1993, pp. 176, 178; Jock Phillips, *A Man's Country? The image of the Pakeha male – a history*, Auckland, 1987, pp. 86–87.

20 Phillips, *A Man's Country?*, pp. 97–98.
21 *Star*, 14 September 1896, p. 4.
22 *Press*, 8 January 1898, p. 10.
23 In their suggestion of a blend of performance and authenticity, and young men taking the opportunity to enjoy a range of roles and personae, Maclay's photographs may be seen as having a connection with the (nonetheless very different) work of William Williams and Robert Gant; see, for example, Chris Brickell, 'At the borders of colonial masculinity: Robert Gant's photographs of men together' in Angela Wanhalla and Erika Wolf, eds, *Early New Zealand Photography: Images and essays*, Dunedin, 2011, pp. 66–71.
24 Maclay, 'Members of Primrose Club, a framed picture with a collage of headshots, Christchurch, c. 1905–26', Ref: 1/1-026182-G, ATL; Maclay, 'Four unidentified men next to the tent doing odd jobs, showing two men doing the dishes, one man chopping wood and the other man cooking, possibly Christchurch district, c. 1902–1903', Ref: 1/1-028804-G, ATL; Maclay, 'Unidentified men doing chores, next to tent, Waterloo camp, probably Christchurch district, c. 1905–26', Ref: 1/1-023572-G, ATL.
25 *Star*, 9 March 1896, p. 2; *Press*, 12 September 1896, p. 5; *Star*, 14 September 1896, p. 4; *Press*, 18 September 1896, p. 2.
26 Anderson, *The Victorian and Edwardian Seaside*, pp. 9, 71; Travis, *The Rise of the Devon Seaside Resorts*, pp. 158–60, 163–64, 180; James Walvin, *Leisure and Society, 1830–1950*, London, 1978, p. 78; Megan Schlase, 'Camping at the seaside: The "fashionable" thing to do in summer', AuthentiCity: The City of Vancouver Archives Blog, 11 July 2013: www.vancouverarchives.ca/2013/07/camping-at-the-seaside-the-fashionable-thing-to-do-in-summer
27 *Press*, 16 September 1896, p. 4; *Star*, 30 September 1896, p. 3; *Star*, 9 December 1896, p. 3; *Star*, 14 January 1897, p. 2; *Press*, 19 January 1897, p. 6.
28 *Star*, 31 December 1896, p. 2; *Press*, 17 February 1897, p. 5; *Press*, 21 November 1903, p. 5; *Press*, 19 January 1906, p. 2.
29 *Press*, 27 November 1907, p. 6; *Star*, 27 November 1908, p. 3; *Press*, 3 December 1908, p. 7; *Press*, 10 December 1908, p. 2.
30 Bill Garner, 'Pegging out the camp: Finding broader histories in camping gear', *reCollections*, 7, 2 (2012), unpaginated, http://recollections.nma.gov.au/issues/volume_7_number_2/papers/pegging_out_the_camp#pageindex

31. An Art Nouveau Jug Collected by Walter Cook

1 J. Rudoe, *Decorative Arts 1850–1950, a catalogue of the British Museum Collection*, London, 1991, p. 62.
2 See Dawson & Co. advertisement for 'Liberty's pewter ware', in *Otago Daily Times*, 22 September 1916, p. 3. Dawsons Limited: Records, MS-3031, HC.
3 A. Calhoun, *The Arts & Crafts Movement in New Zealand, 1870–1940: Women make their mark*, Auckland, 2000, pp. 98–100, 123; *Official Record of the New Zealand and South Seas International Exhibition*, Dunedin, 1926, p. 165.
4 Catalogue note by Walter Cook, 1992.
5 W. Cook, 'Let those dry bones live', unpublished typescript, c. 1992, p. 12.
6 Ibid.
7 Gail Ross, *Hinehauone Coralie Cameron: Printmaker*, Wellington, 2013.
8 I. Spielmann, *The British Government Exhibit at the New Zealand International Exhibition (1906–1907),* London, 1908.
9 Calhoun, *The Arts & Crafts Movement in New Zealand*, p. 123.
10 *Star,* 10 November 1906, p. 7.
11 Cook, 'Let those dry bones live', p. 12.
12 Ibid, p. 8.
13 'Confessions of an obsessive collector', Walter Cook, unpublished essay, 2007, p. 7.
14 Ibid.
15 Ibid.
16 Walter Cook to Dr A.N. Baker, Director, National Museum of New Zealand, 5 November 1991, Te Papa Corporate Records file CO-AD-01-50-1992/105, TPA.

32. Katherine Mansfield's Hei Tiki

1 *Free Lance* (*FL*), 19 October 1907, p. 8.
2 Laurel Harris, Mary Morris and Joanna Woods, eds, *The Material Mansfield: Traces of a writer's life*, Auckland and Wellington, 2008, p. 39.
3 Ibid., p. 43. The note is written on Vera's – Mrs J. Macintosh Bell's – card, which is reproduced. *The Material Mansfield* transcribes this as 'shown and worn' but 'shared and worn' makes more sense.
4 Letter from Charlotte ('Chaddie') Beauchamp to Sylvia Payne, 14 October 1907, quoted in Antony Alpers, *Katherine Mansfield: A biography*, New York, 1954, p. 89. In Alpers' 1980 biography he does not quote the letter: 'After describing all of Kass's birthday presents (greenstone

earrings, Liberty brooches, and so on) …', Antony Alpers, *The Life of Katherine Mansfield*, New York, 1980, p. 55.
5 Joanna Woods, *Katerina: The Russian world of Katherine Mansfield*, Auckland, 2001, p. 56.
6 H.D. Skinner, *The Maori Hei-Tiki*, 2nd edn, appendix by D.R. Skinner, Dunedin, 1966, p. 12.
7 Ngarino Ellis, 'Te Hei Tiki: Between tradition and modernity', *Art New Zealand*, 117, (2005–06), 47–51, p. 48.
8 *FL*, 8 December 1906, p. 8.
9 *Evening Post* (*EP*), 4 September 1907, p. 2.
10 *FL*, 19 April 1902, p. 11.
11 Mildred Amelia (Mīria) Tapapa Woodbine Pōmare. S.P. Andrew Ltd: Portrait negatives, Ref: 1/2-043506-F, Alexander Turnbull Library, Wellington.
12 'Wet afternoon in the library – in March [1908]. I have read the most strange books here – one on the Path to Rome, one of Maori Art': Margaret Scott, ed., *The Katherine Mansfield Notebooks*, vol. 1, Lincoln and Wellington, 1997, p. 152.
13 *EP*, 5 February 1907, p. 2.
14 *FL*, 19 October 1907, p. 8.
15 Quoted in Elizabeth Wilson, *Adorned in Dreams: Fashion and modernity*, rev. edn, London, 2003, p. 214.
16 *Weekly Graphic and New Zealand Mail*, 24 February 1909, p. 35.
17 Alpers, *The Life of Katherine Mansfield*, p. 87.
18 Image of Katherine Mansfield, Murry, John Middleton, 1889–1957: Diaries and notebooks, Ref: MSX-4147-65, Alexander Turnbull Library, Wellington, New Zealand.
19 Scott, *The Katherine Mansfield Notebooks*, vol. 1, p. 67.
20 *Dominion*, 19 October 1907, p. 3.
21 Alpers, *The Life of Katherine Mansfield*, p. 19.

33. Te Pai o Ngā Āhua: The visitors' books at the Lindauer Art Gallery

1 This is a revised version of the essay commissioned for the Auckland Art Gallery's website *Whakamīharo Lindauer Online*, which was launched in July 2010. The project was led by Research Librarian Catherine Hammond; Indigenous Curator Ngahiraka Mason, (Ngāi Tūhoe, Te Arawa, Ngāi Te Rangi); and the gallery's iwi consultant Mere Lodge (Ngāti Porou). Funding was received through the Digital Strategy initiative of the Department of Internal Affairs' Community Partnership Fund, while partnership with Te Taura Whiri i te Reo Māori, the Māori Language Commission, enabled the translation of the book into modern Māori and English. This essay benefited enormously from the translations made by Te Haumihiata Mason (Ngāi Tūhoe, Te Arawa, Ngāi Te Rangi) and Hohepa MacDougall (Ngāi Tūhoe).
2 *Pictures of Old New Zealand: The Partridge Collection of Maori paintings by Gottfried Lindauer, described by James Cowan*, Auckland, 1930. Documenting the entire collection of 62 portraits and eight large scenes of Māori life, this opulent publication builds on an earlier, more modest gallery guidebook, *Maori Biographies: Sketches of old New Zealand, compiled by James Cowan; Descriptive catalogue of Maori portraits painted by Herr G. Lindauer*, Auckland, 1901. In 1901 the collection numbered 40 portraits and one large work, *The Tohunga under Tapu*.

34. Toko Toru Tapu: A tale of four churches

1 *Poverty Bay Herald* (*PBH*), 16 January 1912, p. 2.
2 Ibid.
3 *PBH*, 8 March 1913, p. 2.
4 Ibid., 7 March 1913, p. 4.
5 *Evening Post*, 4 March 1913, p. 3.
6 Ibid.
7 See Richard A. Sundt, *Whare Karakia: Māori church building, decoration & ritual in Aotearoa New Zealand 1834–1863*, Auckland, 2010, pp. 93–97.
8 Richard A. Sundt, 'Reconstruction of a carved Māori church: Controversy and creativity at Manutuke, 1849–1863 (Part 1)', *Journal of the Polynesian Society*, 117, 2 (2008), 129–210, p. 135.
9 Editor, 'Brief reviews of the past history of the missions', *Church Missionary Intelligencer*, III, 2, 1852, 42–48, p. 48.
10 For a description of the manaia and other carving designs, see Julie Paama-Pengelly, *Māori Art and Design: Weaving, painting, carving and architecture*, Auckland, 2010, pp. 133–34.
11 William Williams and Jane Williams, *The Turanga Journals, 1840–1850: Letters and journals of William and Jane Williams, missionaries to Poverty Bay*, ed. Frances Porter, Wellington, 1974, p. 548.
12 Sundt, 'Reconstruction', p. 131.
13 Sundt, *Whare Karakia*, p. 126.
14 Sundt, 'Reconstruction', p. 132.
15 See Roger Neich, *Painted Histories: Early Maori figurative painting*, Auckland, 1993, pp. 85–86.
16 Sundt, 'Reconstruction', p. 136.
17 *PBH*, 28 January 1910, p. 4.
18 *PBH*, 22 January 1913, p. 5.
19 *PBH*, 10 March 1913, p. 5.

35. A Gentleman's Slippers

1 *New Zealand Herald* (*NZH*), 19 April 1898, p. 5.
2 *Evening Post* (*EP*), 26 April 1898, p. 6.
3 For a full list of pallbearers see *NZH*, 13 May 1898, p. 3.
4 Ibid.
5 Anthony Dreaver, 'Te Rangihiwinui, Te Keepa', from the Dictionary of New Zealand Biography: www.TeAra.govt.nz/en/biographies/1t64/te-rangihiwinui-te-keepa
6 *Hawke's Bay Herald*, 16 April 1898, p. 3.
7 Dreaver, 'Te Rangihiwinui, Te Keepa'.
8 Michelle Horwood and Che Wilson, *Te Ara Tapu – Sacred Journeys: Whanganui Regional Museum Taonga Maori Collection*, Auckland, 2008, p. 88.
9 'Te Keepa Te Rangihiwinui (Major Kemp)', New Zealand History Online, Ministry for Culture and Heritage: www.nzhistory.net.nz/people/te-keepa-te-rangihiwinui
10 'Spotlight: The Albert slipper,' The Black Tie Blog, posted 21 February 2014: http://blog.blacktieguide.com/2014/02/21/spotlight-the-albert-slipper/
11 *Wanganui Herald*, 23 July 1887, p. 4.
12 *Press* (Christchurch), 26 April 1898, p. 6.
13 *Horowhenua Chronicle*, 20 May 1915, p. 3.
14 *Horowhenua Chronicle*, 22 May 1915, p. 3.
15 *Wellington Independent*, 20 October 1871, p. 2.
16 *Colonist*, 19 April 1882, p. 3.
17 *Marlborough Express*, 1 December 1906, p. 1.
18 *NZH*, 26 April 1898, p. 5.
19 Accession Number: 1899.183.2; http://collection.wrm.org.nz/search.do?id=1262&db=object&page=1&view=detail
20 Horwood and Wilson, *Te Ara Tapu*, p. 88.
21 Dreaver, 'Te Rangihiwinui, Te Keepa'.

36. Māori Monument or Pākehā Propaganda? The memorial to Keepa Te Rangihiwinui, Whanganui

1 For detail of the memorial's elements, see Ewan Morris, 'Keepa Te Rangihiwinui Memorial', New Zealand History Online, Ministry for Culture and Heritage: www.nzhistory.net.nz/media/photo/keepa-te-rangihiwinui-memorial
2 On Te Keepa's life, see Anthony Dreaver, 'Te Rangihiwinui, Te Keepa', from the Dictionary of New Zealand Biography: www.TeAra.govt.nz/en/biographies/1t64/te-rangihiwinui-te-keepa; David Young, *Woven by Water: Histories from the Whanganui River*, Wellington, 1998, ch. 6.
3 For the Pākaitore occupation, see Mason Durie, *Te Mana, Te Kawanatanga: The politics of Māori self-determination*, Auckland, 1998, pp. 125–29; Paul Moon, *New Zealand in the Twentieth Century: The nation, the people*, Auckland, 2011, pp. 577–82; Young, *Woven by Water*, pp. 98–101.
4 See also Jock Phillips, 'Wanganui: War memorial capital of the world' in Kynan Gentry and Gavin McLean, eds, *Heartlands: New Zealand historians write about places where history happened*, Auckland, 2006, pp. 72–89.
5 *Te Whiringa Taura o Whanganui*, Howard Taylor Productions, 2007. Phillips, too, describes it as 'primarily a Pakeha monument': Phillips, 'Wanganui', pp. 79–80.
6 The painting and the sword are shown in Michelle Horwood and Che Wilson, *Te Ara Tapu: Sacred Journeys: Whanganui Regional Museum Taonga Māori Collection*, Auckland, 2008, pp. 88–89.
7 Thomas Wayth Gudgeon, *The Defenders of New Zealand*, Auckland, 1887, pp. 383–86.
8 *Notes of Meetings Between His Excellency the Governor (Lord Ranfurly), the Rt. Hon. R.J. Seddon, Premier and Native Minister, and the Hon. James Carroll, Member of the Executive Council Representing the Native Race, and the Native Chiefs and People at Each Place, Assembled in Respect of the Proposed Native Land Legislation and Native Affairs Generally, During 1898 and 1899*, Wellington, 1899, pp. 30–39. Porokoru Patapu is named in this account as Porokurua Patupo. See also *Wanganui Chronicle* (*WC*), 17 May 1898, p. 2; *Te Tiupiri*, 17 May 1898, pp. 3–6.
9 Wanganui Borough Council minute book, 8 December 1899, AAF 63/4, Wanganui District Council Archives; *WC*, 13 December 1899, p. 2; James T. Muir to James Carroll, 26 July 1904, James T. Muir to Prime Minister Richard Seddon, 26 February 1906, James T. Muir to Prime Minister J.G. Ward, 10 June 1908, file 1906/282, MA1 876, ANZ.
10 For the construction, see evidence given in the Supreme Court case discussed below (particularly the evidence of Walter Grace, Gray Phillips, John Roderick McDonald and Rora Hakaraia). Transcripts of evidence were printed as part of a booklet prepared for the Court of Appeal case (hereafter *Evidence Booklet*), file 1358, ABIO 6085 C482 113 Box 621, ANZ. There were also detailed reports of the evidence in *Manawatu Evening Standard* (*MES*), 28 May 1913, p. 6, 29 May 1913, p. 3, 30 May 1913, p. 2. The contracts for the construction of the memorial were included in the Statement of Claim and Statement of Defence, *Evidence Booklet*, pp. 4–5, 7–8. There were two contracts, one signed in May 1911 and one in July 1911.
11 *Marlborough Express*, 25 September 1912, p. 4.
12 *Harris v Hakaraia* (1914) 33 NZLR 1074, 1077–78, 1079 (CA).

13 For official records of the trial, see file 13/1913, AAOY W3298 21227 Box 111, ANZ; file 1358, ABIO 6085 C482 113 Box 621, ANZ; *Harris v Hakaraia* (1914) 33 NZLR 1074 (CA). For newspaper accounts see *MES*, 28 May 1913, p. 6, 29 May 1913, p. 3, 30 May 1913, p. 2, 31 May 1913, p. 5; *WC*, 29 May 1913, p. 8, 30 May 1913, p. 2, 31 May 1913, p. 2; *Evening Post* (*EP*), 6 May 1914, p. 8, 7 May 1914, p. 8; *Dominion*, 7 May 1914, p. 9. Rora Hakaraia's obituary is in *WC*, 29 January 1915, p. 2.

14 Comments of James Thomas Muir, stonemason; William Leslie Morrison, sculptor and painter; Denis Seaward, art master at the Wanganui Technical School: *Evidence Booklet*, pp. 21, 23, 24.

15 Evidence of William L. Morrison, reported in *MES*, 30 May 1913, p. 2; Justice Hosking in *EP*, 7 May 1914, p. 8. The Court of Appeal decision noted the opinions of experts that the battle scenes were 'absolutely contemptible in design and execution': *Harris v Hakaraia* (1914) 33 NZLR 1074, 1086 (CA).

16 *EP*, 6 May 1914, p. 8. The meeting at Pūtiki sent a petition to Frank Harris & Co. asking for the statue to be replaced and including a photograph of their preferred image. I have been unable to locate this petition.

17 *Evidence Booklet*, pp. 17 (Gray Phillips), 20 (Frank Harris), 31–32 (Rora Hakaraia).

18 Evidence of George Tuppin, *MES*, 28 May 1913, p. 6; *Evidence Booklet*, p. 15. Harris too was concerned the marble made Keepa 'too much like a white man': *MES*, 29 May 1913, p. 3.

19 *MES*, 30 May 1913, p. 2.

20 *Evidence Booklet*, p. 27.

21 See file 1918/98, MA1 1182, ANZ.

22 See evidence of John McDonald and Rora Hakaraia, *Evidence Booklet*, pp. 29, 31; *MES*, 30 May 1913, p. 2.

23 *Evidence Booklet*, pp. 18, 31. The interpreter shared Grace's commission, a conflict of interest criticised by the Court of Appeal: *Harris v Hakaraia* (1914) 33 NZLR 1074, 1089 (CA).

24 The judge drew attention to this fact in his summing up in the Supreme Court: *MES*, 30 May 1913, p. 2.

25 For the full Māori text, see Morris, 'Keepa Te Rangihiwinui Memorial'.

26 Rāwiri Taonui, 'Whakapapa – Genealogy', Te Ara – the Encyclopedia of New Zealand: www.TeAra.govt.nz/en/whakapapa-genealogy. Te Keepa's whakapapa was published locally after his death: *Te Tiupiri*, 26 April 1898, pp. 2–5, and matches part of that on the memorial.

27 Ruth Wilkie, 'Rere-o-Maki', from the Dictionary of New Zealand Biography: www.TeAra.govt.nz/en/biographies/1r4/rere-o-maki; Young, *Woven by Water*, p. 103.

28 Roger Blackley, *Te Mata: The ethnological portrait*, Wellington, 2010, p. 33; also Roger Neich, *Carved Histories: Rotorua Ngati Tarawhai woodcarving*, Auckland, 2001, pp. 137–45.

29 Dreaver, 'Te Rangihiwinui, Te Keepa'; Young, *Woven by Water*, pp. 104–20.

37. Naturalising Nightingale in the Ashburton Domain: The Florence Nightingale memorial tree and tablet

1 *Ashburton Guardian* (AG), 1 September 1910, p. 3.

2 Michael Roche, 'Transforming the colonial settlement with parks and domains: Scenic beauty in two New Zealand towns 1894 to 1920' in Andrea Gaynor, Elizabeth Gralton, Jenny Gregory and Sarah McQuade, eds, *Urban Transformations: Booms, busts and other catastrophes*, Proceedings of the 11th Australasian Urban History/Planning History Conference, University of Western Australia, 2012, 293–305, p. 298.

3 *AG*, 18 November 1912, p. 5.

4 Michael Roche, 'Ashburton remembers: Celebration and commemoration in a New Zealand town 1903–1928' in L. Finch, ed., *Seachange: New and renewed urban landscapes*, 9th Australasian Urban History/Planning History Conference Proceedings, Caloundra, February 2008, University of the Sunshine Coast, Maroochydore (CD), unpaged.

5 For example see Joan Woodward and Glenys Mitchell, *A Nurse at War: Emily Peter, 1858–1927*, Christchurch, 2008.

6 See Julia Bush, *Edwardian Ladies and Imperial Power*, London, 2000; Katie Pickles, *Female Imperialism and National Identity: Imperial order daughters of the empire*, Manchester, 2002; Katie Pickles, *Transnational Outrage: The death and commemoration of Edith Cavell*, Basingstoke, 2007; Katie Pickles, 'The old and new on parade: Mimesis, Queen Victoria, and carnival queens on Victoria Day in interwar Victoria' in Katie Pickles and Myra Rutherdale, eds, *Contact Zones: Aboriginal and settler women in Canada's colonial past*, Vancouver, 2005, pp. 272–91; Dorothy Thompson, *Queen Victoria: Gender and power*, London, 1990.

7 *AG*, 3 December 1907, p. 2; *Star*, 12 December 1907, p. 2; *Colonist*, 13 December 1907, p. 3. The *Marlborough*

Express, the *Manawatu Standard* and the *Wanganui Chronicle* also carried the Kaiser story.
8 *AG*, 18 May 1910, p. 2.
9 Ibid., 17 August 1910, p. 1.
10 See John A. Mangan, ed., *The Imperial Curriculum: Racial images and education in the British colonial experience*, London, 1983; John A. MacKenzie, *Propaganda and Empire: The manipulation of British public opinion, 1880–1960*, Manchester, 1984.
11 *NAC's New Zealand*, June 1976, p. 10; Glyn Strange, 'I regret the delay …', *Historic Places*, September 1998, pp. 11–14.
12 *Press*, 4 April 1911, p. 8.
13 Ibid., 5 April 1911, p. 3.
14 'Florence Nightingale: Her funeral': www.countryjoe.com/nightingale/funeral.htm
15 Alex Attewell, 'Of lamps and lanterns', *International History of Nursing Journal*, 7, 3, (2003), pp. 94–97.
16 *Poverty Bay Herald*, 19 August 1913, p. 7.
17 *Press*, 24 February 1914, p. 4.
18 *AG*, 15 March 1916, pp. 1, 5.
19 Ibid., 14 October 1919, p. 2.
20 Ibid., 19 May 1916, p. 6.
21 Interview, Ashburton, 2 February 2013.
22 *AG*, 20 January 1911, p. 3.
23 *Evening Post*, 26 May 1939, p. 14.

38. A Bottle of Mineral Water from Te Aroha

1 C.F. Spooner, *A Guide for Invalids and Tourists to the Thermal Springs and Baths of Te Aroha, New Zealand*, Te Aroha, 1895. The publication includes chemical analyses of the hot springs, attributed to James Hector.
2 K.W. Wells, *A Postcard from Te Aroha: An account of taking the waters at Te Aroha's Hot Springs Domain*, Auckland, 2003, p .32.
3 A.S. Wohlmann, *The Mineral Waters and Spas of New Zealand*, Wellington, 1914, p. 107. Subsequent chemical analyses of the water suggested that it contained significant boron and arsenic: D.E. White, J.D. Hem, and G.A. Waring, 'Chapter F, Chemical composition of sub-surface waters' in E. Fleischer, ed., *Data of Geochemistry*, 6th edn, *Geological Survey Professional Paper*, 440-F, 1963, p. F48. 'This spring was in use from 1880–1975. Due to high levels of arsenic and boron, it is not recommended for drinking purposes': Wells, *A Postcard from Te Aroha*, p. 44.
4 E. Stokes, *Wairakei Geothermal Area: Some historical perspectives*, Hamilton, 1991, p. 4.
5 See Ian Rockel, *Taking the Waters: Early spas in New Zealand*, Wellington, 1986.
6 Wohlmann's appointment attracted media interest: *Evening Post*, 2 May 1902, p. 7. Also see R.H. Johnson, 'Arthur Stanley Wohlmann, the first government balneologist in New Zealand', *Medical History*, Supplement No. 10 (1990), pp. 114–26.
7 The information collected by Wohlmann was initially published in 1904 as three pamphlets, covering Te Aroha, Hanmer and Rotorua, under the combined title *The Mineral Waters and Health Resorts of New Zealand*. The pamphlet on Rotorua ('Part 1') was published in 1904 and reprinted in 1906; that for Hanmer ('Part III') was printed in 1905; and all three parts were collected and reprinted in 1907, 1910, 1911 and 1914, by which time, although the book still contained information about the therapeutic benefits of the waters, the title had become *The Mineral Waters and Spas of New Zealand*.
8 Wohlmann, *The Mineral Waters and Spas of New Zealand*, p. 103.
9 J. Cowan, *Official Record of the New Zealand International Exhibition of Arts and Industries, Held at Christchurch 1906–1907, A description and historical account*, Wellington, 1910, p. 145.
10 Annual sales of 'canned' water are given in the reports of the Department of Tourist and Health Resorts in *AJHR*, 1927–36.
11 Wohlmann, *The Mineral Waters and Spas of New Zealand*, p. 94.
12 Patronage data for the Te Aroha resort are provided in some annual reports of the Department of Tourist and Health Resorts, *AJHR*, 1904–24.
13 A 'poster stamp' of the Blue Baths features women in modern one-piece bathing costumes, Ref: Eph-A-TOURISM-1930s-02-cover, ATL.
14 Image Ref: Eph-E-TOURISM-Rotorua-1932-01, ATL.
15 'Two panels with yellow backgrounds showing a man at left and a woman at right, both waving cheerfully', Ref: Eph-A-TOURISM-Rotorua-1930s-02-back, ATL.
16 C. Brickell, *Mates and Lovers: A history of gay New Zealand*, Auckland, 2008, p. 245.
17 R. Cursons, D. Sleigh, D. Hood and D. Pullon, 'A case of ameoebic meningoencephalitis', *New Zealand Medical Journal*, 116, 1187 (2003), pp. 1–5.
18 W.A.J. Mahon, 'Geochemistry and geothermal development' in P.P. Williams, ed., *Chemistry in a Young Country*, Christchurch, 1981, pp. 155–77.

19 R.B. Glover, 'Chemical and physical changes at Geyser Valley, Wairakei, and their relationship to changes in borefield performance', *DSIR Bulletin*, 218 (1977), pp. 19–26. The changes in composition were later attributed to changes in temperature that affect the chemical reactions between the water and the rocks in which it is confined.

20 The development of the Wairakei and Ohaaki geothermal power stations is described in M. Wright, *New Zealand's Engineering Heritage 1870–2000*, Auckland, 1999, pp. 110–13; with the science background explained in: A.J. Ellis, 'The development of geothermal power' in D. Hogan and B. Williamson, eds, *New Zealand is Different: Chemical milestones in New Zealand's history*, Christchurch, 1990, pp. 211–21.

21 Trends in the scientific interest in thermal springs are briefly described in Hodder, P., 'Getting into hot water – II: Wohlmann's legacy', *ChemEd NZ [Chemistry Education in New Zealand]*, 129, 4–11 (2012); the associated implications are described in: Hodder, P., 'Trends in technological use and social relevance of geothermal waters', *Chemistry in New Zealand* (forthcoming, 2015).

39. The Rotorua Bathhouse Radium Activator: From therapeutic device to quack curiosity

1 Report of the balneologist in Annual Report of the Tourist and Health Resorts Department, 1914, *AJHR*, 1914, H.2, p. 9.

2 Wohlmann to General Manager of Department of Tourist and Health Resorts, 25 May 1914, TO1 24/34, ANZ.

3 Arthur Wohlmann, *The Mineral Waters and Spas of New Zealand*, Wellington, 1914, pp. 61–62.

4 Ibid.

5 *Rotorua Times*, 30 October 1914.

6 Wohlmann, *The Mineral Waters and Spas of New Zealand*, pp. 61–62.

7 Wohlmann to General Manager, Department of Tourist and Health Resorts, 30 October 1914, TO1 24/34, ANZ.

8 'On the trail of the elusive millimicrocurie', *New Zealand Truth*, 5 September 1929, p. 1.

9 Duncan to General Manager, Department of Tourist and Health Resorts, 9 June 1922, TO1 24/34, ANZ.

10 Tourist Agent to General Manager, Department of Tourist and Health Resorts, 24 September 1925, TO1 24/34, ANZ.

11 Report of the balneologist in Annual Report of the Tourist and Health Resorts Department, 1914, p. 9.

40. 'Pōua's Cloak': The Haberfield family kahu kiwi

1 See Te Maire Tau and Atholl Anderson, eds, *Ngāi Tahu: A migration history: The Carrington text*, Wellington, 2008, p. 163.

2 Museum of New Zealand Te Papa Tongarewa, 'Feathers – Materials for making Maori cloaks': www.collections.tepapa.govt.nz/topic/3625

3 Hokimate P. Harwood, 'Identification and Description of Feathers in Te Papa's Māori Cloaks', *Tuhinga* 22 (2011), 125–47, pp. 125, 128.

4 Personal communication, Tiny Metzger to author, February 2013.

5 'A weaver might have woven 6000 feathers into a single cloak … one cloak in Te Papa's collection contains more than 12,000 feathers.' Museum of New Zealand Te Papa Tongarewa, 'Feathers – Materials for making Maori cloaks'.

6 Awhina Tamarapa, ed., *Whatu Kākahu: Maori cloaks*, Wellington, 2011, p. 101.

7 Harwood, 'Identification and description of feathers in Te Papa's Māori cloaks', p. 145.

8 See Angela Middleton, *Two Hundred Years on Codfish Island: From cultural encounter to nature conservation*, Invercargill, 2007.

9 Aritaku and Ani had 10 children. Their eldest, Golan (1904–1978), attended Te Aute College before studying medicine at the University of Otago, during which time he spent holidays with Pōua and our wider family at Greenhills and Bluff. See Bradford Haami, *Dr Golan Maaka: Māori doctor*, North Shore City, 1995, pp. 59–60, 66–68, 79–80.

10 Personal communication, Ian Church to author, 11 March 2009.

11 *Otago Witness*, 10 July 1907, p. 36.

12 See *Adventures in Maoriland: Alexander Markey and the making of Hei Tiki*, television documentary, 1985: www.nzonscreen.com/title/adventures-in-maoriland-1985; and Toby Rikihana, 'An outpost of Maoritanga', *Te Ao Hou: The new world*, 15 (July 1956), p. 10.

41. Feathers for a Wartime Bride

1 Postcard from South Africa, 1916, TMP014794, TPA.

2 Fred Waite, *The New Zealanders at Gallipoli*, Wellington, 1919, p. 26.

3 George Bollinger, 19 December 1914, MS-Papers-2350-01, ATL.

4 Anthony S. Travis, 'Decadence, decline and celebration: Raphael Meldola and the Mauve Jubilee of 1906', *History and Technology*, 22, 2 (2006), 131–52, p. 147.

5 Sarah Abrevaya Stein, 'Mediterranean Jewries and global commerce in the modern period: On the trail of the Jewish feather trade', *Jewish Social Studies*, 13, 2 (Winter 2007), n.p.
6 Sarah Abrevaya Stein, '"Falling into feathers": Jews in the transatlantic ostrich feather trade', *Journal of Modern History*, 79 (December 2007), 772–812, p. 773.
7 Ibid., p. 780.

42. 'Badness Personified': Nola Pratt's photograph album

1 PA1-o-883, ATL.
2 Carole van Grondelle, *Angel of the Anzacs: The life of Nola Luxford*, Wellington, 2000, p. 21.
3 Paul Rodaway, *Sensuous Geographies: Body, sense and place*, New York, 2011 [1994].
4 Barbara Brookes, Erik Olssen and Emma Beer, 'Spare time? Leisure, gender and modernity' in Barbara Brookes, Annabel Cooper and Robin Law, eds, *Sites of Gender: Women, men and modernity in South Dunedin, 1890–1939*, Auckland, 2003, 151–89, pp. 177–78.
5 Grondelle, *Angel of the Anzacs*, p. 24.
6 *Star*, 22 April 1905, p. 3.
7 *Evening Post*, 13 February 1914, p. 9.
8 *Grey River Argus*, 8 May 1914, p. 8.
9 *Otago Witness*, 22 July 1908, p. 73.
10 Grondelle, *Angel of the Anzacs*, p. 26.
11 Ibid., p. 13.

43. Hiding and Revealing: The emotional history of a travel diary

1 'Pere' is a loan noun which, among other things, denotes a bell. As Peter Gibbons has discussed, in 'Cultural colonisation and national identity', *New Zealand Journal of History*, 36, 1 (2002), 5–17, p. 11, Pākehā giving Māori place names in this period was one expression of cultural colonisation.
2 Tony Ballantyne and Brian Moloughney, 'Asia in Murihiku: Towards a transnational history of a colonial culture' in Tony Ballantyne and Brian Moloughney, eds, *Disputed Histories: Imagining New Zealand's pasts*, Dunedin, 2006, 65–92, p. 81.
3 Lydia Wevers, *Reading on the Farm: Victorian fiction and the colonial world*, Wellington, 2010, discusses the station and house libraries at Brancepeth in the Wairarapa; leather-bound editions of complete oeuvres were an expected component of a Victorian library.
4 By naming her home Sunny Hill, Bond chose an alternative to Remuera, which Māori used to name this maunga. It is possible that she did so to avoid confusion with the suburb in which she lived, rather than from a desire to replace or erase the Māori history of the place. 'Pere Street' directly references the effects of colonisation: from their home the Bonds could hear the church bells of St Luke's (Presbyterian), St Michael's (Catholic) and St Mark's (Anglican).
5 See, for example, Henrietta Rothwell, Travel Diaries, 1927, MSC 249, Hamilton City Libraries, which comprise 24 small notebooks, sent home as they were completed, or C.W. Collins, Travelogue, 9 April–1 June 1932, Accession MB 95 Box 1, Macmillan Brown Library, University of Canterbury, which was handwritten, and later typed, on loose pages.
6 Bond, '6th Apr.', '9th April', '14th April', '16th April', '18th April', '21st April', '10th May', '1st June', Diary 1, pp. 26, 35, 36, 41, 43, 48, 72, 99, and elsewhere.
7 Between pp. 82 and 83 and after p. 273 Bond included lists of letters, postcards and packages she posted to New Zealand, totalling 11 pages.
8 Ibid., '5th Oct.', p. 265.
9 Ibid.
10 Ibid., '10th July', pp. 172–73.
11 Genevieve de Pont, 'Historicising the Big O.E.: New approaches to New Zealand tourists and travel writing abroad', *History Compass*, 10, 3 (2012), 219–30, especially pp. 223–26.

44. From Polo to Poultry: A planter's legacy

1 'Pour les Intimes': Diary of John Graham, 1937, 6039:7, National Library of Scotland.
2 Alistair Gordon, *George Peters and his Descendants*, London, 2008, p. 248.
3 Martha Langford, *Suspended Conversations: The afterlife of memory in photographic albums*, Montreal, 2001, pp. 155–57.
4 Marianne Hirsch, *Family Frames: Photography, narrative and postmemory*, Cambridge, 1997, p. 248.
5 Annette Kuhn and Kirsten Emiko McAllister, eds, *Locating Memory: Photographic acts*, New York, 2006, pp. 1–2.
6 For details of my project see my website: www.kalimpongkids.org.nz
7 Evidence of this lifestyle is plentiful in the photographic record of tea planters, as well as numerous published memoirs: F.A. Hetherington, *Diary of a Tea Planter*, Sussex, 1994; George Barker, *A Tea Planter's Life in Assam*,

Calcutta, 1884; A.R. Ramsden, *Assam Planter*, London, 1945.

8 Other planters recorded the struggle to make a living from tea. See for example, Tony Ballantyne, 'Mr. Peal's Archive: Mobility and exchange in histories of empire' in Antoinette Burton, ed., *Archive Stories: Facts, fictions and the writing of history*, Durham, 2005, 87–110, p. 89.

9 For a discussion of the persistence of Raj nostalgia, see Elizabeth Buettner, *Empire Families: Britons and late imperial India*, Oxford, 2004, pp. 252–57; and Antoinette Burton, 'India, Inc.? Nostalgia, memory and the empire of things' in Stuart Ward, ed., *British Culture and the End of Empire*, Manchester, 2001, pp. 217–32.

10 Laura Bear, *Lines of the Nation: Indian railway workers, bureaucracy and the intimate historical self*, New York, 2007, pp. 264–67.

11 Buettner, *Empire Families*, ch. 5, 'From somebodies to nobodies: Returning home to Britain and perpetuating overseas connections'.

45. Reconfiguring Cricket Culture in Colonial Sāmoa

1 Accession lot record, 1983/40, TPA.

2 *Western Samoa Mail*, 9 October 1936.

3 *Evening Post* (*EP*), 9 August 1939, p. 9. Accession lot record, 1980/04, TPA.

4 William Churchward, *My Consulate in Samoa*, London, 1887, p. 135.

5 Ibid., p. 143.

6 *Nelson Evening Mail*, 24 September 1897, p. 2.

7 Robert Stevenson, *A Footnote to History: Eighty years of trouble in Samoa*, Auckland, 1996, p. 6.

8 T. Damon I. Salesa, '"Travel-happy" Samoa: Colonialism, Samoan migration and a "brown Pacific"', *New Zealand Journal of History*, 37, 2 (2003), 171–88, p. 182.

9 Brian Levison, *Amazing and Extraordinary Facts: Cricket*, London, 2012, pp. 62–63.

10 *Auckland Star*, 22 April 1925, p. 5. See Malama Melesia, *The Making of Modern Samoa: Traditional authority and colonial administration in the history of Western Samoa*, Suva, 1987, p. 110.

11 Mary Boyd, 'Racial attitudes of New Zealand officials in Western Samoa', *New Zealand Journal of History*, 21, 1 (1987), 139–55, p. 148.

12 *Samoa Times* (*ST*), 25 September 1915.

13 Ibid., 17 July 1915, p. 3.

14 Ibid., 14 August 1915, p. 4.

15 *Press*, 12 January 1915, p. 7.

16 Stephen J. Smith, *The Samoa (N.Z.) Expeditionary Force, 1914–1915: An account based on official records of the seizure and occupation by New Zealand of the German Islands of Western Samoa*, Wellington, 1924, p. 98.

17 *ST*, 27 November 1915, p. 3.

18 See Brian Stoddart and Keith Sandiford, eds, *The Imperial Game: Cricket, culture and society*, Manchester, 1998.

19 *EP*, 19 August 1936, p. 16.

20 *Auckland Star*, 10 July 1936. See Mary Boyd, 'The military administration of Western Samoa, 1914–1919', *New Zealand Journal of History*, 2, 2 (1968), 148–64, p. 162.

21 *EP*, 19 August 1936, p. 16.

46. 'A "Lucky" Snap': Reframing colonial culture through a pictorialist lens

1 'Pleasing pictures: Photography as an art', *Evening Post* (*EP*), 26 May 1930, p. 11.

2 Ibid., 2 December 1938, p. 8.

3 Ibid., 10 March 1938, p. 23.

4 See 'Homeward bound', O.032249; 'Bullock team', O.032254; also 'A bullock team at work Kakahi', O.032129; 'A New Zealand bullock team at work', O.032170, TPA.

5 Compare 'The team', O.031879, with 'The team', O.032243, TPA.

6 David Eggleton, *Into the Light: A history of New Zealand photography*, Nelson, 2006, p. 49.

7 W.J.T. Mitchell, *Landscape and Power*, Chicago, 1994, p. 23; Beth Fowkes Tobin, *Picturing Imperial Power: Colonial subjects in eighteenth century British paintings*, Durham and London, 1999, p. 2.

8 This is most apparent in work linking anthropology, colonialism and photography: Elizabeth Edwards, *Anthropology and Photography, 1860–1920*, London, 1992; Elizabeth Edwards and Christopher Morton, eds, *Photography, Anthropology, and History: Expanding the frame,* Farnham, Surrey; Burlington, 2009; Eleanor M. Hight and Gary D. Sampson, *Colonialist Photography: Imag(in)ing race and place,* London and New York, 2002; Christopher Pinney, *Photography and Anthropology*, London, 2011. Art photography falls outside the scope of James Ryan's *Picturing Empire: Photography and the visualisation of the British Empire*, Chicago, 1997.

9 For a recent exception see Tony Ballantyne, 'Knowledge, sociability and community in Gore's intellectual life, 1875–1914', *New Zealand Journal of History*, 44, 2 (2010), 138–56, p. 139.

10 Tony Ballantyne, 'Colonial knowledge' in Sarah Stockwell, ed., *The British Empire: Themes and perspectives*, Oxford, 2008, 177–98, p. 185.
11 Explorations of New Zealand's colonial culture in the twentieth century are largely clustered around Peter Gibbons' cultural colonisation thesis: examples include Chris Hilliard, 'Island Stories: The writing of New Zealand history, 1920–1940', MA thesis, University of Auckland, 1997; Kirstie Ross, *Going Bush: New Zealanders and nature in the twentieth century*, Auckland, 2008.
12 *EP*, 17 March 1896, p. 4.
13 *Daily Telegraph*, 3 October 1896, p. 4.
14 *EP*, 17 June 1899, p. 2.
15 Gael Newton, 'Australian pictorial photography: Seeing the light' in Thomas Padon ed., *Truth Beauty: Pictorialism and the photograph as art, 1845–1945*, Vancouver, 2008, 97–103, p. 98; *Sharland's New Zealand Photographer* (*SNZP*), 7 March 1905, p. 6.
16 William Main, *Wellington Album*, Wellington, 1998, p. 11; Eggleton, *Into the Light*, p. 49.
17 *New Zealand Observer*, 22 February 1902, p. 22.
18 *SNZP*, 7 November 1899, p. 3.
19 Elizabeth Edwards, 'Unblushing realism and the threat of the pictorial: Photographic survey and the production of evidence 1885–1918', *History of Photography*, 33, 1 (2009), 3–17, p. 9.
20 Eggleton, *Into the Light,* p. 35.
21 *SNZP*, 7 November 1899, p. 3.
22 Sandra Callister, 'Being there: War, women and lantern slides', *Rethinking History,* 12, 3 (2008), 317–37, p. 324.
23 *EP*, 21 July 1919, p. 10.
24 Isobel N. Coulston, ed., *Photographic Endeavours of the Gisborne Camera Club, 1916–1998*, Gisborne, 1998, pp. 3–4.
25 *Auckland Star*, 4 September 1931, p. 3; *EP*, 18 September 1926, p. 13.
26 *SNZP*, No. 39, 7 January 1903, p. 13.
27 *Auckland Star*, 23 June 1934, p. 17.
28 *EP*, 22 August 1930, p. 3.
29 *SNZP*, 7 September 1911, p. 59.
30 Harry Moult, 'The Pensioner's Hut', Camera Pictures of New Zealand, O.032246, TPA.
31 Harry Moult, Record Pictures of New Zealand, O.032189, TPA.
32 For the survey movement and links to clubs, see Elizabeth Edwards, *The Camera as Historian: Amateur photographers and the historical imagination, 1885–1918*, Durham and London, 2012, p. 42; for the link with pictorialism see Edwards, 'Unblushing realism'.
33 Harry Moult, Photograph album – London, AL.000249, and Photograph Album – England, AL.000250, TPA.

47. The 'Smiling Boys': The New Zealand health stamps of 1931

1 A.J. Stallworthy to A.E. Currie (Crown Law Officer), 17 October 1929, T40/538, ANZ.
2 Margaret Tennant, *Children's Health, The Nation's Wealth: A history of children's health camps*, Wellington, 1994, p. 69.
3 R.J.G. Collins, *The Postage Stamps of New Zealand Vol. 1*, Wellington, 1938, p. 404.
4 *Auckland Star*, 17 November 1931, p. 11.
5 Tennant, *Children's Health*, p. 85.
6 Edwin Myers to Michael Watt (Director-General of Health), 22 July 1934, H1 261/4 (1352), ANZ.
7 *Auckland Star*, 4 December 1931, p. 10.
8 *Evening Post*, 14 November 1931, p. 8.
9 *Evening Post*, 20 October 1931, p. 8.
10 Collins, *Postage Stamps*, p. 406.
11 The current Len Jury catalogue values unmounted mint specimens of the stamp at $NZ700 each. See *Len Jury Catalogue of New Zealand Stamps*, Nos 184 and 185: www.lenjury.co.nz/_asp/Catalogue3.asp?ProductGroupCode=31&ImageID=30
12 Robin Gwynn, *Collecting New Zealand Stamps*, Auckland, 1988, p. 92.
13 Tennant, *Children's Health*, p. 83.
14 Neuline Studios, Auckland, *Health Stamps for Health Camps*, 1949. Film held at ANZ.
15 David Scott, email to the author, 22 October 2012.
16 Angus Trumble, *A Brief History of the Smile*, New York, 2004, p. 154.
17 Allen and Frank Mitchell, interview by the author, Wellington, 26 October 2012.
18 David Scott, *European Stamp Design: A semiotic approach to designing messages*, London, 1995, p. 14.
19 The feat was repeated in his complex design for the 1940 commemorative half-crown coin reverse. See Mark Stocker, 'Completing the change: The New Zealand coin reverses of 1940', *British Numismatic Journal*, 81, 2011, 203–22, especially pp. 206–11.

48. The Rin Tin Tin Plaque: A man, his dog and a Japanese prisoner of war

1 Trades and occupations of prisoners, Papers relating to Featherston Prisoner of War Camp, E.H. Thompson Papers, fMS Papers 7014-2, ATL.
2 Commandant 1 PW Camp to Army Headquarters, 15 April 1944, PW4/14, Prisoner of war camps: Featherston Prisoners Japanese, Instructions re: administration, WA112/23, ANZ.
3 Pay office, PW1 Camp, PW working parties, 18 April 1945, Prisoner of war camps: Featherston employment, productive works, WA112/23, item 36, record 11/3/2, ANZ.
4 Cathy Casey, 'Souvenirs of camp life', Editorial features, *Wairarapa Times Age*, 4 August 1992, Featherston prisoner of war camp, Wairarapa Archive (WA).
5 A/Comdt PW1 Camp to HQ, 6 July 1944, Prisoner of war camps: Featherston Prisoners Japanese, Instructions re: administration, WA112/23, ANZ.
6 Ibid.
7 Alister Harman to Kristyn Harman, email correspondence, 8 July 2013.
8 Director of the National Service Department, NS41J Notice calling person up for service with the territorial force, to Mr Ronald Noel Farmer, Registration No. 554160, 28 April 1942, original held in the author's private collection.
9 Private Ronald Noel Farmer to Sheila Evelyn Ruth Farmer, undated letter held in the author's private collection.
10 Ibid. Punctuation as in the original.
11 Elaine Finlay (née Farmer) to Kristyn Harman, email correspondence, 17 April 2013; Pamela Harman (née Farmer) to Kristyn Harman, email correspondence, 22 April 2013.
12 'Prison camp art brings back flood of memories', *Wairarapa News*, 28 August 2002, Featherston prisoner of war camp, WA.
13 Casey, 'Souvenirs of camp life'.
14 Don Farmer, 'Time at POW camp recalled', *Wairarapa Times Age*, 7 November 1994, Featherston prisoner of war camp, WA.
15 Casey, 'Souvenirs of camp life'.
16 Trades and occupations of prisoners, Papers relating to Featherston Prisoner of War Camp, E.H. Thompson Papers, fMS Papers 7014-2, ATL.
17 Yasuhiro Ota, 'Shooting and friendship over Japanese prisoners of war: Differences between Featherston, New Zealand, and Cowra, Australia, in Japanese connections', MA thesis, Massey University, 2013. Mike Nicolaidi, *The Featherson Chronicles: A legacy of war*, Auckland, 1999; Charlotte Carr-Gregg, *Japanese Prisoners of War in Revolt: The outbreaks at Featherston and Cowra during World War Two*, New York, 1978.
18 Mike Nicolaidi, 'Interview with Ron Farmer, Greytown, Jan. 12, 1991', p. 8. Transcript generously shared with the author by the interviewer.

49. The Final Link in the Empire Route: New Zealand and the TEAL Short Solent Flying Boat

1 Alastair Shephard, 'Tasman Empire Airways Limited: The significance of its "Coral Route" Service', *Fukuoka University Review of Commercial Sciences*, 52, 2 (2007), 223–36, p. 225.
2 'Tasman chose solents', *Flight*, June 1950, p. 25.
3 Brian Cassidy, *Flying Empires: Short 'C' Class Empire Flying Boats*, Bath, 2004, p. 86.
4 Leigh Edmonds, 'Australia, Britain and the Empire air mail scheme, 1934–38', *Journal of Transport History* 20, 2 (1999), pp. 91–106.
5 John Gunn, *The Defeat of Distance: Qantas 1919 to 1939,* Brisbane, 1985, p. 239.
6 'Not un-British', *Auckland Star,* 13 July 1935, p. 9.
7 Gunn, *The Defeat of Distance*, p. 239.
8 Shephard, 'Tasman Empire Airways Limited', p. 225.
9 I.A. Thomson, 'A history of TEAL: The origins of Air New Zealand as an international airline, 1940–1967', MA thesis, University of Canterbury, 1968, p. 65.

50. Afterword: The wharenui Mataatua, and some thoughts about things

1 Hirini Moko Mead, 'Nga Karoretanga o Mataatua Whare: The wanderings of the carved house, Mataatua,' *Research Report No. 2*, Whakatane, 1990; Jonathan Mané-Wheoki, *Mataatua: No wai tenei whare tupuna? A Report on Ngati Awa Claim (WAI 46)*, Wellington, 1993; Conal McCarthy, *Exhibiting Maori: A history of colonial cultures of display*, Oxford, 2007; Jonathan Mané-Wheoki, 'Te wharenui, *Mataatua*: From captivity to liberation. A case study in repatriation', Keynote Lecture, Colonial Objects: Inaugural Conference of the Centre for Research on Colonial Culture, Toitū Otago Settlers Museum, Dunedin, 11–13 February 2013. In 1993 Jonathan Mané-Wheoki was commissioned to write the report for the Waitangi Tribunal that successfully

argued the case for the wharenui's repatriation from the Otago Museum to Ngāti Awa. This historic event sent ripples through the international museum community for the precedent it established. In preparation for his keynote address on Mataatua at the Colonial Objects conference, the author contacted Professor Hirini Moko Mead, who was instrumental in the process of the whare's return. Excerpts are taken from the keynote address and the email correspondence with permission.

2 Sidney M. Mead, *Te Toi Whakairo: The art of Maori carving*, Wellington, 1986, pp. 26, 94–95.

3 Conal McCarthy, 'The practice of repatriation: A case study from New Zealand', in Louise Tythacott and Kostos Arvanitis, eds, *Museums and Restitution: New practices, new approaches*, Aldershot, 2014, pp. 71–83.

4 W.J. Phillipps and J.C. Wadmore, *The Great Carved House Mataatua of Whakatane*, Wellington, 1956.

5 Paul Tapsell, *Pukaki: A comet returns*, Auckland, 2000. Conal McCarthy, *Museums and Maori: Heritage professionals, indigenous collections, current practice*, Wellington, 2011.

6 Mead, *Te Toi Whakairo*, p. 26.

7 Sidney M. Mead, *Maori Art on the World Scene: Essays on Maori art*, Wellington, 1997, p. 207.

8 Sidney Moko Mead, 'Nga timunga me nga paringa o te mana Maori/The ebb and flow of mana Maori and the changing context of Maori art', in S.M. Mead, ed., *Te Maori: Maori art from New Zealand collections*, New York, 1984, p. 21.

9 Tony Ballantyne, *Webs of Empire: Locating New Zealand's colonial past*, Wellington, 2012.

10 Judith Binney, *Encircled Lands: Te Urewera, 1820–1921*, Wellington, 2009, p. ix.

11 Neil MacGregor, *A History of the World in 100 Objects*, London, 2011.

12 Nicholas Thomas, *Entangled Objects: Exchange, material culture, and colonialism in the Pacific*, Cambridge, MA, 1991.

13 Bruno Latour, *Reassembling the Social: An introduction to actor-network-theory*, Oxford, 2005.

14 T.J. Barringer and Tom Flynn, *Colonialism and the Object: Empire, material culture, and the museum*, London and New York, 1998.

15 Sarah Longair and John McAleer, eds, *Curating Empire: Museums and the British imperial experience*, Manchester, 2012.

16 Chris Gosden, Frances Larson and Alison Petch, *Knowing Things: Exploring the collections at the Pitt Rivers Museum, 1884–1945*, Oxford, 2007.

17 Rodney Harrison, Sarah Byrne and Annie Clarke, eds, *Unpacking the Collection: Museums as networks of material and social agency*, Santa Fe, 2011.

18 Chris Tilley, Webb Keane, Susanne Küchler, Mike Rowlands and Patricia Spyer, eds, *Handbook of Material Culture*, London, Thousand Oaks and New Delhi, 2006.

19 Thomas J. Schlereth, *Cultural History and Material Culture: Everyday life, landscapes, museums*, Charlottesville, 1990.

20 See for example Karen Harvey, *History and Material Culture: A student's guide to approaching alternative sources*, London and New York, 2009; Sarah Barber, *History Beyond the Text: A student's guide to approaching alternative sources*, London and New York, 2009.

21 Kate Hunter and Kirstie Ross, *Holding on to Home: New Zealand stories and objects of the First World War*, Wellington, 2014.

22 Bronwyn Labrum,'The female past and modernity: Displaying women and things in New Zealand department stores, expositions and museums, 1920s–1960s', in Beth Fowkes Tobin and Maureen Goggin, eds, *Material Women 1750–1950: Consuming desires and collecting practices*, London, 2009, pp. 315–40; Bronwyn Labrum, 'Material histories in Australia and New Zealand: Interweaving distinct material and social domains', *History Compass* 8, (2010), pp. 805–16; Bronwyn Labrum, 'Reliving the colonial past: Histories, heritage, and the exhibition interior in postwar New Zealand', *Interiors: Design, Architecture, Culture. Special Issue: Living in the Past* 2, 1, (2011), pp. 27–44.

23 Labrum, 'Material histories', p. 8.

24 Sandra Dudley, ed., *Museum Objects: Experiencing the properties of things*, Leicester, London and New York, 2012, p. 1.

25 Ibid., p. 2.

26 Ibid., p. 4.

27 Ibid., pp. 5–8.

28 Tony Bennett and Patrick Joyce, eds, *Material Powers: Cultural studies, history and the material turn*, London and New York, 2010.

29 Tim Ingold, 'Making culture and weaving the world', in Dudley, ed., *Museum Objects*, p. 382.

30 Chris Gosden and Chantal Knowles, *Collecting Colonialism: Material culture and colonial change*, London and New York, 2001.

31 Ibid., p. 4.
32 Arjun Appadurai, *The Social Life of Things: Commodities in cultural perspective*, Cambridge, 1986; Igor Kopytoff, 'The cultural biography of things: Commoditization as process', in Appadurai, ed., *The Social Life of Things*, pp. 64–91; Alfred Gell, *Art and Agency: An anthropological theory*, Oxford, 1998.
33 Bill Brown, 'Thing theory', *Critical Inquiry* 28, 1, (2001), pp. 1–22.
34 Tony Bennett and Chris Healy, eds, *Assembling Culture*, London and New York, 2011.
35 Tony Bennett, Ben Dibley and Rodney Harrison, 'Introduction: Anthropology, collecting and colonial governmentalities', *History and Anthropology* 25, 2, (2014), pp. 137–49.
36 Rodney Harrison, *Heritage: Critical approaches*, London and New York, 2013.
37 Amiria Henare, 'Nga Aho Tipuna (Ancestral Threads): Maori cloaks from New Zealand', in Susanne Küchler and Daniel Miller, eds, *Clothing as Material Culture*, Oxford and New York, 2005, pp. 121–38. Amiria Henare, 'Taonga Maori: Encompassing rights and property in New Zealand', in Amiria Henare, Martin Holbraad and Sari Wastell, eds, *Thinking through Things: Theorising artefacts in ethnographic perspective*, London and New York, 2007, pp. 47–67. Paul Tapsell, 'Taonga, Marae, Whenua – Negotiating Custodianship: A Maori tribal response to Te Papa The Museum of New Zealand', in Annie Coombes, ed., *Rethinking Settler Colonialism: History and memory in Australia, Canada, Aotearoa New Zealand and South Africa*, Manchester, 2006, pp. 86–99.
38 Apirana Ngata, 'Some aspects of Maori culture', in Eric Ramsden, ed., *Sir Apirana Ngata and Maori Culture*, Wellington, 1948, p. 85.

Index

Page numbers in **bold r***efer to illustrations.*